Borrowstounness and district

Being historical sket... ...inneil,
Carriden... ...1850

Thomas James Salmon

Alpha Editions

This edition published in 2019

ISBN : 9789353299705

Design and Setting By
Alpha Editions
email - alphaedis@gmail.com

This book is a reproduction of an important historical work. Alpha Editions uses the best technology to reproduce historical work in the same manner it was first published to preserve its original nature. Any marks or number seen are left intentionally to preserve its true form.

BORROWSTOUNNESS AND DISTRICT

The Roman Tablet found at Bridgeness in 1868.

Now in the National Museum of Antiquities, Edinburgh.

BORROWSTOUNNESS
AND DISTRICT

BEING

HISTORICAL SKETCHES OF KINNEIL,
CARRIDEN, AND BO'NESS
c. 1550-1850

BY

THOMAS JAMES SALMON

With Illustrations and Maps

EDINBURGH AND LONDON
WILLIAM HODGE & COMPANY
1913

PRINTED BY
WILLIAM HODGE AND COMPANY
GLASGOW AND EDINBURGH

TO
THEIR GRACES
THE
DUKE AND DUCHESS OF HAMILTON
THIS VOLUME
IS
BY PERMISSION
RESPECTFULLY DEDICATED

PREFACE.

INFLUENCED by a liking for things historical and by the sentiment that my kinsfolk have been closely identified with this district for many generations, I commenced to collect the material which will be found in the following pages by way of a recreation seven years ago. There was at first no idea of the present publication. But as my investigations proceeded I discovered so much of what I believed to be new and interesting information that I felt impelled to preserve it, however imperfectly, in volume form. Many difficulties of treatment and arrangement presented themselves. The chief of these was in deciding whether to continue the narrative to the present time or to end it at the middle of the 19th century. Ultimately the latter method was adopted, and for various reasons. Apart from the comparatively brief narratives in the Old and New Statistical Accounts there was nothing in the nature of a local chronicle; detailed reference to early history was very desirable; the space at disposal for modern events would be wholly inadequate; and compression was not always possible. I decided therefore to leave the more modern period alone.

In all cases the official books and papers have been carefully examined. Each chapter, with two exceptions, is complete in itself, and everything has been done to make the volume reliable. Great care has been taken to avoid errors and omissions, and should any such be discovered it is hoped that they will be put down to the exacting nature of the work.

It does not profess to be a complete history, but rather a series of sketches dealing with various phases of burghal and parish life. Facts and events are stated, but in such a way as to raise pictures of periods, of outstanding events and individuals, of progress and of decay, all of which point their own lessons.

PREFACE.

Throughout my labours I have received the encouragement and assistance of many good friends; and in particular I have to express my thanks to the Faculty of Advocates for permission to use their valuable library; to Mr. W. K. Dickson, LL.D., for useful suggestions concerning the Regality; to Mr. A. P. Simpson, Sheriff-Clerk of Linlithgowshire, for access to the Regality volumes in his official custody; and to Bo'ness Town Council and other local bodies and their officials for access to their books and documents. I am also obliged for special aid in various directions to Mr. Lloyd Verney, of Carriden, and Professor Mounsey, Edinburgh; to Mr. H. M. Cadell, of Grange; to Mr. George Dalziel, W.S., Edinburgh; to Dr. T. F. Barrett, City Librarian, Glasgow; and to Mr. Alex. Ross, Closeburn, Hamilton. Other special aid I have acknowledged throughout the text and appendices and in the illustrations. I also desire to thank Mr. John Watt and Mr. George Salmon for a great deal of practical assistance.

For much of the information in the latter half of the concluding chapter I am indebted to Mr. William Miller, Mr. James Paris, and Mr. William Donaldson.

In conclusion, I heartily express my gratitude to the Rev. T. Ratcliffe Barnett for his careful revision of the proofs and for supplying sketches of old gravestones for reproduction.

THOMAS J. SALMON.

GRANGE TERRACE,
   BO'NESS, *June*, 1913.

CONTENTS.

CHAPTER	PAGE
I. Introductory,	1
II. The House of Hamilton and Kinneil,	23
III. Kinneil,	44
IV. What the Privy Council Registers Reveal. Period 1549-1668,	53
V. Regality Court Book,	78
VI. Regality—the Register of Deeds,	94
VII. The trial and burning of the Borrowstounness witches,	111
VIII. Local Covenanting History and "The Borrowstounness Martyrs,"	123
IX. Grange Estate and its Owners,	147
X. Carriden, (*See also* Appendix)	163
XI. Ecclesiastical,	200
XII. The "Trustees for the two pennies in the pint,"	226
XIII. The "Trustees for the two pennies," continued,	244
XIV. The Representatives of Bo'ness,	275

CONTENTS.

CHAPTER	PAGE
XV. Coal and Coal Mining,	305
XVI. The Borrowstounness and Grangemouth Canal,	325
XVII. Local Societies and Lodges,	335
XVIII. Eminent Natives and Residents,	362
XIX. Conclusion—Educational: Industrial,	394

APPENDICES.

I. The Parish of Carriden 200 years ago,	429
II. The House of Hamilton,	449
III. General Section of the Bo'ness Coalfield,	454
IV. Place-names of the District,	456
V. Botanical Notes,	461
VI. Table of Modern Information,	465

LIST OF ILLUSTRATIONS.

The Bridgeness Tablet,	*Frontispiece*
Bonhard Castle,	Facing Page 12
Lady Anne Cunningham,	,, 24
James, Duke of Hamilton,	,, 36
Kinneil House,	,, 44
Anne, Duchess of Hamilton,	,, 58
Blackness Castle,	,, 76
Gravestones in Kinneil Churchyard (No. 1),	,, 88
,, ,, ,, (No. 2),	,, 106
Old Grange House,	,, 138
William Cadell,	,, 154
Carriden House,	,, 166
The Old Kirk Roads, Carriden,	,, 186
James Duguid,	,, 196
Rev. Kenneth Mackenzie,	,, 208
Page of First Town Minute-Book,	,, 226
The Old Town Hall,	,, 244
James Watt,	,, 270
John Anderson,	,, 284
Dr. Roebuck's Tombstone,	,, 306
Plan of Borrowstounness and Grangemouth Canal,	,, 330
Captain Donald Potter,	,, 352
Colonel Gardiner,	,, 366
Dugald Stewart,	,, 378
Admiral Sir James Hope,	,, 390
Henry Bell,	,, 402
Old Church and Churchyard of Carriden,	,, 430

Borrowstounness and District.

CHAPTER I.

INTRODUCTORY.

1. Topography of district—2. The Roman Wall—3. The Bridgeness Tablet—4. Other traces of the Romans—5. The Seats of the Gentry, and Villages of Olden Days: Northbank and the Setons—6. Bonhard and the Cornwalls—7. Blackness and its Castle—8. State Prison and Covenanting Prisoners—9. Beginnings of Borrowstounness and early architecture—10. What contributed to its rise.

I.

THE seaport town of Borrowstounness is situated on the southern shore of the Firth of Forth, eighteen miles west of Leith. Ecclesiastically the district surrounding it embraces the Parish of Carriden and the Parish of Borrowstounness. Civilly they are now united, and form the Parish of Bo'ness and Carriden. This consists of a strip of land running along the shore from Kinneil to Blackness to a length of six miles and a breadth of from two to three miles. It is bounded by the Forth on the north; by the Parish of Abercorn on the east; by the River Avon on the west; and by the Parish of Linlithgow on the south.

The ground rises in several banks or terraces from the waterside southwards. From the low level of the seaport the outlook, though pleasant, gives little opportunity for sight-seeing. On the high grounds behind, however, there is a complete change. Here the broad river, with its immense bay between Kinneil and Grangemouth, the wooded lands of the northern shores, Culross Abbey, the whole range of the

Ochils, the Wallace Monument at Stirling, Ben Lomond, the outlying spurs of the Grampians, and the Campsie Hills to the south-west make up an almost unrivalled prospect. On the Erngath Hills, two miles to the south of the town, the top of the rise is reached, and from here the prospect is even more extensive, as eastwards we now easily discern Dunfermline and the Forth Bridge, and on clear days Arthur's Seat and the Pentland Hills. Throughout the entire uplands of the parish the prospects to the north, east, and west are magnificent, and more than compensate for the necessarily dingy and grimy state of those parts of our neighbourhood that stretch along the shore. The course of the Forth from Alloa to Borrowstounness is decidedly south-easterly, and the large bay referred to gives the river a stately appearance when the tide is flowing. Opposite Carriden it again takes a south-easterly bend to the Forth Bridge. There is a natural charm about these large and graceful curves which adds greatly to the beauty of the general prospect.

The whole district is interesting from various points of view—geological and otherwise—but many of these are remote from our present purpose. Therefore, save for a necessary but brief notice of the Roman Wall and the Roman occupation, we wish in these pages to confine ourselves mainly to some historical sketches of the district and its inhabitants for three centuries only—from the middle of the sixteenth to the middle of the nineteenth century.

Small as our area is, we could crave for no fairer and no more stimulating environment. In truth, the whole border-lands of our beautiful Firth, north and south, possess historical associations and romantic beauties of the most enlivening and entrancing kind.

The first picture, dim even as it is, which holds our historic sense is that of the Roman occupation of North Britain. The Romans left a much deeper impression in every way in England than in Scotland, yet the evidence of their presence here is still traceable. With little effort of the imagination we can yet see their galleys in the Firth and their legions on the shore. We can picture encampments all along the line of the Forth and Clyde rampart. We can imagine the twenty years' reign of Lollius Urbicus, the governor whom the great Emperor Antoninus appointed to the command in Britain. We recall the courage and ability displayed by this distinguished officer in his attacks on the turbulent tribes of Caledonia; his efforts for maintaining peace and improving the country by the construction of various camps and fortalices, the ruins of which, here and there, may still be seen; the formation of roads and the introduction of useful arts. And we are impressed with the physical fitness and fearless courage of the Roman soldiery.

The facts which justify these observations are matters of common history, and require no detailed recapitulation here. We cannot well omit, however, to summarise what has from time to time been discovered locally concerning the Wall, or Vallum, and other Roman antiquities.

II.

Antiquarian research has long ago indicated, and it is apparently now generally accepted, that when Agricola invaded Scotland (about 80 A.D.) and erected his line of forts between the Forth and Clyde, there was one placed on the high ground at Kinneil, possibly either on the site now occupied by the old church and graveyard or on that of the present mansion-house. This is most likely, as either of these positions would command an extensive view of the Firth, and would prove an excellent situation for a watch-tower. When these forts were connected later (about 140 A.D.) by the Wall of Lollius Urbicus, commonly known as Antonine's Wall, and Grim's or Graham's Dyke, research has again yielded indications that the seventeenth military station was at Inveravon, the eighteenth at Kinneil, and the nineteenth at Bridgeness. The rampart between the Forth and Clyde crossed the River Avon near Inveravon and proceeded in an easterly direction towards Bridgeness or

Carriden. Its track has been denoted by Sibbald on the map in his work,[1] and also on the maps of the Ordnance Surveyors, and is still visible, in places, to the eye of the antiquarian, chiefly west of Kinneil House.

About forty miles in length, the Vallum was built of sods and earth upon a foundation of stone, and its estimated height of twenty feet rested on a base twenty-four feet thick. Along its northern front ran a V-shaped ditch or moat, twenty feet deep by forty feet wide, the sloping sides of which, like those of a large reservoir, thus rendered it almost impassable. While the building plan, so to speak, of this great fortification was simple enough, we cannot but admire the cleverness and security of the whole construction. When we remember, moreover, that 50,000 men were required to garrison it, we begin to form some idea of the life and activity that must have been visible between the Forth and Clyde in those early days.

The Vallum was defended by nineteen forts placed at intervals along the line, and a military road ran within it as a necessary appendage, affording a ready communication between the forts.

Such, we are told, has been the solidity of the construction of the wall that notwithstanding the perishable nature of the materials used, the mound can still be traced after the lapse of seventeen centuries; and inscribed stones have been from time to time discovered in various parts of the line recording that the second legion and detachments from the sixth and twentieth legions, with some auxiliaries, were employed upon the works.

There have been many useful collections of facts and also many theorisings about it, locally and elsewhere, for many long years. The local narratives in the old and new Statistical Accounts are interesting and learned, particularly that of the Rev. Kenneth Mackenzie. Later, Mr. Waldie walked along the wall, and eventually wrote entertainingly and intelligently

---

[1] "History and Description of Linlithgowshire."

on it.[2] And now Dr. Macdonald,[3] with the comparatively recent discoveries of the Glasgow Archæological Society and others before him, has skilfully surveyed the whole body of evidence relating to the subject. The impression which a first perusal of his work gives is that had it been possible to do some of the same spadework in this district as has been done at Castlecary and Roughcastle, there would have been more to describe. On second thoughts, however, we doubt after all if spadework here would yield very much, except perhaps at Inveravon. Assuming that the rampart was quite complete between Inveravon and Bridgeness, and further, that its base between these two points was a stone one of considerable width, what more likely than that during the intervening centuries these stones were mostly removed and used in the construction and reconstruction of Kinneil House and other smaller manor-houses hereabouts. If such was the case, spadework would reveal little or nothing about the rampart. As things are then, Dr. Macdonald has left us very much as we were, save for the observations which he quotes from Mr. A. S. R. Learmonth, who was some time tenant of the farm of Nether-Kinneil. The latter, in 1861, when ploughing in the field known as the Easter Wellacres, came upon a causeway of rough stones, varying in size from one to two feet, the larger stones being on the north or lower side, and the smaller ones on the south side. It was covered with eight or ten inches of soil. The stones were removed because they were liable to break the agricultural implements. Mr. Learmonth also mentioned that his uncles, who preceded him in the farm, had removed many other parts of the causeway in that same field, and in two other fields to the west. When he came across the stone causeway, which was eighteen feet broad, he thought it was the Roman Road, or Military Way. Dr. Macdonald, however, thinks that Mr. Learmonth's description is much more applicable to the stone foundation of

---

[2] "Walks Along the Northern Roman Wall," 1886.
[3] "The Roman Wall in Scotland," 1911.

the rampart. Attention is also called to a slight hollow in the field at the end of the road from Nether Kinneil, known as the Walk, or Summer-house Park, which is supposed to mark the line of the Roman Ditch. When Mr. Learmonth first observed it, this ditch had a depth of six or eight feet, but the hollow had been filled up for the purposes of ploughing and carting.

The ditch, not being so easily removed or effaced as the base of the rampart, a critical examination might reveal more of it than has yet been observed. Of course, the ground, like the ridge to the north of Riverview Terrace, by its natural formation would, in some cases, aid very practically in acting as a barrier, but in other places it had to be extensively cut. This may be seen to the eastward of the enclosures of Kinneil. It is said that the wall could be seen at one time in a field immediately above old Grange House.

III.

We need not here discuss the divergent views which at one time existed concerning the eastern termination of the Wall. Probably the reason for many of these was that it was constructed somewhat gradually, and additional forts or towers came to be erected as it progressed eastwards. That it was not erected in sections running from each end appears to be generally conceded. For a time the termination might thus have been at Kinneil, and later at Bridgeness. That the Vallum went further than the latter place is not likely, although it is very probable that the military way was continued eastwards, by the ridge on which Carriden House now stands, to Cramond and Edinburgh, and ultimately joined Watling Street.

What seemed to settle the eastern termination of the Wall was the finding at Bridgeness, in 1868, on the little rocky promontory close to the shore, what Dr. Macdonald describes as the largest and finest of the legionary tablets. The tablet was presented by Mr. Henry Cadell, of Grange, to the National Museum of the Antiquaries of Scotland,

Edinburgh. It is nine feet two inches long by three feet eleven inches high, and is elaborately decorated. These tablets, a number of which are preserved in Glasgow Museum, seem to have been put up in pairs, one at each end of an assigned piece of work; and the opinion has been expressed that some day the companion tablet to the Bridgeness one may be turned up at Inveravon, unless destroyed long ago.

The rectangular beaded moulding in the centre contains a Latin inscription, well spaced and finely cut, which reads as follows:—

Imp. Cæs. Tito. Ælio
Hadri. Antonino
AVG. Pio P.P. Leg. II.
AVG. Per. M.P. IIIIDCL. II
Fec.

Extended this reads—"Imperatori Cæsari Tito Ælio Hadriano Antonino Augusto, Pio Patriæ, Legio II. Augusta, Per Milia Passuum IIIIDCLII. Fecit." And translated—"To the Emperor Cæsar Titus Ælius Hadrian Antoninus, Augustus, Pious Father of his country, the Second Legion (the Augustan) made [the Vallum] for 4652 passus."[4]

The tablet clearly belongs to the Wall of 139. The Roman pace of two steps was about five feet (4·84), so that the whole of this portion was four miles four hundred and sixty-five yards, the distance to the Avon.

Left and right, within a framework of pillars, are two finely-carved illustrations. The left one depicts a horseman, armed and helmeted, galloping; he carries a shield on his arm, and with spear held in position thrusts downwards at four naked Caledonians; one of the Caledonians is already decapitated, but has been armed with a spear and an oblong shield; another, who is just falling dead, has an oblong shield in his hand, while a sword lies at his side; the remaining two are defenceless. The illustration on the right hand contains a

---

[4] See "The Scottish Antiquary," vol. xv., July, 1900.

number of figures and depicts the important sacrifice of the Suovetaurilia, or ceremony of purification, with which the Romans were wont to initiate battles and other great national undertakings. In the under part of the panel is an altar, and beside it the three animals to be sacrificed—a boar or swine (sus), a sheep (ovis), and a bull (taurus), from which the name is derived. Some antiquarians, in view of this illustration, hold that the Wall really began, in place of terminating, at Bridgeness; but it is hopeless to discuss such arguments.

A facsimile of the inscription has been set up at Bridgeness in a framework of stones found on the spot.

Dr. Macdonald mentions that when found the tablet was lying with its face down, in a sloping direction, and, like all the others regarding which there was detailed information, it had the appearance of being deliberately hidden. Those who were supporters of the contention that the eastern termination of the Wall was at Carriden were inclined to assert that the stone had been removed from its original position for the purpose of concealment either by the Romans themselves on being finally recalled to Rome, or by the Caledonians, who were left in unmolested possession, and who would not particularly relish the memorial which their conquerors had left behind. But, as Dr. Macdonald says, it is not easy to believe that either Roman or Caledonian would have been at the pains to transport so huge a block for more than half a mile before disposing of it.

IV.

The district has shown other evidences of the Roman occupation besides the ditch, rampart, and tablet, and to these we turn for a moment.

Near the farm steading of Upper Kinneil, and a little to the south of the Wall, there was—as will be seen from the map—a small tumulus or cairn, locally known by the name of the Laughing Hill. On its being opened to obtain stones for drains, four stone coffins and four urns were found. The coffins contained black mould, and the urns, which were full of human bones, were inverted and placed upon flat stones. Probably the bodies were burned, and after the calcined bones were collected and put into the urns the remaining ashes were put into the coffins. The bones, when first discovered, were almost white; when exposed to the air they very soon became black and crumbled to dust. Several pieces of charcoal were among them.

A stone coffin and an urn similar to those already mentioned were unearthed in the north side of the eminence called Bell's Knowe, immediately above the town of Bo'ness; also a curious battleaxe, coins, and other antiquities in different parts of the parish.

A gold coin, of the reign of Vespasian, was found upon the site of Carriden House, near which a Roman station was thought to have been situated. Miln, one of the owners of Carriden, Sibbald says, when adding a wing or "jamb" to the house, came on a stone with the head of an eagle engraven upon it, which he placed in the wall. He also got some Roman "potterie" there.

To the south of the farmhouse of Walton there is a flat-topped hillock, now used as a stackyard. Here, in the course of some excavations twenty years ago, a number of coffins, constructed of shale and stone slabs and containing human remains, were discovered. Locally these were pronounced to be Roman, but we have the authority of Dr. Joseph Anderson, of the National Museum of Antiquities, Edinburgh, for saying that the place appears to have been a small cemetery of native origin, and to have had no connection with any Roman remains in the neighbourhood. The find revived in some minds an old contention that the Roman Wall ended here, and not at Bridgeness. Other and stronger evidence, as we have seen, made the contention a weak one, and it made no headway. The name of the farm, too, was said to connect it definitely with "the Wall"; but, again, it was shown that it was far more likely that the name was derived from a "well" or spring in the vicinity. In some maps it is certainly marked "Roman Camp or Station." We must not forget, in considering this matter, that the road which comes east from Upper Kinneil and Rousland and over the Erngath Hills by the golf course and Bonsyde was one of the old Roman roads, though not the Military Way. It may not have run direct from Bonsyde to the Walton, but traces of it have been found about the Boroughmuir and also at Grougfoot, near the Walton.

High on the roadside, a hundred yards or so west of the present farmhouse of Inveravon, stand the ruins of an old tower. Sibbald and some others somewhat hastily pronounced it a Roman watch-tower, but calmer judgments declared it to be one of the corner towers of the Castle of Inveravon built on the site of the Roman station. As bearing out the fact that there was such a castle reference is made to the Auchinleck Chronicle of James II., where it is mentioned that in the beginning of March, 1455, James "kest-down the Castell of Inneraryne and syne incontinent passed till Glasgow."

The plateau at Inveravon, on which, first of all, the old Roman station and then the castle of the Douglases were situated, is in a very conspicuous place. Doubtless both the station and the castle were fairly extensive, and were the plateau properly explored with pick and shovel antiquarians might be rewarded with discoveries. Dr. Rennie[5] notes that in a window of the adjacent farmhouse were several hieroglyphic characters which, although much venerated for their antiquity, were not understood.

V.

Sibbald, writing of our district, remarks that in the seventeenth century this part of the coast had increased much in people. From the Palace of Kinneil for some two miles there were almost continuous buildings upon the coast. Above it, upon the sloping ground from the hills of Irongath (or Erngath), there were several seats of the gentry and several

---

[5] Sinclair's "Statistical Account: Borrowstounness," vol. xviii.

villages well peopled because of the coal pits all over that ground.

The villages referred to would include Borrowstoun, where, besides colliers, there were maltsters and weavers; the Muirhouse, corrupted to Muirhouses and Murrayes in Carriden Parish; Little Carriden, east of this and on the south side of the old burial road; and Bonhard, on the high ground in the vicinity of the old castle or keep of that name. Then, on the shore, there were Thirlestane, Grangepans, Cowdenhill, Bridgeness, and Cuffabouts.

The land in those days was broken up into several small estates, and Sibbald's "seats of the gentry" probably included that old mansion-house and garden near Borrowstoun Farm, now the property of the Laird of Grange; the house and garden of North Kinglass, or Little Kinglass, at one time the home of the Hamiltons of Kinglass; Gauze House, or Gawes, likewise a Hamiltonian domicile; and on a ridge of high land above Bridgeness, Old Grange, recently demolished; and further west Carriden House. In the valley east of Bonhard lay the Walton, then a separate estate, and the seat of Sir Colin Campbell; and further east the small property of Dyland.

On the hill, a mile from the sea, were the mansions of Northbank and Bonhard, the homes of the Setons and the Cornwalls respectively.

The old house of Northbank, now a farm shed, was long one of the domiciles of Sir Walter Seton of Abercorn, Northbank, and Carriden, eldest son of Alexander Seton of Graden.[6] He was a brother of the Rev. Alexander Seton, some time Episcopal incumbent in St. Michael's, Linlithgow, whose ministry was marred with almost continual strife with the Town Council. It is said that Mr. Seton was appointed to Linlithgow by the Bishop of St. Andrews, probably through the influence of Sir Walter. At any rate, when his minister brother became involved with the Linlithgow magistrates, he is said to have done all he could, by conference with the parties and otherwise,

---

[6] "Family of Seton," vol. i., p. 359.

to compose their differences. The breach, however, widened, ending, unfortunately, in the deposition of Mr. Seton in 1690.

Sir Walter was heritable Sheriff of Linlithgowshire, as Laird of Abercorn. He also held the office of Taxmaster of the Customs in the reign of Charles Second, by whom he was created a baronet of Nova Scotia by Royal patent in 1663, under the designation of Abercorn, the designation being to him and his heirs male whatsoever. He appears afterwards to have been designed by the title of Northbank.

His official position as "Fermorer" (farmer) of the Customs, seems to have been the subject of serious contention, but of what nature we do not know. His name often appears, as we shall see, in the Privy Council orders dealing with the plague, and no doubt the instructions there given him were given because of his official position. His wife was a Christian Dunbar, and they had three sons and three daughters. The eldest son, Walter, second baronet, became an advocate and commissary clerk of Edinburgh; the second, Alexander, was the ancestor of the Setons of Preston and Ekolsund; the third, George, factor to the Earl of Winton, died unmarried. One of the daughters, Grisel, was married to Edward Hodge, designed as a shipmaster in Grangepans, by whom she had a son and two daughters.

Walter, the second baronet, died on 3rd January, 1708, and was succeeded by his eldest son, Henry. Northbank is now part of Kinneil estate.

VI.

West of Northbank is Bonhard Castle. This old mansion stands on an excellent site which, in addition to affording some fine prospects to the north over the Firth, looks down on the fertile valley of the Binns and Philpstoun. It has been wonderfully preserved. Although no longer one of the seats of the gentry, it is still inhabited, having been divided into six dwelling-houses. It is a fine old place yet, with its entrance drive, ancient dovecot, and walled garden. One authority[7] tells

---

[7] "Castellated and Domestic Architecture of Scotland."

Bonhard Castle.

(From a photograph by Eric Jamieson, Bo'ness.)

us that, notwithstanding the old-world air about the house, it is quite modern in its arrangements, and retains none of the defensive features which frequently prevailed in Scotland till a late period. Its walls are about three feet thick, and the rooms are provided with fairly large windows. The present entrance door in the south front is an old window opened out to form a door. Of the L plan, the house has an octagonal staircase turret in the re-entering angle, in which also is the original entrance. The place is well worth a visit, and inside there are some finely panelled ceilings and ornamental fireplaces still to be seen.

Concerning the old dovecot, there is to be found on its west gable, says the same authority, all the lettered and heraldic history to be found at Bonhard of the Cornwall family. Not much can be made out at first sight, but on a careful examination the Cornwall arms impaled with the arms of a branch of the Seton family can be satisfactorily traced, above which is the motto, "We Beig, Ze. Se. Varle" (We build, ye see, warily), with the date 1591 and the initials N. C. & M. S. The N. C. has been identified as the initials of Nicholas Cornwall, and the M. S. represent those of his third wife, who was a Marie Seton. Nicholas, who for a period occupied the position of Provost of Linlithgow, died in 1607, aged seventy years.

Peter Cornwall, the father of Nicholas, built a town-house in Linlithgow in 1527, and was the first to assume the above arms. The house was demolished in 1870, and among the stones taken from it was one containing the date, the motto of the Cornwalls, and a matrix for a metal plate. The plate containing the arms crumbled away on being touched. Waldie[8] mentions that it bore the device of a bird, with a stalk of *corn* in its mouth, standing on the top of a *wall*. John, the hero of the family, fell at Flodden. He was one of six who were dressed up in the same style as the king, to whom he bore a great resemblance.

The Cornwalls owned the lands of Flask, now Springfield,

---

[8] "History of Linlithgow," p. 46.

and a large portion of Bonnytoun, and were closely connected, civilly and ecclesiastically, with the royal and ancient burgh. As Dr. Ferguson[9] puts it, a Cornwall was Provost of Linlithgow, a Cornwall was one of the chantry-priests in St. Michael's before the Reformation, and two Cornwalls are found among her Protestant ministers.

The ministers were Robert Cornwall and his son John Cornwall, who died in 1646, after a service of twenty years in St. Michael's. Robert had another son, who was minister of Muiravonside.

But the family was also intimately associated with our own town and seaport. There was a Walter Cornwall of Bonhard, who, in December, 1639, compeared before the Town Council of Linlithgow, along with Mr. Richard Dickson, minister of Kinneil, as a deputation from the Presbytery concerning a matter in which the Rev. John Cornwall was involved. Then, in 1679, we find a James Cornwall of Bonhard appointed as one of the special commission to try six persons in Bo'ness for witchcraft. Again, a Walter Cornwall of Bonhard was appointed bailie of the regality of Borrowstounness about the year 1692. With Thomas Cornwall, his son, it would seem that the connection of the family with the district ceased, and the house and lands, along with those of Northbank, were acquired by James fourth Duke of Hamilton in 1742.

VII.

On the shore at the eastern end of the parish stands sentinel-like the old fortress of Blackness. Situated on a rocky promontory, it projects into the Forth, and seawards represents the hull of a ship. The chief part of the building is a strong oblong tower or keep with a circular staircase tower at the north-east angle. This staircase was probably added at a date subsequent to the erection of the keep. The keep is still preserved, although much altered, and stands

---

[9] See Dr. Ferguson's "Ecclesia Antiqua."

detached, with a considerable space of ground, surrounded with a strong wall. A large part of the wall still remains, and has a thick parapet with large portholes or embrasures for cannon cut through it similar to those at Stirling. The other buildings comprise a combination of old and new structures, and a sketch in the Royal Scottish Academy shows the landward or south front, the interior of which is seen as it now stands. The exterior has been deprived of its parapet, and the walls are heightened and covered with a plain roof.[10] In short, save for its ramparts and dungeons, the castle as we see it is comparatively modern.

The powerful Douglases, who seriously menaced the power of the King in the reign of James II., held the Castles of Inveravon, Blackness, and Abercorn. But in one of the subsequent raids on the Douglas lands Blackness Castle was destroyed. It remained for a time ruinous, and by special charter in 1465 the Burgh of Linlithgow—of which town in its palmy days Blackness was the seaport—received power to demolish the ruin and utilise the stones for the purpose of constructing a new port or pier at Blackness. The hill and rock from St. Ninian's Chapel to the sea, all round the promontory, were to belong in future to the burgh. The principal reason for this grant, Waldie says, was the "vexations, troubles, harassments, and extortions" formerly practised by those who held the castle upon the merchants of the burgh and others frequenting the port. It is almost certain, however, that the burgh never entered into possession under this charter. Besides, the grant was recalled by an Act of 1476 revoking all grants made in the minority of James III., and especially of such places as were considered to be "keys of the kingdom." The foundations of St. Ninian's Chapel are still traceable on the top of the Castlehill.

An English fleet, in 1481, is said to have burnt the shipping at Blackness, then a considerable seaport. The castle, some think, was destroyed at this time also; but, if so, it must have been quickly rebuilt, for in 1489 it was in use as a State

---

[10] See also "Castellated and Domestic Architecture."

prison. Nearly sixty years after this—1548—during the Regency of the Earl of Arran, it was for a time garrisoned by the French. When the Queen Mother, Mary of Guise, was made Regent the castle again came into possession of the French, but in April, 1566, it was taken from them by the Sheriff of Linlithgow. In February, 1571, it was manned with a garrison by Lord Claud Hamilton, a zealous partisan of Queen Mary; and it appears to have been held in her interest until February, 1573, when it was delivered up to the Regent, the Earl of Morton. During their occupancy the Queen's troops, it is said, made an inroad upon the opposite coast, when they "spoulzeit" the towns there, and returned to Blackness with considerable booty. On two occasions during the same period an attack was made upon the castle by the Queen's enemies within the realm. And we also find at this time that a ship of war, well furnished with artillery, was sent from Leith to "asseige" the castle, but was driven from the station where she had cast anchor by the violence of the weather. Once more an attempt was shortly thereafter made to carry the place by surprise. It failed, however, as the garrison was on the alert.

A rather tragic story of the castle is told in connection with the betrayal of Sir James Kirkaldy by his wife to the Regent Morton. Sir James, on arrival from France with the arrears of the Queen's dowry, had been made prisoner by the keeper of the castle, who, in his absence and unknown to him, had gone over to the other side. While in prison Kirkaldy managed to gain over the men, and keep the castle. His wife came to visit him, and he was induced to accompany her for a short way when leaving. He was then seized by the keeper of Linlithgow Palace, who was waiting for him in hiding, and sent next day to Edinburgh. Shortly after this he made his escape, and eight days later his wife was found lying strangled in her bedroom. Kirkaldy was executed the same year.

VIII.

But in contemplating the long history of the castle—its many destructions and its many rebuildings, its many owners and its many uses—the most vital memories circle round the great and successful struggle of our forefathers for the principles of civil and religious liberty. In the reign of James VI. it was the principal State prison of Scotland. As such its dungeons confined many a godly minister and many distinguished persons who were martyrs for the truth. In 1584 Andrew Melville was ordered to be "warded" here. He had disputed the authority of the King and his Council to interfere with the doctrines taught in a sermon he had delivered at St. Andrews. After the warrant was served on him, however, he escaped to Berwick.

During the same year the clergy in and near Edinburgh were apprised that measures prejudicial to "the Kirk and its discipline" were to be resolved on at a meeting of Parliament appointed to be held in May. They prevailed upon David Lindsay, minister at Leith, who was most acceptable to the Court, to intercede with the King for the interposition of his authority till the Assembly should be heard in the matter. When entering the gate of the palace, in discharge of his commission, however, he was apprehended and carried to Blackness. There also the ministers of Edinburgh were condemned to a temporary confinement in 1587 for refusing to pray for Queen Mary.

In 1594 the Earl of Angus, one of the excommunicated lords, was required to deliver himself up to custody in Blackness till he should undergo a trial; but, refusing, was subsequently with the others found guilty of high treason.

From August, 1605, till towards the close of the following year John Welsh, minister of Ayr, who had married John Knox's daughter Elizabeth, and five other clergymen, were confined in the castle for refusing to condemn the Assembly that had met a short time before at Aberdeen in defiance of the King's command. Their trial took place at Linlithgow, where the High Court of Justiciary had been temporarily established, away from the risings and troubles which such an occasion was sure at that time to cause among the populace of Edinburgh. After a notoriously unfair trial the ministers were found guilty by the Court, and "banished the King's dominions upon the pain of death," but were re-committed to Blackness, for a time at least. Welsh was courageously defended by Thomas Hope, afterwards the celebrated Sir Thomas, who, in great contrast to his contemporaries at the bar, was no truckler to the King. Welsh is said to have thanked him in Court for his exertions, remarking that he felt assured that Hope's posterity would rise to the highest honours. The various descendants of Sir Thomas Hope have long been large landowners in the county, and many of them have held important positions in the service of the State.

About the same time a State prisoner of a different description was lodged here for a few days pending his transference to Edinburgh Castle. This was Gilbert Brown, Abbot of New Abbey, described as "a trafficking and seducing Papist."

In 1624 William Rigg, one of the bailies of Edinburgh, was deprived of his office of magistrate, condemned to be imprisoned in Blackness Castle, and fined £50,000 Scots, for challenging the doctrine taught by the Episcopal clergy. He was charged with being the chief ringleader of the non-conformitants in Edinburgh, and with contributing liberally to the printing of books which crossed the course of "conformitie."

John Hamilton, second Lord Bargany, and at that time possessor of Carriden estate, was also a prisoner there in 1679. His offence was that of entertaining notorious rebels in his house and declaring that Scotland would never be well till it was clear of Episcopacy. His trial, however, was never brought on for want of evidence. Another sufferer was John Hay of Lochloy, who was in 1683 committed prisoner for the space of thirteen months, "pairtly in the tolbuith of Edinburgh and pairtly in the Castle of Blackness." His offence was hearing the nonconforming ministers.

Waldie relates that, after his victory at Dunbar, Cromwell, on his advance towards Stirling, made some fortifications at the palace at Linlithgow, and that Blackness Castle surrendered after a short siege in April, 1651. Lord Ochiltree, found guilty of accusing the Duke of Hamilton of treason, lay a prisoner there from 1631, and was one of those released by Cromwell's Government after the battle of Worcester. The cell in which he was so long imprisoned can still be seen. Waldie further states that, according to one record, the castle was "blowne up with a powder traine" on 3rd April, 1652; and he remarks that at its upblowing the devil was seen on its walls. Very congenial to the devil of popular estimation was this kind of work.

Before this time, however, Blackness had become a busy seaport and mart of trade, intimately connected with the county town. It had a large Custom-house, was the centre of a considerable population, and had in its neighbourhood mills, fisheries, coal works, and saltpans. But its seaport and industries have long since ceased to be, and the place is now a modest yet popular summer resort. The castle is in use as a Government military store, under the charge of a military guard from Edinburgh Castle.

IX.

What really led to the decay of Blackness in the seventeenth century was the sudden rise of Borrowstounness, "the town on the Ness," as it was called in its early days to distinguish it from the original "town" of the district, the village of Kinneil. We often hear Bo'ness described as "our ancient town," but this is not correct, for, despite its ancient-like appearance in places, it is far from being old, comparatively speaking. In fact, so far as the records show, it cannot be more than three hundred and fifty years old. We begin to trace mention of it about the end of the sixteenth century and the beginning of the seventeenth. Sibbald, speaking of its sudden rise, tells us of Sir Robert Drummond of Meidhope (Midhope, near Hopetoun), an old laird who lived till after the Restoration (1660). This gentleman, in his old age, was in the habit of telling several of his neighbours that he well remembered the time when there was only one house where Borrowstounness and Carriden then stood. But whose house it was, or where it was situated, we are afraid cannot be discovered now.

By oral tradition we have it that the first settlers were fishers, sailors, and miners. Narrow as the space of flat land along the shore now is, it must have been much narrower in those early days, as the foreshore then lay along the north side of the present North Street. The small building-space thus available on the low or shore ground would account for the irregularity of the early buildings. Houses and huts were evidently put up wherever a spot of ground could be conveniently got. Some of us can remember that many of the old houses, not so long ago demolished, were under the level of the street. This would come about when the shore-ground to the north of them was reclaimed and made up, very likely to a considerable height, above the original level of the ground on the shore border, where the first houses were erected and a street was formed. A jocular reason used to be given for the houses being below the street level. The sailors were so much accustomed going below to their cabins that they preferred to get to their houses by a similar process, and built them accordingly. One candid writer has told us, and truly, that the town is very irregularly built, contrasting unfavourably with the beauty of the situation. In modern descriptions of it we are usually informed that it contains two principal streets, which are narrow, running from west to east for a considerable distance, and converging in one. An early record describes it as a long town consisting only of one street, extending along the shore close to the water, and we have no doubt this accurately described the town in its early years.

It is said to have derived its name from the old village of Borrowstoun, situated on the high ground about a mile to the south on the turnpike road to Linlithgow, and still in existence. Borrowstoun, again, is thought to have meant the town of the borough as being in the vicinity of Linlithgow, the county town. Ness, of course, signifies a naze or point of land projecting into the sea, and, if we look at the configuration of the coast, the projecting naze is yet quite discernible.

The early settlers, as we have indicated, seem to have had little idea of architectural beauty or arrangement, and huddled the houses together. In many cases encroachments in the shape of outside stairs and porches were made on the thoroughfares, thereby making it a very difficult and costly task to accomplish the improvements which had to be undertaken by the Local Authority from time to time in later years. Many of the houses were built gable-on to the sea, a practice common in most seaport towns, and several typical instances of this are yet to be seen both in Borrowstounness and Grangepans.

X.

Mr. Johnston,[11] writing of the "auld-warld" look of the town, suggests that a painter with an eye and a taste for the antique in urban architecture might do worse than try his brush in this quarter. Here he would find some streets narrow enough and tortuous enough and erratic enough to be at once accepted as fit for reproduction on his canvas. He would here discover no lack of strange nooks and corners, and see houses in plenty that have all the quaint characteristics so beloved of artists. This was said in 1890; and before the wholesale demolitions which took place in 1902 in the heart of the town, it is gratifying to know that several artists made numerous water-colour and other sketches of the neighbourhood, and especially of its older quarters. These therefore will long preserve for many of us and our successors the quaint and "auld-warld" features of the seaport.

To what individuals or influences, local or external, Borrowstounness owed its somewhat sudden start in life it is difficult to say. It is not likely that the Forth herring fishing, which at a later date was very successful for a time, was one of these. Nor do we think the quest for whales had then become a craze with the inhabitants. What seems more likely to have contributed to its rise was the presence in the

---

[11] "Records of Bo'ness United General Seabox" (1890).

neighbourhood of the shore of an abundance of coal. Coal had been discovered in the district some centuries before, but it is evident that about the time we are writing of it was being wrought, not, perhaps, at a great depth, but still fairly extensively, by the Hamilton family or their lessees, in what was known as the coal-heugh of Borrowstounness.

The young town had the advantage of a natural harbour or creek, which was situated practically in the vicinity of the present harbour. There was then neither west nor east pier. Vessels were simply loaded and unloaded at low water by means of a causeway run out into the mud, the remains of which were discovered when enlargements and improvements at the harbour were being made long years after. Coal and salt were among early exports, chiefly to Holland and the Baltic. When the Union of the Crowns took place, in 1603, a great impetus was given to the commerce of the country, on the east coast, at any rate, and the infant port evidently shared in it. This prosperous trade induced a number of rich merchants from the west country, shipowners and others, who saw possibilities of great developments in the place, to acquire property or to reside here. The town and population therefore rapidly increased. These were the days, of course, when Glasgow and the Clyde had not yet indicated anything of their coming commercial magnitude, and when a Glasgow Customs officer was appointed to Bo'ness " on promotion."

CHAPTER II.

THE HOUSE OF HAMILTON AND KINNEIL.

1. Friar Hamilton's "Historie" and Sir Gilbert's "Exploit" on Kinneil Muir: The Modern Authorities on the Family—2. The First Lord Hamilton and his Reclamations on Kinneil Foreshore: Marries Princess Mary: Second Lord Hamilton and First Earl of Arran: A Famous Archer and Horseman: Visit of James IV. to Kinneil—3. Second Earl of Arran: Governor during Minority of Queen Mary: His Report on the Forth Landing Places: Duchy of Chatelherault Granted him: Imprisoned Edinburgh Castle—4. The First Marquis of Hamilton: The Spurious Earl of Arran Secures Kinneil: Intimacy between James VI. and Hamilton: King's Amusing Letter—5. Second Marquis: His Historic Actions as the King's Commissioner in Scots Parliament: The Five Articles of Perth Ratified: His Sudden Death at Whitehall: Supposed Treachery—6. Third Marquis and First Duke: King Charles' Commissioner to Settle Religious Disorders in Scotland: Alarming Opposition from Duke's Mother—7. Her Strong Character and Extracts from her Wonderful Will: Duke and the Engagers: Capture and Imprisonment: Beheaded in Palaceyard: Body Sent to Kinneil—8. William, Second Duke: The Commonwealth: Kinneil Lands given to General Monk: William Fights against Cromwell: Wounded at Worcester and Dies there—9. Anne, Duchess of Hamilton in her own right: Marries Lord William Douglas, afterwards Created by Courtesy Duke of Hamilton: Duchess Anne and Duke William and Development of Borrowstounness: Alterations and Enlargements at Kinneil House: Indications of their Local Undertakings: William Strongly Opposes Lauderdale: Welcomes Prince of Orange: Duchess Anne Long Survives her Husband and Son—10. James, Fourth Duke: A Strong Jacobite: Defends the Darien Scheme: His Fickle Behaviour over Union of 1707: Loses Confidence of Scottish people: Created Duke of Brandon by Queen Anne—11. The Duke's Share in Queen's Historic Creation of Peers: His Tragic Death in Duel: His son Lord Anne.

I.

THE representatives of the house of Hamilton have been proprietors of most of the land in the old Parishes of Kinneil and Borrowstounness for nearly six hundred years.

The barony of Kinneil is one of their most ancient possessions, and is associated with many interesting events in the history of the family. According to "Ffrier Mark Hamiltonis Historie"[1] King Robert the Bruce gave all the lands of Kinneil to Sir Gilbert Hamilton "for his trew service and greit manheid," and especially for having slain "for King Robertis pleasour the great lieutennand of Yngland upon Kynnale Muir." Sir Gilbert had been with the Bruce on the field of Bannockburn, and was one of the seven knights that kept the King's person. For Sir Gilbert's exploit upon Kynnale Muir, he tells us, "King Robert gaif till him his armis till weir in Scotland thre sink fuilzies[2] in ane bludy field." In connection with the alleged "exploit" on the muir, Mr. M'Kenzie[3] has stated that in a place formerly known as Kinneil Muir a remarkable stone lay near the road, which was at one time used as a thoroughfare between Linlithgow and Falkirk or Stirling. It was seven feet long, five feet broad, and three feet thick. Its upper surface had been roughly dressed, a groove had been cut round the border with a cross in the centre. The stone had a monumental appearance, but there was no vestige of tradition regarding it. The only explanation that occurs is that it might have been meant to mark the resting-place of "the great lieutennand of Yngland," whoever that worthy was. Early in the nineteenth century the stone, being an obstruction to the plough, was blown to pieces and removed. But to return to "Schir Gilbert." We are told he persevered continually with King Robert "in trew service on till ye end of his dayis, and was at his buriing in ye Abbay of Dunfermling." He appears to have been "ane naturall oratour," and gave the funeral oration on that occasion.

We have no desire to discredit the alluring narrative of the learned "Ffrier" concerning Sir Gilbert and his adventures

---

[1] M.S. Adv. Lib. Also Anderson's "Memoirs of the House of Hamilton," p. 480.
[2] Three Cinquefoils on a red shield.
[3] "New Stat. Ac.," vol. ii., Borrowstounness.

Lady Anne Cuningham, wife of James, Second Marquis of
Hamilton, and mother of James, Third Marquis,
afterwards First Duke.

(Photographed by permission from a painting in Hamilton Palace.)

See page 34.

at Bannockburn, and on Kinneil Muir, but his statements do not accord with the information given in Anderson's "Memoirs of the House of Hamilton," or in the recent work of the Lyon King, Sir J. Balfour Paul.[4]

The present Duke is the twenty-third possessor, and the first of the family is given in both these authorities as Walter Fitz-Gilbert (Walter son of Gilbert). He appears under that designation in 1294 or thereabouts. Walter is reported to have sworn fealty to King Edward I. in 1296 at Berwick, and remained an English partisan till the capture of Bothwell Castle by a detachment of the Scottish army after Bannockburn. Quite evidently there was a Gilbert; but it is difficult to believe that Walter, his son, should have been on King Edward's side at the time of Bannockburn whilst the father, according to the "Ffrier" was with Bruce in that battle, and "ane of the seven knights that kept the King's person." This may have been possible, but it does not seem very probable.

Walter is reported to have joined the Bruce after his capture at Bothwell Castle, and was knighted. Later, King Robert made him several grants of land, and among those the lands of Kinneil. Sir Walter was twice married, and the grant of Kinneil in 1323 was to him and Mary Gordon, his second wife, and to his heirs by her.

II.

In an Appendix will be found a complete list of the Hamilton family in the order of their succession, with a few notes concerning each. Several of its members, however, have figured so conspicuously in Scottish history, as well as in our local affairs, that we must now devote our attention to these for a little.

The first of the family to take a prominent place in Scottish history was the second James of Cadzow, who became the first Lord Hamilton in 1445. He was a strong supporter of the

---

[4] "Scots Peerage," vol. iv., pp. 339-397.

Douglas family, to whom he became allied by his first marriage. When King James II., in 1455, besieged the Castle of Abercorn, then a possession of the Douglas, Hamilton and Douglas mustered a strong force, but were unsuccessful in raising the siege. The Castle of Inveravon, situated about three miles to the west of Bo'ness, also belonging to the Douglas, was next demolished. The Hamiltons then became alienated from the Douglases, and Hamilton, through the influence of an uncle, was raised into the King's favour. In October of the same year he received a special charter of his lands and baronies, including Hamilton and Kinneil.

He devoted much of his energies to the reclamation of land from the sea within his territory of Kinneil by permission of the King. This reclamation was made at great cost. The reclaimed land was secured to him and his second wife,[5] Mary Stewart, sister of King James III., and widow of Thomas Boyd, Earl of Arran, by Royal Charter in 1474, the year of the marriage. The tithes of the ground were to go to a new chapel and hospital which he had built and endowed in the Parish of Shotts.

James, second Lord Hamilton, was the son of the first Lord Hamilton by the Princess Mary. He succeeded in 1479, when only a few years old. James was raised to the dignity of Earl of Arran at Holyrood on 8th August, 1503, when present at the marriage of his cousin, King James IV., to Margaret Tudor, daughter of King Henry VII. of England. The lands and earldom of Arran were bestowed, it is stated, for his nearness of blood, his services, and specially for his labours and expenses at the time of the royal marriage. The Earl had the reputation of being the best archer on horse or foot in Scotland. He kept a famous stud of horses at Kinneil, and his cousin, King James IV., is said to have paid a visit there to see them in 1508.

During the minority of James V. Arran was for a time

---

[5] This marriage connected the Hamiltons with the Royal Family of Scotland.

Regent. Ultimately he was involved in the long series of conflicts for supremacy between the rival factions of Douglas and Hamilton. He died about 1529, when he made his will and gave up an inventory of his effects at his "place" of Kinneil.

III.

James, second Earl of Arran, succeeded his father while yet a minor, and was for a time under the tutory of his uncle. He is said to have been the first builder of the Palace of Hamilton, probably under the supervision of his uncle. The young man favoured the Presbyterian religion, which was then secretly spreading in Scotland. Cardinal Beaton consequently had no love for him. Especially was this so when, on the death of the King after Solway Moss, Beaton saw that Arran was likely to be appointed governor of the realm during the minority of the infant Queen Mary of Scotland. Beaton tried to make out that he, along with three others, had been nominated by the King on his death-bed to be tutors of the Queen and joint governors. This, however, was put aside, and Arran was chosen governor, as being the nearest heir to the throne by descent from Lady Mary Stewart, his grandmother. Arran is said to have been of a gentle nature, with a policy that was weak and vacillating.

During his Regency he, in the year 1544, made a report on the harbours and landing places in the Forth, in which we find—"Kyniell—by este Kallendray (presumably Callendar, Falkirk), a myle from the shore and good landinage with botes at a place cauled Barreston."

After being commended by John Knox for his reforming zeal, Arran was prevailed upon to join Beaton's party. The Duchy of Chatelherault, in France, was granted to him and his heirs about 1549. This gift was prompted by the Queen-mother, Mary of Loraine, as an inducement to resign the Regency of Scotland in her favour. He did not do so, however, until 1554, when he retired into private life. In his later years he once more supported the Reformers, and his name is first on the list of signatures to the Second Reformation Covenant of 1560. He was also present in the Reforming Parliament of August in that year. Arran opposed the marriage of Queen Mary to Darnley, and was forced to retire for a time to France. When he returned Mary had been deposed. He was the chief of Mary's party, and suffered imprisonment in Edinburgh Castle, with much loss and damage to his property. His death took place at Hamilton either in 1574 or 1575. The Duke, as he was called in Scotland (no doubt because of Chatelherault), was survived by his wife, the eldest daughter of the Earl of Morton, who had succeeded the Earl of Lennox as Regent. They had eight children, the eldest of whom was James. This young man showed much promise in his earlier years, and was commander of the Scots Guards in France. He had strong leanings to the Reformers, and the Scots Parliament, in 1560, proposed him as a husband to Queen Elizabeth. Most unhappily, two years later he showed signs of a disordered intellect, and was afterwards pronounced insane. He lingered on until 1609, and during his lifetime was nominally in possession of the title of Earl of Arran.

IV.

The second son having died in youth, next in succession was John, the third son, who became first Marquis of Hamilton. He was over thirty years of age when he succeeded. Like his father he was a devoted supporter of Queen Mary, and, also like him, suffered the loss of much property in her cause, including the forfeiture of the Hamilton estates. In 1578 Regent Morton resigned and James VI. ruled in person, but under the influence of low-born favourites. Chief of these was James Stewart, of Bothwell Muir, who figured as Earl of Arran, the insane young Earl having resigned that title in his favour. The Raid of Ruthven delivered the young King from the influence of this usurper until the escape of James from Ruthven a year later, when the favourite again became supreme.

In the Hamilton papers we find some correspondence which indicates that the spurious Earl had not his sorrows to seek, being evidently hard pressed by many enemies. Among his usurpations he seems to have, at least temporarily, secured Kinneil. One of his letters finishes, "From my houss off Kinnele this 12 Aug. 1585," and is signed "Arraine." He was reported to be still there on 30th August "well accompanied."

In fact, there are several references[6] which point to Kinneil being used as his chief residence. This favourite had great influence with and control over the young King, and we find His Majesty reported on 9th May, 1582, as having gone "to Arran's house of Kinneil."[7] Then on 13th November next year he is again reported as staying at Kinneil with Arran.

These were dangerous times for the House of Hamilton. John first fled to England disguised in a seaman's dress, and thence to France. In 1585 he and some other exiled nobles returned, and, with Queen Elizabeth's permission, entered Scotland, and marched with a force to Stirling, where King James and Arran then were. Arran fled, and the banished lords were admitted to the King's presence. King James, though he had not previously met Hamilton, welcomed him most effusively as a faithful servant of his mother. From then Hamilton speedily rose in the King's favour. At a Parliament at Linlithgow his estates were restored, and he was appointed keeper of the Castle of Dumbarton. The King and he became very intimate friends, and there was frequent correspondence between them, particularly on matters of sport. One of the King's letters to Hamilton is very amusing, and we quote it in full. It is undated and is much destroyed, but it is thought to be about the year 1597, and written from Holyrood :—[8]

"Milorde as I taulde you at youre being withe me I ame

---

[6] P.C. Reg., vol. iv.
[7] P.C. Reg., vol. iii.
[8] Hamilton Report, p. 67.

sa contineuallie braggit uithe Milord Home that I haue to defend the honoure of Scotlande at this tyme; he uill be heir on Weddinsdaye next uith nyne couple of fleing fiends, as they saye, thairfore I pray you to send me with the bearare tua or three of your fleitest and fairest running houndis; and because, in goode faithe, I ame disprouydit of horsis I uill in a hamelie maner praye you to send, lykeuyes with the bearare, Griseld Blackstow,[9] or gif he be not in that cace any other hunting horse and on my honestie na boddie sall ryde on him but myself, and baith he and youre doggis sall be returnid to you immediately . . . I commandit the guidman of Grange[10] to helpe you to choose the doggis. Thus not doubting ye uill be a goode fallou in the aulde maner to this my reasonable request and uith Goddis Grace the Englishe tykis shall be dung doun. I bidd you hair (tilie) fairueill, youre louing freinde in the aulde mainer. James R."

The letter is said to be in the King's best style. It is "hamelie" enough certainly, and we all like to think that the challenge resulted in the honour of Scotland being upheld "in the aulde mainer."

Hamilton was present at Holyrood at the baptism of the Princess Margaret on 15th April, 1549, and then made a peer. Two days after he was installed with great ceremony in His Majesty's great chamber at Holyrood, his title being proclaimed as Marquis of Hamilton, Earl of Arran, and Lord Evan. He died on 6th April, 1604, his last act being to commend his son to the King's favour. Very shortly before his death he bound over his nephew, Lord Abercorn, to see to the interests of his imbecile brother, who was still alive.

Lord John's wife, who survived him, was Margaret, only daughter of John Lyon, [11] seventh Lord Glamis, and widow of Gilbert, fourth Earl of Cassillis.

---

[9] Evidently a special steed of Hamilton's.
[10] Hamilton of Grange, his master-stabler.
[11] It is possible that Castle Lyon, which at one time existed near the shore at Kinneil in the vicinity of the present furnace yard pit, was the Dower House of Lady Margaret.

V.

James, second Marquis of Hamilton, succeeded his father in 1604 about the age of fifteen. He had been styled Lord Evan on his father's promotion to the Marquisate, as his unfortunate uncle still held the title of Earl of Arran. By the time of his succession King James had become King of England, and gone south. The King, however, wished to favour the young man, and was desirous that he should attend Court. But Marquis James preferred to remain in Scotland. In the long run he was prevailed on to go to London, and was there made a Gentleman of the Bed-Chamber, a Lord of the Privy Council, and Steward of the Royal Household. Early in 1617 he attended a Convention of Estates in Scotland, and was residing there when King James revisited it for the first time after leaving to ascend the English throne in 1603. During this visit he was in close attendance on the King, and entertained him at Hamilton Palace on his return journey. In a year or so Hamilton again went south, after endeavouring to induce the Provost of Edinburgh to influence the citizens to submit to the King in matters of ritual. In 1619 the King created him a peer of England as Earl of Cambridge and Lord Innerdale, and in 1621 he was made a Knight of the Garter.

To the second Marquis came the appointment which has made his name prominent in Scottish history. King James, through reckless extravagance, found his finances exhausted, and, having already been repeatedly voted supplies by the English Parliament, he could not at that moment very well make another application. Accordingly, recourse was made to Scotland, and the Marquis of Hamilton was despatched there as the King's representative, with commission to hold a Parliament in Edinburgh, and among other things to raise supplies. He arrived there on the 18th, and the Parliament met on the 25th July, 1621. The Commissioner opened with a long speech extolling His Majesty's merits and explaining his pecuniary necessities. The result was a subsidy equal to about £33,000. It was the King's intention that this same Parliament should ratify the Five Articles of Perth by which Episcopacy was to be imposed upon the Scottish Church, and this delicate matter was next taken up by the Commissioner. After a most determined opposition the Articles were carried by a majority of twenty-seven, on an assurance from the Commissioner that no further innovations would be proposed by the King. Hamilton, it cannot be questioned, manœuvred the whole business, and therefore the ire of zealous Presbyterians was then and afterwards strongly raised against him.

At the close of the sitting, and just at the moment when the Commissioner was about to confirm the Articles by the touch of the sceptre, a terrific thunderstorm suddenly burst over the place. A great darkness came on, illumined only by flashes of lightning. Rain came down in torrents, and hailstones of enormous size also fell. After a delay of nearly a couple of hours the Parliament broke up in confusion and without the usual ceremonial procession. The Presbyterians regarded this storm as an evident token of Divine displeasure against the Parliament for interfering with the spiritual privileges of the people, and the day was long known as "the black Saturday."

The Marquis died suddenly at Whitehall in March, 1625, shortly before his Royal Master. When the King, who himself was then lying ill, heard the news, he is reported to have said, "If the branches be thus cut down, the stock cannot be expected to survive long." It was boldly asserted that Hamilton had been poisoned on grounds of jealousy, either by the Duke of Buckingham or at his instigation. The King died very soon after, and Dr. Egelsham, who had been one of his physicians, expressly accused Buckingham not only of poisoning the King, but the Marquis of Hamilton also. Buckingham, however, was never judicially accused of the crime.[12]

The wife of the Marquis was Anna, daughter of the Earl of Glencairn, who is described as "a lady of firm and masculine

---

[12] See Taylor's "Pictorial History of Scotland," chap. xlii.

character," and of whom we shall have more to say later. They had issue James, third Marquis and first Duke, who succeeded; and William, afterwards second Duke; and three daughters.

VI.

James succeeded at the age of nineteen. For the next three years he remained in Scotland. He then received a pressing message from King Charles to come to Court. This he did, and had the Order of the Garter and a number of other offices bestowed upon him. He was afterwards sent abroad, by the King's desire, to assist Gustavus Adolphus in invading Germany. When Charles visited Scotland in 1633 the Marquis accompanied him and took part in the Coronation ceremonies. After this he seems to have retired from public life, until the people began to openly resist the order to use Laud's Service-Book in all the churches. Charles then specially commissioned the Marquis to settle these disorders; and in this task he naturally incurred a marked degree of popular odium. His efforts were useless, and he was obliged, after many negotiations and two journeys to London, where he seriously consulted and advised with Charles, to proclaim the meeting of the famous General Assembly at Glasgow in November, 1638. Hamilton then went south again, but returned in a year as General and Commander of a fleet with which the King meant to silence the Covenanters. It is related of his mother, Marchioness Anna Cunningham, that when her son the Marquis arrived with his fleet in the Forth she rode up and down the sands of Leith, carrying pistols in her holsters, and threatening to blow out the brains of her son should he cross her path to molest the Covenanters.[13] Whether this scared him we do not know, but at any rate a truce was before long agreed to at Dunse Law, and the Marquis again retired into private life.

In 1641 Charles made his second visit to Scotland, and

---

[13] See Hewison's "Covenanters," vol. i., p. 325.

C

Hamilton, who was with him, was one of the intended victims of a plot known as "The Incident," whereby Argyll, Hamilton, and Lanark, his brother, were to be seized and carried on board a Royal frigate at Leith. The plot was discovered, and these lords withdrew to Kinneil House, and refused to meet the King. It is not clear, however, whether Charles was involved in the affair or not.

In April, 1643, the King, by a charter dated at Oxford, created the Marquis Duke of Hamilton, Marquis of Clydesdale, Earl of Arran and Cambridge, Lord Avon and Innerdale, with remainder to himself and the heirs-male of his body; whom failing, to his brother William and the heirs-male of his body; whom failing, to the eldest heir-female of the Duke's body, without division; and it was under this destination that his daughter, the Duchess Anne, in time succeeded. The Duke and his brother Lanark were slandered to the King, and the former was for a time imprisoned.

VII.

It must be remembered that during all this time the Duke's old mother was still alive. Her son's association with the King against the Covenanters, of whom she was a strong supporter, not only aroused her wrath, as we have seen, but caused her great grief. This can be gathered from her Will.[14] That document was written with her own hand at Holyrood House on 4th November, 1644, and in the introduction she explains that she considers it her duty to put her house in order, lest she "should be chapit at on ane soudentie." Referring apparently to this imprisonment of her son, "my lord douck," she, in making him her executor and heir, leaves him her blessing, and prays the Lord to direct him and to grant that he may make the right use of this "visitation" that is laid upon him; also that he may have God's glory before his eyes, and look more to that than to all this world can give him. Then she says, there is one thing that she would beseech him to do above any other earthly thing, if ever he got out

---

[14] Hamilton Report, pp. 55-7.

of prison, and that was to "mack chois of soum good woman to mache with," so that if it pleased the Lord his father's house might stand in his person, which she prayed the Lord might be. (His first wife had died some years before, and their two sons had died young.) In her bequests she leaves him her rights and leases of her coal of Kinneil, and mentions that it had cost her much money, and servants did reap the profit; but now it was in so good case that he could not but make great benefit out of it. She counsels him to put faithful servants to it, and never to put it out of his own hands. She leaves him all her salt-pans, and advises him to build more, for she believes the profit will be great if God sent peace. She also leaves him the plenishing in her house in Kinneil, her new tapestry, and all other movables she either made or bought, except her silver saltfit and some little silver porringers which she left to her "dochtir." She further requested him to be "caynd to his sister and hir childring," for she believed she was a good woman and feared the Lord.

As for her son Lanark, who had also been, as a Royalist, opposed to the Covenanters, she prayed the Lord to hold his heart upright before Him, and make him now, after his past wanderings, a faithful servant in His cause, and let him never fall back from Him, lest his last state be worse than his first; she prayed God also to take a grip of his heart and reveal Himself, and let him know that in the day of death there is no comfort to be found but in Him, for all the monarchs and monarchies in the world could not give one moment's ease. A blink of the face of a reconciled God was a sweet thing; therefore, for Christ's sake, he was to seek Him in time, and away with the follies of Courts, for their ways were but wicked, and all their delights and sweetness in the end would bring bitterness. These maternal solicitations concluded with, "Remembir this is the last saying of ane louing mother."

The closing events in the reign of King Charles are all so well known that they need not be recalled here. We must remember, however, that when the King was captured the

Duke did all he could to obtain his release, just as he before that had—hopelessly, however, because of the King's obstinacy in repudiating the Covenant—done what he could to advance the King's interests. And we must also remember that when a last effort was made to rescue the King from the hands of Cromwell, the "Engagers" or band of Scottish Royalists who did so were led by the Duke. Cromwell easily defeated this force near Preston in 1648. The Duke was taken and imprisoned in various places, Windsor Castle being the last. He had an affecting interview with the King here on the latter's last journey to London. After the King's execution in January, 1649, the Duke escaped, but was re-taken. He was then tried at Westminster, and beheaded in the Palace Yard on 9th March. His remains were first sent to his house of Kinneil, and from there taken to Hamilton, where they were buried. He is said to have been of an affectionate and kindly temperament, and strongly attached to his brother. It was a good thing that his poor old mother was spared the grief of his trial and execution, she having been "chapit at," and left this troublesome world some little time before. The Duke did not marry a second time. He left two daughters—Anne, who became Duchess of Hamilton in her own right, and Susanna, who married the seventh Earl of Cassillis.

VIII.

William, second Duke of Hamilton, was James' brother and successor, and the "Lainrick" of his mother's Will. He had been closely associated with his brother's Royalist exploits, and in 1640 was made Secretary for Scotland. William had frequently been in danger of imprisonment, but made wonderful escapes. While James was the leader of the "Engagers," it was William who conducted the correspondence with the English Royalists in connection with the movement; and when James went to Preston to meet his defeat William remained in Scotland, and did his best to uphold the King's party. William

James, First Duke of Hamilton.

(After the painting by Vandyck in Hamilton Palace.)

Photographed by permission from the copy recently hung in the Scottish National Portrait Gallery.

The House of Hamilton and Kinneil

was seeking safety abroad when his brother was executed, and Scotland being then ostensibly under the Commonwealth and in a particularly unsettled state, he remained away. Cromwell about this time seems to have appropriated the lands of Kinneil, and bestowed them along with other appropriated possessions on General Monk for his military services in Scotland. King Charles II.—himself abroad—found William at The Hague, and they returned to Scotland together in 1650. William's return was objected to, and he withdrew from the Court and remained in retirement for a year. He then entered the Civil strife, and was actively engaged in attacking the English garrisons that were quartered in Lanarkshire. He was also prominent in the march of the Scots army with the King and General Leslie at its head, and in the defeats of that army at the hands of Cromwell at Dunbar Drove and Worcester. At Worcester he fought bravely, but was severely wounded, his leg being crushed and broken by a shot. Had the limb been at once amputated it is believed he would have recovered. This was delayed until it was too late, and he died on 12th September, 1651, nine days after the battle, aged thirty-five. Thus his brief career was closed. His wife was the eldest daughter of the Earl of Dirleton, and they had one son, who died an infant, and five daughters.

IX.

We have now reached that member of the Hamilton family whose interest in Kinneil and Borrowstounness was very great. This was Anne, Duchess of Hamilton in her own right. As her uncle William left no male issue, she succeeded him, in terms of the destination in the charter of Charles I. to her father. The Duchess Anne, or Anna as she is sometimes named, was born about 1636, and so was about fifteen when her uncle died. She lived to the long age of eighty, but her long and useful life was not without its heavy sorrows. When she was thirteen her father, the first Duke, was executed, and she lived to bemoan the termination of the career of her son, the fourth Duke, in a duel with Lord Mohun. She was a lady of great constancy of mind, evenness of temper, solidity of judgment, and unaffected piety.

In April, 1656, she married William Douglas, eldest son of the second marriage of William, first Marquis of Douglas. Four years after the marriage came the Restoration, when Charles II. returned from France and was restored to kingship at Whitehall, amid great rejoicing, in May, 1660. Duchess Anne and her husband soon came under Royal favour, and in September of the same year the King bestowed upon the latter for life the titles of Duke of Hamilton, Marquis of Clydesdale, Earl of Arran, Lanark, and Selkirk. A year later the Duchess received from the King a re-grant of all the lands and baronies of Hamilton, Kinneil, and others which had been resigned by her uncle to the King when they were together at The Hague in 1650.

The Duke's first business was to remove the burden of debt under which the Hamilton estates lay. He then gave some attention to public affairs.

To Duchess Anne and Duke William, her husband, much credit is due for the early development of "the village" of Borrowstounness. With them commenced a thoroughly practical interest in the struggling town and in their own House of Kinneil. On the latter they made very considerable alterations, greatly enlarging and embellishing it. And there is no doubt whatever that they made it a frequent place of residence. The reign of Charles II., as we know, was full of bitterness and bloodshed for Scotland over religious difficulties. In all this the inhabitants of the young town and of the surrounding district had their share; and, loyal as the Duke had originally been to the King, he seems to have resented the repeated attempts of Charles to put down Presbyterianism.

Hamilton most strongly and openly opposed the Duke of Lauderdale, who had become Secretary for Scotland, and was, unfortunately, exercising a remarkable influence over the King. Lauderdale, in the former reign, had been a zealous Covenanter.

He now turned about and became as bitter and severe against Covenanters and conventicles as he had hitherto been zealous for them. There is good evidence locally to show that Duke William was a keen practical business man, and we are not surprised to find that he strongly condemned Lauderdale's Government, setting forth a variety of grievances in the law, revenue, and commerce. This attitude lost him all favour at Court. On the accession of James II. that monarch was anxious to get the Duke's support for his schemes of toleration during his short reign of three years, but he does not appear to have succeeded. On the contrary, it is stated that the Duke was one of the first in Scotland to welcome the coming of William, Prince of Orange. Moreover, he was President of the Convention of Estates, which met in 1690, and accepted William and Mary as King and Queen of Scotland. He died in April, 1694, at Holyrood, and was buried at Hamilton. William, we read, was not of polished manners; he was rough, but candid and sincere. His temper was boisterous, less calculated to submit than to govern. He wrote well, but spoke ill. It is said also that he had an expert knowledge of the families, laws, and history of his country.

To revert to their local connection, we will find in the first chapter on the Regality that King Charles II., in January, 1668, granted a charter in favour of Duchess Anne and her heirs, creating the lands and baronies of Kinneil, Carriden, and others, and the town of Borrowstounness, into a Regality, and naming the town to be the head burgh of the Regality. This was the first important step towards the proper local government of the district. An Act of the Scots Parliament in 1669, doubtless on the supplication of the Duke and Duchess, embodied the above charter, and, in addition, gave the burgh the privilege of a free port and harbour. There can be no doubt that the Regality Charter was obtained by the Duchess on her own and her husband's initiative in the interests of a town and district which seemed full of possibilities for superior and vassal alike. Then, in 1669, we discover the Duke and Duchess Anne supplicating Parliament and getting the

Kirk and Parish of Kinneil suppressed and included in the Parish of Bo'ness, the Kirk of Bo'ness declared to be the Kirk of the United Parish, and appointing the Duke and Duchess to provide a manse and glebe in Bo'ness in place of the old manse and glebe of Kinneil.

Again, we find an Act of the Scots Parliament in favour of Duchess Anne changing the fourth fair of Borrowstounness from 18th November to the second Tuesday of July. Another Act is also found in 1672 authorising the Duke and Duchess to appropriate the vacant stipend to the repair of the Kirk and manse of Bo'ness. And in the "Register of Bandes" of our Regality Court there is recorded in October, 1717, an Obligement by the Duchess Anne to contribute £5 sterling yearly for defraying the expense of the communion elements at the celebration of the sacrament in the Kirk of Bo'ness.

X.

We close this narrative with a sketch of Duchess Anne's son, James, Earl of Arran, fourth Duke of Hamilton. And here we may fitly say that the tragic termination of his life practically saw the withdrawal of the House of Hamilton from its important place in the historical annals of Scotland.

As we have already hinted, Duchess Anne long survived her husband, and she even outlived her son by four years. The Earl was thirty-six when his father died, and while the father, as we have seen, became alienated from Charles and from James, the son appears to have developed strong Jacobite leanings. It is very remarkable to find the father receiving William of Orange with open arms, while the son maintained his close adherence to the deposed James. In fact, it has been asserted that he was implicated in a treasonable correspondence, and twice imprisoned in the Tower of London, but released without prosecution. When his father died Duchess Anne, in the unusual circumstances just referred to, continued to manage her own affairs. Five years after, however, she, as Duchess in her own right, resigned all her titles into the hands of King William III. The King then, in August of the same year (1698), by a charter dated at Loo, conferred upon the Earl the titles and dignities of Duke of Hamilton, Marquis of Clydesdale, Earl of Arran, Lanark, Cambridge, and others. The grant, we are told, came as a great surprise to the governing party, as the Earl's disaffection was well known. It was, we may be sure, not given out of respect for himself, but clearly as a recognition of the loyal services of his father and mother to the King and Queen. When he became Duke he remained as much a curious personality as ever. During Queen Anne's reign he bulked very largely and somewhat romantically in our national history. He formed a party in the Scots Parliament in defence of the Darien scheme for the colonisation of Panama, but did not carry his views. He at first strongly opposed the proposal for the Union of the Parliaments in 1707, but failed his party at a critical moment in the final stages of the struggle, and the measure was passed. This failure lost Hamilton the confidence of the Scottish people, and historians have severely criticised his actions at this time, fickleness, treachery, and self-seeking being among the things laid to his charge. We must recollect, in considering these things, that the Duke had a difficult position to fill. Though lukewarm towards William, it was different with Queen Anne, who was his kinswoman, and looked upon him as leader of the Scottish nobles, and as a personal friend and adviser as well. The Queen was strong for the Union. Hamilton was strong against it. The Queen implored Hamilton to withdraw his opposition, and the Queen prevailed.

When an attempt on behalf of the Pretender was made, in 1708, the Duke's Jacobite ardour seems by this time to have cooled, for he disapproved of it. In June that year he was chosen as a Representative Peer of Scotland, and on 11th September, 1711, Queen Anne created him a peer of Great Britain, as Duke of Brandon, County Suffolk, and Baron Dutton, County Chester. Any questioning of the Royal prerogative in such matters appears unconstitutional to a degree. But such was the high tension at which party politics stood, and so intense were the feelings of rage and jealousy which the bestowal of such a signal mark of Royal approval engendered in some breasts that an objection was entered against the dukedom. The points of objection and all other details connected with the fight on the Hamilton patent, although very interesting, cannot be given here.

XI.

The Duke, perfectly entitled as he was to take his seat as Duke of Brandon in spite of all objections and oppositions, evidently did not care to do so, and his descendants were deprived of the honour until 1782, when the point was decided in favour of Douglas, eighth Duke of Hamilton, who petitioned George III. to be summoned to Parliament as Duke of Brandon. The request was referred to the judges of the House of Lords, and they immediately decided he was entitled to such summons.

One significant and historically interesting action of the Duke's when he became a power at the Court of Queen Anne must not be omitted. We refer to the precedent by which, largely on the advice of the Duke, and by way of getting rid of the Marlboroughs, Queen Anne created twelve new peers, thus swamping the Whig lords with the new creations. Those days, it seems, were as sensational politically as any we have had since.

On 26th October, 1712, Queen Anne invested Hamilton with the Order of the Garter in addition to that of the Thistle, which he already held. Soon afterwards, on 15th November, 1712, his career was terminated in the celebrated duel in London with Lord Mohun, a notorious bully, both parties being killed. Thackeray, in his "Henry Esmond," introduces the Duke as one of his characters, and also describes the duel.

The Duke was buried at Hamilton. He was twice married,

The House of Hamilton and Kinneil

first to the eldest daughter of the second Earl of Sunderland, who died at Kinneil in her twenty-fourth year. She had two daughters who died in infancy. The Duke's second wife was the only child and heiress of the fifth Lord Gerard. By her he had three sons and four daughters. The sons were James, who succeeded as fifth Duke; William, who became M.P. for Lanark in 1734, and died shortly after; and Lord Anne, a son born 1709, who received his feminine name from Queen Anne, who was his godmother.

The name and career of Lord Anne Hamilton, or Lord Anne Edwards Hamilton, as he came to style himself, are of more than passing interest to us, because it is from him that the thirteenth and present Duke is directly descended. The genealogical history, however, is too long to be here referred to.

CHAPTER III.

KINNEIL.

1. Kinneil House—2. The Village and Parish—3. The Church and Churchyard—4. The Ministers of Kinneil.

I.

KINNEIL HOUSE, the ancient seat of the Hamiltons, is beautifully situated about a mile west from Bo'ness and just a little beyond Casteloan. Originally the building must have been of the nature of the ordinary feudal keep, and occupied much the same site as the existing structure. Its strategical position on a high and naturally protected site made it well-nigh impregnable.

Historians and antiquarians have all along been anxious to have a complete history of the building from its earliest days. Professor Dugald Stewart, when in residence at Kinneil, wrote to Rome in quest of information. He is said to have succeeded in getting traces of its history for several hundred years back, but these notes have been lost.

The house was pillaged in December, 1559, during popular commotions, burned in February following, and again burned in 1570 by some of the English army who had invaded Scotland. The Duke of Chatelherault, who was reputed to be the first builder of Hamilton Palace, is said to have also made large repairs at Kinneil, and these quite possibly were made by him both before and after the two burnings.

Sibbald had a great partiality for "Kinneil Palace," as he calls it. To his mind, it ranked amongst the finest seats in Britain. His descriptions not only of the woods and gardens,

Kinneil House.

(From a photograph by W. S. Andrew, Carriden.)

but of the mansion, its rooms, staircases, and of the furniture and pictures by great masters, furnish us with some idea of the former grandeur of "this princely seat, once the abode of nobles and the retreat of kings."

Dr. Rennie and Mr. M'Kenzie both give descriptions of the building. The following notes, however, are based on a much more recent and very complete architectural account of it[1]:—

"As will be seen from the illustration the structure consists of two parts, namely, an oblong keep (the original and centre building), with wings north and south added in later times, and a block of buildings to the north-east originally forming a separate house. In length the keep runs to fifty-six feet six inches, and to thirty-one feet six inches in width, with walls fully six feet in thickness. On the ground floor level in the western or back wall are still to be seen three shot-holes of the horizontal kind two feet six inches in length by six inches in height. The first floor contains a great hall, forty-one feet six inches long by twenty feet broad; but in other respects the structure has been completely transformed through subsequent additions and alterations. Where the original entrance doorway and staircases were cannot now be traced, and few features remain to indicate the date of the keep. The old building, as we have seen, passed through many vicissitudes. With the advent of the seventeenth century came quieter times. It was then considered more suitable to erect a new and detached mansion to the north-east, keeps at this period being often abandoned and newer and more comfortable dwellings erected. This new house was of the L plan, with the staircase in the re-entering angle, as can still be observed from the north side. Some of the rooms in this building have the appearance of an awkward addition, and, especially opposite the staircase, do not fit in as if they formed part of the original design. The elevation shows a good deal of the character of a Scottish seventeenth century mansion. During the reign of Charles II. the Duchess Anne and her husband

---

[1] "Castellated and Dom. Arch. of Scotland."

resolved to combine the keep and the detached mansion into an imposing edifice. They therefore added the wings at the north and south ends of the old keep. The north wing served to unite the keep and the detached mansion, the internal communication being obtained by means of a skewed doorway. At the same time the existing great square staircase, with its heavy stone balustrade, was erected in the south wing. It only leads to the first floor, however, the upper wings being reached by two circular staircases. The roof of the keep was also at this time crowned with a classic cornice and balustrade, just as we find it now; and its windows were enlarged and arranged in regular rows to match those in the symmetrical wings. A central doorway with classical mouldings completed the transformation. On the front of the north wing is a fine panel which attracts much attention. This contains the arms of the authors of the transformation just decribed. In the right shield are to be found the Hamilton arms and motto, and on the left what appear to be the Hamilton and Douglas Arms quartered, probably for the Duchess Anne and her husband, Lord William Douglas. The house now became a great but rambling edifice, the hall of the ancient keep serving as the dining-room, while the hall of the formerly detached mansion became the modern drawing-room. Internally the building was once richly decorated, but the upper floors of the keep seem never to have been finished."

No mention is made of the approach to the keep. In all likelihood this would be from the west, where a drawbridge would be used over the natural moat formed by the wide and deep ravine of the burn. And there is still evidence of a pillar, probably connected with the drawbridge, on the east bank of the ravine to the rear of the house.

There are now two beautiful approaches, one named the Hamilton Ride, entering from the south at Hamilton Lodge The other, from the east, is across the bridge which spans the Dean burn, and along a wide and beautiful avenue of stately beech trees.

Kinneil policies are greatly enhanced by two beautifully

wooded rivulets, the Dean burn and the Gil burn. The former runs under the main approach near the entrance, while the latter forms the western boundary of the house. Both fall into the Firth near the Snab. The glen of the Gil burn, according to tradition, is haunted by the wraith of Ailie or Alice, Lady Lilburne. The story is that she was the wife of a colonel of Cromwell's, who was for some time resident at Kinneil, and that she committed suicide by throwing herself into the ravine from one of the back windows. Another legend is to the effect that there was a subterranean communication between Kinneil House and Linlithgow Palace; but it is too foolish for credence.

II.

There is little doubt that the village of Kinneil, now no more, sprang up in feudal times. It was built, we are told, to the west of Kinneil House near the site of the Roman Wall, and had the causeway or base of the rampart as its street. The proprietors of the soil in those days fostered such villages in the neighbourhood of their keeps. Thus in troublous times they had their vassals and retainers ready at any time to guard and defend them. With the advent of more peaceful times, however, many of the old feudal obligations fell into disuse, and, as a consequence, these feudal villages were broken up. But Kinneil village long survived feudal times, and latterly assumed quite a modern character. In time the district became the Parish of Kinneil, which was bounded on the north by the sea, on the west by the River Avon, on the east by the castle wall, commonly called "Capies Wall,"[2] and on the south by Linlithgow. Malt-making and brewing were in the seventeenth century the occupations of the villagers and parishioners to a great extent. Indeed, many of the early feuars in Bo'ness were bound by their titles to go to the Brewlands of Kinneil to have their barley made into malt.

---

[2] A point of shore land east of Snab was known as "Capies Point."

It is recorded[3] that Kinneil was a considerable town long before any population had collected at the Ness, and also that in the year 1661 there were 559 "communicable" persons in the parish, the greater number of whom resided in the town of Kinneil. In 1691 the village was almost wholly demolished, only a few families remaining. As with Blackness in the east, so with Kinneil in the west, the rapid rise of the new town and port of Borrowstounness practically led to its extinction. But even in 1843, long after the Kirk and Parish of Kinneil had been suppressed and a new church opened in Borrowstounness, the inhabitants of the Barony of Kinneil still observed some old customs connected with the ancient parish. This appeared particularly in the management of their poor, which was quite distinct from that of Bo'ness. Kinneil folks put their church-door collections for the poor into the old ladle of Kinneil Church, whilst the inhabitants of the town put their quota into a different receptacle. After the poor belonging to Kinneil were supplied, the remainder of the funds that could be spared was distributed to the poor of the town. These funds were occasionally augmented by voluntary contributions from a Hearse Society connected with the barony, and were always more than sufficient for supplying their poor. It is greatly to be regretted that information concerning the parish and village is so scant. Unfortunately, the Church records were lost some hundreds of years ago. In a historical sense this is a calamity, for with them a great deal of interesting and valuable information must have gone for ever.

III.

On a knoll to the west of the ravine at the back of Kinneil House are yet to be seen the ruins of the Church of Kinneil. The building ran east and west, and the western gable, containing a belfry apparently for two bells placed adjacently, is nearly all that remains. In consequence of its ruinous state

---

[3] "New Stat. Ac.," vol. ii.

it is now difficult to form much idea of what the church was like. Its length cannot be traced, but there appear to have been buildings, at a distance eastwards of about sixty-four feet. From indications it seems to have consisted of a large nave, with a transept on the south side only. On the north several small chapels may have been grouped, as there are evidences, though slight, of buildings here. The west gable measures twenty-six feet wide outside, and is three feet nine inches thick. Entrance was gained by doors opposite each other on the north and south sides, a few feet from the west gable. Short flights of steps led into the church, the floor of which was below the ground level. There is no trace of the eastern gable, or of where the entrances from that end, if any, were situated. The floor appears to have been covered, in places at least, with slabs. Some of these bear devices and initials, and it is very probable that interments had taken place inside the building.

At what date the church was built we cannot learn. In the twelfth century it was common for the feudal lord to provide a place of worship for his family and retainers, and doubtless the building was erected early in the century by some of the Hamiltons.

According to an authority[4] quoted by Sibbald, Kinneil was in the diocese of St. Andrews and deanery of Linlithgow about the year 1176, and was rated at twenty five merks. It had been given to the Canons of Holyrood in the twelfth and thirteenth centuries, and was confirmed to them by the Bishop of St. Andrews in 1240. The canons enjoyed the revenues, and the cure was served by a vicar. We find[5] also that in 1512 John Stirling granted £10 sterling yearly from his lands of Easter Crackey to a chaplain for performing divine service at one of the altars of Kinneil Church. A manse and glebe, we know, came to be attached to the charge in later years. The site of the former cannot be located, but it possibly lay to the north or west of the church.

---

[4] "New Stat. Ac.," vol. ii.
[5] Ibid.

A bell belonging to the church is now in the possession of the Kirk Session of Bo'ness. It is thought to be one of two, inasmuch as the inscription is incomplete, and is supposed to have been continued on the other. The double belfry lends support to this supposition. The inscription is in ornamental Lombardic capitals—"+en Katerina: vocor: ut: per: me: virginis: aline:" Diameter, 23¾ inches. This bell was on view in the Scottish Exhibition of National History, Art, and Industry, Glasgow, 1911.

Around the remains of the church lies the old churchyard. To the west and south the flat tombstones lie in abundance; and it is believed there are also many graves and tombstones to the north, though not now visible. Few of the tombstones to be seen are now in their original positions. Laid flat on the grave, and with little but their own weight to keep them in position, they could be easily displaced; and it is evident that many of them have from time to time been removed and cleaned, with the object of deciphering the emblems and dates. The stones are generally about six and a half feet long and three feet broad. Inscriptions there are none, and names but few. Initials, however, are common; and the names, when given, are usually cut round the borders of the stone. Very many have a shield on them, generally in relief, but sometimes simply cut into the stone; and it is supposed that many of these indicate the graves of some of the numerous cadets of the House of Hamilton at one time resident in our neighbourhood.

Some of the stones have symbols indicating the occupation of the deceased. There is, for example, one with an anchor; another with a small hammer in the centre of a shield, with initials; another with what is evidently a maltster's shovel; and several with collier's pick and hammer.

The members of the Ducal House were generally buried at Hamilton Palace. Alexander, the tenth Duke, constructed the famous mausoleum there, which cost £150,000, and took twelve years to build.

IV.

Undernoted is a list of the ministers of Kinneil[6] from the Reformation.

The first is Mr. Thomas Peblis, and the year of his appointment is given as 1588. He was presented to Bathgate in 1592, but preferred to remain at Kinneil; was a member of Assembly in 1602, 1610, and 1617; and had a son, boarded in the New College, St. Andrews, in 1616. It is thought that he became the minister of Kirkmichael.

Mr. Peblis was succeeded, in 1618, by Mr John Peblis, A.M., who studied at the University of Edinburgh, and attained his degree three years before. He died in March, 1625, aged about thirty, and in the seventh year of his ministry. There is nothing to show that he was a relative of the former minister.

The successor of Mr. John Peblis was Mr. Richard Dicksone, A.M., formerly of St. Cuthbert's. He was presented here by old Marchioness Anna of Hamilton. There was delay over his settlement. During the reign of James, or early in that of Charles, he had been confined in Dumbarton Castle. When nominated by the Duchess, the Bishop of St. Andrews continued the collation until he acquainted King Charles, and meanwhile steps were taken to "keep order" at Kinneil. The King's authority was obtained, release followed, and the Bishop directed Mr. Dicksone "not to exercise his gifts elsequhair than at the Kirk of Kinneil." He was a member of the General Assembly in 1638, and died in 1648, aged about seventy-two. He was married first to Bessie Pantoune, by whom he had a family of two daughters and five sons. His second wife, Elizabeth, daughter of Robert Hamilton, merchant, Edinburgh, survived him.

The last minister of Kinneil was Mr. William Wishart, A.M. He graduated at Edinburgh University in April, 1645, of which his son and grandson became the twelfth and fifteenth

---

[6] Scott's Fasti: Synod Lothian and Tweeddale

Principals respectively. He was admitted in August, 1649, but there is some uncertainty as to the year in which he entered the charge. Details of his trials and troubles while minister here and afterwards will be found in the chapter on the Covenanters. References to his brilliant family will also be found elsewhere.

Kinneil Parish and Church were finally suppressed by an Act of the Scottish Parliament in 1669.[7]

---

[7] In order to stimulate public interest in the historical associations of Kinneil the Rev. R. Gardner, present parish minister of Bo'ness, conducted divine service in the ruins of the old church on three occasions between 1898 and 1900.

CHAPTER IV.

WHAT THE PRIVY COUNCIL REGISTERS REVEAL.

Period 1549-1668.

1. Kinneil and the Fort on Inchkeith: Carriden Man, Keeper of Haven of Bo'ness, 1565: Saltmaking an Early Industry: Regulations as to Salt Export—2. Protective Measures Concerning Plague: The Mercat Cross, Kinneil: Opposition from Linlithgow—3. The Royal Visit of 1617—4. Attempt to Evade Customs: Restrictions Regarding Coal Exportation: The Troubles of Roger Duncanson, Coalmaster—5. Threatened Invasion by Spain—6. Plague Precautions of 1635: A Bellicose Gentleman—7. Regulation of Coal Supply and Charges: An Echo of Commonwealth: A Re-edified Kirk Seat—8. Extraordinary Rioting at Caldwall of Grange—9. Peremptory Measures Anent Plague—10. Linlithgow Magistrates in Trouble—11. The "Clenging" of Goods and Vessels: Letters of Marque: The Old Roadways of Borrowstounness.

I.

The Privy Council of Scotland was practically the executive body of the Scots Parliament. It was a very excellent institution, as its Acts and minute-books show. The scope of its business embraced nearly every kind of question—civil, criminal, and administrative. Particular attention was paid to measures to preserve the peace, and to regulations for preventing the country from being infested by plague and pestilence. The registers of this important Council naturally contain much of historical value concerning all parts of Scotland. There are many things of very considerable local interest. Instead of giving the local complaints and supplications in all their quaint detail, we now refer to them in short narratives, and only give the original phrasing when specially interesting.

On 22nd June, 1549,[1] the Council Ordered Kinneil (no word yet of Bo'ness), as one of "the borrowis on the sydes of

---

[1] P.C. Reg., vol. xiv. (appen. vol.), p. 8.

Forth and great tounes and throuchfares that lyis within tua myles to the coist of the samen," to send its quota of men to assist in building a fort on Inchkeith for resisting the old enemies of England. It appears the number of "pioneers," as they were termed, needed to assist in the work was 400, and that they were to get 2s. per day (Scots).

We find the first reference to Bo'ness on 19th October, 1565.[2] It indicates the beginning of life at the port. On this date the Council appointed Patrick Cruming of Carriddin " keeper of the haven of Borrowistounness, and all the bounds betwixt the same and Blakness for watching the passage of any of the enemies of their Majesties."[3] This gentleman's name we have also noticed in connection with the ownership of certain land in Wester Carriden. He is there designed as " Patrick Crumbie in Carriden, first janitor to the then Queen's Majesty."

During the sixteenth and seventeenth centuries both shores of the Firth of Forth were studded with salt pans, and a big export trade was developed. Locally there are references to Kinneil pans, or the Duke's pans, situated in the vicinity of the present slaughter-house at Corbiehall; to the Grange pans —the pans connected with Grange estate; to Bonhard pans— connected apparently with the estate of Bonhard, but situated on the Carriden shore near the present tollhouse; and to Caris pans, evidently the pans on Carriden estate, situated a few hundred yards to the east of the present Burnfoot.

The local and other saltmasters had for some time prior to 13th October, 1573,[4] exported very largely. So much so that the lieges could only procure what salt they desired for home use at a ridiculously high price. They complained to the Council, and an order was pronounced prohibiting the export of salt for three years. The panmasters then complained that they could not live if the export were altogether stopped,

---

[2] P.C. Reg., vol. i., pp. 380-2.
[3] Mary and Darnley.
[4] P.C. Reg., vol. ii., pp. 286-7.

and they offered to supply the natives with what salt they required at 8s. the boll, if liberty was granted them to export the rest. This was agreed to by the Council. Fulfilment of the agreement was delayed by the panmasters of Culross, Kinneil, and some other places. On this being reported, the Lords ordained proclamation to these panmasters to be made in the neighbouring towns of Stirling and Linlithgow, ordaining them to sell, and the lieges to buy the said salt at not more than 8s. the boll—the former to open their cellars and girnels to that effect at once, otherwise their lordships would force them, or, as it is put, "make open doors."

It would appear that the saltmasters resented the order, and honoured it more in the breach than in the observance, because on 20th September[5] of the next year, the Lords ordained that their proclamation be again made, and among other places, at the Mercat Cross of Borrowstounness.

The salt exportation question was again brought up during the administration of Regent Morton. The panmasters of Borrowstounness, Culross, and Fordell, on 10th January, 1574-5,[6] humbly offered the Regent and Council that of every going pan in these places three bolls of salt, Kirkcaldy measure, would be delivered to such person as should have the commission of the Council to receive the same at 10s. the boll under a penalty of three bolls for each boll wanting. This was to continue till 25th February, and such salt was for the service of the country. A few days later an order was pronounced directing the panmasters of "Barrestounes" and others to compear before the Council and receive their commissions for furnishing and disposing of their salt.

II.

On 20th September, 1580,[7] proclamation was to be made at, among other places, "the Mercat Crose of Kynneill," against

---

[5] P.C. Reg., vol. ii., p. 407.
[6] P.C. Reg., vol. ii., pp. 427-9.
[7] P.C. Reg., vol. iii., p. 314.

the landing of the passengers of a plague-infected ship which had arrived in the Firth of Forth.

We find evidence, on 29th September, 1601,[8] of what we think is the first of several very natural attempts on the part of the royal burgh of Linlithgow to prevent the seaport of Bo'ness from developing into a rival of the county town, and particularly of its seaport of Blackness.

On this date a complaint was tabled by the Provost, Bailies, Council, and community of Linlithgow against the town of Borrowstounness. A Signature, the narrative states, had been presented to His Majesty in name of James, Earl of Arran,[9] and John Marquis of Hamilton, his tutor, for erecting the town of Borrowstounness, alleged by the complainers to be within a mile of the port of Blackness, into a burgh of barony, and his Highness had subscribed the same. The signature granted to Borrowstounness, among other privileges, the liberties of "ane frie port of packing, peilling, lossing, laidning, and selling of staple wairis, sic as skynis, hydis, woll, wyne, wax, and all uther kynd of merchandice and wairis usit to be sould and bocht within any burgh Regale within this realm, with all customes and ankerages belonging to a port and heaven of a frie burgh." This, Linlithgow pleaded, was to the "grite wrak and decay of thair burgh end heaven (Blackness) quhilk is biggit and repairit be thame for saiftie of schipis and boittis upoun thair grit expensses." The provost and bailies of Linlithgow appeared personally, and the signature was produced. The lords ordained it to be expede through the Register and Seals till the pursuers be warned and heard to the contrary.

What resulted does not appear to be recorded. Apparently Borrowstounness was made a port, notwithstanding the protest, for we find that on 27th April, 1602, the Privy Council

---

[8] P.C. Reg., vol. vi., pp. 289-90.
[9] This James, Earl of Arran, appears to have been the heir who lost his reason—the tutor, of course, was his brother John, first Marquis of Hamilton.

discharged it from being a port along with numerous other places because of the smuggling that went on.

The year 1617 was a busy and exciting one for the Privy Council. That year James VI. visited Scotland for the first time after leaving to ascend the throne of England in 1603. Nowadays, with railways, royal trains, and motor cars, a royal tour in Scotland causes little or no upheaval in the daily round of the people. In these days it was the very opposite. The visit took place in June, and comprised a fortnight's hunting in the north of Scotland, chiefly in the Kingdom of Fife, a stay of a week or two at Holyrood, and among other places visits to Stirling, Perth, and St. Andrews. We are concerned here only with the journey from Holyrood to Stirling. The chief work of the Privy Council was that of making arrangements for the carriage of His Majesty's luggage, including a great quantity of silver plate for the use of His Majesty during his stay in Scotland. Meeting after meeting was held, and the reports of these detail the preparations in the different sheriffdoms concerned.

III.

One minute discloses the order made concerning Fife, and another a similar order "anent the carriage through Linlithgowshire." The latter is dated at Edinburgh, 13th May, 1617, and embodies the report from "the Commissionaris and Justices of Peace within the Schirefdome of Lynlythgow," who had been appointed by the Privy Council to arrange the supply of horses for this county. Each parish had to furnish a certain number of horses. In Fifeshire the lands within every parish were reckoned up " according to thair plewis, appointing everie pleugh of land to send ane horsse with all necessair furnissing." Presumably the horses, on account of the wretched roads, were to be used as pack horses, as there is no mention of carts. Special " constablis " were appointed in each parish to see to the mustering of the horses, and the justices also appointed two general constables for the whole sheriffdom, "quho sal be answerable to the Maister of the cariage that the constablis in the particular parrocheis foirsaidis sall haif the horsse of the parrocheis in reddynes at the tymes and placeis to be appointed."

The special constables and number of horses from our district are referred to thus—"That is to say, in the parrochynnis of Kynneill and Carribdin quhair Richard Bryce, Officiair of Kynneill; James Wilsoun, Officiair in Carribdin, David Galbraith, in Kynneill; and Johnne Hendersoun, in Murehous, ar Constablis, fourescoir horsse."

A part of the luggage was to be lifted at "Haliruidhous" upon Saturday, 28th June, and to be carried from there to Stirling, and the remainder was to be taken upon Monday, the last day of June. The parishes were all to obey their special constables; and they in turn were to answer and obey the two general constables for the whole shire. The parishes and constables jointly were directed to "caus the number of horsse abone written, sufficientlie providit with all furnitour necessair fer cariage, to be send in dew and laughfull tyme the saidis dayis about the brek of daye to the pallice of Haliruidhous and thair to lift his Majestie's cariage and to carye the same thairfra to the said burgh of Striviling."

Payment was to be made to the owners of the horses; but if any failed to appear as appointed, there was to be a fine of "sax pundis for everie horsse that salbe absent, and warding of the ownaris for the space of ane month."

Particulars of the great receptions accorded the King on this occasion in Leith, Edinburgh, and elsewhere, with copies of the speeches and poems delivered will be found in the Edinburgh volume of 1618 called "The Muses Welcome." William Drummond, of Hawthornden, wrote one of the poems for the occasion in "ryhyming heroics" entitled "Forth Feasting: A panegyricke to the King." It is put first in the volume among all the literary relics of the King's visit. Subjoined are a few of the opening lines. The river Forth is supposed to be speaking them—

Anne, Duchess of Hamilton.

(Photographed by permission from a painting in Hamilton Palace.)

See page 38.

> What blustering noise now interrupts my sleep?
> What echoing shouts thus cleave my crystal deep,
> And call me hence from out my watery Court?
> What melody, what sounds of joy and sport,
> Be these here hailed from every neighbor Spring?
> With what wild rumours all the mountains ring,
> Which in unusual pomp on tiptoes stand,
> And full of wonder overlook the land?
> Whence come these glittering throngs, these meteors bright,
> These golden people set unto my sight?

It should be noted in connection with this Royal visit that James, second Marquis of Hamilton, and proprietor and superior of Kinneil and Bo'ness, took a prominent part in it, being in attendance on the King the whole time. He was then a young man, and held in high esteem by his Sovereign. On the King's southward journey the Marquis entertained him for two days at Hamilton Palace.

IV.

On 14th December, 1620,[10] the Council disposed of complaint at the instance of the King's Advocate against Gabriel Rankine, younger, John Johnstoun, William Damahoy, and Gilbert Lothiane, all merchant burgesses of Edinburgh. They were charged with having by themselves or their factors packed a great quantity of merchant gear in trunks and coffers at a port in Flanders. They there found a Flemish ship coming to this country for coals, and resolved "to mak thair advantage of that occasioune and to send hame thair guidis in the said ship thinking thairby that trunkis, kistis, and cofferis wald be concealed and that they would releive thamselffis of his Majesteis Customes." The goods were taken on board, and on the ship arriving at "Barristounnes" the "searchers" and "customaris" in attendance there desired the merchants to make a lawful entry of their gear and to open their trunks and coffers in order that the goods "might have been sighted and some course and ordour tane for the assureance of his Majesteis

---
[10] P.C. Reg., 2nd series, vol. xii., p. 389.

customes." The defenders, however, not only refused to do so, but quietly removed their cargo, and so defrauded His Majesty of his customs. Gabriel and Gilbert appeared personally before the Council, and the former was found guilty and ordered into the ward in the Tolbooth of Edinburgh. Gilbert was assoilzied on his own oath of verity, and the two absent defenders were denounced rebels.

A proclamation was made by the Council on 29th November, 1621,[11] for remedy of the sufferings of the lieges owing to the extreme scarcity of coal or other fuel, and ordained that the owners of coal-heughs on both sides of the water of Forth should let the lieges be first served with coal expeditiously and at the old prices before the foreign dealers frequenting the Forth for coal should be served therewith. Notwithstanding this, we find that on 12th February, 1622, they had before them the complaint of George Mairtyne, George Harper, John Law, James Gib, elder, and David Hirrene, all of Borrowstounness, against Roger Duncanson, tacksman and owner of the coal and coal-heugh of Borrowstounness, for having ignored the above proclamation. They narrated that, having gone to Duncanson, "and earnestly desired him to sell them their lading of coals at the ordinary price and measure, he not only wrongouslie refusit to do the same and preferrit strangeris unto thame, but he highted the pryce of his coillis ane mark upoun the chalder and hes maid ane grite chang and alteratioun in his measure diminishing the same verrie far." Patrick Glen (not before named) appearing personally for himself and the other pursuers, and the defender being also present, the lords found the complaint not sufficiently proved and assoilzied the defender.

On 27th February, 1623,[12] the same Roger Duncanson, designed merchant-burgess of Edinburgh, complained that on 24th October last,[13] as he was riding from Leith to Bo'ness alone and unarmed, about the business of his coal-heughs, John

---

[11] P.C. Reg., 2nd series, vol. xii., pp. 645-9.
[12] P.C. Reg., vol. xiii., pp. 180-1.
[13] P.C. Reg., vol. xiii., pp. 751-2.

Houston followed him from Leith on horseback, and having overtaken him at Ecclymure, drew his whinger to kill him. Duncanson took the whinger from him, and then Houston struck him with his "nieve" and a stick. Houston swore he did nothing of the kind, and was acquitted.

Again we find a petiton by Roger Duncanson, in which he narrates that he for many years at great expense erected and maintained works for keeping out the water, in so much that by the daily attention required the revenue had never exceeded the outlay. That when at last he hoped to have found some profit, David Kerse and Archibald Liddell " pierced a strong wall and bulwork " he had erected for keeping out the water, which thus gaining entrance had drowned nine of the best heads of the heugh. For long he could make no discovery of those who did the mischief. In course of time, however, information came out, and Kerse, fearing lest one Mungo Adie would give evidence against him, made an attack upon him (Adie) with a whinger in the petitioner's chamber "on a Sabbath night at ten o'clock two days ago, and has since lain in wait for him with a sword." He craved the citation of Kerse and Liddell, and this was ordered to be done. There is no record of the result of the complaint.

V.

On 17th June, 1623,[14] the Council desired proclamation to be made at the Mercat Cross of Borrowstounness against throwing ballast into the Forth above Queensferry indiscriminately. Eight years later proclamation was again ordered to be made at, among other places, "the mercat croce of Borowstounnesse" to the same effect.

A minute of date 1st April, 1625,[15] runs—"It has pleasit God to visite the toune of Borrowstounes with some little infection of the contagious seeknes of the pest, whilk (in

---

[14] P.C. Reg., p. 263.
[15] P.C. Reg., vol. i., 2nd series, pp. 9-10.

respect of the confused multitude of poore people within the same) may haif some forder growth and progress" Therefore Sir John Hamilton, of Grange, and Mr. Alexander Hamilton, of Kinglass, are appointed special justices within the said town and parishes of Kinneil and Carriden to take measures to prevent its spreading. They are empowered to hold Courts and punish transgressors of their Acts.

It was reported to the Council on 4th October, 1625,[16] that a Dunkirk barque, pretending to be a Hollander come for coals, was then lying about Caribden, and had been along the whole coast of the Forth on both sides plumbing the water. Commission was therefore given to Sir John Hamilton, of Grange, and Alexander Bruce to seize the ship and send the skipper to Edinburgh for examination.

On 11th July, 1626,[17] owing to a threatened invasion by Spain, the burghs on the Firth, including Borrowstounness, were ordered to send commissioners to confer with the Council and to say what they were prepared to do in the manning of a navy for defence of the coasts. The commissioners compeared on 25th July, and stated that they could not do anything. Owing to the long peace the best of their ships were either sold or absent on voyages, nothing but small, unarmed barques remaining. As for the sailors, the most of them belonged to Fife and were at the fishing in the Isles. They would not return till September. In connection with the same matter the bailies of Bo'ness were, on 23rd August,[18] ordered to send six mariners out of this town towards the Scottish contingent for H.M. Navy. By 20th September[19] they had not done so, and the Council ordered a charge of horning to be directed against them to do it.

The Council had news, on 14th November, 1626,[20] of a "Flemis" ship in Leith harbour which was said to have contained implements for making counterfeit coin. These,

---

[16] P.C. Reg., vol. i., 2nd series, p. 148.
[17] P.C. Reg., vol. i., 2nd series, pp. 383-5.
[18] P.C. Reg., vol. i., 2nd series, p. 390.
[19] P.C. Reg., vol. i., 2nd series, p. 408.
[20] P.C. Reg., vol. i., 2nd series, p. 440.

What the Privy Council Registers Reveal 63

it was reported, had now been transferred to another "Flemis" ship lying about Caribden with the view to being taken out of the kingdom. Order was then given to H.M. Customs at Caribden to board that ship and make search for these implements, and if found to send them to the Council.

In the report afterwards[21] made the ship was given out to be a Holland ship driven back by contrary winds. Search had been duly carried out, but nothing found.

Relative to another royal visit to Linlithgow and Stirling —that of Charles I. in 1633—we find the Council as usual made all arrangements for the conveyance of His Majesty's baggage. These were similar to those made in 1617, only now we find "carts and wains" stipulated for in addition to horses. The local order ran—"For the Parishes of Kinneil and Caribden, James Gib, in Kinneill Kers, Richard Bryce, officer of Kinneill, and Thomas Napier, officer of Caribdin ar appointed Constablis and ar to provide from the inhabitants eighty horses with carts and wains."

VI.

The low countries being infected with the plague, the Council, on 29th September, 1635,[22] proceeded to take means for preventing ships from thence entering Scottish ports till they were known to be clean. The committee appointed by the Council to see their orders carried out in Borrowstounness and Caribden were Sir John Hamilton of Grange, James Hamilton, his eldest son, Walter Cornwall of Bonhard, William Drummond of Rickartoun, Thomas Dalyell of Binns, Mr. Alexander Hamilton of Kinglass, John Hamilton, Chamberlain of Kinneil, the Provost and Bailies of Linlithgow, and Sir John Hamilton, Younger of Bargaine.

Some Holland ships having gone up the Firth, on 4th November,[23] towards Caribden to discharge their cargoes and get

---

[21] P.C. Reg., vol. i., 2nd series, p. 471.
[22] P.C. Reg., vol. vi., pp. 118-9.
[23] P.C. Reg., vol. vi., p. 123.

coals, the Lords ordain that the goods in the ship of which George Henderson is skipper and those in the other Flemish ships shall be returned therein to the low countries. They, however, allowed John Maill and his wife and all other native passengers to come ashore and bring their kists and clothes with them, where they are to be "closed up and sett apart in loodges to abide there tryall" for the space of "sax weeks." The Lords further directed the magistrates of Linlithgow and Borrowstounness to provide lodges for them, and "to see thame handle thair kists and cloathes and to be cleanged." The said passengers were not to violate the orders of the magistrates on pain of death. Coals were to be supplied to the ships, but the carriers to the ships' sides were not to enter the ships.

On 12th November, 1635,[24] Alexander Downie, merchant burgess of Edinburgh, explained to the Council he had some tarred tackling in a ship of Rotterdam, lying at Borrowstoune, to which the Council had given permission to receive coals. Downie urged the tackling was not a thing likely to carry infection, and craved delivery of it. The Lords remitted the matter to the discretion of the local Commissioners.

Report was made on 7th June, 1636,[25] concerning one Alexander Park, merchant burgess of Linlithgow. He five weeks before had loaded a ship with grain at Rotterdam which eight days ago had arrived at Borrowstounness. The ship was free from sickness, but the Commissioners refused to allow the grain to be unloaded. It was heating, and would soon spoil, and Park supplicated the Council's permission to land it. The Lords permitted the ship's company and such workmen as the magistrates of Linlithgow should think fit to discharge the cargo and store the grain in some lofts and other convenient places at Blackness or Caribdin to preserve it from spoiling. The ship's company and workmen were to remain apart by themselves with the grain till such time as the magistrates should prescribe their trial.

John Gordon of Innermerkie was charged, on 8th Septem-

---

[24] P.C. Reg., vol. vi., p. 137.
[25] P.C. Reg., vol. vi., p. 254.

ber,[26] to "betake himself" to prison at Blackness. It was complained of him that he frequented public places openly, and in particular it was said "he repairs publicly to Borrowstounness market and fairs wearing his hagbut and pistols."

On 19th April, 1642,[27] Thomas Mure, merchant in Edinburgh, complained that "certain goods and spicery" with iron ware which he had shipped at Amsterdam in Robert Mitchell's ship of Bo'ness had been with said ship put under arrest, and he craved delivery. The Lords directed delivery to be given on his finding caution to the arresters.

VII.

On 19th October, 1643,[28] a committee was appointed for visiting the whole coal-heughs of Linlithgowshire to determine the amount to be supplied by each for the use of the shire. Sir William Dick of Braid declared his willingness to supply from the coal of Caribdin his just proportion. He was then lessee of the coalfield.

General complaint made, on 9th November, [29] by two burghs against the coalmasters for exporting their coal, insufficiently supplying the country, and keeping the price too high. Charge was given the coalmasters to answer. The Lords fixed the prices at which the coal was to be sold at the different places, "and the chalder of coals at Caribdin, Grange, Bonhard, and Borrowstoun, quhilk is the double of Alloway measure to be sold at six pounds, and the land laid, being ane measure of ane water boll at six shillings." (The Alloa chalder is £3. Sir George Preston of Valliefield's measure is more than double that of Bo'ness, and four and a half times that of Alloa, and he is to charge £12 the chalder.)

Oliver Cromwell's chief agent in Scotland was General Monk. He and some of his colleagues were rewarded, or rewarded themselves, with the lands of several of those nobles

---

[26] P.C. Beg., vol. vi., p. 320.
[27] P.C. Reg., vol. vii., p. 565.
[28] P.C. Reg., vol. viii., p. 10.
[29] P.C. Reg., vol. viii., p. 16.

whose estates the Protector had been pleased to declare forfeited to the Commonwealth. An echo of this period was heard on 16th February, 1665,[30] when the Duke of Hamilton presented to the Council a report on behalf of the Commissioners who had some time previously been appointed "to consider the claims of such persons as were forfeited by the late usurpers." They had considered, among others, the claims made by Duchess Anne and himself for relief from certain payments of interest and annual rents which were demanded from them by several persons, but which, owing to the seizure of their estates for eight years in the time of the Commonwealth (from which estates these sums were due), they did not consider they should be called upon to pay. The Commissioners agreed with them, and reported accordingly. The Duke and Duchess were heavy sufferers in that time, and, among others, Kinneil and its belongings, coal, salt, &c., were seized by General Monk, who would not relinquish them until he got payment therefor. The whole furniture of Kinneil House was carried off by the English.

The Council, on 16th January, 1662,[31] had to deal with a night attack at Kinneil Church. That day Sir John Fletcher, Knight, His Majesty's Advocate, and Mr. William Crauford, portioner of Kinneill, complained against David Murray, farmer in Borrowstoun; David Murray, younger, his son; James Hardy, maltman, there; George Mitchell, smith, there; George Mitchell, younger, his son, there; Archibald Gib, farmer, there; Alexander Hardy, younger, farmer, there; James Brown, coalier, there; James Hardy, weaver in Borrowstoun; and Janet Aitkinheid, there. Crauford and his predecessors had been in peaceful possession of a seat in the Parish Church of Kinneil past all memory of man. The complaint narrates that the seat had lately been "re-edified" by him, and that he had continued to possess same until the above defenders "having casten off all fear of God and reverence and respect to His Majesty's authority and laws on . . .

---

[30] P.C. Reg., 3rd series, vol. ii., pp. 26-28.
[31] P.C. Reg.,   „   vol. i., p. 138.

January instant entered the said kirk in a violent and tumultuarie maner under silence and cloud of night, being armed with swords, staffes, axes, and such lyke weapons, resolving to have the lyfe of any person that should offer to resist them, and most violentlie and unwarrantablie with axes and other instruments of purpose prepared, destroyed and cutted the said dask all in pieces."

Parties being cited, and the complainer compearing, but none of the defenders, the Lords ordained the latter to be put to the horn and escheated.

VIII.

On 8th April, 1668,[32] the Lords had to deal with two very serious complaints.

The complainers were Dame Christian Forrester, Lady Grange, widow of Sir James Hamilton of Grange, and Mr. John Wauch, minister of Borrestounnesse, "now her spouse." Mr. Wauch was the first minister of Bo'ness after it was disjoined from Kinneil. Evidently he had been a widower, with a family, when he espoused Lady Grange. The two, at any rate, conceived a vigorous destructive policy for "redding things up" at the Caldwall. The complaint states that the predecessors and authors of the complainers had beyond the memory of man been in possession of the lands and barony of Grange, coal heughs thereof, sinks, watergangs, and levels of the same, and particularly "of ane levell wrought diverse years ago by Sir George and Elexander Bruces, tacksmen of the coall of Grange, and the Lairds of Grange runing throw that pairt of the said lands called the Caldwall." And that on a certain recent date James Riddell, merchant, indweller in Leith, and present tacksman of the coal works of Kinglassie, "without any warrand or order of law accompanyed with Hendrie Measson, his oversman; Thomas Measson, William Measson, Alexander Whyt, Thomas Brown, Thomas Cairns, Arthur Cairns, Alexander Cairns, and Andrew Patoun, coal-

[32] P.C. Reg., vol. ii., pp. 427-432.

heughers; Alexander Henderson, his coall grieve; John Harvie, cairter; William Ker in the Nesse, and diverse others, their complices, all boddin and provydit with spades, shovels, and other materialls, did in ane tumultuary maner come to the ground of the said lands of Grange called the Caldwall, and by force and violence entered to the digging and casting up of the said levell; off which ryott and oppression the said Lady Grange haveing gotten notice she accompanied with some few servants, haveing in ane peaceable maner gone to the place and offered to make interruption, the fornamed persons did most cruelly assault them and beat and stroak some of her servants to the effusion of ther blood and perill and hazard of ther lyves," and for which they craved the offenders ought to be punished.

There was a counter complaint at the instance of the said James Riddell, who is designed as merchant in Leith, and heritable proprietor of the lands, coal, and saltworks of Kinglassie, which gives another version of the disturbance. He and his authors since the year 1638 had been in peaceable possession of " ane levell and water passage throw the lands of Grange frae Munsholl coall to the sea, conform to ane right and disposition made by umquhile Sir James Hamiltoun of Grange, with consent of Dame Christian Forrester, his spous, and Alexander Bruce of Alva, to John Hamiltoun of Kinglassie, his author, dated the 8th of April, 1638, off wh. water course & level the said John Hamiltoun, his author, continued in peaceable possession untill the year 1650; that the said coall works were destroyed, ruined, and drowned by the English; att which tyme he, being unable of himself to recover the saids coall works, did engadge the said complainer to erect & sett up the same agayn; & the said compleaner, out of affection to the mantinance of trade, haveing erected agayne the said coall works with great trouble & in draneing of water, setting doune of sinks, running of levells & water courses & maintaining the wayes & passages & enjynes belonging thereto, expended above the soume of fourescore thousand merkes; & conforme to the forsaid disposition, haveing entered to & continued in possession of the forsaid levell ther twelve years past being the only mean wherby the said coall may be dryed & made profitable without stop or interruption, till about Lambus last Mr. Johne Wauch, present spouse to the said Dame Christian Forrester, Lady Grange, out of meer malice and envye, without any warrand or order of law, did att his owne hand stop & dame up the said levell & water course. Against which violence the said compleaner then protested & took instruments. And now in the spring season the said compleaner, with some of his servants, in a peaceable maner being goeing about the clearing of the said water passage, without fear of any hazard or prejudice, true it is that upon the twentie-eight of March last bypast the persons underwritten, viz., the said Dame Christian Forrester, Sara Wauch, in Grange Place; Rachell Wauch, Issobell Wauch, Margaret Baillie, Henrieta Baillie, Andrew Allan, in Grangepans; Johne Johnson, bellman; Johne Love, officer; Robert Adam, in Kinneill; Johne Pollock, coal hewer to Grange; Thomas Davie, James Cairns, Robert Wilson, Johne Browne, the barne; James Robinson and John Mutter, coal hewers, there; Robert Mitchell, footman to Mr. John Wauch; Matthew Riddock, William Dishington, James Anderson, Alexander Cowie, Johne Boyd and Johne Patoun, salters; Isobell Wyllie, Christian Gibson, wyf to Johne Campble; Margaret Drysdaill, Agnes Dick, coall bearers; Margaret Ritchie, salt bearer; Robert Baillie, salter; Catherin Miller, wyf to Edward Hodg, coall bearer; and Agnas Davie, wyf to John Porteous, of the specially causing, sending, hunding out, and direction of the said Mr. John Wauch, all boddin in fear of wear, airmed with swords, staffs, stones, battons, and other weapons invasive, did in ane violent and hostile manner fall upon the said compleaner (Riddell) and his servants, and gave them many bauch and blae stroaks to the perill and hazard of thir lyves and effusion of their blood in great quantity, by which rable and multitud of wicked and insolent persons they were necessitate to flee for safetie, who, notwithstanding of the violence done to the saids compleaners, a great multitud of them, and especially fyve or sex woman of the said Mr. Johne Wauch, his family, did persew them most cruely and unchristianly, and trew att them above the number of fyve hundreth stones to the great hazard of ther lyves, and by God's providence very narrowlie escaped, as instruments taken upon the civill behaviour and cariage of the said compleaner and his servants and of the forsaid insolence and violence produced bears. By which bangstry and oppression not only is the said compleaner in hazard to be ruined in his private fortune and estate, the publick trade and commerce greatlie prejudged, and the customs bullion and other publick dueties impaired, bot above the number of fyve hundreth poor persons, who, these twelve years bypast have had ther only lyvlihead by the saids works, are in hazard to be starved and famished. Wherefor in all justice, equity, and reason the said Mr. Johne Wauch ought not onlie be decerned to make and keep open the said levell in all tyme comeing to the effect that the said compleaner may have the use and benefite thereof for draining of his saids coallworks as he has formerlie been in possession conforme to his just rights, and to make payment to him of the damage sustained by him throw the said oppression, bot otherwayes exemplary punished in his person and goods to the terror of others to committ and doe the lyke in tyme comeing." Charge having been given to both parties, and both compearing personally, the Lords, having heard the complaints and answers, granted commission to the Earls of Linlithgow and Kincairdin, "with thair first conveiniency to visite the levell in debate and to hear both parties thereanent; and, if they find cause, with power to examine witnesses upon oath for clearing the whole mater lybelled, and to endeavour to agree the pairties, or otherwayes to report the next Councill day."

The Commissioners had presumably managed to "agree the pairties," for the minutes contain no further reference to the matter.

IX.

The plague raged with so great virulence in Holland, and

the trade of this kingdom with that country was so great that the Council had once more to take the strictest precautions by the issue of peremptory orders and proclamations to prevent the disease being carried to this country. The following entries give us some idea of how these measures were carried out locally.

On 22nd December, 1663,[33] the Lords were informed that, notwithstanding their orders prohibiting ships from Holland entering any of the harbours or ports of Scotland until they had lain in quarantine for forty days, several ships, after being debarred from entering the harbours of Queensferry and Borrowstounness, had landed at Grange and other places betwixt the said two ports to the endangering of the country. Therefore the Lords gave "warrand, power, and command to the magistrattes of Linlithgow and Queensferrie, and to my Lord Duke Hamilton and his baylie of Kinneil, or any of them, to debar and stop the entry of all shipes, or landing of persons and goods from Holland at any place betwixt the saids two ports of Queensferrie and Borrowstounnesse."

On 2nd February, 1664,[34] they considered a petition by Andro Burnsyd, John Dumore, and Robert Allan, shipmasters in Borrowstounness; Thomas Fleming, Edward Hodge, and Andro Duncan, shipmasters in Grangpannes, craving for a relaxation of the prohibition. In support they stated that upon information from Sir William Davidson, Conservatour in Holland, and Mr. John Hog, Minister at Rotterdam, together with his elders, the plague was much arrested in Amsterdam, and that there was no infection for the present in Rotterdam. The Lords in this case ordained that the quarantine should only be "Threttie dayes after they come to the porte." The magistrates of Linlithgow and Queensferry and the Duke of Hamilton's bailie were to see the quarantine punctually observed "by making of the said shipmasters and their company keip themselves within ship boord in the road, setting of

---

[33] P.C. Reg., 3rd series, vol. i., p. 473.
[34] P.C. Reg., 3rd series, vol. i., p. 492.

watches for that purpose, and prescryving of such other orders as they should think expedient."

The Lords gave warrant and command on 16th February, 1664,[35] to the magistrates of Queensferry, the Laird of Grange, and the Duke's bailie, or any of them, to arrest several Dutch skippers, whose names are not given, for refusing obedience to the orders, and, as the complaint asserts, had "landed at Cuffabout Pannes, and doe at their pleasure goe abroad in severall places of the countrey." When seized they were to be "Shutt up and keipt close" until the forty days' quarantine expired, "and in the meantyme the saills and roes to be taken from their mastes."

On 23rd February, 1664,[36] Major Robert Hamilton, the Duke's bailie, reported that John Umphra (Humphrey), skipper in Borrowstounness, had asked permission to store his goods in cellars till the quarantine expired, and as he (the bailie) could not comply until he had warrant for so doing from the Council he craved accordingly. The Major was authorised to allow the skipper "to liver his goods and put them in sellars by themselves till the expiry of the time of trial," and the Earl of Linlithgow was recommended to see this done.

Information was supplied the Council on 14th July, 1664,[37] that two Dutch ships and other two ships, one belonging to one Duncan and the other to one Weightman, were loading goods contrary to the orders prescribed by the Acts of Council, "and doe most contumaciously refuse to be hindered or stopped by those having power from the Councill." The Council therefore commanded and ordained the ships to go out of the harbour and port of Borrowstounness within forty-eight hours, after intimation, "and if they disobey and remove not within the said space the lords doe give warrand and command to Major Hamilton, the Lord Duke Hamiltounnes baylie, to fyre and burn the saids shipes."

The Lords were also informed that same day that five ships

---

[35] P.C. Reg., 3rd series, vol. i., p. 501.
[36] P.C. Reg., 3rd series, vol. i., p. 515.
[37] P.C. Reg., 3rd series, vol. i., p. 567.

had lately arrived at Grangepans or Borrowstounness, and were there loading contrary to the orders of Council. These were also commanded and ordained "to goe to sea and remove from these places within twenty-four hours after intimation; and in case they doe not give obedience, the said lords gives warrant and command to the Lord Duke Hamiltoun's baylie to sett fyre to the shipes and burn them."

X

The Lords of the Privy Council, on 17th August, 1664,[38] ordained that "Gavin Marshall, merchand in Linlithgow, be sett at liberty out of the Tolbuith of Borrowstounnesse, and recommended Major Hamiltoun, the Lord Duke Hamiltoune's baylie, to take sufficient caution for the appearance of the said Gavin before the Councill upon Tuesday nixt under the pains of ane hundredth lib. stg." A feasible explanation of the cause of Marshall's imprisonment is furnished at the sederunt of the Council a fortnight later—6th September[39]—when Robert Mill, bailie of Linlithgow, Alexander Mill, and Gavin Marshall, bailies there, and Hamiltoun of Grange, were all summoned to appear to answer for loading a Dutch ship with coal in contravention of the Council's order. These persons appeared, also Major Robert Hamiltoun, bailie of Kinneil, to whom the execution of the orders of the Council were entrusted. The Lords found that the said Alexander and Robert Mills and Gavin Marshall had transgressed, as they well knew, of the orders of the Council. They, therefore, ordained them to enter the Tolbooth of Edinburgh as prisoners during their Lordships' pleasure, and to pay 200 merks to the said Major Hamiltoun for the charges and expense he had been put to in the execution of the Council's orders. The contravention in this case was all the more flagrant and inexcusable inasmuch as the bailies of Linlithgow were, as we have seen, among the special

---

[38] P.C. Reg., 3rd series, vol. i., p. 590.
[39] P.C. Reg., 3rd series, vol. i., p. 597.

Commissioners appointed by the Council to see that their orders for the prevention of the plague were duly carried out.

On 3rd November, 1664,[40] Major Robert Hamilton petitioned the Council for guidance "anent thrie severall ships lately come from Holland & Zealand, and driven in upon the port of Borrowstounesse by the stresse of weather." A petition, in name of the three skippers, George Cassills, Alexander Drysdale, and Thomas Knox, and also in name of several merchants and the owners thereof, "desiring a warrant for coming ashore and livering the goods in the said ships," seems also to have been presented at the same time. The Council remitted this to the Earl of Linlithgow, Lord Bellenden, Lord Lie, and Sir Robert Murray, with power to them or any two of them to call the parties interested before them, "and to hear if they can offer any proposalls anent the livering of the saids shipes and landing of the persons therein, which may secure the country from danger, and to make report to the Councill."

A week after the report of above special committee was given in as follows:—"As to the said Geo. Cassills' ship, she may be allowed to land, and both the persons and goods may be putt in Sir Walter Seatoun's houses and girnells in Borrowstounness, or such houses in the said place as he shall appoint, where they may be keipt through the space prescryved by the Councill's Act by a guard of souldiers consisting of such a number as the Lord Commissioner His Grace shall appoint; and in the meantime both the ship and goods may be clenged (cleansed) by clengers, and the magistrates of Edinburgh may appoint some honest man to sie that the said clengers doe their duety; and as to the charges of keiping of the guard and clenging of the ship it is our opinion that the same be proportioned betwixt the merchands and skippers and owners, at the sight of Sir Walter Seatoun and the Dean of Guild of Edinburgh, and that the merchands pay the whole charges for clenging of the goods. And, as for the two ships belonging to Alexr. Drysdale and Thomas Knox, it is our opinion that the

---

[40] P.C. Reg., 3rd series, vol. i., p. 617.

What the Privy Council Registers Reveal 75

men may come ashore and be kept through the ordinar tyme in such houses as Majour Hamilton shall provyd for them by a guard of souldiers to be maintained upon the charges of the merchands, skippers, and owners, which charges may be proportioned in maner above sett down.

"As for the goods—being only iron and barrells of ayle—the same may be clenged by being pott in the sea for the space of thrie tydes, which Majour Hamilton may be appointed to sie done accordingly."

The Council approved of this report, and ordained that the suggestions made therein be carried out, with this addition, that such of the goods as could not be cleansed, be burned and destroyed; and that after the cleansing of the goods the whole persons on board—passengers and others—be kept till they abide the ordinary trial or quarantine of forty days. Further, the Council made another remit to the Reporting Committee, this time "to call before them the magistrates of Edinburgh, and advise them seriously to have great care in cleansing the said goods."

XI.

On 22nd December, 1664,[41] Robert Allan, skipper in Borrowstounness, supplicated the Council, and explained that he had lately come from Rotterdam "in ane small heuker belonging to Thomas Burnet, in Aberdeen, wherewith there is ane Glasgow merchand only, ane towmaker, with his wyfe and chyld and some merchand goods, such as iron, meather, and the lyk whereof there can be no hazard of infection, neither is there any suspition at Rotterdam, the pestilence there being, by the mercy of God, nearly wholly gone." He therefore desired warrant to set the passengers and goods ashore. The Lords granted same, Major Hamilton, as usual, to provide houses for the goods and persons, and see the goods cleansed, and set guards at the petitioners' expense.

The same year we find the Council ordering the Earl of

---

[41] P.C. Reg., 3rd series, vol. ii., p. 639.

Linlithgow to levy men to meet the wants of the Royal Navy—
"Six men out of Cuffaboutpannes and Grange, and thirty-four
men out of Borrowstounness."

The Lords considered supplication, on 7th February, 1665,[42] by James Peacock, skipper of the good ship called the "Love of Enster"; Robert Craufurd, merchant of Linlithgow, and the rest of the merchants, owners of the goods in the said ship. The petition explained that on 15th December last the said James Peacock "sett sail from Rotterdam, and throw ane great tempest of storm was constrained to goe in to Skaerburgh, in England, where he continued the space of thrie weikes, or thairby, not having the occasion or opportunity of fair wind and weather. Thereafter he removed, and upon the eleventh of January last he arryved at Borrowstounnesse, where the ship hath ever since lyen, not entered or disloadened be reason of ane late proclamation." The petitioners craved that, as the ship was altogether free from any hazard of infection, she might be permitted to enter and unload. The Lords granted licence to unload the vessel, and to the Collector of Custom or his deputes to receive an entry thereof and goods therein.

About same date Thomas Burnett, merchant of Aberdeen, and Robert Allan, skipper, explained that they had lately come to the port of Borrowstounness about their lawful affairs with a little vessel belonging to them. They further explained that it was their intention "to goe back to Aberdeen and some other necessar places," but that they were detained by Major Hamiltoun upon pretext of the late Act of Council, even although they had offered caution conform to the tenor of the said Act. Liberty was craved to sail. It was granted—Hamilton to see that sufficient caution was received.

On 12th July, 1666,[43] the Council directed Commissions for "privat men of warr" against the French King, King of Denmark, and States of the United Provinces in favour of Captain Jon Black, of the "Thistle"; Captain Alexander Allan,

---

[42] P.C. Reg., 3rd series, vol. i., p. 639.
[43] P.C. Reg., 3rd series, vol. i., p. 179.

Blackness Castle.

(*From a pen and ink sketch by the late John Paris, Bo'ness, taken from an old print of the Castle looking west.*)

See page 15.

of the "Christian," of Borrowstounness; and Captain Jon Brown, of the "Lamb."

The following interesting supplication concerning the old roadways of Borrowstounness was submitted to a meeting of the Privy Council on 19th November, 1668,[44] by Robert Hamilton, chamberlain to William and Anna, Duke and Duchess of Hamilton, at Kinneil:—"There is within the lands and barony of Kinneill a high common way and passage from Borrowstounes towards Linlithgow and Borrowstoune, and those wayes, southward; and from Borrowstounes to Kinneill, westward, which of necessitie must be calsayed for the ease and accommodation of horse and others comeing and goeing there throw, otherwayes the samen, being so deep, will become altogether impassible, wh. will heavilie tend to the hurt and prejudice of the inhabitants within the said lands and baronie." Crave was made for the imposition of a custom or tax, "seing that the calsayeing of the said highwayes will be ane considerable expense and charge wh. the inhabitants of the said baronie are not able to undergoe and bear altogether." The Lords, on consideration thereof, granted warrant to the petitioner, and those having commission from him, "to exact for each loadned horse, each head of cattle, and everie ten sheip four pennies, and for everie loadned cairt eight pennies Scots money wh. shall happen to pass or repass from Borrowstounes to Borrowstoun, Kinneill, or Linlithgow, the wayes forsaids, and that during the space of fyve yeirs following the date of this presents."

---

[44] P.C. Reg., 3rd series, vol. i., p. 560.

CHAPTER V.

REGALITY COURT BOOK.

1. Unsuccessful Attempt to Form Royal Burgh: Regality Charter to Duchess Anne: Opening Ceremonies of Regality Court—2. The Burgh Tolbooth: Terms of Regality Charter—3. Roll of Heritors and Vassals from Kinneil and Carriden—4. Statutes Enacted by Bailie: Acts Against Shooting Wild Fowl: "Anent the Toun Well": Regarding Pasturage in Kerse Lands: And "Anent Profane Language"—5. Acts Anent Exaction of Town's Custom Dues, Damaging Trees and "Yeards," and against "Flytting and Scolding"—6. Acts Anent Building of Houses, Pasturage of Cattle, and Harbouring Sturdie Beggars: The Various Sittings and Magistrates —7. Illustration of a Day's Work in Court—8. Protection against Accusation of Witchcraft: Tariff for "Penny Brydells."

I.

BORROWSTOUNNESS was erected into a Burgh of Regality by a charter of Charles the Second, dated 8th January, 1668, and remained such until the passing of the Heritable Jurisdictions Act, 1747.

In early days great ambition prevailed among the inhabitants of the populous and thriving places in Scotland to obtain Royal charters of incorporation, or, in other words, to have their towns made into Royal burghs. These Royal burghs were superior to the other orders of burgh of the time, and were not afterwards abolished by the Jurisdictions Act, like the burghs of regality and burghs of barony. The Royal burgh had by its constitution its Provost, Bailie, Dean of Guild, Treasurer, and Common Council, and the general dignity attaching to it was greatly valued. A perusal of the Old Scots Acts, where we find many enactments regulating the trade in Royal Burghs and defining the privileges of the magistrates and burgesses, gives us an idea of their importance.

We are glad to find evidence that some years before 1668, namely, in October, 1661, "Deuk Hamilton" put forth an effort to get "the village of Borrowstounness" erected into a Burgh Royal, or, failing that, a Burgh of Barony or of Regality. Linlithgow Council strongly opposed this, and the Convention of Burghs supported the protest. The opposition did not prevail, however, as regards the Regality. In a Burgh of Regality there was neither Provost nor Council. The Corporation, so to speak, consisted of the inhabitants of a certain determined area which comprised the Regality, and these inhabitants were subjected to the government of a magistrate or magistrates. The right of electing these was vested by the Charter of Erection, sometimes in the Lord of Regality (as superior of the land), and sometimes in the inhabitants themselves. Our Regality Charter conferred the right of election of a bailie or magistrate on the Duchess Anne, in whose favour it was granted.

The day of the formal constitution of the Regality Court was an historic one indeed in the annals of the town and district. Among the many notable personages then assembled were the Duke William, his lawyer, James Johnstone, Writer to the Signet, Edinburgh, and the bailie-elect. We have referred in another place to the Hamiltons and the lands and barony of Kinneil, and we have seen from the Privy Council registers that Major Robert Hamilton of Dechmont was the Duke's bailie of the barony, and resided at Kinneil. His duties as such appear from these registers to have been many and varied, and he was factor or chamberlain as well. With the opening of the Regality Court, however, more important duties and enlarged responsibilities awaited him. He was then made Bailie of the newly erected Regality, and thus became not only our first local judge in nearly all matters, civil and criminal, but the framer of the laws for his Court as well. Some indication of what took place on this historic day is to be found in the opening pages of the Book of the Regality Court. It is inscribed, "*Liber Curiarum Burgi Regalitatis de Borrowstounness.* Begun the 2nd April, 1669."

II.

The place of meeting was the Tolbooth[1] of the Burgh, and as will be seen from the subjoined lists, there was a large gathering of vassals and tenants. These were obliged to give suit and presence thereat personally, or by proxy. After the heading, wherein it is stated that the Court was solemnly fenced in name of the King and the Duke and Duchess of Hamilton, comes the legal narrative, which reads, "The whilk day the said Noble Prince William Duke of Hamiltoune being personally present, and for himself and in name and on behalf of his said lady, produced ane Chairtour under his Majesty's Seill of the date at Whythall, the 8th day of January, 1668 years, granted to and in favours of the said Noble Princess Anna, Duchess of Hamiltoune, and her airs of ALL and HAILL the lands, lordship, and regalitie of Polmonte; the lands and baronnies of Kinneil, Carriden, and Ketlestoune, with the pertinents thereof, and with divers and sundrie other lands, lordships, and baronies, erecting the same in the foresaid Dukedom, Lordship, and Regalitie of Hammiltoune and the said town of Borrowstounness in ane burghe of Regalitie, and naming samen to be the head burghe for the said lands and lordship of Polmonte and the said lands and baronies of Kinneil, Carriden, and Kettlestoune, with power to the said Duches to make and constitute Bailys, Clarks, Officers, Pror fiscolls, dempsters, and all other members necessary. Which Chairtour the said William Duke of Hammiltounne caused James Johnstone, Writer to his Majesties Signet, to read in presence of the haill vassells and other persons assembled. Thereafter the said Noble Prince for himself and his lady created Major Robert Hammiltoun of Dechmont, their Graces Baily of the Burgh of Borrowstounness haill lands and baronies thereof, and created and admitted Rodolph Weir, Notary, to be procurator fiscal, and Robert Bellenden, John Bryce, John Bantan, and Thomas Eastoun, Officers of the foresaid bounds and...............

---

[1] The property, now Nos. 13 and 15 Smith Street, which has for long been in the possession of the Paris family is described in the old titles as "the high and laigh Tolbooths."

dempster of said Court, and caused the oath *de fideli administratione* to be administered to the same. Lyk-as the said Noble Prince William Duke of Hammiltounne produced ane Commissione subscribed be him and the said Noble Dutches to the said Major Robert Hamiltoune for being their Graces Baillie within the foresaid bounds, and caused the said James Johnstone lykwayes read the samen publicklie in presence of the said vassels and others then present, after reading whairof the said Major Robert Hamiltoune asked and took instruments upon the public reading and intimation thereof, and desyred the samen commissione might be recordit in the Court Books of ye said regalitie. Whilk the said Noble Prince for himself and in name of ye said Noble Dutches, his said lady, ordeaned to be doon."

The Commission in favour of the Bailie is then recorded, and from it we learn he had full power to make and appoint all members of Court needful, and to determine in all cases, civil and criminal, competent within the foresaid bounds, and to do all things required thereanent.

The document was signed "at our Castell of Kinneill," and the witnesses were Mr. John Hairpour, Cambus, advocate; John Hamiltoun, yr. of Kinglass; James Johnstone, W.S.; and Rudolph Weir.

III.

After this ceremony there was the further and lengthy one

ERRATUM

Page 80.—*In footnote read* South Street *instead of* Smith Street.

II.

The place of meeting was the Tolbooth[1] of the Burgh, and as will be seen from the subjoined lists, there was a large gathering of vassals and tenants. These were obliged to give suit and presence thereat personally, or by proxy. After the heading, wherein it is stated that the Court was solemnly fenced in name of the King and the Duke and Duchess of Hamilton, comes the legal narrative, which reads, " The whilk day the said Noble Prince William Duke of Hamiltoune being personally present, and for himself and in name and on behalf of his said lady, produced ane Chairtour under his Majesty's Seill of the date at Whythall, the 8th day of January, 1668 years, granted to and in favours of the said Noble Princess Anna, Duchess of Hamiltoune, and her airs of ALL and HAILL the lands, lordship, and regalitie of Polmonte; the lands and baronnies of Kinneil, Carriden, and Ketlestoune, with the pertinents thereof, and with divers and sundrie other lands, lordships, and baronies, erecting the same in the foresaid Dukedom, Lordship, and Regalitie of Hammiltoune and the said town of Borrowstounness in ane burghe of Regalitie, and naming samen to be the head burghe for the said lands and lordship of Polmonte and the said lands and barronies of Kinneil, Carriden, and Kettlestoune, with power to the said Duches to make and constitute Bailys, Clarks, Officers, Pror fiscolls, dempsters, and all other members necessary. Which Chairtour the said William Duke of Hammiltounne caused James J...

dempster of said Court, and caused the oath *de fideli administratione* to be administered to the same. Lyk-as the said Noble Prince William Duke of Hammiltounne produced ane Commissione subscribed be him and the said Noble Dutches to the said Major Robert Hamiltoune for being their Graces Baillie within the foresaid bounds, and caused the said James Johnstone lykwayes read the samen publicklie in presence of the said vassels and others then present, after reading whairof the said Major Robert Hamiltoune asked and took instruments upon the public reading and intimation thereof, and desyred the samen commissione might be recordit in the Court Books of ye said regalitie. Whilk the said Noble Prince for himself and in name of ye said Noble Dutches, his said lady, ordeaned to be doon."

The Commission in favour of the Bailie is then recorded, and from it we learn he had full power to make and appoint all members of Court needful, and to determine in all cases, civil and criminal, competent within the foresaid bounds, and to do all things required thereanent.

The document was signed "at our Castell of Kinneill," and the witnesses were Mr. John Hairpour, Cambus, advocate; John Hamiltoun, yr. of Kinglass; James Johnstone, W.S.; and Rudolph Weir.

III.

After this ceremony there was the further and lengthy one of calling the roll of the vassals and tenants. We reproduce the lists so that some idea of the names and number of the chief residenters in Kinneil and Carriden at that date may be gathered. Kinneil Barony, it must be remembered, then included Balderston, Murehouse, Borrowstoun, and Borrowstounness. Lists of the heritors and vassals from Kettleston and Polmont also appear in the book, but their reproduction here is unnecessary. We must not forget, however, that the vassals from these districts were as often in and about Borrowstounness in those days as the other vassals and tenants within the Regality. Head Courts at which all the vassals had to give their presence were frequently held.

From the barony of Kinneil the following heritors and vassals were present:—Alexander Lord Almond, for the lands of Whytrig and a part of the Mumrells (present by attorney); James Hamiltoun of Balderstoun; James Monteath of Auldcathie, for his lands thereof; the said Laird of Balderstoune, and minister of Borrowstounness, for the lands of Muirehouse; Robert Forrest, for his part of the lands of Rousland; Margaret Hamilton, widoe of William Levrance, liferentrix of the Gawes (compearing by James Sandie, her son-in-law); James Thomsone, for his lands in Borrowstoune; the relict of David Langlands, for certain acres of land in Deanefield, as liferentrix thereof; the relict of David Thomson, for certain acres there, as liferentrix thereof; Thomas Dounie, for his lands there; the relict of John Huttone, for certain lands there, as liferentrix thereof; Duncan Mure, for his lands there; Andrew Burnsyd, for the lands of Wairdes (by attorney); Robert Mitchell, for his lands there and houses in Bo'ness (by attorney); Alexander Hardie, elder, for his lands and houses in and about Bo'ness; William Carss, for his houses and lands there; Mr. David Adinstoun, for the Pann acre (by John Johnstoun, as attorney for him); the relict of George Allan, for certain houses and lands in Bo'ness, as liferentrix thereof; the relict of Alexander Allan, for certain lands there, as liferentrix thereof; Alexander Ritchie, skipper, for certain houses and lands there; John Ritchie, "called Leivetennent," for two acres of land there; Richard Hardie, Maltman, for certain houses and lands there. Also for certain houses in Bo'ness— John Paterson; John Hunter; Margaret Mitchell; Alexander Grintoun; the heirs of the deceased John Harper (by John Dunmore, skipper, son-in-law of the defunct, for himself and as attorney for the remanent heirs-portioners); James M'Kinnlay; Elizabeth Allan, as liferentrix; John Gib (present by Richard Dawling, his attorney); Alexander Cornwall; Thomas Mitchell, Alexander Law, John Meldrum, and the heirs of James Fumertoun; William Horne and the heirs of Patrick Dunckane; James Thomsone, in Rowsland; the relict of John Hendersone, as liferentrix; John Gray; Mr. William

Hendersone (present by attorney); William Baird; Alexander Walker; John Drysdaill (by attorney); John Burne; Richard Hamiltoun; John Ritchie, skipper; John Monteith (as liferenter); Richard Hardie, "Laird"; the heirs of Alexander Robiesone (present by attorney); James Gib, in Kinneill Carse; John Maistertoun (by William Wallace); John Maither, smith; Alexander Gib; John Aitkine; Janet Cornwall, as liferentrix; the widow of Duncan Bennet (as liferentrix); John Mairschell; Thomas Aitkinheid; the heirs of Alexander Simpsone (present by attorney); Janet Baveritch; Thomas Dunmure; John Stevin; Richard Thomsone; Andrew Saidler (by attorney); John Campbell; Janet Edward; James Wawghe; George Bennet; James Hunter (present by Robert Forrest as attorney for him); James Slush; William Beattie; John Short; James Turnbull; Isobel Carstoun; Andrew Bennet, younger; Walter Andersone; Thomas Smyth; Andrew Bennet, elder; Elizabeth Wilsone; the heirs of George Gib (present by Robert Forrest, their attorney); James Robb; Alexander Drysdaill; Margaret Reid; Thomas Eastoun; Eupham Andersone; the heirs of Patrick Harper (present by attorney); John Dunmure; Andrew Cowie; David Wallwood; Marion Falkoner and John Hendersone, her husband, for his interest; Robert Learmont; and Patrick Smyth.

The following heritors and vassals from Kinneil barony were absent:—The Earl of Callander, for the lands of Lairber and Brumadge; David Gawdie, for his lands in Bo'ness; James Cassilles, for his lands there; the heirs of the deceased Thomas Smyth; the relict or heirs of James Gib, skipper; Mr. Andrew Ker; the relict and heirs of the deceased John Dick; James Crawfaird; Robert Broun; William Willsone, all for certain houses there.

From the barony of Cariddin there were present—John, Lord Bargany, for the lands of Cariddin (by Thomas Dick, his attorney); John Hamiltoun of Grainge, for the lands of Lyttill Cariddin; Dame Christian Forrester, Lady Grainge, liferentrix thereof, and Mr. John Wawghe, her husband, for his interest; the Laird of Bonhard, for the lands of Bonhard; the heirs of

Thomas Drummond of Rickartoun, for his part of the lands of Murrayes (present by attorney); Sir Colin Campbell, for the lands of Walltoun; Thomas Edward, for the Lochmylne; Christian Mylne, for the lands of Stackes, liferentrix thereof. Heritors absent—None mentioned.

"Doome given upon the absents—The bally amerciats and fynes ilk absent heritor from the said head court in the sowme of fiftie pounds Scots money, and ilk absent tennent in fyve pounds money foiresaid."

IV.

On 11th May, 1669, the Court again met. The roll of vassals is again entered, and the following statutes are enacted:—

"*Act anent Shooting of Wyld Foules.*—The whilk day the said Major Robert Hammiltoun of Dechmont, bally forisaid, sitteand in judgement, statuts, enactes, and ordeanes, That no persoun or persounes whatsomever at any tyme heirafter shoot or kill within any place or pairt of the haill bounds and jurisdictione of the said regalitie, any land foule, wyld beast, and others within the samen whilkes are prohibet to be killed or shott be the actes of Parliament, lawes, and statutes of this kingdome, and especially all and sundrie peatricks, dowes, plovers, haires, duik and draik, and others of that natour resaiding within the foirsaid bounds, without speciall libertie and licence of the lord of the said regalitie or his substitut be first had and obtained in the favours of those personnes who shall happen to medle with the wyld foule and others above written, and that under the paine of ten pounds Scotis money of liquidat expenss to be payed be ilk persounes contraveiner to the bally of the said regalitie for ilk falzie of the premiss or ony pairt thairof. And sickelyk that no countrieman be found walking or goeing within the feilds of the bounds foirsaid with musketts, yagbutts, grewens, or any shooting instrument, without libertie foirsaid had and obtained under the lyk penaltie."

"*Act anent Compeiring of Witnesses and Assisting of Officers.*—Item, statuts and ordeans that ilk persoun within the bounds foirsaid who shall happen to be ceited as ane witnes befoir the court of the said regalitie for proving of whatsomever actione and cause depending befoir the said court in relatione to ryots, shall compear befoir the said court at the peremptor day and houre wherto they shall happen to be lawfully ceited, under the pain of fourtie shilling Scotis for the first tyme and thrie pound for the secound tyme; and sicklyke ordeanes that no persoun or persounes presum to refuise to assist any of the officers within the said bounds in the execution of their offices whensoever they shall be desyred thereto, and that under the paine of tuentie pounds to be payed be ilk persoun contraveiner for ilk falzie."

"*Act anent Welles and Funtanes.*—Ordeanes that no persoun or persounes, in any tyme heirafter, hinder or stope any of the running wells, watters, or fountains within the said haill bounds in prejudice of their neighboure, but that they shall have their full course and frie passage of running according to old use and wont; and that there be no bleitching therat bot at such pleaces allenarlly (only) wher they were in use and wont to bleitch; and that under the paine of ten pounds Scotis."

"*Act anent the Toune Well.*—Statuts and ordeanes that no person wash any cloathes within six ells of the comone toune well of the said brught of regalitie of Borroustounes, and that under the paine of fyve pounds Scotis."

"*Act for Bestiall Passing upon ther Maisters Head Roume to ther Pasturage.*—Enactes and ordeanes the haill tennants within the baronie of Kinneill who have land in the Kerse feild, to cause ther goods and bestiall go to and from the samen upon ther awen head rowmes and not upon ther neighbours, when they resolve to cause ther bestiall pasture upon the severall proportiones of gress in the said Carse feild, except such passages and wayes as are comone to them; and that under the paine of fyve pounds.

"*Act anent Profane Language.*—Statuts, enactes, and ordeanes that no persoun or persounes within the haill foirsaids bounds speike any profaine langwage in any tyme coming, or yet be found to vent any calumnies or reproatches on others, and that under the lyk penaltie."

V.

"*Act for Paying the Customes of Eggs and Others, and for Weighting Vendable Goods at the Weight-house.*—Enactes and ordeanes that all and sundrie persounes whatsomever who shall happen heirafter to bring butter, eggs, meill, or any other comoditie to the town of Borroustounes to be sold there shall, in the first place befoir they sell the samen or any pairt thairof, pay the ordinar customes dew to be payed therfoir to the customers of the said brught of regalitie; and that they tak such of the saids commodities as are to be weighted to the comone weght-house of the said brughe, ther to be weighted with the weghtes of the said weight-house and with no other weghtes whatsomever, and that under the paine of fyve pounds money foirsaid."

"*Act anent Brecking of Yeards, Pulling of Peise, Eating and Spoyling of Grase.*—Enacts that no persoune or persounes within the said brughe, lands, and barrounies of Polmont, Kinneill, Carrideine, and Ketlestoune, presum nor tak upon hand at any tyme after the daite heirof to breck any yeard or yeards by pulling of the fruit of the trees thereof, or spoiling any of the trees in any manner of way whatsomever, or wronging or damnifieing any yeard or yeards within the haill bounds foirsaids in any sort; and specially, but (without) prejudice of the generallitie foirsaid, of ane noble and potent Prince and Princess William and Anna, Duke and Dutches of Hamiltoune, ther haill yeards, woods, pairkes, and others perteaning to them within the said barounie of Kinneill. And that no persone or persounes make any wayes or passadges throw any pairt of the samen woods and others foirsaids more then is allowed be the awners thereof; or yet gather any fallin timber or cutt broom or whins therein, without speciall libertie of the awners foirsaids of the samen; And sickelyke that no persounes whatsomever, upon whatsomever cullar or pretext, pull or spoyle any of their neighbours peise, aither be codd or ruite, when the samen shall happen to be growing, or yet eat, tramp, or trade (tread) any of thair neighebours cornes or grase with their bestiall or goods, under the paine of fyve pounds Scotis money, to be payed be ilk persoun contraveiner of any pairt of the premiss for ilk falzie; and that by and attour (over and above) satisfactione be given be them for the skaith to the partie or parties who shall happen to be damnified by them."

"*Act against Flytting.*—Statuts, enactes, and ordeanes that no persoun or persounes whatsomever within the haill foirsaids bounds in any tyme coming flyt or scold one with another or misbehave themselves anywayes uncivilie towards uthers, or mak any disturbance within the saids bounds under the lyke penaltie of fyve pounds to be payed be each contraveiner; and enactes in lyke mainer that ilk persoune who shall happen to give in any complent to the court against any other persounes whatsomever for flyting, scolding, or any other sclanderous cariadge and misbehaviour shall, befoir they be heard anent the said complent, consigne in the clerk of court his hands threttie shillings monney forisaid, therein to remayne ay and quhill they make out and prove the haill artacles they shall happen to lybell against the contrair partie; and ordaines the samen to be given to the poore in caise it be not delivred up again to the saids complainers bot be losed be them throw their falzie in order to the premiss.

VI.

"*Act anent Building of House.*—It is statut and ordeaned that no persoun or persounes whatsomever presum or tak upon hand to build any house or any other building within the said brughe of regalitie of Borroustounes without acquenting my Lord Duke of Hamiltoun his Graces bally thereof and obtaining his libertie thereto: to the effect that no persoun or persounes may any wayes be prejudged therintill; and that under the paine of ane hundreth pounds Scots money of penaltie for ilk falzie."

"*Act against the Bringing of Horse with Cairts or Sledds bot throw the ordinar passadge wayes.*—The said bally enactes and ordeanes that no persounes bring any horss with cairts, sledds, or any other instruments quherin coalls uses to be brought from the respective coalle-hughes within the baronie of Kinneill, and specially throw or allongs thes aikers of land in Deanfield and other aikers lyand within the said bounds neir Borrowstounes, and that under the penaltie of ten pundes, except allenarlly (only) throw the ordinar and patent passadge wayes used and wont."

"*Act anent Pasturing upon Others' Ground.*—Enactes and ordeanes that no persoun or persounes pastour upon others' ground with their bestiall, aither outfeild or infeild, aither in seed tyme, sommer, or harvest, or to trowble or molest them in their sykes, bogs, or any other pleace belonging to their neighboure in any manner of way whatsomever in tyme coming, under the paine of ten pounds."

"*Act anent Encrotching upon Hie Wayes.*—Enacts and ordeanes that no persoune or persounes incrotch upon any hie wayes and passadges within the haill bounds foirsaids by delving and spayling thereof or casting divotts therupon in any pairt neir unto the samen, nor yet to delve or cast up any ground or mak any ditches or shankes, or anything whatsomever without their awen proper lands and heritadges, and that under the paine of tuelf pounds money foirsaid."

"*Act against Resseting of Sturdie Beggars.*—Enactes and ordeanes that no persoun or persounes within any pairt of the foirsaids bounds lodge, harbour, haunt, or ressett within any of their possessiounes any sturdie beggers, tincklers, or any suchlyk persounes in any tyme heirafter, and that under the paine of fyve pound Scotis for ilk fault."

A case of debt came up on the day when these statutes were enacted. It was disposed of, and resulted in William Thomson, maltman in Bo'ness, being ordained to pay to

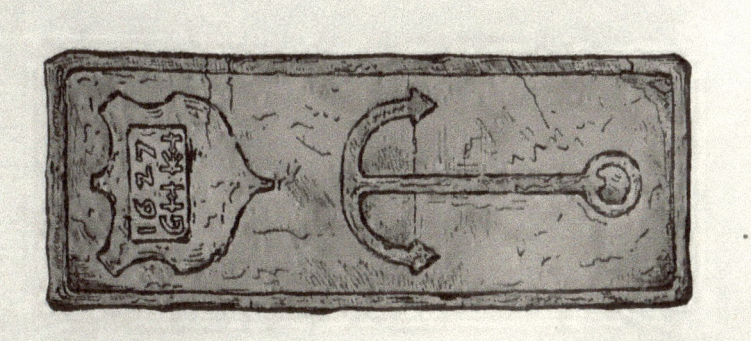

Gravestones in Kinneil Churchyard (No. 1).

(From sketches by the Rev. T. Ratcliffe Barnett, F.S.A. Scot., Bo'ness.)

See page 50.

Margaret Hamilton, widow of David Thomson, skipper, £75 Scots as the price of some "bear."

Another Court was held on the 25th of May, six Courts were held in June, four in July, three in August, and two in September, all in 1669, and all presided over by Major Hamilton. On two subsequent occasions, 11th and 12th October, 1669, they were presided over by Alexander Gibb, skipper in Bo'ness, bailie-depute, whose letter of deputation is duly recorded, bearing date at Kinneil, 11th October, 1669. Hamilton presided on 23rd October; Gibb on 2nd November and 16th November; and Hamilton again on other five occasions in November and December of that year.

The volume records the proceedings of the Court with regularity until June, 1673, when there is a hiatus until October, 1680. From then it records proceedings until March, 1681, when there is another blank until October, 1692. From that date it goes on until 17th April, 1693, which is the latest date of the Court proceedings. The Bailie, Major Hamilton, presided in Court most frequently. During 1670, when the average was three to four sessions each month, Gibb only presided three times, in 1671 twice, in 1672 ten times, and in 1673 twice. He does not again appear as Bailie-depute after 25th May of that year. Hamilton was still Bailie in 1680-1681. James Nisbet, writer in Bo'ness, now became his depute, but presided in Court only on 3rd and 10th January and 14th February, 1681. After the lapse between March, 1681, and October, 1692, Walter Cornwall, of Bonhard, appears as Bailie, and no depute is noticed.

There must have been another "*Liber*" coming down to about the middle of the eighteenth century, when Regalities were abolished, but we have not discovered it. When we come to examine the "Register of Bandes" we will see that it continues, with breaks now and again, until 1722, and discloses William Bell, of Avontoun, Robert Gregorie, and others as the Bailies of Regality between 1693 and 1722.

At the three Head Courts held respectively in February, May, and October of each year, lists are given of the heritors and vassals present, and also of those absent, the latter being as usual fined.

VII.

The following is an illustration of a day's work in Court as recorded in the "*Liber*":—

On 29th June, 1669, the Court of Regality was held in the Tolbooth of the Burgh of Regality of Bo'ness, by Robert Hamilton, of Dechmont, bailie; and the Court having been lawfully fenced, decreet is given against Matthew Robertson, salter in Snab, to pay to Janet Bow, spouse of Thomas Devine, in Borroustounes, and the said Thomas for his interest, £8 8s. Scots as the price of certain ale purchased from her by him, and also to pay expenses of Court. The defender did not compear although personally cited by John Buntein, officer.

Fines Janet Konochie, spouse to James Brucklay, cooper, a rex dollar for "stryking, beating, and abusing of" Elizabeth Archbald, spouse to James M'Kennall, on Wednesday last, the evidence being proven by witnesses. She is not to "goe forth of prisone until shoe mak payment thairof."

Action of removal being intended at the instance of William and Anna, Duke and Duchess of Hamilton, against John Hamilton, elder, of Kinglass, and Alexander Cornwale, in Bo'ness, as "pretendit" tenants and possessors of "ane great ludging" at the east end of Bo'ness and yards thereof, as also of lands called the Park with the "braes and links adjacent therto lying on the south-east of the said great ludging," and a considerable number of others who are tenants thereabouts, for their removing from these lands, decreet is given against them for this purpose.

Decreet is given against John Dick, in Woodhead, to pay Agnes Gibb, spouse of Alexander Hardie, in Nether Kineill, and her said husband £8 Scots " as buit and niffer promised be him to the said Alexander in the exchynging of ane horse of the said John Dickis with ane horse of his ten years since or thereby"; also £5 8s. received in borrowing by him from the said pursuer, and four merks for ale furnished to him at several times since then. The defender, being summoned to give his oath anent the foregoing, failed to appear, and decreet was given in absence, with expenses.

William Hunter, in North Kinneill, is sued by Robert Brash, in Kingcavil, for £18 Scots as the balance of the price of ten bolls of oats purchased by him from the pursuer in the end of March last. Compearing along with John Graham, writer in Linlithgow, his procurator, and being put on oath, he deponed that he only received six bolls and two pecks of "Clurttie oattes" at £4 the boll from the pursuer, and paid £21 10s. of the price thereof, and he now produced £3 1s. 4d., which he consigned in the hands of the clerk of Court as the balance of the price. He is therefore assoilzied.

VIII.

Complaint was made by Janet Conochie, spouse to James Brucklay, cooper in Bo'ness, that several persons in the said burgh did daily and continually "asperse, reproatch, and callummniat hir good name with the name of ane witch and divers other opprobrious and scandallous speitches." For remeid whereof the bailie ordains that no person hereafter call the said Janet Conochie a witch or otherwise abuse her good name under the penalty of £5 Scots. Janet has, as we have just seen, been fined this day for fighting. This poor woman, as we will find in another place, was afterwards among three tried here for witchcraft, found guilty, and burned at Corbiehall. It will be noted that mostly all the names we have yet referred to are Lowland names. Janet, however, judging from her maiden surname of Conochie, seems to have been of Highland origin, and very probably possessing in a considerable degree the mysticism and superstition of the Highlander, she was soon marked out in this community as a "witch."

Some of the statutes already recorded were afterwards

re-enacted, and others were added from time to time. One such relates to the curious marriage custom of "penny brydells," and it was made on 8th February, 1670, and reads as follows:—

"The samen day complent given in be severall persones within the foirsaid brughe of regality and barounie of Kinneill anent the hudge and exorbitent pryces of penny brydells made and sett within the foirsaid bounds whilks are exacted and collected from the persones who comes therto be those who maks and setts the samen, contrair to equity, reasone, and justice, and to just legall and orderlie customes used and observed in other places of the contrie theranent. Said bally for remeid and redres of quhilk abuise for the futur, and after matur deliberatioun and serious consideratioun had be him in order to the premises, heirby statuts, enacts, and ordeanes that no persone or persones whatsomever within the said brughe or regality and barounie above writtin under whatsomever cullar or pretext presum or tak upon hand at any tyme heirafter to exact or receave any more from ilk persone who comes to the said penny brydell for the brydell denner then the pryces respective underwrittin, to wit—Ten shilling Scots money at the brydells within the said brughe of regality, and nyne shilling money foirsaid at the brydells within the said barounie, and those persones who maks and affoords the saids penny brydells are to furnish to ilk mease consisting of four persones for the foirsaids raites and pryces the particular victwalls following—to witt, two plaitts full of broath, ane soddin of beife, ane rost of mutton or veill, according to the season of the year; four wheat loaffes, and ane quart of ale, with sufficient trunchers, servitors, and spoones: provyding nevertheles, in caise the setters and makers of the saids penny brydells provyd and affoord to ilk mease ane sufficient henn by and attour the victwalls above specifeit then and in that caise it is heirby declaired that it shall be leisum for them to exact and receave tua shillings money foirsaid from ilk person who comes to the said denner over and above the raites and pryces above specifeit: And the said bally ordeanes thir presents to be punctwally observed be the haill inhabitants of the foirsaid brughe of regality and barony foirsaid in all tyme coming under the paine of ten pounds Scots money foirsaid to be payed be ilk person contraveiner of the premiss for ilk falzie; also ordaines thir presents to be affixed upon the mercat place of the said brughe of regality that non pretend ignorance heirof."

CHAPTER VI.

REGALITY—THE REGISTER OF DEEDS.

1. Court Book Continued: Statutes Against Ignoring Jurisdiction and Receiving Strangers Without Character Certificates—2. Inhabitants "Thirled" to Mills of Kinneil; Regulations for Sale of Fish—3. A Peculiar Jury—4. Perambulations of Marches—5. The Register of "Bands": Arbitration Regarding Wages of Coalhewers—6. Shipmasters' Will and Testament: Duchess Anne's Grant for Communion Elements—7. More Arbitration: Seamen's Box and Fleshers' Box: Writers and Notaries—8. Examples of Surnames and Employments: Regality abolished.

I.

THE Court was troubled by persons declining its jurisdiction, and on 7th November, 1670, this is dealt with as follows:—

"The samen day the said bally upon severale complents made to him be severall off the inhabitants mentioning that ther are severall persones residing within the bounds who doth call and persew divers and sundrie of the said inhabitants before the Commissers of Edinbrugh and other inferior judicatories at ane great distance from the said inhabitants. . . . For remeed wherof and for preventing of prejudicies and inconveniencies for the futur, enacts and ordeanes, that no persone or persones whatsomever leaving (living) and reseiding within the said brught of regallitie and haill bounds forsaid take upon hand under whatsomever cullar or pretext in any tyme coming, to ceit, charge, call, or persew, any of the saids inhabitants and residenters within the forsaid bounds, for any civill debt, or any other cause or occasione whatsomever befor any other inferior judicatorie within this kingdome bot allenarllie[1] befor the said regallitie court of

---
[1] Only.

Borroustounes, and that under the paine of tuentie pounds Scots money to be payed to the procurator fiscall of court be ilk persone who shall happen to contraveine the premiss. Ordeanes thir presentts to be publictlie published to the inhabitants at the publict head court ensewing, that non pretend ignorance heirof."

A statute was passed on 14th February, 1671, against resetting of fugitives and strangers—

"Enacts and ordeans that no heritor, tennant, or any other persone quhatsomevir inhabitant within the said brught of regalitie and hail bounds of the lands and barounies annexed to the samen, presum or tak upon hand, at any tyme heirafter directlie or indirectlie upon whatsomevir cullor or pretext to harbour, receave, or resset any subtennants, craters, servants, or other persones whatsomever without sufficient and valid testimonialls from the pairtes and places they last reseided duellie subscrivit be the minister, elders, and session-clarks of the saids pairtes and places, and alls be the magistrat or justice of peace thairof, bearing and conteaning them to be frie of any knowen or publict scandell, and that the heritors and others abovewritten within the said brught of regallities befor the harboring, resetting, or recaveing of any of the saids persones, with their saids testimonialls, in the first place acquent the said Major Robert Hamilton, baillie foirsaid, or his baillie deput therwith; and procure and obtaine the names of the saids persones insert and recorded in the particular book appointed for that effect, under the clark of the said brught his hand; and that under the paine of tuentie pounds Scots money to be payed be ilk persone, heritor, master, tennant, or others, who shall happen to contravein any pairt of the premiss and that for ilk falzie."

II.

Statutes were passed on 9th May, 1671, with relation to thirlage and forestalling of fish as under—

"*Act Compelling the Inhabitants of Kinneil Barony to take their Grindable Corns and other Grain to the Mills of*

Kinneil only.—The whilk day the said bally in corroboration of the haill former acts of court and acts of thirlage made be whatsomever baillie within the foirsaids bounds of Kinneill and brught of regallitie of Borroustounes anent comeing with grindable corines, malt, and other graine to my Lord Duke of Hamilton his Graces mylnes of Kinneill to be ground thereat according to use and wont, statuts, enacts, and ordeanes that no persone or persones whatsomevir within the said baronie and brught of regallitie foirsaid goe by the said mylnes in any tyme comeing with any of ther grindable corines or other grain bot come convenientlie with the samen therunto to be ground therat and to pay multor and knavship therfoir according to use and wont and as was in use to be payed in the lyfetyme of the deceist Dame Anna Cunynghame, Lady Marques of Hamilton, of worthie memorie; and ordaines ilke persone contraveiner to pay for the first fault fyve pounds Scots, and to the fermeror of the mylnes dowble multor for what quantatie can be made appear is abstracted from the said mylnes; and for the second fault ten pounds money foirsaid, and to the said fermeror dowble multor; and sua furth dowbling thairof alls oft and sua oft as they shall happen to contravein the premiss."

"*Act enacting that Fresh and Salt Fish shall not be Sold in the District until the Inhabitants be first served.*—The said baillie statuts, enacts, and ordaines that no persone or persones whatsomevir resorting to this brughe at any tyme heirafter with any kynd of fish, aither fresh or salt, shall make sale and offer the samen to any persone or persones quhatsomevir untill such tyme that they send throw the bell therfoir and serve the haill inhabitants of the said brught with the samen and sua continow the selling thairof for the spaces following— to witt, the said fresh fish for the space of six hours, and the dry fish for the space of eight hours, to the effect the saids inhabitants may be then sufficientlie served thereof; and that under the paine of fyve pounds Scots money to be payed be ilk persone contraveinen for ilk falzie *toties quoties;* and sicklyke statuts, enacts, and ordeans that no persone, dreipster, or other persones quhatsomever attempt presum or take upon hand in any tyme comeing to medle or bargane with such persone or persones who shall happen to resort to the said brught with such fishes as are befoir mentioned heirafter whill and untill advertizment beis made of the samen as said is be the publict bellman of the said brught, and alls whill the saids spaces respective foirsaids be fhllie expyred; and that under the paine of fyve pundes money foirsaid to be payed be ilk contraveiner of the premiss."

III.

These statutes were always passed at the Head Courts, and it is noticeable that it was also a practice at this Head Court to empanel a jury of inquest. The object of this was not to deal with the cases of persons brought before them, but, like the elders of the kirk session, each member of the jury was called upon to delate offenders. Here is a record of this procedure on the foresaid day—

"Compeared Robert Cunyngham, in Bonhard; Allexander Watson, in Little Carriddin; Thomas Faupe, in Murrayes; William Drysdaill, in Bonhardpanes; John Davisone, salter there; John Hairt, in Redding; James Goffe, there; Hendry Hardie, in Whysyd; Thomas Whyt, in Gilstoune; Allexander Hardie, there; James Dobbie, in Kinneill; Alexander Gibb, in Inneraven; James Thomson, in Over Kinneill; James Thomsone, in Rousland; John Glen, in Inneraven; and John Ritchie, in Borroustounes. Whilks persones of inqueist being all lawfully sumond, suorn, receaved, and admitted and includit be themselves, and having be plurality of voyces choysen the said Hendry Hardie Chancellar, and being interrogatt be him be vertes of his office of chancellarie whither or not they knew any faultes, wronges, or injuries doen or committed within the foirsaids bounds undelaited, they delaite and declair as follows:—

"The said Allexander Hardie declaires that he saw John Cuthell, in Carsiebank, careing ane gun within this fournight, and lykewayes did sie him shoot with the samen, bot did kill nothing; as also saw John Shaw in Gilston shoot with ane gun.

"The said Thomas Whyt declaires that he saw Allexander Cowie and the said John Cuthell careing gunes within the barouny.

"The said John Ritchie declaires he saw Allexander Randie, Thomas Padyeon, John, James, and Allexander Gibbs also carieing gunes; and alse James Cowan in Corbiehall and James Maither carieing gunes.

"The said John Heart declaires that ther is ane yew in his custodie whilk does not belong to him, both declaires the samen does belong to John Johnston, his hird, and that James Goffe gifted the samen to him; as also declaires that there was ane rugh sheip in sommer last goeing amongest John Cloggie in Midlerig his sheip.

"The said John Glen declaires that upon the saboth day last, the 13 of February, he saw James Burn shoot ane gun in Clarkstoun bounds, lykeas depones that ther was some persones shotte dowes besyd Kinneill kerse, but knowes not what they wer; saw James Mungal in Borroustounes with them, and that he took up the dowes that wer shotte; and farder declaires that upon Yooles evin he saw the said James Burn goeing with ane gun in his hand and shot dowes in his other hand.

"The said James Dobbie declaired he saw James and Allexander Gibbs, Thomas Padzeon, and William Gibb, tuentie dayes since carieing guns bot saw them shoote non.

"The said William Drysdaill declaires he saw Thomas Gillespie cary a gun.

"The said Robert Cunyngham declaires that he saw James Robertson, in Bonhard, shoote ane dove bot alledges that he had ane order from the shirref-deput to shoot al suck doves he could find in respect they prejudged his dovecott.

"And the remayent persones of the said inqueist being lykewayes posed and interrogatt be the said Henry Hardie, chancellor, declared that they knew of no wrongs nor injuries doen or committed within the haill foirsaids bounds."

Among other business done by the Regality Court was the

appointment of curators to persons under age. There is at least one instance of this. On 19th April, 1670, at the instance of William Jaupe, who was a minor, but past the years of pupillarity and tutory, charge is given to John Robertson, in Muiredge, and another Robertson, in Bonhard, who are his nearest of kin on the father's side, and to Alexander and Thomas Smith, sailors in Grangepans, who are the nearest of kin to him on the mother's side, to attend and see and hear curators chosen for the said minor for the management of his affairs until he attain the age of twenty-one years. They did not compear, but evidence having been given of their being lawfully cited, the Bailie asked the minor whom he wished, and he chose John Fod and Duncan Alan, both in Bonhard, to be his curators. They accepted the office, gave their oaths, and became cautioners each for the other for the faithful discharge of the duty.

IV.

The Court also dealt with the perambulation of properties, of which there are several instances in the volume. The first is on 27th June, 1670, and is occasioned by the complaint on the part of John Meldrum, tailor in Bo'ness, against William Horn, skipper there, and Agnes Hardie, his spouse, who in building a shop on the east side of their house had encroached upon the pursuer's property, especially in appropriating a stone gable which was mutual between them. For determining the matter an inquest of fifteen persons was sworn, and inspection made not only of the properties, but of the pursuer's and defender's titles, the pursuer producing a disposition by Alexander Law, tailor in Bo'ness, to the pursuer and Marion Law, his spouse, dated 15th March, 1642, showing forth the bounds of the subjects disponed. There also compeared William Fumertoun, in Nether Kinneill, in right of an apprising led at the instance of his deceased father, James Fumertoun, in Kinneill, against the said Alexander Law, of the foresaid house, protesting that he might not be wronged by the new building, and especially that his stair on the north side of his house might not be encroached upon nor made use of by the said Agnes Hardie. The judgment of the Court conserved the said stair to William Fumertoun, but the jury declared they could not determine as to the property of the mutual gable, and in the end the judge declared that it should be mutual to both parties.

Another case occurred on 23rd November the same year, in which the Court was asked to declare the meiths and marches and to set up march stones between the properties of Richard Thomson, maltman in Bo'ness, son of the deceased William Thomson, maltman there, and Andrew Burnsyde, skipper in Bo'ness, for Andrew Burnsyde, younger, his eldest lawful son. This was done by means of empanelling a jury of inquest, who determined the bounds between the properties.

On 16th March, 1671, there were no fewer than four cases of perambulation on hand. In the first William Horn, skipper in Bo'ness, wished to build a shop on his own ground there, and desired that the same might be defined. The jury having considered the whole circumstances, ordained him to build his shop between the vennel and the east side of his own house, with certain restrictions, among which was that he was not to injure the lights of other houses.

The second was a dispute between John Paterson, sailor in Bo'ness, and Marjory Cassillis, spouse to Andrew Burnsyde, elder, in Bo'ness, and Eupheme Cassillis, spouse to James Cassillis, elder, skipper there, and their said husbands. It was found that the properties were divided by a mutual dyke, but that Paterson had right to his own gable, and the road for horses and carts to his kiln and barns in the close. Within the close there was a spring well. It was to be public for the inhabitants of the burgh who might require to make use of it. The said properties were upon the High Street, and in building both parties were enjoined to keep that street "sufficiently broad, fully large, wide, and spacious."

The third case was the settlement of a march between the property of Alexander Grintoun, in Grange, in that part of the burgh called the Boig, and that of Robert Mitchell, skipper in Bo'ness.

The fourth dealt with a public right of way which had been stopped to the south-west of the house and yard belonging to the heirs of David Thomson, skipper in Bo'ness, and led from the High Street to some fields on the south. The jury decided it should be re-opened for the use of the inhabitants, with horses and creels, as it had formerly been past memory of man.

The last case in the volume is on 9th January, 1673, when a Court of perambulation was held to decide a dispute as to the boundaries between the houses and yard of Alexander Gibb, skipper in Bo'ness, and the glebe of the minister, which lay to the south of Gibb's property; also the boundary between the said glebe and the Paundiker, belonging to Robert Mitchell, skipper in Bo'ness. The jury found that Alexander Gibb had built a wall too far south, which encroached on the property belonging to the minister; ordered him to have it removed and rebuilt where the old marchstone was still standing. Further, declared that the minister's glebe "marches to the south-side wall of John Johnstone, maltman in Bo'ness, his kiln and barn, and the said Pandiker belonging to the said Robert Mitchell on the north."

(End of "*Liber Curiarum*.)

V.

Besides the "*Liber Curiarum*" there is another register of the Court which gives us interesting glimpses in other directions of the life of the inhabitants more than two centuries ago. This book is inscribed "Register of Bandes and Uther Wryttes of the Burgh of Regality of Borrowstounes, Landes & Baronies thereto anexit; Begun the 2nd day of Appryll 1669." The volume is in a fairly good state of preservation. Registration seems to have gone on until the end of July, 1673. There is then a break until 1st November, 1692—nearly twenty years—when it is resumed, and goes on until the end of May, 1695. There is then another break of about twenty years until October, 1713, when the book is turned upside down and a fresh beginning made. From then registration goes on until 20th November, 1722, where the two sections meet in the middle of the volume. It is more than likely that there would be another volume running on to the extinction of the Regality in 1748, but we have not found it.

The deeds recorded in this register are heritable bonds and other obligations, agreements, discharges, tacks, marriage contracts, and, so far as we have observed, one testamentary settlement. Submissions and decrees-arbitral and protested bills occupy a considerable portion of the book, the protested bills being especially numerous after 1713. To make a selection from such a mass in order to enable the reader to form a reasonable picture of the business life of the district at that period has been no easy matter. It is hoped the following will prove illustrative:—

Discharge by "Maister John Waugh, Minister at Borrowstouness" to the representatives for "compleat payment and full satisfaction of all stipend due." This is the first document recorded.

Commission by Duke William and Duchess Anne of Hamilton to John Mayne, writer in Linlithgow, to be procurator-fiscal of the Burgh of Regality of Borrowstouness, during pleasure, dated at Kinneil, 2nd April, 1669, recorded 14th April. This was presumably in addition to Rudolph Weir referred to in the "*Liber*" as being appointed fiscal on the opening day.

Submission and decree-arbitral relating to a dispute over the "platform" of a house in Grangepans. The parties concerned were Flor. Gairdner, "bally of the Baronie of Grange," on the one part; and Thomas Smith, wright in Borrowstouness, on the other part. The judge-arbitrators were Thomas Edgar, in Grange, and Robert Forest, in Borrowstouness. Recorded 9th October, 1669.

Gairdner was, we understand, a near relative of Colonel James Gairdner, who was born at Burnfoot, Carriden.

Contract of marriage, dated at Linlithgow 6th April, 1655, between William Kerse in Falconhous, with consent of Richard Kerse in Bo'ness, his eldest lawful brother, and Helen Tennent, lawful daughter of the deceased John Tennent of Burncheid. She has a brother William Tennent, of Wester Dykeheid, who is due her 500 merks, and this debt, with another 1000 merks due by Mr. George Dundas of Maner, she presents to her husband as tocher. Among the witnesses are David Tennent and Mr. William Crawfurd, son of William Crawfurd, of Dean. Recorded 23rd May, 1670.

Commission by William and Anna, Duke and Duchess of Hamilton, to Robert Ballenden of Parkend, to uplift the rents of the baronies of Kinneil, Polmont, Carriden, and Kettlestoun, dated at Hamilton, 16th November, 1670.

Submission and decreet arbitral between John Mayne, writer in Linlithgow and tacksman of the coal works of Balderston, and William Rae and George and William Robertson, his coal hewers, as to the prices to be paid to the latter and their bearers and servants. The judges were John Fod and James Mitchell in Bonhard, John Robertson there, and Robert Cornwall in Kinglass. The submission is dated at Bo'ness and Bonhard, 5th and 9th December, 1672, and until the decision is given the hewers agree to proceed with their work diligently and truly as other coal hewers, and have found cautioners that they will do so. The decreet is dated at Bonhard 10th December, 1672, and in it the judges ordain the said coal hewers and their bearers and the said servants to attend dutifully their work at the coal heugh of Balderstone and not absent themselves without consent any working day, health and strength permitting, and continue, not by starts but for nine hours each day at least, and if they absent themselves without leave they shall forfeit 20s. Scots for each day they do so, with a corresponding part from their yearly bonus. Sixteenpence Scots is the price presently paid per load for the coals won, but as the owner is willing to augment this, it is agreed that the third part of what is obtained by the sale of the coals shall be the share belonging to the coal hewers, and the owner is to increase the price of the coal to 5s. and 7s. Scots *per mett*. The coal hewers also agree to relieve the owner of the labour of making the levels, &c., and working the coal, under certain conditions, provision being specially made in the case of "troble." Further, the coal hewers being in the habit of carrying home as many coals as they require to burn in their own houses nightly, they in return for these are to deliver a load of coals weekly to the master as formerly upon the coal hill, and this they are not to sell or part with to their neighbours under a penalty of 30s. Scots per load.

VI.

6th January, 1693.—Contract of marriage dated at Bo'ness, 23rd February, 1691, between Robert M'Kindley, merchant in Bo'ness, and Katherine Esplin, lawful daughter of the deceased John Esplin, maltman there, with consent of Lybra Smyth, her mother, and Thomas Padgen, maltman there, now her spouse. Her tocher is 600 merks. There is also a deed by Lybra Smyth to Robert M'Kindley.

Will and Testament of a Borrowstounness Shipmaster.— This is recorded 13th January, 1714, and is very interesting. The introduction runs—"To all and sundry whom it effeirs, or to whose knowledge these presents shall come: Be it known that I, ..., being for the present infirm in my body, though perfect in memorie and judgment, blessed be God; and considering the frailty of this short and transitory life, with the certainty of death and uncertainty as to the time and manner thereof (that being referred to the Omniscient wisdom of God): Therefore to the effect I may the better prepare against the time of my transmutation when the samen att the pleasure of God shall happen, I have thought fit to make my Latter Will and Testament as follows:—Imprimus I recommen and entirely resign myself soul and body to the hands of God Almighty my great and bountiful Creatour and Redeemer; and declare that I am a Protestant professing the true religion by God's mercy presently professed and taught in the reformed Churches of Christ according to the written word of God and summarly contained in the Confession of faith in this Church, and ratified and approved be ye Statutes of Parliament of Scotland; and declares that my hope of Salvation depends only upon the free love and mercy of God and the merits and intercession of Jesus Christ my only Saviour and Mediatour:" Like the prophet of old, he gave commandment concerning his bones thus: Ordains and wills that when it pleased God to separate his soul and body, his body should be interred amongst his friends, decently in a Christian manner. Then comes the disposal of his estate to his wife and daughter. We have an impression that the declaration that he was a Protestant, if not absolutely necessary, was at that time safe and desirable in view of the disabilities which affected Roman Catholics.

Factory and commission by John Cassils, skipper, in Borrowstounness, in favour of Jean Melvin, his well-beloved wife. He narrates that "for as much as I am necessarily called abroad furth of this kingdome in pursuance of my employment, and being desirous that my business at home be not neglected, and having intire trust and confidence in the fitness and integrity of the said Jean Melvin," he appointed her his sole acting factrix and commissioner for him with full powers. This document is recorded 22nd May, 1714.

Obligement.—The Duchess of Hamilton to the Kirk Session of Bo'ness for paying Communion elements; recorded 31st October, 1717. It runs—"We, Ann Dutches of Hamilton and Chatlerault, considering that we have been in use those many years bygone to pay to the Ministers and Kirk Session of Bo'ness the soume of Five pounds Sterling yearly for defraying the expense of the Communion elements att the celebration of the Sacrament of the Lord's Supper att the Kirk of Bo'ness, for the payment of which the said Kirk Session has no security but our use of payment; and we being willing to grant to them the security underwritten for payment thereof; Therefore we hereby bind and oblige us, our heirs and successors to make good and thankful payment to the Minister or Kirk Session of said Kirk of Bo'ness and to their successors in office the soume of five pounds Sterline yearly for defraying the expences of the Communion elements at celebrating the Sacrament in the said Kirk, and that within ten days after the celebration of the said Sacrament yearly, beginning the first year's payment of the said soume for this instant year 1713 and so forth yearly thereafter in all time coming: And, in case it shall happen by the troubles of the times or by any other accident it shall happen that the Sacrament shall not be celebrat yearly, we oblige us and our foresaids to pay the said soume of five pounds Sterline yearly during the years the said Sacrament shall not happen to be celebrat att the said Kirk to the Minister or Kirk Sessione of the said paroch for the use and behoove of the poor thereof: In Witness Whereof we have subscribed thir presents att our Palace of Hamilton the twenty-eight day of Aprile 1713 years, before these witnesses, James Hamilton of Pencaitland, one of the Senators of the Colledge of Justice; and David Crawford, our Secretary; and Alexander Hamilton, Writer to the Signet, Wryter hereof."

VII.

Submission and decree arbitral in a succession dispute between John Brice, merchant in Bo'ness, only son then in life to the deceased William Brice, weaver in Muiredge, on the one part, and Thomas Knox, in Muirhouse of Grange, for himself and Elizabeth Brice, his spouse, daughter to the said William and sister to the said John Brice, on the other part. John Hardie, maltman in Borrowstounness, was the arbiter chosen by John Brice; and James Stephen, schoolmaster of Carriden, was chosen by the said Thomas Knox for himself and spouse. It was decided that John Brice should succeed to the just and equal half of the houses in Muiredge with the lands and "aker" of land pertaining and belonging to the deceased weaver, his father; also to a half of the household plenishing,

Gravestones in Kinneill Churchyard (No. 2).

(From sketches by the Rev. T. Ratcliffe Barnett, F.S.A. Scot., Bo'ness.)

and sole right to the deceased's "wearing" clothes. The other half of the heritable and movable subjects were to be divided, one-half to Thomas Knox and his spouse, and the other equal half of foresaid half to belong to Agnes Knox, their daughter, in liferent, "and the heirs to be lawfully procreat of a suitable marriage to be entered into by her, whom failing, to the said John Brice his heirs." In the squaring up, the one-half of the value of an iron chimney and a piece of "cloath," value £17 Scots (both taken by John Brice) was to be accounted in part payment of the funeral and other expenses disbursed by him, he to give credit for the equal half thereof in his accounts. The deed is recorded 1st March, 1719.

Submission and decree-arbitral in dispute between John Guthrie, officer of Excise at Bo'ness, on the one hand, and George Galbrath, tacksman of the milns of Kinneill, on the other part. The arbiter for Guthrie was Thomas Buchanan, officer of Excise at Grangepans, and for Galbrath one John Burn, in Parkhead, of Linlithgow. Duncan Glasford, shipmaster in Bo'ness, was the oversman chosen by the arbiters. We have not noted the precise nature of the dispute, but the result was that Guthrie had to content and pay Galbrath the sum of five pounds in full satisfaction of his claim. This submission is recorded 20th November, 1722.

To take a few more examples we find recorded on 14th September, 1694, an agreement amongst the seamen of Borrowstounness about a box, one Walter Nimmo being boxmaster. About the same time appears a bond by a maltman for 50 merks Scots borrowed from Gilbert Marshall, "Boxmaster of the Fleshers' Box of Borrowstounness." And on 17th June, 1714, there is a tack recorded betwixt John Mairtoun, chirurgeon in Borrowstounness, and John Egglinton, flesher there, whereby the doctor sets "two aikers" of land of the lands of Deanfield belonging to him. We find also commission by the Dowager Duchess Elizabeth of Hamilton in favour of Archibald Grosert, merchant in Bo'ness, her factor and chamberlain in her lands of Kinneil, Carriden, and others;

also factory by John Edmonston, writer in Edinburgh, as factor in Scotland for the said Dowager Elizabeth in favour of Archibald Grosert, merchant in Bo'ness, her factor in virtue of factory, dated 20th July, 1725, whereby he constituted John Hay, of Balbethan, his depute, to uplift and receive all rents, profits, and duties due and belonging to said Duchess furth of the lands and barony of Kinneil and others liferented by her. Mention is also made in a document in 1721 of a John Main, manager of His Grace the Duke of Hamilton's coal works at Kinglass.

Writers and notaries flourished in the seaport during the Regality period. In addition to Rudolph Weir, we frequently come across James Tailfer, John Wilson, Andrew Wilson, William Wilson, David Jervay, and William Keir, "wrytter in Grangepans." These were the procurators and conveyancers about the place from time to time, and are not to be confused with the mere "servitors," *i.e.*, the clerks or apprentices. One Donald Blair, described for years as a "servitor" to Weir, in time blossoms into a procurator on his own account, and similarly a Robert Blair, some time "servitor" to Andrew Wilson.

VIII.

The following are examples of common surnames to be found in this register:—Baird, Bell, Blair, Callender, Drysdail, Downie, Gairdner, Gray, Grinlay, Hardie, Hendry, Johnston, Kincaid, Marshall, Mitchell, Muir, Paterson, Ramsay, Rankine. Shepherd, Smith, Snadden, Stewart, and Thomson. There are also to be found a Richard Maltman, maltster in Bo'ness. and a James Watchman, merchant there.

As for employments, there are many maltmen, skippers, boatmen, sailors, fleshers, wrights, baxters (bakers), and some coal-hewers.

A sample or two of the wording of the bills in those days may also interest—

"Pay to myself or order at my dwellinghouse in Bo'ness

two hundred and eightie seven pounds six shillings Scots money, the value in your hands and oblige your friend."

"Sir, Be pleased to pay to me or order upon the............ at my dwellinghouse in Grangepans the soume of.............. Scots value in your own hands. Make thankfull payment and oblidge. Sir, Your most humble Servant."

"Please to pay to...............at or between the............... at his own dwellinghouse the soume of...............Scots value in your own hand. Make thankfull payment and oblidge. Your humble Servant."

The following entries appear on one of the back pages of the volume:—"The 28 of August, 1728.—Then the whole warrands of all Registers in this Regality were revised and seen by Hew Markaill, Deput to Ventris Columbine, Inspector Generall of the Stamp-duties."

"Wednesday, the 25th of September, 1728.—David Rennie, Merchant, Admitted Quarter-Master of this Town by the Baillie, and sworne *de fideli*."

"Tuesday, the 18th Feb., 1729.—John Cram, Maltman, Admitted Conjunct Quarter-Master with Robert Main in room of David Rennie deceast, and sworne *de fideli*."

We close these two old books reluctantly. They are full of local interest to those who care about conjuring up the past from the facts they set forth. In great contrast to many other places the government of this district during the period of Regality appears to have been in every way efficient and beneficial. But in the north especially, the heads of clans and feudal lords were said to have obtained complete sway over their vassals and retainers by the unjust and terrifying exercise of their powers of criminal and other jurisdiction. These lords, in the knowledge of the support they could thus depend on became frequently rebellious against the Government, even to armed insurrection. The Rebellion of 1745 brought matters to a crisis. After passing an Act vesting in the Crown the estates of the insurgent lords of the '45, it was followed up in 1747 by a general Act abolishing all these heritable jurisdictions. Henceforth all jurisdictions, powers, and authorities were vested in the Court of Session and its inferior Courts. "So ended," says a writer on the subject,[2] "a system which had been part of the national life since the dawn of history, and which only perished when it had become quite incompatible with the conditions of modern life."

---

[2] See "Juridical Review," 1897, article "Heritable Jurisdictions," W. K. Dickson.

CHAPTER VII.

THE TRIAL AND BURNING OF THE BORROWSTOUNNESS WITCHES.

1. Prevalence of Witchcraft and Superstition in Scotland—2. Local Confessions of Charming: Commission Granted for Trial of Six Carriden Witches: Supplication of Isobel Wilson: the Case of Margaret Finlayson—3. Trial for Witchcraft of Six Women and One Man in Borrowstounness Tolbooth — 4. The Indictment: the Verdict and Commitment—5. Cases of Superstition and Witchcraft in Carriden Parish.

I.

THE history of witchcraft and superstition in Scotland presents many strange and unaccountable phenomena, although the whole subject, as was recently said by an authority,[1] deserves to be examined carefully, without disbelief, without fear, rejecting all impostures, and studying the residuum of truth that is left behind.

Notwithstanding the strong religious feelings which prevailed, witchcraft was rife all over the country during the seventeenth and part of the eighteenth century. So strange and foreign to most modern minds are those superstitions that, had we not definite and undeniable records of the occurrences, we should never believe the things at all. The state of matters is well put by Graham[2] when he says, "Superstition was spread amongst all classes; there was not an event of their lives from birth to death which was free from it; omens were seen in a myriad coincidences; charms were used to ward off every form of evil. Some superstitions were relics of paganism, others

---

[1] Mr. Brodie-Innes.
[2] Social life in Scotland.

were relics of Popish days, while many were due to those instinctive fears and associations with mysterious events of Nature common to humanity everywhere."

These curious beliefs gave rise to a criminal code of great severity. Sorcery and witchcraft, according to the law of Scotland, were very serious crimes, and offenders were rigorously dealt with. The Ecclesiastical Courts, too, kept a watchful eye on suspected persons, and enforced disciplinary measures without fail. When we recall the punishments and deaths of so many persons who, after all, were innocent of any actual crime, we are amazed at the results of this peculiar phase of the mental state of all classes in the nation at that time.

The chief actor in all this hurly-burly, as is revealed in the indictments of the cases which came to trial, was his satanic majesty the devil. Let us take one example. The countryside down by Tranent, especially a place called Saltpans, probably Prestonpans, was kept in terror for a time by the strange doings of one Doctor Fian, alias John Cunningham, master of the school at Saltpans, and his female associates. According to one record,[3] a company of at least two hundred females assembled there on "Allhallon-Even," and set out to sea, each one in a riddle or "cive." They went in the same, "very sustantially," as it is put, with flagons of wine, "making merrie and drinking by the way to the Kirke of North Barrick." After landing, they took hands and danced a reel, singing as they danced. They afterwards formed a procession, and one of their number, accompanied by Fian, went before them, playing a reel on "a small trumpe called a Jewe's trump, until they entered into the Kerk of North Barrick." The devil was in waiting for them, and, as they had tarried on the way and were late, he made them all do penance in a most revolting and abasing fashion. His satanic majesty then delivered his ungodly exhortations from the pulpit, and, after receiving their oaths for good and true service, they returned to sea, and so home again. What a length the imaginations of our

---

[3] See Sharpe's "History of Witchcraft," chap. iii., p. 60.

forefathers must have gone to in this direction! The sea voyage as narrated, for one thing, was utterly impossible in fact. Fian was convicted before the King and Privy Council for this and other like offences, and burned at Edinburgh in January, 1591. This is just a feeble sample of what went on and what was believed. The King sat often with the Privy Council during the trials for sorcery and witchcraft, and he, "in respect of the strangeness of these matters, took great delight to be present at the examinations."

II.

That the district of Borrowstounness was not any freer than its neighbours from these strange happenings the Privy Council and other records show. Take the following as an example:—

It is to be found among the confessions of charming (1617-21) by one Jonet Anderson, in Stirling.[4]

"The said Jonet Andersone confesses that ane tailyour in the Falkirk, callit Sandie Wear, came to hir with ane sark of ane bairne of the Chalmerlane of Kinneil, and desyrit the sark mycht be charmit. He affirmit that she soght ane knyf to that effect. The said Jonet confesses that she charmit the said sark, and that in the tyme thereof she had ane knyf in hir hand, bot denyes she soght any: and confesses she said to the tailyour, 'Ye neid not seik this charme; the bairne will be ded or ye cam hame.' And, being demanded quhow she knew the bairne wad be ded, answered that she wald not receave meat quhen the same man cam fra hir."

On 27th January, 1648, the Council had before it a supplication by the Presbytery of Linlithgow, signed by Mr. Pa. Shiells, moderator, and Mr. Ro. Row, clerk. The supplication narrates that the Council had on a former occasion, also on the application of the Presbytery, granted a commission to several gentlemen for the trial of six witches in the Parish of Carriden,

---

[4] P.C. Reg., vol. viii., 2nd series, p. 346.

and that these (the witches apparently) had been duly executed. They had made confessions, and therein had denounced other persons, not only in Carriden, but in adjacent parishes. This supplication therefore craved the appointment of a Standing Commission to deal with such. The Council refused the request as unreasonable, and stated that, when any particular case was offered for their consideration, they would deal with it as might be necessary.

We have been unable to trace any evidence of the trial of these Carriden witches. More than likely it took place, and, if it did, there can be little doubt as to the result. The trial of the Bo'ness witches was thirty or forty years after this.

In the following year—1649—we find the Council considering the supplication of one Isobel Wilson, in Carraden, who had been imprisoned on a false charge of witchcraft, but since liberated by their lordships. Fearing she would be annoyed by her accusers and brought up for trial locally, she craved that in such a case she might be tried before the Justice Court, as she would then have the benefit of advocates to plead for her. Isobel apparently, though she wished the benefit of an advocate, was also afraid, and not without reason, that a Court composed of local assizers or jurymen would not be to her advantage. The Council do not appear to have disposed of the request.

In articles proven before the Council on 26th February, 1650, against a witch, Margaret Finlayson, of the parish of Renfrew, the following item occurs:—

"A man called Bargans, fugitive from Borrowstounness for the alleaged cryme of sorcerie, that was never known in that place of the counterie befor, being in Alexander Duglass house in the Yoker, said if he knew quhere Margaret Finlayson were shoe would give him a bunnock; and quhen it was told him that shoe lived in the nixt house he went in to hire, & shoe immediately following him out with a bunnock as he hade said, & they drank tua chappins of aile together in Alexander Duglass house befor they pairted."

If this is a sample of the sort of thing people were branded sorcerers and witches for, suffering in many cases death by torture, we may well feel utterly confounded at human credulity. Plainly Bargans knew Margaret Finlayson in Yoker, just as any one here to-day might know some one there also. But he did not know where she stayed, and naturally inquired at Douglass' house (presumably an ale-house) into which he had gone. Evidently hungry, he mentioned that, if he knew where Margaret Finlayson stayed, and called for her, she would be sure to give him a "bunnock." It turned out, as we have seen, that she lived next door. He called, got his bunnock, and, in return, brought her into the inn, where they drank "tua chappins of aile together." And yet this was evidently sorcerie and witchcraft.

III.

But the worst case of all was still to come. In the year 1679 the Privy Council named Cochran of Barbbachlay; Richard Elphinstown; Saindelands of Hilderstown; Cornwall of Bonhard; Robert Hamilton of Dechmont, Bailzie of the Regality of Borrowstounness; Sir John Harper, advocate; Mr. William Dundas and Mr. John Prestowne, advocates, Commissioners of Justiciary, specially constituted, nominated, and appointed for the trial and judging of the persons afternamed, viz.—Annaple Thomsone, widow in Borrowstounness; Margaret Pringle, relict of the deceist John Cambell, sivewright there; Margaret Hamilton, relict of the deceist James Pollwart there; William Craw, indweller there; Bessie Vickar, relict of the deceased James Pennie, indweller there; and Margaret Hamilton, relict of the deceist Thomas Mitchell. The parties had been duly apprehended and imprisoned in the "tolbuith" of Borrowstounness. There they had served upon them a copy of the precept or charge, wherein it was stated they were suspected "guilty of the abominable crime of witchcraft, by entering into paction with the devill, and renouncing their baptizme." In the name of the Sovereign they were commanded to "compear" before the abovenamed Commissioners, or any three of them (three being a quorum), within the "said tolbuith of Borrowstounness" upon the 19th day of December, 1679, there "to underlye the lawe for the crymes above specifiet," and that under the ".paines" contained in the new Acts of Parliament. Officers of Court were likewise commanded to summon, warn, and charge an assize or jury "of honest and famous persons, not exceeding the number of fortie-five," also such witnesses who best knew the "veritie" of the persons above complained upon.

The precept concluded thus—"Given under our hands at Borrowstounes the twentie-nynt day of November, ane thousande six hunder and seventie-nyne yeirs."

It was signed "R. Hamilton, J. Cornwall, Rich. Elphinstone, W. Dundas."

IV.

The indictment makes painful and in some places revolting reading. But it furnishes a good illustration of the very superstitious state of the country two centuries and a half ago. We reproduce the document[4] underneath, save the unreadable parts, which are left blank.

The accused are named and designed as already noted, and it proceeds—

"Yee, and ilk ane of you ar indytted & accused that whereas, notwithstanding be the law of God, particularlie set down in the 20 chapter of Leviticus and eighteen chap. of Dewtronomie, & be the lawes & Actes of Parliament of this kingdome, and constant practis thereof, particularlie be the 73 Act of Parliament, 2 Marie, the cryme of witchcraft is declaired to be ane horid, abominable, and capitall cryme, punishable with the paines of death & confiscatioun of moveables; nevertheless it is of veritie that you have committed and are gwyltie of the said cryme of witchcraft in so far as ye have entered in pactioun with the devill, the enemie of your salvatioun, & have renounced our blessed Lord and Saviour, and your baptisme, and have given yourselffes, both soulles and bodies, to the devill, and have bein severall meetings with the devill, and wyth sundrie witches

---

[4] See "Scots Magazine," vol. 34, 1772.

in diverse places; and particularie ye, the said Annaple Thomsone, had a meeting with the devill the tyme of your weidowhood, befoer you was married to your last husband, in your coming betwixt Linlithgow and Borrowstownes, when the devill, in the lykness of ane black man, told you that you wis ane poore puddled bodie, and had ane evill lyiff and difficultie to win throw the world: and promesed iff ye wald follow him and go alongst with him you should never want, but have ane better lyiff: and about fyve wekes therefter the devill appeired to you when you wis goeing to the Coal-hill about sevin aclock in the morning: having renewed his former tentatiown, you did condeschend thereto, and declared yourselff content to follow him & becum his servant, whereupon the devill threw you to the ground. . . .

"And ye, and each person of you, wis at several mettings with the devill in the linkes of Borrowstounes, and in the house of you, Bessie Vickar, and ye did eatt and drink with the devill and with ane anither, and with witches in her house in the night tyme: and the devill and the said William Craw brought the ale which ye drank, extending to about sevin gallons, and from the hous of Elizabeth Hamilton: and you, the said Annaple, had ane other metting about fyve wekes ago, when you wis goeing to the Coal-hill of Grange, and he inveitted you to go alongst and drink with him in the Grangepannes:

"And you, the said Margaret Pringle, have bein ane witch thir many yeers bygane, had renounced your baptizme and becum the devill's servant, and promeist to follow him: and the devill . . . and tuik you by the right hand, whereby it was for eight dayes grevouslie paind, but having it twitched of new againe it imediatlie becam haill:

"And you, the said Margaret Hamilton, has bein the devill's servant these eight or nyne yeeres bygane: and he appered and conversed with you at the toun-well of Borrowstownes and several tymes in your awin hous, and drank severall choppins of ale with you, and thereafter . . . and the devill gave you ane fyve merk piece of gold whilk a lyttell efter becam ane sklaittstane:

"And you, the said Margaret Hamilton, relict of James Pullwart, has bein ane witch and the devill's servant thirtie yeeres since, haith renounced your baptizme as said is, and has . . . with the devil in the lyknes of ane black dowg.

"And ye, and ilk ane of you, wis at ane metting with the devill and other witches at the croce of Murestane, above Kinneil, upon the threttin of October last, where you all danced, and the devill acted the pyper, and when you endeavored to have distroyed Andrew Mitchell, sone to John Mitchell, elder in Dean of Kinneil."

We had hoped to supply a list of the names of the jurymen or assizers in this case, but, unfortunately, the justiciary records of the period have gone amissing.

Here is a copy of the verdict and commitment—

"Forasmeikle as (then here follows the names of the five women and the man), prisoners in the Tolbuith of Borrowstownes, are found guiltie be ane assyse of the abominable cryme of witchcraft, comitted be them in manner mentioned in their dittayes, and are decerned and adjudged be us under-subscryvers (Commissioners of Justiciary speciallie appoynted to this effect), to be taken to the west end of Borrowstownes, the ordinary place of execution, ther upon Tuesday, the twentie-third day of December current, betwixt two and four o'cloack in the afternoon, and ther to be wirried at a steack till they be dead, and therefter to have their bodies burnt to ashes: these therefoir require and command the baylie-principal off the Regalitie of Borrowstowness and his deputts to see the said sentence and doom put to dew execution in all poynts as yee will be answerable: given under our hands at Borrowstounes, the nynteenth day of December, 1679 years: W. Dundas, Rich. Elphinstone, Wa. Sandilands, Jn. Cornwall, R. Hamilton." And duly and punctually, we must sorrowfully say, was this sentence of death carried out on the flat glebe land at the west end of Corbiehall, on the afternoon of the 23rd of December, 1679.[5]

---

[5] The site is now occupied by the works of Messrs. Jas. Calder & Co., Ltd.

We have heard it stated that the Bo'ness witch burning was the last, or about the last, in Scotland, but this is not so. There were witch trials and witch burnings long after the one here narrated.

V.

No other local case seems to have gone to trial, but the Carriden Kirk Session records show not a few references to superstitions.[6] One Margaret Thompson was cited for "using magicall arte in burning of a corn riddle to find out some money she wanted, and that on Sabbath last, April 5th."

A man, Thomas Rolland, compeared against Christian Henderson, and alleged that, if she did not call his mother a witch, she did mean as much, in that she should have come to his said mother and "asked the health of her son for God's sake: and should have taken bread from his said mother to her said chylde."

One woman, Anna Wood by name, was accused in 1704 of witchcraft. She was brought before the session, and witnesses appeared to prove her a witch.

Robert Nimmo, seaman, being called and required to declare what he saw or knew anent Anna Wood, declared as follows:— "That upon Monday, the 29th January last, about 7 o'clock at night, as he was coming from Linlithgow to the waterside (Carriden shore), he met with six catts, who followed him homewards till he came to Sir Walter Seton's Park Dyke at Northbank, at which place they appeared to him as women; that he knew one of them to be Anna Wood, and that he did speak to her, and that she did bid kill him; and that all of them convoyed him a considerable space and then appeared as birds fleeing by him and about him, and after that appeared again as women and went alongst with him till he came to the Grange, when they left him; and that he knew the said Anna to be one of them this time also.

See also "Sharpe's History of Witchcraft.'

"The said Anna Wood, cited and compearing, was interrogate what envye she had at Robert Nimmo that she should have offered to kill him. Answered that she had no envye at him: indeed she had no envye at the young man. Was asked when she was at Holland last. Answered not there twelve years. Was asked if she dreamed she was there since. Answered she never dreamed such a thing. Interrogate whether she met with Robert Nimmo 29th January, at such time and in such a place. Answer—Denyed it. Was interrogate whether she forbade him to mention her name to the Session. Answered she never said such a thing. Was interrogate where she was that night at that time, for she was found to be missing, for she had left work till nyne o'clock at night. Answered in Thomas Henderson's and Archibald Campbell's, in Coudonhill. Was further interrogate whether she was at Sir Walter Seton's Park Dyke that night, the 29th January, and other five women with her. Denyed it, saying she was free of such scandall.

"John and James Craig were deputed to find out whether she was in Thomas Henderson's and Archibald Campbell's such a night, and report next day. And the said Anna to be summoned against the next day, with other witnesses, and the said Robert Nimmo.

VI.

"Next day first Robert Nimmo was interrogated whether he had seen Anna Wood since the 29th January last, answered he saw her not since. Declared further that upon Saturday last, the 17th inst., betwixt Cowdenhill and Bridgeness, at night, he heard women say to him, 'Robine, declare what ye saw,' and that on Friday night he heard them on shipboard also distinctly cry to him to declare what he saw. He was asked what he thought was the ground of her hatred at him. Answered that about two years ago, on his refusall of a commission from her to Holland, she then said to him she would do him an ill turn. He further declared that he saw the said Anna Wood aboard their ship when the said ship was lying at Cuffabouts; and also that she had a candle in her hand, and that she went fore and eft the ship, and that the half of ane hogshead of sack was drunk out that night, for it was wanting on the morrow, they knew not how: Also, that ane day, in Isabel Nimmo's, the said Anna Wood did forbid him to speak of her name to the Session. He further declared that eight nights before the night he met them coming from Linlithgow three women came aboard their ship and kept him from sleeping and speaking.

"James Linlithgow, seaman, cited and compearing, declared that he saw the said Anna Wood aboard their ship, that she went fore and eft with a candle in her hand, and he, being admonished to take good heed what he said, asserted that he really knew it to be Anna Wood, and that he could depone upon it before any judge in the world, and further declared that he saw her another night aboard a ship when he was aboard with Robert Nimmo.

"John Craig reported that Euphaim Allan declared that Anna Wood, on 29th January last, left her work in the said Euphaim's house about seven hours at night, and was not in again till nine o'clock.

"James Steidman, skipper, declared that if ever he saw Anna Wood in his days, he saw her at the Briell, in Holland, in his ship cabin, when he was last there, anno 1693, otherwise the devill in her likeness, at which time he lost a boy.

"The said Anna Wood, cited, called, and non-compearing, it was told the Session that she was fled, whereupon the clerk was ordered to draw out the whole process against her, to be sent to Edinburgh: and referred to the magistrate, and in particular to the Bailie of Grange, to make search for her: all which was done."

It was well for Anna Wood that she fled, for her life was in serious danger. In that very year a woman was burned on the opposite shore of Torryburn for witchcraft, and the evidence recorded above shows that the Session and Parish of Carriden might have been guilty of a similar crime had the opportunity not been snatched from them.

The laws against witchcraft in Scotland were afterwards

abolished. As Graham says[7]—"It was a terrible blow to the credulous and pious when the old Act against witchcraft was abolished, in 1736, and, instead of death being passed on all 'traffickers with Satan,' there was a prosaic, rational statute left making liable to a year's imprisonment and three months in the pillory all vulgar practisers of occult arts ' who pretended to tell fortunes and discover stolen goods.' "

We have now as a nation strong views on the sacredness of human life, which is doubtless a reaction from the carelessness of former generations. But although witchcraft has been legally abolished, the cult of the witch is so dear to humanity that it is in some aspects as prevalent to-day as it was some centuries ago.

---

[7] "Social Life in Scotland," p. 488.

CHAPTER VIII.

LOCAL COVENANTING HISTORY AND "THE BORROWSTOUNNESS MARTYRS."

1. Introduction—The National Covenant—2. The Solemn League and Covenant—3. The Seaport a Haunt of Covenanting Fugitives: Zeal and Steadfastness of Inhabitants—4. Persecution of Rev. William Wishart: Sufferings of his Family: His Continual Enthusiasm—5. Visits of Rev. John Blackader, Field Preacher: His Conventicle at Hilderston; Linlithgow Magistrates and their "Deluded Townsmen"—6. The Rev. Donald Cargill and his Escapes: Carriden Hiding-Places—7. Sir Robert Hamilton: Residence and Death in Borrowstounness: His "Faithful Testimony"—8. The Four Borrowstounness Martyrs: Archibald Stewart and his Testimony—9. Marion Harvie, Serving-maid: Her Own Story—10. Before Privy Council—11. Before Justiciary Court: Her Written Testimony—12. On the Scaffold: Her Last Testimony—13. William Gouger and William Cuthill—14. The Gibbites, or Sweet Singers of Borrowstounness—Rev. Donald Cargill's Fruitless Mission: What the Dragoons Did.

I.

THE life-story of the Scottish people contains no finer chapter than that concerning the Covenants and Covenanters. All phases of Covenanting history are exceptionally interesting, and the interest is intensified to those whose lot has been cast in districts which specially contributed to it. Hereabouts we have been accustomed to associate that history with the southern counties—Dumfriesshire, Galloway, Ayrshire, and Lanarkshire—the land of hills, moss-hags, deer-slunks, declarations, conventicles, and Covenanting battles. But it will come as a revelation to many when they find that the district of Borrowstounness has an honoured place in the Covenanting story.

In our day the exceedingly long and tortuous railway routes to the southern counties give us the impression that these are further off than they really are. In Covenanting times there could be no such delusion. Lying directly to the north of the Covenanting counties, it would be comparatively easy for horsemen, and even for pedestrians, to come by the hill roads to the shores of the Forth from the uplands of Lanarkshire and further south. As we shall see, there must have been a considerable traffic to the seaport from these centres.

Before relating the events which interest us locally we may be pardoned for recalling a few of the outstanding facts of the national struggle.

Although there were the first and second Covenants of 1557 and 1559, whereby certain Scottish nobles agreed to resist attempts made in these years to revive the Roman Catholic religion, the Covenanters derived their name chiefly from the National Covenant, signed in the spring of 1638, and the Solemn League and Covenant, signed in 1642. The cause of revolt was the misguided persistence of King James, and his son and grandsons, in holding to the doctrine that they were Kings by "Divine Right," and that the will of the people did not enter into the scheme of government at all. Scotland had no sooner cast off the Roman Catholic religion and established Presbyterianism at the Reformation than first James, and then the others in their turn, sought, despite promises to the contrary, to impose Episcopacy. Passive resistance more or less to James, however, blazed into open rebellion in the early years of his son. According to King Charles and his spiritual adviser, Archbishop Laud, the Scottish Church, as established by Knox and the other Reformation heroes, eighty years before, had to go—presbyteries, kirk sessions, and elders. For the future the bishops were to rule, and Laud's Service-book was ordered to be used in all churches. Upon this the Lowland people of all classes rose in united protest and flocked to Edinburgh. Popular tumult for a time was quietened by the appointment of four committees of four each—drawn from the nobles, the gentry, the clergy, and the citizens—to see to their interests. This body was known as the Tables, or the Four Tables. The King ignored it, supported the bishops, and pronounced all protestors conspirators. The Tables recalled the people to Edinburgh, and the result was that historic declaration, the National Covenant, signed by thousands in Greyfriars' Church and Churchyard, Edinburgh, on the 1st of March, 1638, and following days, and afterwards throughout the whole country. Its chief terms were a passionate profession of the Reformed faith, a resolution to continue in it against all errors and corruptions, and also a resolution to support the religion, liberties, and laws of the realm. It was distinctly national, and it was not, as the King tried to make out, a treasonable document. It clearly indicated that the people wished to be loyal to the King in matters of ordinary government, but that they declined to accept him as the dictator of what religion they should profess. Interference with their freedom of conscience they could not and would not accept under any pretext. The wrath of Charles and the bishops at this strong exhibition of spiritual independence, or, as they called it, treason, was extreme. Duke of Hamilton's useless mission on behalf of his King, who prudently remained in England, and other events now well-known matters of national history, followed.

II.

The Solemn League and Covenant, to turn to it for a moment, was of more than national import. The King had been as high-handed with the Puritans in England as he was with the Scottish nation. When their Civil War broke out the Puritan leaders sent to the Scottish Convention of Estates for help, and the Estates willingly agreed to send a Scottish army to their aid. The Alliance then entered into between the two kingdoms was known as the Solemn League and Covenant. Both countries were to strive for the uprooting of Prelacy and Popery, and to labour for the reformation of religion in the Kingdoms of England and of Ireland in doctrine, in worship, discipline, and polity, according to the Word of God and the example of the best Reformed Church.

During the Covenanting struggle various Declarations, notably two at Sanquhar and one at Rutherglen, were made by the Covenanting leaders from time to time. These Declarations, of course, like the Covenants, were viewed by the Throne as treasonable, only more so. Certainly the terms in which the King and others of the Royal House were spoken of in these documents became more pronounced as the issue resolved itself more and more distinctly into a fight for mastery in spiritual matters between a tyrannical Royalty and an independent people. But the circumstances were such that it could scarcely be otherwise. The haughty Stuarts thought of the people only as so many pawns to be used for the Royal purposes. The idea of treating them as rational human beings never once entered their minds. The Covenanters, seeing this, had either to succumb without a murmur to this blind driving force or to assert themselves as rational units. They asserted themselves. The result of Declaration after Declaration was that the rigour of the persecutors was redoubled, and the Covenanters were ruthlessly hunted and done to death. These, indeed, were "the killing times," times, as Crockett puts it, of "many headings, hangings, hidings, chasings, outcastings, and weary wanderings."

The position and action of the Covenanters have in many cases been misunderstood for lack of complete knowledge of the facts, and in others they have been sorely misrepresented. However, as the facts of their history come to be more generally known in detail, pieced together, and studied as an epoch by themselves. what the Covenanters did for Scotland and the Presbyterian religion will, we doubt not, duly receive the intelligent and permanent recognition which it deserves.

III.

Borrowstounness, at the time when the struggle became acute, had frequent and intimate commercial intercourse with

Holland, and, as Holland was the favourite resort of expatriated Covenanters, and the base, so to speak, of many of their banished leaders, the seaport became a regular haunt of Covenanting fugitives from the southern counties and elsewhere. The minister of Bo'ness, for a time at least, and the minister of Carriden entirely, were King's men. But the people of the town and district, being inspired by the Rev. John Blackader, the great field-preacher, and many others, strenuously opposed the endeavours of King Charles to crush out the national religion. James, first Duke of Hamilton, was, as we have stated elsewhere, unfortunately employed as one of the chief instruments of King Charles for opposing the Covenanters. It is clear, however, that this fact did not in the slightest way tend to abate the Covenanting zeal of his many vassals, both here and in Clydesdale. And no doubt among the crowds who flocked to Edinburgh to demonstrate against the Duke during his futile endeavour to discharge his commission from Charles, there were large numbers of his own vassals from Bo'ness and Clydesdale.

Speaking of the seaport as a place of refuge for the persecuted, it can easily be conceived, says Mr. Johnston,[1] that the skippers of Bo'ness, who loathed Prelacy and all its works, did much to help the persecuted Covenanters to escape. They could usually count on finding there a good ship, commanded by a sympathetic master and manned by an honest crew, ready to put them beyond the reach of their foes. We know, too, that, as the Press at home was under a strict censorship, the Presbyterians found it necessary to get their literature printed abroad, much of it—to the great annoyance of the Government—being smuggled over to Borrowstounness from various Dutch cities in which Scottish exiles had taken up their quarters.

Many of the sons and daughters of the seaport were distinguished for their zeal and steadfastness. And when the struggle became an armed one on both sides raids and persecutions against those who upheld the Covenants were frequent in this neighbourhood, for Edinburgh, the seat of the

---

[1] Records of Bo'ness Seabox.

civil authority, was near, and nearer still was Binns, the seat of Sir Thomas Dalyell—the bloody Dalyell, as he was called.

IV.

One of the earliest local victims of the persecution was the Rev. William Wishart, the last minister of the Parish of Kinneil. From the first he had been a vigorous protestor, forming one of the Dissenting Presbytery from 1651 to 1659. On 15th September, 1660, by the authority of the Committee of Estates, he was seized in Edinburgh, where he had apparently been staying at the time, and confined to his chamber. Five days later he was imprisoned in the Tolbooth. He remained in prison for thirteen months. His offences were two—not disowning the Remonstrance and refusing to sign the Bond for keeping the peace. Part of his imprisonment seems to have been in the Castle of Stirling, for we find his spouse, Christian Burne, petitioning Parliament early in 1661 for assistance, and showing "the sad condition of Mr. Wishart, now prisoner in the Castle of Stirling, throw want of means while ane numerous familie are dependant." As a result, an Act was passed on 29th January, 1661, in her favour, whereby "all the arrears of stipend restand awand (resting owing) preceiding 1660 were ordeaned to be payed to her be the persons lyable in payment thereof." In November, 1661, we find three Commissioners, of whom Mr. John Waugh, first minister of Bo'ness, was one, supplicating the Privy Council for themselves, and in name and on behalf of the "remanent bretherin" of the Presbytery of Linlithgow. They narrated that Kinneil, owing to the imprisonment of its minister, Mr. Wishart, had for thirteen months been without the "settled administration of the ordinances." The Presbytery had done what they could, but this "had been but little, having eight kirks beside that to provide with preaching." They craved for his release, so that access could be had for the "planting of that kirk with some other whom the patron should be pleased to name." The petition having been carefully considered by the Privy Council, they were pleased to order his release. From this contemplated "planting" we are inclined to think that Mr. Wishart did no duty at Kinneil after his release. If he did his ministrations must have been of a perfunctory character. In any event, Kinneil Parish and the Church were soon suppressed. On 17th December, that same year, the Council had before them another supplication from the Presbytery It craved the Lords to remove the sequestration which then lay on Mr. Wishart's stipend for that year. Parliament had taken it off for the previous year, so that "the said Mr. William and his numerous family would have at least a viaticuus for keeping them from starving for a tyme." The Lords granted what was craved, and ordained all heritors and others liable in payment of the minister's stipend within the said parish to make payment of their respective proportions to the said William Wishart.

But if Mr. Wishart had through his imprisonment lost his charge, it did not make him lose his enthusiasm for the cause of the Covenants. For the next fourteen stormy years he appears to have been a leader in the field meetings or conventicles, and on 6th August, 1675, was intercommuned by the Privy Council for taking part in these. We do not expect these letters of intercommuning would cause him to abate his enthusiasm in the slightest. On the contrary, we fear that imprisonment followed, as we do not discover anything of him for the next ten years. On 5th February, 1685, he was ordered to be sent to His Majesty's plantations for refusing the abjuration or test, and was only liberated from prison on the 24th of the same month owing to the death of King Charles II.

When King James VII. issued in 1687 his Declarations of Indulgence, under which the majority of the Presbyterian ministers returned to their parishes, Mr. Wishart began to preach again, and took charge of the congregation at Leith, where he had his residence, promising to continue until a minister was settled. However, he stands enrolled as a minister of the Presbytery of Linlithgow on 25th July, 1688. He died in

February, 1692, aged about sixty-seven, in the forty-third year of his ministry.

V.

Another noted Covenanter whose voice was often uplifted in this district was the Rev. John Blackader. He was immediately descended from the Blackaders of Tulliallan, and more remotely from a famous Berwickshire family—father and seven sons—once a terror to the English, and known as "the Black Band of the Blackaders." Mr. Blackader was trained at the College of Glasgow, but did not find a charge until he was thirty-seven. He was then ordained over the Parish of Troqueer, in the Presbytery of Dumfries, where he did great work for seven years in the face of serious difficulties. Refusing to bow the knee on the passing of Middleton's Glasgow Act, the dragoons came after him, and he had to seek refuge in Galloway, beyond the bounds of his Presbytery. Soon, however, he became one of the chiefs in the great conventicles of the time. He had his headquarters in Edinburgh, but hastened here and there all over the country on his Divine errands.

We do well then to remember the frequent presence in our neighbourhood of this famous field-preacher. In the spring of 1671 he held one of his great meetings at Hilderston House, near Torphichen. Kettlestone, which was within the Regality of Borrowstounness, was also in that direction. It is interesting to recall here[2] that William Sandilands, brother of the fourth Lord Torphichen and tutor to his nephew, the fifth Lord, was Laird of Hilderston. He married the second daughter of Cunningham of Cunninghamhead, in Ayrshire, a gentleman distinguished even in that period for his sincere piety. Hilderston and his lady were both remarkable for their attachment to the Presbyterian principles of the Scottish Church, and their mansion-house of Hilderston

---

[2] See New Stat. Account, Torphichen, vol. ii.

was often the hospitable resort of the persecuted Covenanters. There Mr. Blackader and others often held conventicles, and heavy fines were on that account imposed upon the family.

On this occasion Mr. Blackader had gone to visit Lady Hilderston, and, being indisposed, intended to remain private. Early on the Sabbath morning, however, the house was surrounded by multitudes. Numbers attended from Linlithgow, which through all the persecution remained loyal to the King. Indeed, its inhabitants became noted for their hostility to the Covenants and conventicles. Blackader did not wish to have more present than the family. But when the morning Psalm was being sung the gates of the court were opened. Speedily the large hall, holding about eight hundred people, was filled, besides the rooms beneath, many people also standing in the court. Before the meeting a serious accident occurred to "a very honest gentlewoman in Lithgow," who on her way thither fell off horseback from behind her husband and broke her arm. In spite of the pain, the pious and plucky lady went to the service, at which she was present all forenoon listening composedly without fainting. Had it not been for the minister, who desired her husband to take her home, she would have remained for the afternoon worship also, being "so earnest to hear and to see such a day in that part of the country."

The Provost of Linlithgow, Crichton[3] states, punished this fanaticism of his deluded townsmen with severe fines to keep up the loyalty of his burgh. Many were summoned and apprehended the same afternoon, and some imprisoned that very night. All cheerfully paid their penalties—some three hundred merks, some fifty pounds, some one hundred pounds sterling. The lady and her son, the young laird, were brought before the Council; she was fined in four hundred merks for suffering a meeting in her house, and her son in a like sum for not disclosing the name of the minister. The activity of the magistracy was stimulated and emboldened by the

---

[3] Memoirs of Rev. John Blackader.

presence of the Earls of Linlithgow and Kincardine, two of the Lords of the Privy Council who happened to be at the palace, and "were brought into the Council-room for a terror." These noblemen had been on a crusade to the west with six or seven of the ablest and subtlest curates essaying with flattering and insinuating speeches to draw the people to conformity. They offered money to the poorer sort, but with no effect; so they "returned disappointed of that poor senseless wyle."

At a later date Mr. Blackader was once more in Borrowstounness, where the meeting was dispersed by the soldiers from Blackness, and he himself nearly taken prisoner. On that occasion his son Adam was seized, and sent to Blackness Castle. In his autobiography the son says they told him he was to be put into a dungeon full of puddocks and toads. "This was for being at Borrowstounness, where my father had been preaching and baptised twenty-six children. They made my worthy old father climb dykes and hedges from one yard to another on a dark night till he got up the hill, where there was a barn in which he lay down all night."

VI.

Yet another of the faithful who was often in this district was the Rev. Donald Cargill, one time minister of the Barony Church of Glasgow, whose saintly character and career are well known to those acquainted with Covenanting history. It was through means of a scheme intended to entrap Cargill, while in the neighbourhood, that Marion Harvie and Archibald Stewart, two of the Borrowstounness martyrs, were apprehended between Edinburgh and Queensferry in November, 1680. Cargill on this occasion got warning of his danger in the nick of time, and escaped. He had on the 3rd of June previous an even narrower escape at Queensferry. Strolling[4] between Bo'ness and Queensferry the minister of Carriden, one

---

[4] Hewison's "Covenanters," vol. ii., p. 328.

John Pairk, and James Hamilton, fourth minister of Bo'ness, recognised Cargill, and sent word to the Governor of Blackness Castle. The latter followed quickly to Queensferry, found Cargill in a hostelry, and arrested him. Henry Hall, who was also arested, drew steel and overcame Middleton, the Governor. Meanwhile Cargill made off on Middleton's horse. Pairk's action was much resented by the faithful, and his life threatened. He apparently appealed to the Privy Council for protection, and we find the Council in June, 1680, recommending him to the Lords of the Treasury "for some allowance for this good service," *i.e.*, discovery of Mr. Cargill. As we will see in another chapter, Pairk was a worthless creature.

In the rising ground to the south of the Kinningars Park, Grange, there are several caves which are said to have been hiding-places of the Covenanters. Some were also to be found in the Carriden woods.

Stevenson, in "Kidnapped," makes Alan Breck and David Balfour, after being rowed across the Firth by a Limekilns lass, land "on the Lothian shore not far from Carriden"; and we read also that the two wanderers rested "in a den on the seashore." Though occurring in a work of fiction, we expect Stevenson had either seen the caves himself or been told of their existence. These hiding places were not, of course, caves in the geological sense, there being no rocks to speak of in this part of the Forth coast.

It was Donald Cargill, too, who some little time before his execution made a pilgrimage of faithfulness and love to the "Gibbites" in the Pentland Hills. He addressed to them a long letter of kindly remonstrance while in prison. We shall refer fully to the Gibbites later.

VII.

A prominent but unfortunate Covenanting leader who lived and died in Bo'ness was Mr. Robert Hamilton, afterwards Sir Robert. He himself neither appropriated the title nor entered upon possession of the family estates. Historians have charged him with having shown cowardice while in command at Drumclog and at Bothwell Brig, and of being a "feckless" general. We think the cowardice quite a mistaken and unfounded charge. "Fecklessness" there apparently was at Bothwell Brig, but it was more, we believe, a result of the bickerings and strivings which arose prior to the battle among the varied sects of the Covenanters themselves than inherent inability on Hamilton's part.

He was born in 1650, being the younger son of Sir William Hamilton, of Preston and Fingalton, who signed the Covenant in 1638, and of the same stock as Sir John Hamilton, of Preston, who defied King James's Commissioner, the second Marquis of Hamilton, at Edinburgh, in 1621, by boldly voting against the ratification of the Five Articles of Perth. Robert was educated under his relative, Gilbert Burnet, at Glasgow. Burnet thought him a promising youth, but held that the company of Dissenters early turned his head. He leagued himself with the party of Richard Cameron and Donald Cargill, and was the leading spirit in the Rutherglen Manifesto shortly before Drumclog. This document declared against all the statutes for overturning the Reformation and setting up the Royal Supremacy. Shortly after Bothwell Hamilton fled to Holland, and had to keep away, as an order was out for his execution. He visited Germany and Switzerland as Commissioner for the Scottish Presbyterian Church, and persuaded the Presbytery of Gronnigen to ordain Mr. James Renwick. Throughout his wanderings he passed through many hazards and difficulties. He returned home at the Revolution, about which time his brother, Sir William, died, and he fell heir to the estates and honours. But he felt he could not in conscience enter into possession unless he owned the title of the Prince and Princess of Orange, and this he could not bring himself to do. After his return he again became active for his cause. He took a prominent share in publishing the Sanquhar Declaration of 1692, for which he was apprehended, taken to Edinburgh, and there and elsewhere kept prisoner until May, 1693.

On being examined by the Privy Council he declined to recognise them as competent judges, because they were not qualified according to the Word of God and the Covenants. Asked if he would take the Oath of Allegiance, he answered "No," it being an unlimited oath "not bottomed upon the Covenants." Asked if he would give his security for obedience and peaceable living, he answered, "I marvel why such questions are asked at me, who have lived so retiredly, neither found plotting with York, France, or Monmouth, or any such as the rumour was; nor acting contrary to the laws of the nation enacted in the time of the purity of Presbytery." Upon Lothian remarking they were ashamed of him he replied, "Better you be ashamed of me than I be ashamed of the laws of the Church and nation whereof you seem to be ashamed."

Before his liberation he gave in two protests against what he termed his unjust imprisonment for adhering to the fundamental laws and constitution of the Church and Covenanted nation. Until his death, eight years after, he continued faithful in his contendings, and greatly strengthened the rest of the suffering remnant. During a portion of this period he seems to have taken up his residence at Borrowstounness, but whether in the town or at Kinneil we cannot say. He died here in 1701, at the age of fifty-one, after a sore affliction of some years, which he endured with great fortitude and in a spirit of holy submission to the will of God. His remains rest in one of the local churchyards. In drawing near his end he wrote a faithful testimony, dated Borrowstounness, 5th September, 1701,[5] in which he says—"As for my case, I bless God it is many years since my interest in Him was secured, and under all my afflictions from all airths He hath been a present help in time of my greatest need. I have been a man of reproatch, a man of contention; but praise to Him it was not for my ain things, but for the things of my Lord Jesus Christ."

---

[5] See "Scots Worthies," pp. 501-510, 1824 edition.

Renwick always called him "mi Pater," and had ever a great regard for him. The last letter Renwick wrote, just on the eve of his execution, was to Hamilton. There he says—"If I had lived and been qualified for writing a book, and if it had been dedicated to any, you would have been the man, for I have loved you, and I have peace before God in that; and I bless His name that I have been acquainted with you."

For soundness in the faith, true piety, exercise of real godliness, a conversation becoming the Gospel, and a true understanding of the state of the Lord's cause in every part thereof, says one judgment of him, he was an honour to the name of Hamilton, and to his nation.

Crockett, in his "Men of the Moss Hags," introduces Sir Robert, Renwick, Cargill, Cameron, and other Covenanters, and describes their characters.

VIII.

The Borrowstounness victims of the persecution were—(1) Archibald Stewart, who suffered death at the Cross of Edinburgh on 1st December, 1680; (2) Marion Harvie, executed in the Grassmarket of Edinburgh on 26th January, 1681; (3) William Gougar, executed at Edinburgh, 11th March, 1681; and (4) William Cuthill, seaman, also executed there on 27th July, 1681. A short account of each, with their answers to the questions put to them when brought before the Privy Council, and full copies of their written testimonies prior to death, are to be found in the "Cloud."[6] This book, it is interesting to recall, was first published in 1714, and there have been many editions since. The idea of it originated with the "United Societies" so far back as 1686, and its object, as explained in a letter to Sir Robert Hamilton in 1688, was to have an account of those who suffered under the tyranny of Charles II. and James, his son. The societies considered it a duty laid

---

[6] "Cloud of Witnesses or last Speeches and Testimonies of those who Suffered for the Faith in Scotland since 1680"; last edition.

"The Borrowstounness Martyrs" 137

upon them to hand down to their posterity "such a rich treasure as the fragrant and refreshing account of the sufferings of the martyrs, witnesses, and confessors of Christ."

When the Privy Council registers of that period come to be printed we shall doubtless find therein the official report of what passed for a trial of Stewart and the others. There is, however, in the "Cloud" and more recent volumes[7] of Covenanting history sufficient to enable us to give a brief sketch of each of the local martyrs.

Archibald Stewart.—There is no indication of this man's occupation or where he lived in the town. We simply read that he belonged to Borrowstounness, that he had been in Holland, and that he was converted by what he heard there and at home. Stewart was several times before the Privy Council, and on 15th November, 1680, was examined by torture. The Council feared a scheme was on foot to kill King Charles and the Duke of York, and applied the torture of the boot to many of their prisoners to see if they could thus cruelly extort information. We have no details of Stewart's torture, but we find that Robert Hamilton, son of Major Robert Hamilton, the Duke's chamberlain, was put to the torture at the same time. The Committee of the Council conducting the examination reported that Stewart confessed to being at Airsmoss, and that he, in addition, described to them a number of Mr. Cargill's haunts and places of hiding.

The Duke of York and General Dalyell—both of them arch-persecutors, and loathed by the Covenanters—were present among many others at most of these examinations by torture, and took evident pleasure in them.

Stewart's testimony is dated on the day of his execution. The martyrs evidently considered these testimonies absolutely and sacredly necessary, both as a public protest against their sentences and as an incentive to their former associates to stand firm for the cause. They seem to have been all carefully

---

[7] Hewison's "Covenanters"; Smellie's "Men and Women of the Covenant."

written out before their executions, mayhap by themselves, but more likely with the assistance of some of the zealous Covenanting preachers.

In considering Stewart's testimony, and that of Marion Harvie, we must remember the excellent caution given by the original compilers of the "Cloud." They ask that the statements by the martyrs as to leaving their blood on the heads of their persecutors are not to be understood as the effects of a revengeful, ungospel spirit, but rather as a simple declaration of their persecutors' blood-guiltiness in condemning them.

Stewart was executed along with James Skene, brother of the Laird of Skene, and John Potter, a farmer at Uphall. Upon the scaffold he sang the 2nd Psalm, and read the 3rd chapter of Malachi. While attempting to pray his voice was purposely drowned by the beating of drums, and while at his devotions he was launched into eternity.

In the testimony we find these sentences—

"It is like the most part of you are come here to gaze and wonder upon me. It is no wonder you count us fools, for while I was in black nature myself I was as mad as any of you all. But blessings to His Glorious and Holy Name, whereas once I was blind now I see: and therefore I abhor myself in dust and ashes, and I desire the more to magnify His free Grace for all that He hath done for me.

"I leave my testimony against those tyrants that have fore-faulted (forfeited) all the rights that they now lay claim to and usurp over the people of the Lord, and of the whole land, and all their unjust laws; but especially that accursed supremacy, by which they set up a miserable, adulterous and wretched man in Christ's room who thinks to wrong our Lord and carry His Crown. But it will be too heavy for him. Though all the wicked Lords, Prelates, Malignants and Indulged be joining hand in hand to hold it on, down it shall come and whosoever wears that Crown."

And down both came in the next reign.

IX.

Marion Harvie.—Marion was born in Borrowstounness

Old Grange House.—Erected in 1564; Demolished 1906.

(From a photo. in 1896 by W. S. Andrew, Carriden.)

See page 148.

about 1660, and followed the occupation of a servant maid there. In what house she was born or with whom she served we unfortunately cannot say. Her father, she tells us, had sworn the Covenants, so it is most likely she enjoyed the advantage of a religious education. But, according to her own story, she was fifteen before religious teaching produced a good effect upon her mind. Richard Cameron appears to have been among the field preachers who visited this district, for Marion says that it was a sermon of Cameron's which awakened her to a sense of sin. Thenceforward she embraced every opportunity of hearing the persecuted preachers. She speaks of having attended the preachings of Donald Cargill, John Welch, Archibald Riddell, and Richard Cameron, and of being particularly refreshed with the hearing of the latter at a communion in Carrick, to which she had gone. Marion was taken prisoner in 1680 along with Archibald Stewart, between Edinburgh and Queensferry, after having been to the city to see Cargill. She was brought before the Justiciary Court on 6th December that year, and the following extracts from the Court records explain what took place.

"Compeared Marion Harvie, prisoner, and being examined adheres to the fourth Article of the fanatics' New Covenant, the same being read to her, and disowns the King and his authority and the authority of the Lords of Justiciary. She approves of Mr. Cargill excommunicating the King. Declares she can write, but refuses to sign the same." Her indictment was drawn up from this statement, and she was tried, and found guilty on Monday, 17th January, 1681.

Those who desire full details must refer to the "Cloud," where they can read (1) Marion's last Speech and Testimony, containing (a) an account of her answers before the Privy Council; (b) her discourse before the Justiciary Court; (c) her dying testimony and last words; and (2) a description of her behaviour on the morning of her execution and on the scaffold.

She and Isobel Alison, the latter described as having lived very privately in Perth, suffered together in the Grassmarket. No execution of those cruel times excited more sympathy or a deeper interest throughout the country. Peden has testified that these martyrs were "two honest worthy lasses." As showing the hatred and scorn which their persecutors had of them, the girls were executed along with some three or four wicked women guilty of murdering their own children, and other villainies.

X.

The following paragraphs should help the reader to frame a picture of the character and personality of Marion:—

From her Account of her Answers before the Privy Council.—
"They said, 'Do ye own these to be lawful?' I said, 'Yes; because they are according to the Scripture and our Covenants which ye swore yourselves, and my father swore them.'

"They said, 'Yea; but the Covenant does not bind you to deny the King's authority.' I said, 'So long as the King held by the truths of God which he swore we were obliged to own him; but when he break his oath and robbed Christ of his kingly rights which do not belong to him we were bound to disown him, and ye also.'

"They said, 'Do ye know what ye say?' I said, 'Yes.' They said, 'Were ye ever mad?' I answered, 'I have all the wit that ever God gave me. Do ye see any mad act in me?'

"They said, 'Where were you born?' I said, 'In Borrowstounness.'

"They asked, 'What was your occupation there?' I told them, 'I served.'

"They said, 'Did ye serve the woman that gave Mr. Donald Cargill quarters?' I said, 'That is a question which I will not answer.'

"They said, 'Who did ground you in these principles?' I answered, 'Christ, by His Word.'

"Then they asked, 'What age I was of?' I answered, 'I cannot tell.'

"They said among themselves that I would be about twenty years of age, and began to regret my case, and said, 'Would

"The Borrowstounness Martyrs" 141

I cast away myself so?' I answered, 'I love my life as well as any of ye do; but would not redeem it upon sinful terms.'

"They said, 'A rock,[8] the cod, and bobbins were as fit for me to meddle with as these things.'"

XI.

From her Narrative of her "Discourse" before the Justiciary Court.—"When the Assize (15 Jurymen) were set in a place by themselves, I said to them, 'Now, beware what ye are doing, for they (her accusers) have nothing to say against me but only for owning Jesus Christ.'

"The Advocate said, 'We do not desire to take their lives, for we have dealt with them many ways, and sent Ministers to deal with them, and we cannot prevail with them.' I said, 'We are not concerned with you and your Ministers.'

"The Advocate said, 'It is not for religion we are pursuing you, but for treason.' I answered, 'It is for religion ye are pursuing me. I am of the same religion that ye all are sworn to be of, but ye are all gone blind. I am a true Presbyterian in my judgment.'"

From her Testimony and Last Words.—Marion's testimonies against her persecutors were many and elaborately stated.

She begins by adhering to the Covenants and declarations in detail, and "to the holy and sweet Scriptures of God which have been my rule in all I have done and in which my soul has been refreshed."

She left her blood upon the King and the Duke of York, who she says "was sitting in Council when I was examined the first day." Then on James Henderson, in the North Ferry, whom she describes as the Judas who sold Archibald Stewart, Mr. Skene, and her to the soldiers. On the Criminal Lords, then especially on the Lord Advocate Mackenzie and "on that excommunicate traitor, Thomas Dalziel, who was porter that day that I was first before them, and threatened me with the Boots."

---

[8] A Distaff, a Pin Cushion, and a Bobbin of Thread.

The testimony concludes—

"Farewell, brothers; farewell, sisters; farewell, Christian acquaintances; farewell, sun, moon, and stars, and now welcome my lovely and heartsome Christ Jesus into whose hands I commit my spirit throughout all eternity. I may say, 'Few and evil have the days of the years of my pilgrimage been, I being about 20 years of age. From the Tolbooth of Edinburgh, the Women-house on the east side of the prison. Jany. 11th, 1681."

Dr. Smellie tells us of the visit of Mr. Archibald Riddell, the minister sent by the judges to see the girls. He was well enough known to Marion, as she had attended his field meetings before he accepted the Indulgence. He was a good man, but he had blurred and enfeebled his former efforts in the eyes of all Cameronians by accepting the Indulgence. Mr. Riddell's duty was to persuade the girls to conform; but he might as well, says this writer, have tried to soften into velvet and silk the brute-mass of the Castle Rock. This is a part of the account of the interview—"He offered to pray. We said, 'We were not clear to join with him in prayer.' He said, 'Wherefore?' We said, 'We know the strain of your prayers will be like your discourse.' He said, 'I shall not mention any of your principles in my prayer, but only desire the Lord to let you see the evil of your doings.' We told him we desired none of his prayers at all. The Goodman[2] of the Tolbooth and some of the gentlemen said, 'Would we not be content to hear him?' We said, 'Forced prayers have no virtue.'"

XII.

On the morning of their execution they were once more led into the Council Chamber. Bishop Paterson endeavoured to worry and grieve them, and said, "Marion, ye said ye would never hear a curate; now you shall be forced to hear one," and he commanded one of his suffragans to pray, but he was outwitted. "Come, Isobel," said the unconquerable Marion.

---

[2] Prison Governor.

"let us sing the 23rd Psalm." Line by line she repeated the calm and uplifting words, and line by line, as Dr. Smellie touchingly puts it, these two who were appointed to death sang of the Lord their Shepherd and of the valley of the shadow where his rod and staff sustained them, and of God's house in which for evermore their dwelling-place should be. And not a petition of the curate's prayer was heard!

On the scaffold Isobel sang the 84th Psalm and read the 16th chapter of St. Mark. Marion chose the 74th Psalm and the 3rd chapter of Malachi. After this Marion, who it is apparent had the gift of fluent utterance to a degree, and was always calm, clear-headed, and self-possessed, gave the assembled populace a narrative of her capture, trial, and sentence, and a summary of her written testimony. Towards the close she said, "They say I would murder. I could not take the life of a chicken but my heart shrinked!"

Going up the ladder preparatory to being cast off by the hangman she turned round, sat down coolly, and said, "I am not come here for murder, but only for my judgment. I am about twenty years of age. At fourteen or fifteen I was a hearer of the curates, and indulged. And while I was a hearer of these I was a blasphemer and Sabbath-breaker, and a chapter of the Bible was a burden to me. But since I heard this persecuted Gospel I durst not blaspheme nor break the Sabbath, and the Bible became my delight."

This further speech highly irritated the major in charge of the soldiers, for he peremptorily called to the hangman to cast her over. And as the "Cloud" has it, "the murderer presently choked her."

XIII.

William Gouger and William Cuthill.—On the 11th of March, 1681, William Gouger, of Borrowstounness, was executed in Edinburgh, along with Robert Sangster and Christopher Miller, two Stirlingshire men. Gouger had been present at the battle of Bothwell Brig, and to the last he resolutely avowed the principles of the Covenanters. On the 27th of July the same year William Cuthill, a sailor belonging to the port, suffered along with the great Donald Cargill, Walter Smith, student of divinity, and William Thomson, a Fife man, in the Grassmarket of the capital for non-conformity and rebellion. We learn, as the narrative in the "Cloud" puts it, that the hangman "hacked and nagged off all their heads with an axe." Mr. Cargill's, Mr. Smith's, and Mr. Boig's heads were fixed upon the Netherbow Port, William Cuthill's and William Thomson's upon the West Port.

It is but right, then, that we should fervently and reverently remember those four martyrs of Borrowstounness, who have their names inscribed in the long death roll of the Scottish Covenanters. Yet, in the town and parish to which they belonged the humblest memorial has never been erected in their honour.

XIV.

In concluding this chapter it may not be inappropriate to refer to a curious sect which originated here shortly after the death of the local Covenanting martyrs. Either the spiritual and physical trials of the persecution or, more likely, the excitement created among the poorer classes of the community caused a number of the people to lose that strong but calm faith which was such a noble characteristic of the zealous Covenanter. At all events, there unfortunately arose—and to the grief of all wise and godly men—a little sect of fanatics with what has been described as "demented enthusiastical delusions." They were known as the Gibbites, or Sweet Singers of Borrowstounness. Their leader was John Gibb, a local sailor of gigantic stature, and familiarly known as "Muckle Jock Gibb." In the eyes of John Gibb and his followers all the field preachers were considered backsliders and enemies. The Gibbites would pay no taxes, denounced the King, and protested against Covenants and confessions. They also called for vengeance on the murderers of the local martyrs, Stewart and Potter, whose blood they carried about and exhibited on handkerchiefs. Part of their programme was to indulge extensively in fasting, and this naturally did not improve their already nervous condition. They were continually rushing about the streets of the town singing their penitential and dirgelike Psalms, the 74th, the 79th, the 80th, the 83rd, the 137th, and declaring in a frenzied fashion against the abounding evils of the day. They condemned everything as wrong, both in Church and State. They refused to recognise even the very days of the week. The number of Gibb's hallucinations were many. He had tremendous energy, and expressed himself with much eloquence. By his followers, who were chiefly women, he was accepted as the favoured and inspired of Heaven, and they did homage to him as King Solomon. Ultimately one wintry day early in the year 1681 the poor Gibbites—four men and six-and-twenty women—left their houses, families, and occupations for the desert places of the Pentland Hills. There they imagined they should be free from snares and sins. Some of them declared that here they would remain until they saw the smoke and ruin of the bloody city of Edinburgh, as they termed it.

To these poor demented creatures the great Donald Cargill, a short time before his execution, made, in the words of Dr. Smellie, a pilgrimage of faithfulness and love. He found them in the midst of a great flow-moss betwixt Clydesdale and Lothian, and earnestly strove to bring them to a better mind. Out on the moor he stayed on a night of cold easterly wet fog trying every device to effect their rescue from the phantasms which had mastered them. But the hour of penitence, although not far off for most of them, had not yet arrived, and Mr. Cargill, the messenger of pity, had to take his departure with disappointment in his soul.

Shortly after Cargill's visit to them the wretched creatures fell into the hands of a troop of dragoons at a very desert placed called Wool-hill Craigs. Carried to Edinburgh, the men were lodged in the Canongate Tolbooth and the women in the

Correction House, and a sound flogging was administered to them all round. After suffering a term of imprisonment, they were liberated. It is said that most of them regained their proper senses, and quietly settled down again in their native town. As for John himself, he never seems to have quite got over his ridiculous and absurd fancies. A few years later he got into further trouble with the authorities, and was once more placed under lock and key. He died in America, whence he had either gone voluntarily or been banished.

Mr. Crockett[3] has given us a lively description of a scene with these Sweet Singers at the Deer-Slunk after Mr. Cargill's fruitless visit to them. The novelist treats the situation so aptly that our only regret is that the sound thrashing which he makes one of his characters administer to the " muckle man of Borrowstounness " did not actually take place.

---

[3] "Men of the Moss Hags."

CHAPTER IX.

GRANGE ESTATE AND ITS OWNERS.

1. Early History: Description of Old Grange House—2. The Hamiltons of Grange: Family Traditions: Dame Christian Forrester and the Whale: Mrs. Nimmo and Lord Forrester—3. Family History of the Cadells: William Cadell, "Merchant Burgess" of Haddington: William Cadell, Secundus: Friend of Roebuck and one of the Founders of the Carron Company—4. The Third William Cadell: Manager at Carron: Resigns in 1769: Takes Lease of Grange Coalfield Along with his Brother John: Formation of Grange Coal Company: Extracts from Old Colliery Minute Book—5. The "Miller's Pit" Fatality and its Result—6. James John Cadell: The Second Mansion-House of Grange—7. Erection of Vitriol Work: Description of the Salt Making: Henry Cadell: Bridgeness Furnaces.

I.

GRANGE estate has an area of about three hundred and fifty acres, and lies between the lands of Carriden and Kinneil. We do not find any reference to it as a separate holding until the sixteenth century. Its history before that time is bound up with that of the pre-Reformation Church and the House of Hamilton. The lands in early times were largely Church lands held by the monks, who had their domicile near Culross. Tradition says they named this district the Grange because it was used as their grange or farm. Their possession of it, of course, terminated with the Reformation. When we begin to find separate mention of Grange after this, it had in part, like Carriden, come from the Duke of Hamilton into the possession of some of the numerous cadets of that House. It was then called Grange-Hamilton.

The old mansion-house or manor-place was only recently demolished (1906), and its site at the west end of Grange Loan is still vacant. The house, according to the date over the doorway, was built in 1564, and the initials on the pediments of the windows indicated Sir John Hamilton as its first proprietor. The building[1] was of simple but picturesque design, being a long parallelogram in plan, with a square projection near the centre of the south side (containing circular staircase), thus giving it the shape of the letter T. A small stair in an angle turret led to a chamber in the top storey of the staircase projection, the roof or ceiling of which was carved. The basement was vaulted, and contained the kitchen at the west end, with a large fireplace and oven, and inlet and outlet drains for water. At the east end there was a lean-to building of later date than the original house. This was used for a stable previous to the demolition. The upper floors were each divided into three rooms. Among its picturesque details were the angularly-placed and detached chimneys and the skew-putts of the crow-stepped gables. Two hundred yards to the east, on the site of part of what is now Grange Loan, was the gateway of the entrance drive, which led through an avenue of fine trees, some of which still remain. About the beginning of last century it ceased to be the residence of the lairds of Grange. From then until 1898 it was occupied as a small dairy farm. After that it was found to be dangerous as a habitation.

There was a considerable quantity of valuable coal underneath the house. This was in time worked out. The undermining was very harmful to the building for long, and at last a collapse took place on the north side. The site, on an eminence overlooking the Forth, was a most excellent one, and the house was one of the landmarks on the Admiralty Chart.

II.

No less than five of the owners of the estate from the sixteenth century bore the name of John Hamilton, and this is at times confusing. The first mentioned is John

---

[1] See Castellated and Domestic Architecture.

Hamilton, designed as of Grange and "the Bailzie of Kinneal." He appears to have occupied the post of Master Stabler to King James VI., and is evidently the "guidman of Grange" referred to in the King's letter to John, first Marquis of Hamilton, already mentioned. He was one of those who rode with the King in hot haste from Falkland to Perth on 5th August, 1600, where in the evening the King was attacked in Gowrie House. Hamilton seems to have been knighted, and lived to a long age. It is during his possession that the titles first contain reference to the town of Grange as a free Burgh of Barony. There are references in later times to the Bailie of Grange and the Bailie in Grangepans, but there is no evidence to show that any measure of autonomy or self-government was ever exercised within its bounds. The bailie's position was apparently quite a nominal one. This is doubtless accounted for by the fact that Grange estate, like that of Carriden, was included in the Regality of Borrowstounness, and would be under the jurisdiction of the Bailie of Regality there.

In 1615 James VI. granted a Signature or Warrant in favour of John Hamilton, eldest son of Sir John, on the 26th of December. The purpose of the warrant was to give John, jun., a royal charter of the lands of "Grange Philpenstane." Why this addition was now made to the territorial designation it is difficult to say authoritatively, for in the title of his father they are simply the lands of Grange. It has been suggested that Philpenstane was the revival of an old name used in the days when Grange formed part of the Church lands, and were possibly identified with some Philip. A more likely theory is that the Hamiltons interested in getting this charter were descendants of Sir James Hamilton, eldest natural son of the first Earl of Arran, whose grandson was a Robert Hamilton "of Philipstoun," in this county.

The signature, after the reference to the lands of "Grange Philpenstane," continues, "with the town thereof, manor-place, houses, biggings, lands, orchards, and mills; also the salt pans thereupon and the coals great and small." These lands, it is narrated, had at one time been held by James, Lord Colville of Culross, immediately under his Sovereign, and were resigned by him to this Sovereign. John, jun., in time became Sir John, and the next mention we find of the lands is in a deed of 1631 infefting therein on certain conditions "an excellent young man," James Hamilton, lawful son of Sir John. James, afterwards Sir James, married Christian, third daughter of the first Lord Forrester of Corstorphine, in 1631. Three years after, Hamilton, for some reason not apparent, transferred the Grange to his father-in-law. James and Christian had a son John, and in 1653 one David German, described as some time Bailie Burgess of Dunfermline, ignoring the conveyance to Lord Forrester, got a decreet of apprising of the lands of Grange Philpingstone against John Hamilton. This led to complications with Lord Forrester's heirs. By 1670, however, John Hamilton appears to have come into his own again, for there are then to be found conveyances to him both by his mother, Dame Christian Forrester, and David German. In 1705 a fourth John Hamilton completed his title as heir to his father, and in 1741 comes the fifth and last John. This laird's affairs became embarrassed, and the estate was sold by decree of the Court in 1750 to one David Main. He first of all disponed it to James Stewart, Edinburgh, and again to William Belchier, banker and money broker, London, under burden of Stewart's disposition. In course of time litigation ensued at the instance of John Belchier and others, and in 1788 the lands were acquired by John Buchan, W.S., on behalf of William and John Cadell.

The Hamiltons disappear entirely from their old patrimony in 1750. Many of them were of the dare-devil type, and of very easy virtue. The Old Grange, therefore, is not without its many and curious traditions. The wife of Sir James was, as already stated, Christian Forrester, and they had a family. On Sir James' death the widow married John Waugh, minister of Borrowstounness, and of their rioting at the Caldwall we have already heard. Whether they lived at the Grange or in the Dower or Jointure House in Grangepans we cannot say.

At all events, the Dame, in her early widowhood, had resided at the latter place.[2] The back door of this house bordered on the beach, on which, on one occasion, a whale got stranded. Lady Hamilton claimed it as her property, and stood astride it as the factor to the Duke of Hamilton approached. There then arose an angry dispute as to ownership, the factor, in turn, claiming it as the Duke's property. The squabble ended by his pushing Lady Hamilton unceremoniously off it. Mortally offended, she hastened to Grange House to acquaint her son of the occurrence. He traced the factor to a tavern in Borrowstounness, entered it, and, recognising his man, shot him dead with a pistol. A hue and cry got up. Sir John was followed to the mansion-house, where he mounted a horse and had to flee for his life. So goes the story. But the Dame had trouble with her daughter Christian. This young lady, contrary to the wishes of her family, had married an Edinburgh burgess named James Nimmo.[3] She also made an unholy alliance with her uncle, the second Lord Forrester, a man of extravagant habits and dissolute life. Mrs. Nimmo was a woman of violent temper; and, having in course of time quarrelled with Lord Forrester, she, on the 27th of August, 1679, stabbed him with his own sword in the garden of Corstorphine. He died immediately, and she was speedily captured and put in prison. On the 29th of September she succeeded in escaping. Next day, however, she was recaptured, and on 12th November was executed at the Cross of Edinburgh.

The arms of the Hamiltons of Grange were *gules, a lion rampant argent, between three cinquefoils ermine*.

III.

Before dealing with the lands of Grange under the Cadell

---

[2] A new property now occupies the old site. A stone on the front (a pediment on one of the original windows of the two-roomed dower house) bears the lettering "S.J.H., D.C.F., 1647." It also states: "Here for two and a half centuries stood the old jointure house of Grange, inhabited in 1647 by Dame Christian Forrester of Corstorphine, widow of Sir James Hamilton of Grange, both of whose initials are preserved on the above pediment."

[3] See "Scots Peerage," vol. iv., p. 92.

family, we must refer to their early family history and how they came to Grange.

In East Lothian the name of Cadell stood for much in the history of the commercial development of that county during the last two centuries. The first of the family was William Cadell, merchant in Haddington (b. 1668, d. 1728). This gentleman, in the course of a busy life, acquired some property at Cockenzie. His tombstone, which is still in fair preservation, stands within the unroofed entrance of the Abbey Church of Haddington, and the inscription states that he was a " merchant burgess " of the town. Among other children, he had a son who became William Cadell of Cockenzie (b. 1708, d. 1777). Mr. M'Neill[4] tells us that this second William Cadell was a very clever and enterprising man, that he carried on a large mercantile trade (chiefly in iron and timber) at Port Seton, and had vessels which sailed to the Baltic, the Mediterranean, and other places then considered distant. He was also lessee of the Tranent Collieries after the Setons. Among his friends was Dr. John Roebuck, who, though a Sheffield man, did much when he settled in East Lothian to advance practical science in Scotland. Utilising a chemical discovery, he superseded the old method by the use of leaden chambers, and erected at Prestonpans large vitriol works. His process was kept a profound secret; the premises were surrounded by very high walls; and no stranger was allowed within. Mr. Cadell established potteries on a fairly large scale in the neighbourhood. The clay from Devonshire and the flint from London were brought by sea to Port Seton.

Mr. Cadell, anxious always to promote more industries, now came to the conclusion that iron, instead of being imported, might well be manufactured at home from the native ore. He therefore proposed to start an iron foundry near Cockenzie, and consulted with Dr. Roebuck and Mr. Samuel Garbett on the subject. They favoured the idea, but on a much bigger scale. And so, after prolonged investigations and considerable

---

[4] " Tranent and Neighbourhood " (M'Neill) 1884, pp. 8-9.

prospecting, they, in 1759, established the now famous Carron Company, under the style of Roebucks, Garbett & Cadells. We have elsewhere referred to the copartnery, and the whole details connected with this historic enterprise are given by Mr. H. M. Cadell in his recently-published book.[5]

The machinery invented for the new works and the adaptation of water, and afterwards of steam power, were thought to be among the engineering wonders of the day. The great adventure was inaugurated at Carron on the 1st of January, 1760. Before daylight the workmen were at their posts. Dr. Roebuck and Mr. Cadell were early upon the scene for the reception and entertainment of their visitors. The great water-wheel and bellows were kept going throughout the night, while the air furnaces had also been charged, so that everything would be in readiness. At length Dr. Roebuck personally pierced the furnace breast, when a fiery stream of molten metal flowed upon the mould. Mr. Cadell then called for a bumper to the works—"Long years of prosperity to Carron and Dr. Roebuck."

IV.

William Cadell secundus had two sons—John, who inherited Cockenzie, and afterwards acquired Tranent, and William (*b.* 1737, *d.* 1819). This third William Cadell was a man of great business capacity and energy. Along with his father he was one of the original partners in the Carron Company, and when only twenty-three was appointed its first manager. This post he held for nine strenuous and anxious year. In 1763 he built Carron Park, so that he could be on the ground. And four years later he bought the estate of Banton, where he discovered a good seam of ironstone, and let it to the Carron Company at a royalty of £4 per 100 tons.

On leaving the Carron Company Mr. Cadell and his brother John, in 1770, took a lease from William Belchier, of the Grange coalfield and salt works, which were then standing idle. They

---

[5] "The Story of the Forth" (chapters ix. and x.), 1913.

also leased Pitfirrane and other coalfields in the district, and carried on large ironworks at Cramond. These collieries were managed under the name of Grange Coal Company, and the partners were the two Cadells and one or two others. In the lease William Cadell is designed as merchant at Carron, and John merchant at Cockenzie. When the lessees arrived they found the works in a state of dilapidation. The five saltpans were without a roof, and were "greatly consumed by rust." The "Buckett Pond" was reported much "mudded up," the top of the walls washed away by the sea, and the sluice in great disrepair. The fourteen colliers' houses at the pans, with the two at the House of Grange, were in a very bad condition, and at so great a distance from the works that they were of little value. Regarding the ten colliers' houses built some time previously at Graham's Dyke, and then vacant, they were in good order, except for the want of a few tiles. A conspicuous landmark at this time was the old tower above Bridgeness (now remodelled and surmounted by a castellated top). It was originally built for a windmill, and one of the lintels bore the date 1750. Though the coalfield was said to have been fairly well exhausted, yet the Cadells were enterprising, and believed there was still a quantity of coal, and possibly ironstone too, which could be profitably worked for a few years at least, and they expected also to have the Carron Company as their chief customer, both for coal and ironstone. Among the many resolutions which are to be found carefully recorded in the old minute-book of the colliery is one in January, 1772—"Not to allow any agent employed by us to keep a Publick House, the consequence thereof being destruction to the works."

On becoming joint owners, in 1788, when the proprietor had to sell Grange as part of his bankrupt estate, the Messrs. Cadell actively set to work to develop the coal, and sunk what were then known as moat pits Nos. 1, 2, and 3, and afterwards Nos. 4 and 5, on the shore, where coal had never been worked before. They

William Cadell (b. 1737 d. 1819).
From a portrait by Raeburn.
(*By permission from Mr. H. M. Cadell's* "*Story of the Forth.*")

also practically rebuilt the harbour at Bridgeness, and appeared, after numerous struggles and difficulties, to have made the place prosper. The Grange Coal Company still continued to carry on as before, and, in 1789, were anxiously considering "the ruinous effects of the overseer of the works keeping a public-house." They passed a resolution calling upon the overseer to give up his public-house, failing which his appointment would be cancelled. He did not resign, and dismissal followed. In May, 1792, it is recorded that several of the bound colliers had lately gone off to Sandyhills and other collieries. It was thereupon resolved to send John Donaldson immediately in quest of them with a justice of peace warrant and with orders to incarcerate such of them as did not return with him peaceably. In the event of the coalmasters refusing to part with the colliers without having refunded to them any money advanced, it was an instruction that he should carry the collier claimed before a justice of peace, who was to determine whose property he was. The same year complaints were made against another oversman for keeping a public-house, in respect that five of the Grange colliers came out of his premises drunk and vicious, and committed several outrages in the neighbourhood. The Company ordained him to give it up, and again expressed the opinion that oversmen or other officials should not keep alehouses.

On 22nd June, 1797, we find the company appointing William Smith, writer, in Bo'ness, Baron Bailie of the Barony of Grange. They also resolved to immediately put into his hands all the accounts due by the "fewers," with a recommendation "to examine their titles to see which of them were in a state of non-entry, that they might enter and pay up their arrears of feu-duty according to law, and, in default of this, to obtain possession of the subjects, and make the best of them."

V.

We revert for a little to the period when the Cadells were

only lessees of Grange Colliery. That coalfield adjoined the Duke's coalfield, and the Chance pit, which was sunk by Dr. Roebuck's trustees, was situated near the march between Borrowstounness and Grange. This pit led to a very expensive and troublesome litigation in the Court of Session between the lessees of the two collieries. John Allansen and John Grieve were the managers for Dr. Roebuck and his trustees, who were the Duke's lessees. Allansen superintended the sinking of the pit, and had an intimate knowledge of all the underground workings in that vicinity, and so had Grieve. In 1773 Allansen left Roebuck, and shortly after was engaged as manager at Grange. Grieve had also by this time left and become one of the partners of the Grange Coal Company. The position of affairs between the two collieries is explained by the following letter to Mr. John Grieve & Co. from Mr. John Burrel, snab, the Duke's factor. It is dated 9th October, 1775:—

"Litigious contests and differences betwixt neighbours from my beginning to this day I have uniformly endeavoured to compromise and never to foment. This can only be known to you with regard to my conduct with regard to the differences seemingly commenced between you and your company and our company and me, we alleging that you have made an encroachment by working and taking part of Duke Hamilton's coals from below the lands of Kinglass, and you alleging we have made an encroachment by taking part of your coal from below the lands of Grange." To end this controversy each party was to survey the wastes of the other. The Grange Company were able to make the survey of the Duke's wastes, but Mr. Burrel had been quite unable to examine the Grange workings because of the water. Mr. Burrel then thought that an excambion would settle the whole question, and this was agreed to between them. The Grange Company were to have immediate liberty to take so much of the Easter main coal from below the lands of Kinglass, but not exceeding ten Scots acres, on condition that the Duke's lessees got a like quantity of the same coal from below the lands of Grange that lay contiguous to the Chance pit. This arrangement, instead of being a success, only bred more suspicion. It appears from the papers in the case that Dr. Roebuck, Mr. William Cadell, and Mr. John Grieve had a meeting at Borrowstounness shortly before the commencement of the litigation. Mr. Grieve had in his mind "a proposed communication or junction of the two collieries." He stated it to the doctor, who "absolutely refused to consent." Upon which Mr. Grieve said with some heat, "Well, doctor, I know what I will do," or words to that purpose; and added at the same time, "Do you know that we can communicate levels?" To which the doctor replied, "If you attempt to communicate levels, I shall be obliged to defend myself in the best way I can. I have weathered many a storm, and must do the best I can to get clear of it." We have found other references to this desire of Mr. Grieve to amalgamate the two collieries. Some people thought that Roebuck was ill-advised in rejecting it; but Mr. Grieve always maintained that the doctor would find he would be obliged to do it at last. Both parties raised actions, and, these being conjoined, a very long proof was taken on commission at Borrowstounness. Dr. Roebuck's action was one of suspension and interdict against the Grange Coal Company from working within the limits of the excambed coal. Interim interdict was granted, but, upon a further hearing, was withdrawn. The doctor then appealed to the Inner House. During the interim interdict Messrs. Cadell and Grieve, as partners of the Grange Coal Company, raised an action against his Grace the Duke of Hamilton and Dr. Roebuck, in which they complained that interdict had been obtained against them "upon certain frivolous pretences and groundless allegations, whereby they had suffered great damages." They accused the doctor of making "various encroachments upon the coal on the estate of Grange and wrought out the same, applying the grounds to his own use, and refusing to account for the value thereof." They claimed £5000 as the damages sustained and such further damages as might be incurred during the continuance of the interdict. They also claimed £2000 as the value of the coal taken out of the bounds of the estate of Grange by Dr. Roebuck. A perusal of the pleadings and evidence reveals much of interest concerning the old mineral workings of Bonhard, Grange, and Borrowstounness. There are references to an old pit named Balfour's pit, which was situated where Riverview Terrace now stands; to a pit upon the south-east corner of David Cornwall's farm of Kinglass, called Causewayside Well pit; to one called Mary Buchanan's pit, upon the south-east corner of Drum farm; to the Boat pit, distant from the Schoolyard or Borrowstounness Engine pit, about three hundred fathoms; and to one or two others now unheard of. The evidence of the oversmen, colliers, and bearers of both collieries is particularly interesting. Even in those days we find numerous Grants, Sneddons, Robertsons, and Hamiltons among the colliers. An amusing sidelight on the colliery life of those times is revealed in the evidence of one of the women coal-bearers. Speaking to the date of a certain event, she states that she " recollects Elizabeth Nisbet bringing down a 'hot pint' to her master, James Grant, upon a Yule evening." This was corroborated by one of the colliers, who further states that it was " upon a Christmas Eve, and that, so far as he can now recollect, it was ten years past the last Christmas Eve, old stile." In fact, the evidence shows that there were several " hot pints " taken down to the colliers on this occasion, so that they did not neglect their annual celebration even when engaged underground. More than one attempt was made to have this big litigation settled by arbitration. Whether this was ultimately agreed to we do not know. Neither have we discovered any record of the decision of the Inner House.

VI.

Like most Scottish lairds, Mr. William Cadell was involved in a costly law plea during his ownership of Grange. This case[6] raised the question of liability for accidents to third parties. Incidentally it gave rise to the name of the

---

[6] Appeal, Cadell v. Black. Paton's Reports, vol. v., pp. 567-573.

Miller or Miller's pit. The circumstances were these. Henry Black was an industrious farmer in Scotstoun, in the parish of Abercorn. He was a tenant of Sir James Dalyell of Binns, married early, and had a wife and family of three sons and nine daughters. Black also had a meal mill, and was prospering and rearing up his family, the eldest of whom, a son, was twenty-eight years of age, and the youngest three years at the end of 1800. On 5th January, 1801, Black set out on horseback to Bo'ness on business, and to the alarm of his wife and family did not return in the evening. Next morning his son went to seek him at Bo'ness, and found that his father had left between five and six the previous evening quite sober, going by the road southwards up the hill from Grangepans to the point where the road branches eastwards to the Muirhouses. In the angle at the fork of the roads there was an old pit which had been used as an engine or pumping pit since William Cadell acquired the estate. By 1800, however, this was disused, and left uncovered, like other old shafts of that time, and with a wall 18 inches high round its mouth. It was only 4 feet from the side of the road running eastward, and had 50 fathoms of water standing in it. The miller's son traced the horse's footmarks to this pit, and the appearance of a stone having been removed, as if it had recently fallen in, raised in his mind the dreadful suspicion that his father had in the dark plunged into the pit. After two or three days' search the body of Mr. Black was found. This event so deeply affected the miller's wife, who was in delicate health, that from the day of his death she never left her room, and died in three months' time.

Mr. Cadell offered to pay 100 guineas and the price of the horse, not in reparation, but out of sympathy. But this was refused, and an action was raised by the family in the Court of Session (first) for £2000 as reparation for the loss of their father; (second) for £23 as the expense incurred in recovering the body; and (third) for £20 as the value of the horse.

The Lord Ordinary on 12th November, 1801, reported the

cause to the Court. In his defence Mr. Cadell pleaded that the pit was in existence before he had bought Grange estate, and that it was at the time of the accident in no way more dangerous than it had always been. At the time the miller lost his life he was a trespasser and off the road, and no complaint had ever been made by the public authority as to the fence being insufficient to prevent cattle grazing or the land falling in. The situation of the pit, moreover, was known to all the neighbourhood. After hearing the case on 9th March, 1805, the Court decided that the defender, Mr. William Cadell, was liable in £800 damages, with £100 expenses, each child under fourteen to have double the share of each over fourteen years of age. On 2nd July, 1805, both parties reclaimed, but the Court adhered, and against this decision the case was appealed to the House of Lords by Mr. Cadell. That Court on 20th February, 1812, eleven years after the accident, dismissed the appeal with £200 costs, so that the whole litigation and its result would involve him in close upon £2000.

VII.

William Cadell had five sons, and on his death in 1819 his second surviving son, James John Cadell (*b.* 1779, *d.* 1858), succeeded to the eastern half of Grange, the western half having gone to William Archibald Cadell. On his death, in 1855, however, his trustees conveyed it to James John Cadell, so that he became proprietor of both halves, and the estate has since remained intact. About 1816 a sad mining calamity occurred at Grange. As the result of an explosion of fire-damp in the smithy coal seam of No. 4 pit several lives were lost. The fire in the workings raged fiercely, and to extinguish it the sea was let in by a cutting to the shore. All the workings were drowned, and the whole colliery abandoned. During the next forty years no coal was produced on Grange estate. Mr. Cadell meantime leased part of Kinneil colliery, but many troubles attended the work. He devoted himself with far more success to agriculture, and kept his own lands in a high state of cultivation. Considerable attention was given to the development of the salt industry, and a vitriol work was also established at Bridgeness.

Grange House, in Kinningars Park, originated in a modest way. It was at the beginning of the nineteenth century a small, old-fashioned dwelling-house, tenanted by Sir Henry Seton, the collector of Customs. On his death, in 1803, Mr. Cadell took possession of the dwelling, and altered and added to it just as his successors did in later years.

As we have just stated, saltmaking was an important industry in Grangepans in Mr. Cadell's time, as it was a century ago at many other places on the Firth of Forth. There were at one time thirteen pans in full swing. The sea water was originally pumped up to the pans by large pumps handled by several men or women, often with young people helping them, and it was a sight to see the pumps at work. As the sea water was found too fresh, rock salt was, in later times, brought from Liverpool and Carrickfergus to strengthen the Grange salt. A ton of salt was carted regularly to Falkirk every week to supply the inhabitants of that town. Although the salt cost 11s. per half cwt., people came from far and near to the Grange saltpans, as the local product was considered particularly good. The Government duty was heavy, and a Revenue officer was stationed at the pans. In consequence of the duty smuggling was very prevalent. The salt was stored in large cellars or "girnels" barred by strong doors, sealed up by a Custom-house officer, just as the bonded stores of the present day are sealed. It was not allowed to be taken out again until the duty was paid. The sea water and raw rock salt were full of mud and other impurities, and these were extracted by the additions of evil-smelling clotted blood to the boiling liquor. The albumen in the blood coagulated in the hot water, and floated up in a thick scum, which was skimmed off, leaving the solution perfectly clear. It was an interesting sight to watch the red blood spreading through the seething water, and coming to the surface in dirty brown or grey froth. The pans becoming unremunerative, gradually

L

diminished in number in course of time, and the year 1889 saw the last of the saltmaking in this part of the Forth.

Mr. Cadell was married three times, his first wife being Isabella Moubray, daughter of Henry Moubray of Calderbank, who died in 1832; his second, Agnes, daughter of John Hamilton Dundas of Duddingston; and his third, his cousin, Martha Cadell. There were five sons, the second eldest, Henry (*b.* 1812, *d.* 1888), succeeding to Grange on his father's death, and to Banton in 1872. In 1863 he built the Bridgeness Ironworks, but only one of the two furnaces was ever in blast. There was no railway then, and the furnace only went for about six months. It was restarted in 1870, and went on intermittently till the iron trade declined in 1874. The works were pulled down in 1890. The district from Cowdenhill to Bridgeness in the beginning of the nineteenth century was quite different to what it is now. There was then no shore road; and the old road ran in a south-easterly direction in front of Cowdenhill along by Peter Muir's house and Grindlay's garden wall. The present road along by the shore was formed by Henry Cadell. On his death Mr. Cadell was succeeded by his third son, Henry Moubray Cadell (*b.* 1860), the present laird of Grange and Banton.

The arms of the Cadells of Grange, as registered at the Lyon Office, are—" *Or, a stag's head couped in chief gu and in base 3 oval buckles, two and one, tongues fesswise az. within a bordure of the second.*"

Crest—A stag's head ppr.   Motto—*Vigilantia non cadet*.

CHAPTER X.

CARRIDEN.

1. Boundaries of Parish: the Lands and Barony of Carriden and their Owners—2. Carriden House and its Policies—3. The Old Church and Churchyard: First Manse and Glebe: First Excambion of Glebe Lands—4. New Church and Churchyard at Cuffabouts—5. Rioting at a Burial and Subsequent Prosecution—6. Details of the Evidence—7. More Evidence: an Unfortunate Sequel: Second Excambion of Glebe—8. Closing of the Old Church Road from Carrisgates—9. Suggested Improvements at Old Burial Ground Resented: Mr. James White and his Committee on the Alert: Lord President Hope as Peacemaker—10. His Lordship's Character and Career, Lowering of Wall, Erection of Iron Railing and Other Improvements Undertaken by the First Admiral's Trustees: Letter of Assurance from Trustees: the Heritors and Burials in Old Churchyard—11. Improvement of Part of Old Burial Road Resented: Mr. White and his Committee again Assert Themselves: a False Alarm—12. Captain Hope Petitions Justices to Close Old Burial Roads: Mr. James Duguid becomes People's Champion: Important Meeting in Church—13. Details of the Meeting: Committee of Justices Inspect the Roads and Report: Petition Withdrawn—14. Another Misunderstanding with the Admiral: Proposal to Remove the Railing: Mr. Duguid and the Obligations of "Moral and Accountable Beings"—15. The Ministers of Carriden—16. Binn's House: General Dalyell and his Scots Greys.

I.

ABOUT twenty years ago the Parishes of Borrowstounness and Carriden were for civil purposes combined. Ecclesiastically, however, they remain distinct, and it is around its ecclesiastical affairs that the real and abiding history of the Parish of Carriden clusters.

According to a survey in 1817 the parish is 4¼ miles square. It is bounded on the east by the Parish of Abercorn; on the west by the Parish of Borrowstounness; on the north by the Forth; and on the south by the Parish of Linlithgow. Altogether it presents the appearance of an irregular four-sided figure, the longest side stretching along the shores of the Forth. Its surface is very unequal, rising from the shore by a quick ascent with a varied undulating form for about a mile, and then declining to the south. The most elevated ground lies to the south-west, near the Irongath Hills. The highest point is 519 feet above the level of the sea. In the west end of the parish we have Thirlstane, Grangepans, Cowdenhill, Bridgeness, and Cuffabouts, and in this stretch of shore-ground is now to be found as busy a hive of modern industry as can be seen in Scotland. Coal mines, potteries, woodyards, sawmills, and other works occupy almost all the available industrial space in the neighbourhood—and a romantic touch is given by the quaint old harbour or haven of Bridgeness.

Long ago the estate of Carriden was smaller than it is now, the Stacks, Dyland, Walton, and other farms being then separate holdings. Carriden lands, like those of Grange, were originally in part Church lands. We find more than one reference to the "Dominical lands of Carriden," and we know also that the coal there was worked in early times by the monks. The remainder of the lands of Carriden have a long history,[1] in which we find references to Sir William de Veteriponte or Vipont, proprietor of Langton, in Berwickshire; also to Sir Alexander de Cockburn, who married Sir William's daughter Mary. He succeeded to Langton in right of his wife, and obtained the Barony of Carriden from David the Second in 1358. With the Cockburns the estate remained until 1541, when Sir James Cockburn of Langton granted a feu charter to one Patrick Abercromby. In 1598 the property descended to Patrick Abercromby, junior, who, in 1601, disponed it to Sir John Hamilton of Letterick. Sir John afterwards became the first

---

[1] In the sixteenth century titles it is clear the Mill of the Barony of Carriden was at Linlithgow:—"The Mill of the Barony of Carriden called the Lochmill with the water gang of the King's loch of Linlithgow." About two centuries later it was conveyed to James Glen of Longcroft.

Lord Bargany, and in 1632 conveyed the subjects to John Hamilton, his son, and Jean Douglas, his son's spouse. Lord Bargany died soon after, and in the following year John, the second Lord Bargany, completed his title. In the Sea Box records it appears that his lordship had a loan over the estate from that society, and they for a time held the title deeds in security for the advance. Of this laird the couplet was written—

"Kind Bargany, faithful to his word,
Whom Heaven made good and social though a Lord."

Bargany, in 1667, disposed of Carriden to his neighbour, Sir Walter Seton of Abercorn and Northbank. He did not hold it very long, for in 1678 he sold the estate to Walter Cornwall, younger, of Bonhard, and James Cornwall, his father. But the Cornwalls no sooner got it than they sold it to Alexander Miln, designed as some time Provost of Linlithgow. Miln held the place for twenty years, but after that many varied transmissions took place until it came into the hands of the Dalhousie family, in whose possession it remained for long. The details of the transmissions are as follows:—Miln, in 1696, sold to Colonel John Erskine, who in six years' time sold to General George Ramsay. In 1705 Mrs. Jean Ramsay, his daughter and heir, succeeded, and she in turn was in 1708 succeeded by her heir, William Earl of Dalhousie. Four years later his sister, Lady Elizabeth Ramsay, followed, and she again in two years' time was succeeded by her son, Francis, Master of Hawley, as heir of entail. Then in 1719 we find a decree of sale of the lands of Carriden Law, Dyland, Waltoun, Woolston, and Groughfoot, whereby these lands were vested in Colonel Francis Charteris of Amisfield. Two years later this gentleman entailed his estates, and in 1736 his son, the Honourable Francis Charteris, succeeded as heir of entail. A family dispute seems now to have arisen at the instance of Francis against his sister, the Countess of Wemyss and the Earl of Wemyss, in the course of which she was called on to enter as heir in general of her father. This resulted in a decree by the Lords of Council and Session in 1744 decerning the Earl and Countess to make up titles to and denude themselves of the estate of the deceased colonel in favour of Francis. This was done, and the latter held the estate until 1764, when he disponed it to Colonel Campbell Dalrymple. This gentleman held for three years only, when he sold to William Maxwell primus. Maxwell was succeeded by William Maxwell secundus, and the trustees of the latter in 1814 sold to Admiral Sir George Johnston Hope. The Admiral was succeeded about 1829 by his son James (first Captain and afterwards Admiral Sir James Hope). On his death Carriden was for a time liferented by his widow, and then held by his sister, Miss Helen Hope. On her death, in 1890, it passed to Colonel George Hope Lloyd Verney, second son of Sir Harry Verney of Claydon, Bucks, whose mother was a sister of the Admiral's. On the Colonel's death he was succeeded by his eldest son, James, who died three years ago. The estate then went to his brother, the present proprietor, Mr. Harry Lloyd Lloyd Verney.

II.

The mansion-house of Carriden is the principal seat in the parish, and is built in the Scottish baronial style. It occupies a site on the high bank above the shore overlooking the Firth and Royal Dunfermline, the ancient capital of Scotland. The present house, in our view, is not the original building, although the site may be practically the same. It is probable that there was a "place" or keep of feudal times here, before and during the fifteenth century. As we have seen, the estate had several owners before it came into the hands of the first Lord Bargany in 1601. The year 1602 is given as the date when the eastern part—that with the turrets—was built, so that it may be readily assumed that Bargany, or Hamilton of Letterick as he then was, at once set about enlarging, and, in fact, completely transforming the original structure. Carriden House then, as we know it, was erected about the beginning of the seventeenth century, and it is stated that the ceiling of

Carriden House.

(From a photograph by W. S. Andrew, Carriden.)

the study was executed by Italian workmen brought from Holyrood House. One of the owners was, as we have said, Alexander Miln. His family had for long been master builders to the King, and in his time we once more find evidences of alterations. In fact, it was during these that the discovery was made that the house actually stood on what had been a Roman station in connection with the Roman wall.

The mansion-house is now surrounded on the east, west, and south by well-laid-out grounds and fine trees. On the north the ground falls suddenly, and forms a richly wooded slope extending about a mile along the shore, recessing itself into picturesque glens intersected with many pretty walks. At one time the garden was east of the house, but it is now in a fine enclosure considerably to the west of it. The extent of the estate is 734 acres, divided thus—Home farm and policies, 150 arable acres; farms of Stacks and Walton, 480 arable acres; woods, lawn, and garden ground, 91 acres; buildings, yards, and roads, 13 acres. Burnfoot did not form part of the estate. It was always separately held until 1891. In 1647 it belonged to Florence or Laurance Gairdner, designed as bailie in Grangepans. Later he disponed to Patrick Gairdner, and afterwards it was possessed by James Kid, "Seaman and Mariner in Carriden Burnfoot." The latter was a gentleman of very independent character and bearing, as will be seen in his stormy interviews with Carriden Kirk Session. After this it was in the possession, first, of Andrew Cruickshanks, and then of John Cruickshanks.[2] Burnfoot was bought by George Hope Lloyd Verney from R. R. Simpson, W.S., in 1885, and was included in the entail of the estate executed by G. H. L. Verney and J. H. L. Verney in 1891. It is held of and under H. M. Cadell of Grange.

No information is available to indicate the date of the erection of the first church of Carriden, the ruins of which are yet to be found to the south-west of the mansion-house. We have an impression that the first house and the church, with its adjacent burial-ground, would all originate about the same

---

[2] The place is still known as "Crookies."

period. The church, like that of Kinneil, was a pre-Reformation chapel, and the old collection plate is impressed with the Bishop's mitre. In feudal days it was common to find—and Kinneil is an instance—the feudal mansion, the feudal village, and the feudal lord's chapel and burying-ground all within a stone's throw of each other. And at Carriden, when we glance at the ancient title deeds of the main estate and of the smaller holdings in the near neighbourhood, we can readily construct circumstances similar to those of Kinneil. We can imagine the old place or keep, the chapel and burying-ground to the west, and further west still the one-time populous but now long-demolished feudal village of Little Carriden.

III.

The church is described elsewhere.[3] As to the location of the first manse and glebe, the manse was situated on the flat shore land, in what is now the wood west of Burnfoot. Here were found the remains of an old well and indications of a garden and a walk leading up to the old church road. There are a number of interesting references[4] to manse and glebe in the Presbytery records during the ministry of the Rev. Andrew Keir, who was presented to Carriden in 1621. On 16th July, 1628, he craved a visitation of his church, and presented a precept for designation of his manse and glebe from the Archbishop of St. Andrews direct to the Moderator. The Presbytery therefore fixed the visitation for 24th July, and appointed eight of their brethren for that purpose. Shortly after follows this quaint entry:—

> "Die 23 July 1628: The visitation of Carriden is remembered again to be keiped the morne and the visitouiris nominat *ut supra*."

The explanation of this anxious reminder lies in the fact that the Carriden minister was also clerk to the Presbytery.

---

[3] See Appendix I.
[4] What is quoted here and elsewhere from the Presbytery and Heritors Records is from certified extracts.

When the important event took place " the sermon was maid be Mr. Thomas Spittall upon 2 Tim. 8-17, quherin was handled the dutie and dignity of ministeris. Efter the sermoun the holl gentilmen of the said parochin being present—to witt Sir John Hamiltoun off Lettrik, Sir Jhone Hammiltoun of Grange, Walter Cornwall of Ballinhard, Mr Alexander Hammiltoun of Kinglass, the Laird of Cleghorne, Alexander Bruce, David Carmichall, Constabil of Blacknes, with the holl elderis and deconis off that paroche—the brethren ordeined Mr Jhone Drysdall to be Clark to the said visitation becaus Mr Andrew Keir, Clerk to the Presbytery is Minister to this Kirk of Caridenn and is to be removed now that the visitouris may try off his doctrin, disciplin, and conversatioun."

The precept from the Archbishop was then " red publictly," and the brethren signified that they would again attend before the third Thursday in November, when they " wold tak a course for the designatioun off the said manse and gleib." On 4th March the following year a report was made to the Presbytery of the " designatioun of the gleib off Caridenn out off the landis off Grange neirest to the said kirk." This was in the time of the Hamiltons of Grange, and also when they were possessed of portions of ground near Carriden House. A year after it was pointed out to the Presbytery on behalf of Sir John Hamilton that he was prepared to give them in exchange for the parts of his lands designed the year before to be the manse and glebe of Carriden, other parts of his lands " far neirer and more ewous" to the kirk of Carriden. While making this offer he stipulated that " iff it were fund that these landis off Grange designed befoir wer better land than these his other lands wuhilk he now offeris that, upon the astimatioun and valuation of three or four honest skilled men off the paroche of Cariddenn, he suld gie so much mor land in quantatie as may mak out the equalitie of the ane land with the other, and offeris also to mak a disposition or resignatioun off these lands in the hands of the kirk to be ane manse and gleib in all tym coming." The brethren consulted with Mr. Keir. A fortnight later they agreed to the excambion, and instructed the manse and glebe to be designed. This was done on the afternoon of 30th March, 1630.

IV.

The documentary evidence concerning the removal of the church at Carriden House to Cuffabouts and the opening of a new burial-ground there is curiously meagre. At a meeting of the Presbytery held at Linlithgow on the 3rd of April, 1765, Colonel Campbell Dalrymple of Carriden represented that the church and churchyard dykes of Carriden were ruinous, and needed repair. The Presbytery therefore appointed Messrs. Hogg, Baillie (of Bo'ness), and Ritchie as a committee of their number to meet at Carriden with properly qualified tradesmen in order to make up estimates of the repairs wanted and to report. They also appointed edictal citation to be given and letters to be written to the non-residing heritors. On the 26th of the same month the committee gave in their report in writing bearing that they, with proper tradesmen, upon oath, had found the church and churchyard dykes in a ruinous condition, and that the tradesmen had made up estimates for repairing the same, amounting to the sum of £174 8s. 8d. They also reported that there was a design to remove the church and churchyard near to the village of Bonhard-pans. This place they had inspected, and were of opinion that it was very convenient. Further, a cast of the assessment among the several heritors according to their respective valuations had at the same time been made. The Presbytery therefore having read this report and examined the cast of the assessment approved of the whole in all points, and decerned accordingly, humbly beseeching the Lords of Council to interpose their authority.

This is really all the authoritative information on the subject, for it seems a search was made in later years in the minutes of the heritors and of the kirk session, but without anything being found on the subject. It was also about the same time stated that there had been a process between Colonel Campbell Dalrymple and the other heritors of the parish over the expense of building the new church. Extensive searches were accordingly made in the Court of Session records, and amongst the printed papers in the Advocates and Writers to the Signet Libraries, but no trace could be got of any such proceedings. A search was also made amongst the papers at Hopetoun House, but without discovering any document relating to the process in question.

The change of church site has all along been laid at the door of the Colonel and his family, who were said to have wished the church and churchyard to be more distant from their mansion-house. For this reason, and with the view of quieting the minds of the parishioners, and so doing away with all opposition, the tenantry and other householders, it was said, were permitted to remove the seats or pews of the old church and place them in the new one as they thought proper. In this way, and without any other right or title whatever, the greater portion of the area, and even part of the lofts or galleries of the church, were possessed to the great inconvenience of the other heritors and their tenants.

This irregularity gave, in subsequent years, very considerable trouble. As a consequence, the heritors, consisting of his Grace the Duke of Hamilton, the Hon. the Earl of Hopetoun, Sir James Dalyell, Bart. of Binns; James John Cadell, Esq. of Grange; and James Johnston, Esq. of Straiton, submitted a memorial to Mr. John Connell, advocate, for his opinion.

In answer he held that the possession above described was illegal, and could be annulled by the patron and heritors. And had it not been for the long possession which the occupiers had had of their seats, a process of removing before the Sheriff would have been sufficient. In view of this possession, however, he thought it would be more advisable to bring an action of declarator before the Court of Session.

Although this opinion would have warranted what we might fitly term a "redistribution of seats," we have not found that any steps were taken, so that things apparently remained much as they were.

V.

Considerable excitement was caused in Grangepans throughout most of the year 1767 over the circumstances attending the burial of a child in the old churchyard at Carriden. The direct result of this burial was the serving of a complaint at the instance of James Watsone, the procurator-fiscal for the county, against several local people in the month of February. The accused were John Sword, jun., mason in Grangepans; George Younger and James Gibb, indwellers there; Christian Crocket, spouse of George Thomson, sailor in Grangepans; Barbara Nicol, spouse of James Donaldson, salter in Thirlestane; Katherine Drummond, spouse of Gilbert M'Naughton, salter; Euphaim Ritchie, spouse of John Drummond, salter; Magdalene Govan, spouse of Thomas Robertson, indweller in Cuffabouts; Robert Waldie, farmer in Muirhouses; James Kidd, indweller there; and James Anderson, sailor. They were each and all of them charged with breach of the peace, assault, and housebreaking. The circumstances, as set forth in the complaint, were these—A male child belonging to Robert Scott, salt watchman, in Grangepans, having died there on the 20th day of January, the father on the day following went in quest of the gravedigger, whom he found at Muirhouses, and desired him to dig a grave for his child in the new churchyard of Carriden. When Scott was upon this mission the accused were said to have assembled in a riotous and tumultuous manner along with a number of other persons, and attacked him when returning home from the Muirhouses at or near Coulthenhill, and gave him many blows with sticks, snowballs, and other offensive weapons, by which he was much hurt and severely wounded to the effusion of his blood. On the evening of the same day they also in a most outrageous and forcible manner went into Scott's house by breaking open the doors and insisting in carrying off the body of the dead child, using at the same time threatening expressions against Scott and his family, whereby they were put in terror of their lives. With great difficulty the accused were ultimately prevailed upon to desist from carrying off the body. Having gone out of the house, however, they did notwithstanding continue till about three o'clock next morning throwing stones at Scott's door, uttering the while many threatening expressions against him. Next day—22nd January—the accused once more came to Scott's house, and forcibly and without his consent carried off the body, which they interred in the old churchyard. It was craved that upon the charges being proven the defenders ought to be fined in the sum of £100 sterling, conjunctly and severally, and otherways punished in their persons and effects to the terror of others in time coming.

On 6th March all the accused appeared in Court, attended by Walter Forrester, their procurator. The fiscal craved for the apprehension and imprisonment of all the accused until they found caution to attend all the diets of the Court. The Sheriff granted this crave, and also allowed a full proof. Due caution seems to have been found. The proof was conducted in a very leisurely way, only the evidence of one or two witnesses being taken at a sitting. Even by the month of December the case does not appear to have been decided. Unfortunately we have not been able to discover what was the Sheriff's decision. The complaint may have ultimately been withdrawn, but, judging from the evidence we have read, we do not expect the complaint was proved. It is quite evident there was considerable feeling on the part of the lairholders in the old churchyard over the suggestion that they should abandon it and use the new burial place.

VI.

In the course of the proof, notes of which we subjoin, the statement in the complaint that Robert Scott ordered the gravedigger to dig a grave in the new churchyard was emphatically denied. Agnes Bell, spouse to Alexander Smith, sailor in Grangepans, and mentioned as being "aged twenty and upwards," said that the day after the child died she heard the bell go through the town of Grangepans in the forenoon, and intimation made to the people to come against three o'clock in the afternoon, and bury the child in the old churchyard of Carriden. She saw the bellman come to Scott's house with the hand-spokes about three o'clock, set them down, and go in. She also saw Sir Alexander Brown go up to the house, and go in, but by this time the bellman had left in order to again ring the bell for the people to come to the burying. But during Sir Alexander's presence in Scott's house he was called back, where he stayed but a short time. When he came out again he told Marion Blackater, in presence of the deponent, that he had got orders to go away, but he did not mention who gave them, and the child was not buried that afternoon. Scott was in a somewhat difficult position. Here on the one hand was his superior officer, Sir Alexander Brown, making a strong personal appeal to him; and it is evident that Sir Alexander was one of those who were most anxious to get the parishioners prevailed upon to abandon the old burial ground. It was reported, too, that Scott was even to get some money, presumably to induce him to bury the child in the new churchyard. On the other hand Scott and his wife distinctly wanted the child buried in the old churchyard "alongst with its brothers and sisters." Scott in his dilemma apparently played the part of diplomat. He, we fear, feigned illness the next day, and indicated to Charles Wood, weaver, Grangepans, that he wished he and some of the neighbours would attend the burying, saying at the same time that if it had not been for Sir Alexander Brown, who had stopped the bellman, the child would have been buried the day before in the old churchyard, as the grave had been digged there for that purpose. Agnes, we should have said, testified that Scott's wife joined with her husband in wishing that some honest neighbours would come and bury their child, that they both repeated it twice, and wished to God it were so. Scott, she mentioned, said he was indisposed and unable to go to the burial himself. She further stated that on the afternoon of the burial Mrs. Scott came out to her stairhead along with the defender Barbara Nicol, who had the dead child in her arms, and that Mrs. Scott called to

James Gibb to come and take her dear child or dear baby. There were, she said, very few persons at the burial except children.

Some further light on the subject is afforded by the evidence of Magdalene Mein, spouse to Adam Taylor, salter in Grangepans. She was standing at a neighbour's door the day of the burial. She saw the accused Barbara Nicol and one Margaret Young bring the corpse out of Scott's house. Mrs. Scott came to the stairhead after them, and Magdalene heard her desire the defender James Gibb, who was standing at the stairfoot, to receive the corpse and carry it away. Gibb refused at first, and asked where the father was that he might carry it. To this Mrs. Scott answered that he was not well, and was unable to go to the interment himself. She again desired Gibb to take the corpse and inter it, declaring it was perfectly agreeable to her inclination that he should do so, and desired the other people who were present to stand until they received a shilling from her to pay the bellman for digging the grave. Thereafter Mrs. Scott delivered the shilling to Walter Miller, who delivered it to Thomas Walker, to be given by him to the bellman. Mrs. Taylor did not see any mob or tumult at this time. Those assembled went off calmly with the corpse.

VII.

Margaret Young, an appropriately youthful witness of fourteen, daughter of William Young, flesher in Grangepans, deponed that she, with the accused Barbara Nicol and Catherine Drummond, went into Scott's house on the day the child was buried; that the two latter on entering wished Scott and his wife good-day, and asked if they intended to bury their child that day. To this Scott answered "Yes," adding that there was his child, coffined and mortclothed, and all in decency and desired them to carry it away and bury it in the old churchyard beside its three brothers, for he was not able to go to the burial himself. Upon the saying of which Scott went into his bed. After this Scott's wife lifted the coffin and gave it to Barbara Nicol and Catherine Drummond, who carried it out of the house and delivered it to James Gibb at the stairfoot. She further stated that Gibb asked Mrs. Scott, who came out to the stairhead, if she desired her child to be buried, to which she answered "O yes." Gibb then came off with the child, and was joined by several people at a small distance from the house. Margaret accompanied the corpse to the place of interment. She returned to Scott's house with Nicol and Drummond, and there told the Scotts that their child was decently buried in the old churchyard, and they thoroughly approved of what had been done.

A few weeks after this burial Thomas Brown, the beadle and gravedigger, was dismissed. From a minute of the Carriden session, of date 22nd February, 1767, we find a letter addressed to the Rev. Mr. Ellis, and signed by Galloway A. Hamilton, Willm. Muir, Arch. Stewart, and And. Stewart. It ran— "Reverend Sir, Whereas we are informed that Thomas Brown, Beadle and Gravedigger at Carriden, did lately refuse to do his duty by digging a grave to a child when ordered to do so, which delay in some measure occasioned the late riot, we therefore desire that you in concurrence with the Session and heritors would displace the said Thomas Brown and appoint another beadle in his place of whom we will approve, and are, Reverend Sir, Your most humble Servants."

The following concurrence is likewise recorded in the same minute:—

"I William Maxwell of Carriden do concur with the tutors of his Grace the Duke of Hamilton in depriving Thomas Brown of his office of Beadle, Gravedigger, and Session Officer of the parish of Carriden, and the said Thomas Brown is hereby from this day deprived of and is declared to have no right to any fees, perquisites, or dues that might arise in any manner of way from said office which is hereby declared vacant until it be supplied by the heritors of the parish or by the majority of the valued rent: and whoever shall presume to employ him or pay him as Beadle, &c., will be accountable to the heritors, and prosecute according to law.—(Signed) William Maxwell."

Then the minute proceeds—

"The Session hereby considered the same; they neither approve of riots nor any that will contribute to them, or do not pretend to employ any officer or beadle that the heritors or the majority of the valued rent think proper to turn out, and will concur with them in any fit person that they shall approve of for that office, and appoints the same to be inserted in their minutes. Adjourns till Sabbath next, and concludes with prayer."

One of the results of the removal of the church and churchyard to Cuffabouts was the removal in course of time of the glebe also. This came about by the Presbytery giving up the old glebe lands which lay in the vicinity of Carriden House for a new glebe, which was designed by them out of Admiral Sir George Hope's lands at Cuffabouts. The process was effected by an excambion or exchange of the old glebe lands for new lands.

VIII.

Towards the close of the life of the second William Maxwell of Carriden, application was made by him to the Commissioners of the roads for the Parish of Carriden under date 30th April, 1802, for authority to close one of the old church roads running through his estate. This was the road originally used by the Blackness people. It began, his petition said, to the east on the shore at Carrispans, then in ruins, passed to the east and south of Carriden House, and terminated at the village of Muirhouses to the west. Of so little importance was it and so little used that it had not been repaired by the Parish Commissioners for upwards of forty years before the application. In fact, it was said to be of no importance whatever to the inhabitants of the parish. Besides it had been long almost impassable, for during the spring tides the east end of it could not be approached from the east or west, the shore road being then, at high water, covered by the sea in several places. Moreover, it was explained, that within the period of forty years, before mentioned, a more convenient, and in every

M

respect a better, road had been made in a new line from Blackness by Burnshot and Waltoun to Bonhard and the Muirhouses, which were the only places to which this road could be considered to lead. Mr. Maxwell also alleged that the old road was a great inconvenience to him, as it enabled idle and disorderly people to pass at all times through the grounds and within a few yards of Carriden House. These people, besides leaving open the gates which he by immemorial practice had a right to have upon the road, frequently committed wanton mischief to his great detriment. He therefore craved the Commissioners to give their consent to the shutting up of the old road in all time coming, and that it be no longer considered as a public road nor any person suffered to pass the same. The Commissioners, who were James Dalyell and James John Cadell, gave their consent. The matter in course came before the justices for their confirmation, and they appointed a committee to examine the road. A quorum of this committee, consisting of James Dalyell, Alexander Marjoribanks, Dav. Falconer, and Patrick Baron Seton, reported, under date Carriden, 26th June, 1805, that having met and examined the road, they considered it of no use to the public, and that it ought to be shut up. The Quarter Sessions therefore, on 10th November, 1805—the sederunt consisting of Sir Alexander Seton of Preston, Dr. Patrick Baron Seton, Yr. of Preston, William Napier of Dales, and James Watson of Bridge Castle (Sir Alexr. Seton, preses)— having taken the petition and report into consideration, approved thereof, and condemned the road, finding it of no use or utility to the public, and authorising Mr. Maxwell to shut up the same. The petition and whole proceedings were at the same time ordained to be engrossed in the books of the Quarter Sessions.

In the light of what is related further on regarding the strenuous objections which were taken to proposals to shut up the other church roads throughout the estate it seems surprising that this road was closed without the slightest opposition. It may have been that the road was, in truth, of little or no public service, because of the opening of the newer road by Burnshot.

But the main reason would seem to lie in this, that the proposal came before the days of James White and James Duguid, who in turn were the leaders and champions of the parishioners in all such matters. We may be sure that, whether the road was used or not, they would have fought against its closing as an infringement of a long-recognised public right. As it was, though no objection was taken in Mr. Maxwell's time, the matter gave his successors considerable apprehension until it had been closed for forty years, for it came to be whispered that the procedure taken was not in order, inasmuch as it was closed by the wrong authority.

IX.

In the month of January, 1819, a meeting of proprietors of burying-ground in the old churchyard of Carriden was held in the house of Mr. James White, wright in Grangepans. Those at the meeting were under the impression that Lady Hope, the widow of Admiral Sir George Hope, intended to remove the walls of the burying-ground, which were then in a most dilapidated state. Such action, it was thought, would have the effect of doing away with the place as a burial-ground altogether, thus compelling those who had still a right of burial there to use the new churchyard at Cuffabouts. The meeting unanimously determined that the walls should be rebuilt, and they expressed the view that in taking them down a right was being exercised which was unjustifiable in law or in any other sense whatever. It was mentioned at the same meeting that an attempt had previously been made on two other occasions to remove the burial-ground, first by Colonel Dalrymple, and latterly by Mr. Maxwell, and that money had been transmitted from different parts of the Continent to resist it. Mr. White, as the preses of the meeting, was instructed to communicate the above resolution to Lord President Hope, who was one of the trustees of the late Admiral, which he accordingly did in very courteous and respectful terms.

The Lord President immediately acknowledged Mr. White's letter at considerable length, and expressed extreme regret at the evident misunderstanding which had arisen. He assured him that it never was the intention of Lady Hope or of Sir George's trustees to remove the burying-ground or to violate it in any way that might hurt the feelings of those whose relations were buried there. He stated that the old ruinous wall which surrounded it was not only a great deformity to the place of Carriden, but actually rendered the lower part of the south front of the house dark. It was therefore proposed merely to take down part of the wall and erect a handsome and substantial iron railing in its place, which should be sufficient not only to exclude man and cattle as effectually as the old wall, but even to exclude dogs. He explained that it had been his intention to have spoken to the principal persons concerned before operations were commenced, but that Lady Hope had misunderstood him, and wishing to employ the stones for some other purpose had begun to take down the wall before he had had an opportunity of conversing with the people concerned. He goes on to say, however, that he understood from Mr. Keir, Philpstoun, who on his behalf attended a recent meeting in the churchyard, that it had been explained there that there was no intention to remove or touch the burying-ground, and that the people then present had expressed themselves satisfied with the assurance he gave them that a substantial iron railing was to be immediately erected.

In consequence of the consent then given, or at least certainly understood by Mr. Keir to be given, the trustees had concluded that Lady Hope might proceed to take down the wall; and the iron railing would have been finished and probably erected by that time if they had not been obliged to stop it in consequence of hearing that there was some opposition going forward. His lordship further pointed out that it was not intended to touch the west side of the wall, against which alone any monuments ever were erected; and no headstone or flat stone would be defaced or touched in any shape. He then says that while the old walls stood the inside of the burying-ground was not visible, and no attention had ever been paid to it. It was overgrown with nettles, thistles, and wild raspberries, and was as dirty and unpleasant a looking place as could well be imagined. If enclosed with an iron railing the greatest care would be taken to keep it clear of weeds and the turf clean and neat, but without touching it with a spade. There, therefore, seemed to him, when the matter was explained, nothing to go to law about, for the trustees had not the most distant intention of removing the burying-ground; and as the people concerned could have no interest but to have it properly secured and enclosed both parties would be just where they were, only Mr. White and the others would have a neat and creditable-looking burying-ground instead of a place full of weeds and dirt and rubbish not fit for a dog to lie in, and enclosed with a strong iron rail, which the trustees would keep in repair, instead of an old ruinous wall, which would soon have required repair at the public expense. His lordship then concludes his epistle in the following paragraphs:—

"Therefore as you, James, by your letter seem to be a man of sense and education, I trust you will explain all this to the people, who have thus misconceived our intentions. To rebuild the wall would cost us not one quarter of the price of an iron railing; and while it would not be so good and secure an enclosure to the burying-ground, it would be a great deformity to the place, which Lady Hope is very fond of, and where she hopes to live, doing as much good to her poor neighbours as she can.

"If you wish for any further explanation, and will yourself with one or two more of your friends, come to town I shall be glad to see you, and most willingly pay your expenses out and home. You will find me generally about one o'clock at my chambers in Hill Street, Edinburgh, every day except Monday, on which day you will be almost certain of finding me at my house at Granton, on the Banks of the Forth, about 2 miles from Crammond."

X.

The writer of this very gracious and peace-making epistle

was, as we have indicated, Lord President Hope, otherwise Charles Hope of Granton, son of John Hope and grandson of the first Earl of Hopetoun. He was born in 1763, admitted to the Bar at twenty-one years of age, appointed Lord Advocate in 1801, Lord Justice-Clerk in 1804, and Lord President in 1811. He retired in 1841, and died ten years after. Lord Cockburn[5] has left us this description of his friend. "He was tall and well set up, and had a most admirable voice—full, deep, and distinct, its very whisper heard along a line of a thousand men (Hope being a most ardent Volunteer and Colonel of his regiment). Kind, friendly, and honourable, private life could neither enjoy nor desire a character more excellent. No breast, indeed," continues Cockburn, "could be more clear than Hope's of everything paltry or malevolent; and indirectness was so entirely foreign to his manly nature that even in his plainest error his adversaries had always whatever advantage was to be gained from an honest disclosure of his principles and objects."

To the letter of the Lord President Mr. White replied that he had submitted it to his committee, who had ordered a general meeting to be called to consider it on 3rd February. We have not seen any record of this meeting, but it appears that it had been resolved to meet his lordship on the ground. Accordingly we find from another document that he had met the committee at Carriden on 17th March, and had no difficulty in arranging everything to their mutual satisfaction. The enclosure was to consist of a wall of only 2 feet high, including the coping, which was to be 8 inches thick in the centre, sloping to 6 inches at the edges—the wall to be surmounted with an iron railing, double at the bottom; the railing to be 4½ feet high, including the arrowheads at the top. The committee most readily agreed that the north-east corner next the house, in which there were no graves, should be rounded off, and pins were accordingly fixed in. They mentioned at the meeting that the people were impatient till the work was begun, and his

---

[5] "Cockburn's Memorials of his Time."

lordship had pledged himself that it should be gone about directly. The new wall was to be "founded" exactly on the old, except at the curve at the north-east. The committee also agreed to transfer the gate to the south-west corner furthest from the house, so that the old west wall was to be finished off with a substantial stone pillar for hanging one check of the gate upon, and another was to be built for hanging the east check. The west wall, it was agreed by the representatives of the Hopes, should be pointed up with lime on the outside and the top; and there was to be a pillar at the north end of it to receive the bars of the railing. The committee, lastly, had agreed to give up the old burial road, and to use the back entry in front of the garden instead of it.

The railing was to be supplied and erected by Thompson, Lady Hope's smith, and one Gib was to be the mason. Weir, the gardener, was to superintend generally. These alterations were all carried out, and the place to-day is pretty much as just described.

The vigilant Mr. White and his committee, however, thought it right and proper to get a letter from the Earl of Hopetoun and the Lord President, the late Admiral's trustees, on the subject of the removal of the gate to the south-west corner. As it was considered of great importance to the public, and might easily have been mislaid or lost, Mr. White, for himself and the others interested, petitioned the Kirk Session of Carriden on 5th August, 1820, to record it in the register of the Kirk Session. We do not expect that this request would be acceded to, as the matter was for the records of the heritors, not of the session. The letter was dated Edinburgh, 23rd June, 1819, and is addressed to Mr. White, as Preses of the Committee on the Old Churchyard of Carriden. It runs—"Some apprehensions having been expressed on the part of those having an interest in the old burial-ground at Carriden that the trustees of the Carriden estate, in removing the gate of the churchyard from the south-east to the south-west corner of said churchyard, in conformity to what had been agreed on between the trustees and the committee, have in view to interrupt access to the burial-ground, now we, on the part of the trustees, have no hesitation in assuring you and all concerned that there does not exist any intention of such interruption, and that the access by the new gate shall be free as formerly by the old one, and that the trustees will be ready, if necessary, to enter into any written obligation to guarantee the old burial road or the one by the garden instead of it, and access to the burial-ground by the new gate as formerly enjoyed. (Signed) Hopetoun: C. Hope."

For a time, therefore, public anxiety with regard to the preservation of the rights of proprietors in the burial-ground was ended.

The following is an excerpt from minute of a general meeting of the heritors of the Parish of Carriden held upon the 19th day of June, 1801:—

"The Meeting considering that some person has lately been interred in the old Churchyard near to Carriden House without its having been ascertained that the individual had any right of burial there, direct that henceforth the Beadle shall not be allowed to dig any grave or permit burial in the old Churchyard without the sanction of the Minister and Kirk Session, who shall make particular enquiry that the predecessors of the defunct have enjoyed the uninterrupted right of burial in that churchyard before they authorise the Beadle to break ground therein."

XI.

Lady Hope, about April, 1825, desiring to improve the old burial road (there being about the middle of it a bend or crooked part which occupied only a very short distance, but was extremely awkward both for the road and the adjoining lands), had the road made perfectly straight at that place. This improvement was completed without objection from any person whatever. Some time after this her ladyship gave orders for planting the piece of ground which had been taken from the old road to effect the above improvement. Thereupon as a document dealing with the subject has it, "Certain individuals in the village of Muirhouses and others actuated by troublesome dispositions or some other unreasonable motives began to complain of the alterations on the road, alleging that Lady Hope was not entitled to have made such alterations without their concurrence and consent previously obtained, and they then threatened to prevent the piece of the old road which was superseded from being planted."

The planting, however, proceeded, and was finished without any interruption. The objectors apparently were James White, wright at Grangepans, Bo'ness; John Aitken, residing at Muirhouses; James Duguid, residing there; William Moodie, smith, there; and Alexander Findlay, residing there. The innocent and well-meant action of her ladyship had once more raised their suspicions, and made them again become exceedingly zealous in the public interest. It was said that these persons in name of themselves and others addressed letters to some of the curators of James Hope, son of Sir George, threatening in a very alarming tone to restore the road to its former situation by their own operations and horses and carts. It was expected that if they did so they would destroy the fences which were erected at both ends of the bend, and would root up the young trees planted. It was also anticipated that they would create a great disturbance in the vicinity of Carriden House, and perhaps under the influence of violent dispositions do a great deal of other mischief and injury which could not be calculated. Therefore young James Hope, with the advice and consent of the Honourable Dames Georgiana Mary Ann Hope, relict of Vice-Admiral Sir George Hope of Carriden, K.C.B.; Miss Margaret Hope, residing at Hastings; the Right Honourable Charles Hope, Lord President; and the Honourable Sir Alexander Hope of Waughton, G.C.B., accepting and surviving curators and guardians appointed to the said James Hope by his deceased father, applied to the Court of Session to suspend and interdict James White and the others from proceeding with their threatened operations. On 10th June interim interdict was pronounced, and the respondents ordered to see and answer the complaint within fourteen days. The matter apparently ended here, for we have no further trace of it. The parties with the "troublesome dispositions" no doubt, on taking legal advice, were assured that Lady Hope had acted in perfectly good faith, and that their legal rights were not being jeopardised in the slightest degree by the improvement which had been carried out.

XII.

In 1838 Captain James Hope, as he then was, desiring to more efficiently protect his pleasure grounds, but without any intention of prejudicing the rights of the proprietors of lairs in the old burial-ground, petitioned the county justices for authority to shut up the old church road running from the manse entry at Cuffabouts up through the glebe lands to the old church and churchyard at Carriden, and also the road running from there on to the Muirhouses. In lieu of these he offered a public access to the churchyard by the road leading along the south side of Carriden garden (from the west lodge eastwards). This new access he held, being shorter and more direct than the old one, would be much more convenient for all concerned. A sketch of the old lines of road and also the proposed new access was lodged with his application. The petition was brought before the justices, because they were vested with certain powers relating to the county roads, and especially the power to alter the direction and course of improper and inconvenient roads and to shut up superfluous and useless ones. It was first considered on 4th October, when there were present Sir James Dalyell, Bart. of Binns, preses; Sir William Baillie, Bart. of Polkemet; John Stewart, Esq. of Binny; Major Norman Sharp of Houston; William Baillie, Esq., younger of Polkemet; James John Cadell, Esq. of Grange; John Ferrier Hamilton, Esq. of Westport; and William Wilson, Esq. of Dechmont. A remit was then made to a committee, consisting of Sir James Dalyell, Bart. of Binns; James Dundas,

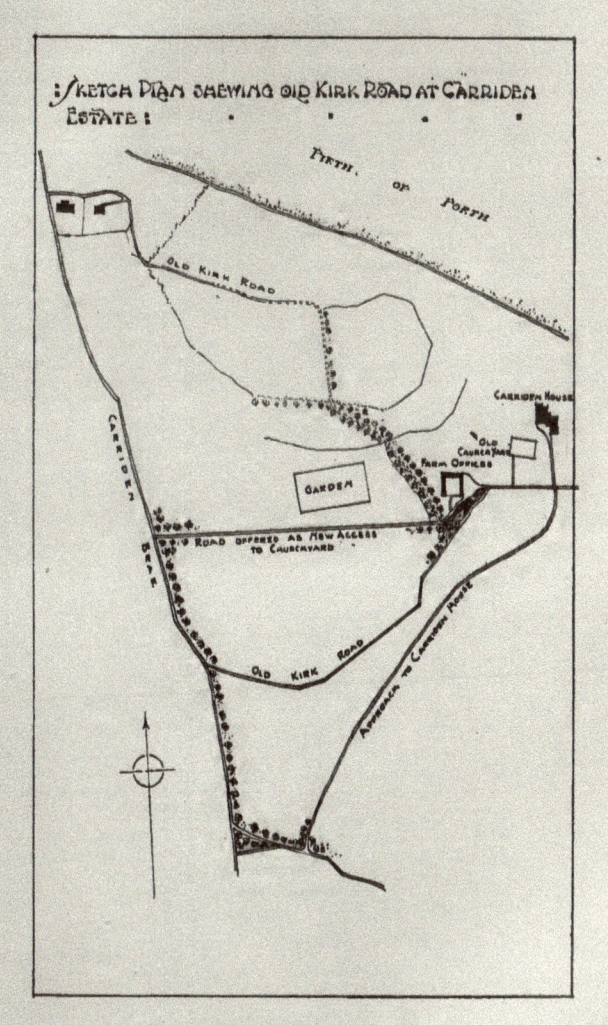

The Old Kirk Roads, Carriden.

(*Sketched by permission of Mr. Lloyd Verney, by Matt. Steele, Bo'ness, from an old plan.*)

Esq. of Dundas; James John Cadell, Esq. of Grange; John Stewart, Esq. of Binny; Gabriel Hamilton Dundas, Esq. of Duddingstone; and Major Norman Shairp of Houston, any three a quorum, and Sir James Dalyell, convener. They also ordered the public intimation required by the Act.

As a result of this remit there assembled within the church of Carriden at one o'clock, on the 21st day of November, 1838, the following members of committee:—Sir James Dalyell, Gabriel Hamilton Dundas, and John Stewart. The petition, with the deliverance thereon, the plan of the roads, the Act of Parliament, and also an execution by William Hendrie, constable, bearing that he had made public intimation of the petition on Sundays, the 7th and 14th days of October, at the principal door of the parish church, and a further execution by him that he, on 11th November, had given notice at same place of the intention of the committee to meet at this place and hour when all parties would be heard for their interest, were all produced, read, and particularly examined by the committee. A number of the inhabitants of the parish also assembled that day in the church, and produced answers, and requested that these be publicly read, which was done. They thereafter desired that the same be entered in the minutes of the committee, which was also done.

The answers bear that they were for James Duguid, shoemaker, Muirhouses; John M'Gregor, labourer, there; John Black, cooper, Grangepans; James Stanners, sailor there; and Thomas Christie, labourer, Gladhill, the committee appointed by a meeting of the inhabitants of the Parish of Carriden having right to the old churchyard as a place of sepulchre held on 20th October, 1838. They then go on to argue in some detail that the roads were neither useless nor superfluous, and, moreover, that the Merrilees Turnpike Act did not apply to the present case. With respect to the new road proposed, it was pointed out that were it accepted the respondents would be deprived of a vested right to the roads in question, which they at present held by prescription. They also felt if they agreed to the new proposal that they would then be compelled to accept of a sufferance from the petitioner, which might afterwards be a source of vexatious litigation. It was further stated by the respondents that by the granting of the petition (which, however, they could not for a moment suppose would be the result) the petitioner would be enabled to improve his estate, and would also acquire several acres of excellent land and £40 or £50 worth of full-grown timber, to which, they alleged, he had "no more right than the man in the moon, if there was such a personage." Several cases in point are quoted, and then the respondents close by remarking that they had no doubt their honours would dismiss the application and find them entitled to expenses. The answers are signed by all the respondents themselves, not by an agent.

XIII.

Turning again to the official narrative of the proceedings in the church we find that the petitioner and various other persons, having been heard verbally, and the committee having thereafter in their presence perambulated, examined, and inspected the road, reported that the road desired to be closed was awkward, ill-formed, in a bad state of repair, and would not in their opinion admit of a funeral procession passing along it; that the road proposed to be substituted was not only in an excellent state of repair, but also on the whole formed a more direct approach to the old churchyard. They were further of opinion that the proposed alteration would be of no disadvantage to those interested. On the contrary, they deemed it would be a distinct advantage, and they proposed that warrant should be given petitioner for shutting up the old line of road and substituting the other line by the south side of the garden in all time coming.

On the 4th December, same year, the justices assembled at Linlithgow in adjourned Quarter Sessions. Having again considered the petition, productions, and the report of their committtee, and also heard John Hardy, procurator of Court, on behalf of James Duguid and others who had lodged answers, they ordained that before further answer the respondents should see the whole process for ten days; that they then lodge objections to the report of committee as craved, the petitioners to lodge answers to such objections within other ten days thereafter.

The respondents, in obedience to this order, lodged further answers, in which they proceeded to largely incorporate their original answers. They again strongly and at considerable length argued that it was not competent for their honours to entertain the petition at all. In particular, they held that this road was not one of those public roads which did fall within their jurisdiction, but, on the contrary, was just that description of road from which their jurisdiction was altogether excluded. Cases in point were quoted very extensively, especially those going to show that no foot or horse or cart road to kirk or mill could be closed. Coming to the report of the committee, the objectors held, with great deference, that it by no means came up to the point necessary to be reached in order to justify the change proposed. The most substantial conclusion of the committee only said the road was an awkward and ill-formed one, in a very bad state of repair. But this in the objectors' view was no sort of reason for shutting it up. In fact, so very ridiculous was the argument for shutting it that they thought they would be trifling with the subject to pursue the topic, because the mere fact of a road being out of repair could never for a single instant be sustained as a reason for shutting it up and opening another one. There must be, they argued, something in the character of the road itself independent of its mere state of repair to justify the proceeding. The old road must be proved in the clearest and most indisputable manner to be disadvantageous to those using it before their honours could be warranted in interfering. In closing they pressed that it would not suffice to merely say the road on the whole was as good as the others, or even that on a critical balancing of their merits somebody might be led to pronounce the new one rather the better of the two. It must, they held, be made out in a strong and unequivocal manner that under the words of the Act the road proposed to be shut up was positively "improper and inconvenient" for those who used it. With all deference they submitted there was nothing of the kind established. The objections were drawn by William Penney, advocate, and signed by John Hardy, writer, Linlithgow.

The strenuous and unflinching opposition thus put forward, and very particularly the strong legal argument that the justices had really no jurisdiction to deal with his petition, caused Captain Hope considerable perturbation, and made him take the opinion of counsel. This was Mr. John Hope, Dean of Faculty, son of the Lord President, and latterly also a judge. Following upon a long memorial of the whole facts and circumstances, counsel, upon what he terms a full and calm consideration of the whole matter, was clearly of opinion that the justices had no jurisdiction. He therefore advised that the proceedings be withdrawn as the object of the petition was beyond the power of the justices. This was in January, 1839, and, so far as we can make out, all proceedings were then dropped. Nevertheless, Captain Hope, though disappointed that he had gone to the wrong tribunal, remained firmly convinced that his plan was really in the end the best for all parties concerned. He took further legal advice, and was advised to repeat his application in the Court of Session. Owing, however, to his many enforced absences and a keen desire not to be misunderstood or misrepresented by his people, he never sought to press the matter further. So the burial roads remain to this day as they were in old times.

XIV.

In the year 1853 yet another misunderstanding arose over the old churchyard. The cause was the blowing down of a portion of the iron railing erected in 1819. Admiral Sir James Hope was abroad at the time, and Mr. George Davidson, his land steward, not having any instructions one way or the other, and apparently not knowing of the terms of the arrangement in 1819, would neither have the railing re-erected on behalf of the Admiral nor allow those interested on behalf of the public to do so. Mr. White was by this time dead, and his mantle had descended on the shoulders of Mr. James Duguid. The latter made diligent search among the writings connected with the churchyard, and came upon the letter of the Lord President, of 22nd January, 1819, wherein he had, on behalf of the Admiral's trustees, pledged himself to put up the railing and to keep it always in repair. Satisfied with this, Mr. Duguid, on 4th July, wrote the Admiral explaining the situation, and on behalf of the committee respectfully requested him to have the broken-down railing put in proper repair as speedily as possible. The Admiral replied on the 5th that the request would be complied with, although until he examined the papers on the subject that day the existence of the obligation of the Lord President was unknown to him. He added that he should have felt mortified if the committee had gone to any expense on the subject themselves, and he should have supposed they were too well acquainted with him ever to have seriously entertained such an intention.

Sir James now conceived the idea of coming to some clear understanding for all time coming regarding the old burial-ground, and wrote Mr. Duguid to call a meeting of the parties interested at which his proposals might be submitted. He mentioned that the only papers he had in his possession relative to the kirkyard were the protest by R. Campbell and others, dated 7th January, 1819; Mr. White's letter to the Lord President, of 19th January; the Lord President's letter, of 22nd January; Mr. White's reply, of 27th January; and the joint letter of Lord Hopetoun and the Lord President, dated 23rd June. If there were any other letters or papers which the parties interested considered of importance he would be happy to have a complete copy made of those just named and such others as might be furnished, and have them all placed in the Kirk Session records for future reference. He also desired that the parties interested should elect two trustees, one resident in the Muirhouses and the other at Grangepans, who should be authorised by them to communicate with him as to the mode in which the kirkyard was kept or any other subject connected with it on which they desired their wishes to be made known. He explained that he rented the grass in the kirkyard merely for the purpose of keeping it in a decent state, and not for any profit, and he should at all times be glad to meet their views on this subject. But now came the vital part of his communication. He was, in pursuance of his letter of 5th July, in the course of having the damaged coping replaced and the railing re-erected, but before giving the final directions he made them this proposal. Their right to have the railing put up being clear and undoubted, would they be disposed to waive that right in his favour and permit the entire railing to be taken down, leaving only the dwarf wall as a boundary? Those parties, he said, who wished to do so could use the railing to fence their own particular burying-places, which they could keep locked, as was usual in such cases. The dwarf wall would remain as a clear and sufficient boundary of the kirkyard, which might be visited and reported on once a year on a regular day by the trustees, while the views of those parties would be met who would like their burying-places more strictly enclosed. His lawns were never pastured, and no accident had ever happened to the numerous evergreens about them. He therefore considered that the kirkyard would be effectually secured in the future from all intrusion as it was then. The improvement to the cheerfulness and amenity of Carriden House was obvious, and he could not help thinking that even those who did not at first like the idea would in a very short time consider the kirkyard much improved by what he proposed. He would be obliged by their taking a month to consider. In a second letter sent the next day he made particular reference to this last proposal, and observed that while on the one hand he considered both he and his family were entitled to, and did enjoy, the goodwill of their neighbours to a very considerable extent (and that this was most undoubtedly an occasion on which that goodwill should be exercised), still, on the other hand, he both respected and fully understood the feelings which prevailed relative to the old kirkyard amongst those who had friends interred there and who intended to be buried there themselves. Whatever decision, therefore, they might come to on the subject they might rest assured that it would make no difference to those feelings of cordiality which he desired to entertain for his neighbours of all classes.

Mr. Duguid and his committee did not, as the Admiral suggested, take a month to consider. A meeting was called immediately, and their decision was communicated by letter dated 26th July, signed by Mr. Duguid as preses. It was pointed out in that letter that the Admiral was already possessed of all the letters of any importance which the committee had, and no reference was made to the suggestion to appoint two trustees. With regard to the chief proposal, they were all decidedly of opinion that the iron rail should be repaired and kept up round about the churchyard, as formerly agreed upon. The letter closed with this somewhat stern, blunt, and no doubt characteristic paragraph—

"As you appear to wish to keep up friendly feelings with us, the committee desire me to say that those feelings are likeliest to last longest when each party shall fulfil all those duties and obligations which as moral and accountable beings rest upon us; therefore, we trust that you will go on with the necessary repair without delay."

So the public rights in the old churchyard were once more vindicated, and the "necessary repair" carried through.

XV.

Scott[6] in his references to the ministers of Carriden makes a note, that after the Reformation the charge was joined with Linlithgow and afterwards with Kinneil.

The first minister he refers to is Andrew Keir, A.M. As already mentioned, he was presented to Carriden—the old church beside Carriden House—in July, 1621, and remained there until his death in November, 1653, in the fifty-fifth year

---

[6] See Fasti.

of his age and the twenty-third of his ministry. Mr. Keir was clerk to the Presbytery in 1629 and for many years thereafter. He was a member of the General Assembly in 1638. Apparently he was translated to Linlithgow. The Assembly confirmed the translation, but the Presbytery declared it null, and he refused, on 31st December, 1641, to transport himself. For preaching for the Engagement in 1648 he was suspended. When he died a few years after, his executor raised a question regarding the stipend alleged as due; and in 1661 the Lords found that the suspension of the minister did not make the stipend vacant, and that the annat or ann needed no confirmation. His wife was Euffame Primrose, and they had three sons and three daughters.

Mr. Keir's successor was Robert Steedman, A.M., of Edinburgh University. He seems to have been made Mr. Keir's colleague and helper in July, 1646, probably at the time of his suspension. He was one of the protesting ministers of the Presbytery, and had to escape after the English entered the Lothians in 1651; he officiated for some time at Cleish; was loosed and deposed in August, 1661. Mr. Steedman then seems to have taken to field-preaching, for we find him denounced by the Privy Council in August, 1676, for keeping conventicles. After the toleration was granted he returned to Carriden, and once more became its minister, as we shall see.

The church evidently was without a minister for a time, for the next name is that of Mr. James Hamilton, A.M., of Edinburgh University. He was first of all schoolmaster at Colinton; was presented to Carriden in March, and ordained in April, 1663. A year after he was translated to Bedrule.

Mr. Hamilton's successor was Mr. John Pairk, an Episcopalian curate, already alluded to in our Covenanting chapter as the discoverer of Donald Cargill and others. He was licensed by the Bishop of Edinburgh, and ordained here on 9th June, 1665. For his behaviour towards the local Covenanters and their leaders he was much disliked. At the Revolution he held to his old opinions and doctrines, and was, in September, 1689, accused before the Privy Council of not reading the Proclamation of the Estates and not praying for William and Mary; he was further accused of baptising the children of scandalous persons without demanding satisfaction; and of praying that the walls of the Castle of Edinburgh might be as brass about George Duke of Gordon. He was acquitted by the Council, but having fallen into drunken and other evil habits he was deposed on 28th August, 1690. When he left, he carried off the parochial registers.

As we have said, Mr. Steedman returned here after the Declaration of Indulgence in 1687, and was chosen moderator of the Presbytery when it was constituted at Bo'ness on 30th November of that year. He was one of those restored by Act of Parliament in April, 1690. His death occurred in September, 1710, in his seventy-sixth year and the fifty-second of a very chequered ministerial career. Mrs. Steedman was a daughter of Sir Alexander Inglis, of Ingliston, and she survived her husband by ten years. Their son became one of the ministers of Edinburgh.

The next ordination at Carriden was that of Mr. John Tod, a Glasgow student, on 19th January, 1704, so that he appears to have been minister some years prior to Mr. Steedman's death. We know nothing further of Mr. Tod except that he died in January, 1720, and was survived by his widow. His marriage took place a few months after his settlement at Carriden, his bride being the relict of George Dundas, skipper, at Queensferry.

The parish seems to have been without a minister for the next five years, when Mr. Alexander Pyott, sometime schoolmaster of Benholme, and afterwards chaplain to the Marquis of Tweeddale, was settled here on 29th October, 1725. Eight years after he was translated to Dunbar. Things were not done hurriedly at Carriden, for another interval without a minister followed. However, in 1734 Mr. James Gair, who two years before had been licensed by the Presbytery of Zetland, was presented to the parish by James Duke of Hamilton. Mr. Gair was not ordained until September of the following year, and he was translated to Campvere in April, 1739.

The names to follow are not unfamiliar to Carriden people. The first is Mr. George Ellis, who in April, 1740, commenced his long ministry of fifty-five years. It was during his incumbency that the church and churchyard were removed from Carriden House and established at the village of Cuffabouts. He died in March, 1795, in his eighty-third year. Four years before, he had contributed the account of the parish which stands under his name in Sinclair's Statistical Account. It is very short. That, however, is not to be wondered at considering his great age, and it is much to the point. One of his brief observations is to the effect, that the living would have supported a family fifty years ago better than £120 sterling could do at the time he wrote. His wife, who was a Miss Alice Drummond, died in 1790; they had a daughter, Katherine.

On the death of Mr. Ellis the Duke presented Mr. John Bell, who was licensed by the Presbytery of Lanark in 1786, and who, it would appear, had not entered the ministry until he was middle-aged. He was ordained here on 21st January, 1796, and died unmarried on 14th December, 1815, in the seventieth year of his age and the twentieth of his ministry. It is recorded of him that he possessed the dispositions to charity and benevolence without ostentation, and that, though worn out by weakness and infirmity, he persevered without intermission in discharging his ministerial duties to the end. His tombstone in Carriden Churchyard bears the following words:—" Good and just in action, charitable in speaking of the character of others, and void of envy and detraction. Erected out of grateful remembrance of his worth by his nephews."

The last of the Carriden ministers in the period we are treating of was Mr. David Fleming, A.M., who was licensed by the Presbytery of Hamilton in June, 1813. He was presented here by Alexander Marquis of Douglas, and ordained on 22nd August, 1816. Mr. Fleming ministered at Carriden for forty-four years, dying there on 19th January, 1860.

James Duguid.
b. Little Carriden, 1796; d. Muirhouses, 1887.
(*From a photograph in possession of Mr. Wm. Duguid, Bo'ness.*)

See page 192.

XVI.

The parish includes other landowners than the proprietor of Carriden estate. Among them is Lord Linlithgow, who owns the farm of Burnshott. Fully three hundred of the acres of Binns estate also lie within it, including the farms of Champany and Cauldcots and parts of Mannerston. And on the east side of the Castlehill, Blackness, there is a strip of land known as Binns Beach.

Binns House itself lies in the parish of Abercorn. An irregular mass of building garnished with turrets and embrasures, it is beautifully placed on the western slope of Binns Hill. Built in 1623, it has been enlarged from time to time. The park around is highly picturesque, the grassy acclivities of the hill being interspersed with scattered trees and groups of evergreens. The policies are further adorned by two avenues and fine gardens. On the summit of the hill is a high, round tower forming a conspicuous landmark, and affording excellent views. It is said to have been erected to surmount the difficulty of seeing past the belt of trees to the eastward. The land in this part originally belonged to the Binns, but was sold to one of the Earls of Hopetoun.

Binns has been the residence of the family of Dalyell for upwards of three centuries. The famous general, Sir Thomas Dalyell, son of Thomas Dalyell, of Binns, was born in Abercorn Parish, but not, we think, in the present house.

In the dining-room of Binns House appears a portrait with the following inscription:—"Lieutenant-General Thomas Dalyell of Binns, a general in the Russian Service; Commander of the Forces in Scotland 1666 to 1685; raised a regiment of infantry 1666, and the Scots Greys in 1681."

The name of the foot regiment is apparently not known, nor can its place in the military lists be traced.

In the blue room is another portrait, and below is given the year of Dalyell's birth, 1599, and that of his death, 1685, together with the following note:—"After he had procured himself a lasting name in the wars, here it was" (evidently referring to Binns) "that he rested his old age, and pleased himself with the culture of curious flowers and plants."

There stands in the front hall an inlaid table of ivory, measuring five feet by three feet, at which Dalyell, so legend says, played cards with the devil. Another version is that the House of Binns was ransacked by Dalyell's enemies—and he must have had many—and all suitable furniture was carried off. The heavier furniture was said to have been consigned to the sergeant's pond, situated close to the house, from which the table was recovered many years later.

In one of the bedrooms the Royal arms appear over the fireplace, the King[7] having, it is said, passed one night at least at Binns. The ceiling of this room is very artistic, and bears, among others, the heads in plaster of King David and King Alexander. There is also a very handsome frieze. Other bedrooms also have richly decorated ceilings. This work is stated to have been executed by the Italian workmen engaged at the embellishment of Linlithgow Palace during the residence of Queen Mary.

Downstairs, in the south-east part of the building, is a dungeon-like apartment known as the oven where Dalyell baked the bread for the regiment of Scots Greys which he raised here. Not far from the oven is to be found the entrance to the underground passage which is said to have existed at one time between Binns House and Blackness.

The family vault erected in 1623 is attached to the Abercorn Church. The general died in Edinburgh, but there is no record of his place of sepulture so far as we have seen.

It has been written[8] of him that his private eccentricities furnished scope for the sarcastic pen of Swift in the memoirs of Captain Creighton, while his public history forms an important element in the narratives of the troubles of the Kirk of Scotland. Undaunted courage and blind, devoted fidelity to his Sovereign were conspicuous traits in his character. He was so much attached to Charles I. that, when the King was

---

[7] Possibly Charles II.
[8] See New Stat. A/c., vol. ii., Abercorn.

beheaded, Dalyell, to show his grief, never afterwards shaved his beard. At the battle of Worcester he was taken prisoner, committed to the Tower, and his estates forfeited. After the Restoration Charles II. restored his estates, appointed him Commander-in-chief of the Forces, and a Privy Councillor. On the accession of James VII. he received a new and enlarged commission, but died soon afterwards.

The comb with which Dalyell used to dress his wonderful beard is still preserved at Binns.

CHAPTER XI.

ECCLESIASTICAL.

1. First Parish Church: Description of Building: Dutch Pulpit: Geneva Bible and Beza's New Testament; Seating Accommodation—2. Ministers 1648-1746—3. Rev. Patrick Baillie: He and the Representatives Resist Captain John Ritchie: Rev. Dr. Rennie—4. Reminiscences of Dr. Rennie: The Rev. Kenneth Mackenzie: His Contribution to New Statistical Account—5. Extracts from the Benefice Lectures.—6. The Secession Church: No Original Secession Church here—7. The Anti-Burghers at Little Carriden: New Meeting House and Graveyard in Bo'ness—8. The Anti-Burghers and their Pastors—9. The Burghers: Their Building Troubles: Formation of United Associates 1820—10. Mr. Harper's Ministry: Succeeded by Mr. Connell: Managers in 1838: Session-Clerks: Secession and Relief Union: Captain Duncan's Bequests—11. Result of Disruption in 1843: Formation of Free Church Congregation: Erection of Church at Thirlestane: Mr. Irving's Labours: Mr. Dempster.

I.

MANY of the ministers of the church of Borrowstounness from its erection in 1636 to 1866 were men of outstanding merit in their day. In considering the earlier of these we must remember that, though the Papal Church in Scotland was abolished by Act of Parliament in 1560, and the doctrine of the Reformed Church formally recognised, Episcopacy, owing to the leanings of King James, also existed in a modified form for over thirty years. What happened after its supposed abolition on 5th June, 1592, we have already dealt with in our chapter on the Covenanters, but we recall that a modified form of Episcopacy was once more adopted, and this time with sanction, in 1618. Owing, therefore, to the ecclesiastical changes of those times, we find curious and, unless we remember our

history, somewhat puzzling things in Church affairs right on to
the Revolution. Some Presbyterians, while retaining their own
doctrine, seem to have consented to their Church being
governed after the method of Episcopacy. Hence the frequent
references to bishops. In other districts, however, Presbyterians
and Episcopalians kept apart, and certain ministers were to
be found who altogether refused to be ordained except by
Presbyterian ministers.

In our chapter on the Representatives, mention is made of
the circumstances attending the erection (1636-1638) of the
first Parish Church of Borrowstounness. It was originally built
only man-height, but in 1672, a year or two after Kinneil
Church was done away with, the Duke added a large aisle for
himself and his tenants. In this form it continued until 1776,
when, pursuant to an agreement between the town and the
Duke's Commissioners, the aisle was taken down and the
church almost entirely rebuilt in an oblong figure, sixty-nine feet
by forty-eight within the walls. This will probably account for
the presence of the Hamilton coat of arms, which can still be
seen in the centre of the north wall of the church. The walls
and ceiling were, we are told, handsomely "plaistered" and
ornamented, but the galleries were heavy and ill-constructed.

In 1820 the south wall and part of the east wall were rebuilt,
and the galleries reconstructed and made uniform. Mr.
M'Kenzie reminds us that the congregation possessed some
curious memorials of the frequent intercourse between Holland
and Bo'ness. The pulpit, for instance, came from there, and
was, he tells us, a curious specimen of ancient art and taste.
The oldest pulpit Bible was an Amsterdam edition of the
Geneva Bible reprinted from an Edinburgh edition of 1610,
having several of the usual maps and figurative illustrations;
and the New Testament was an English translation by L.
Tomson of Beza's version, clasped and ornamented with brass.
The pulpit is now in the new church, on Pan Brae Road, and
Bible and Testament are yet preserved.

The church, he continues, was seated for the accommodation
of nine hundred and fifty, but might have accommodated a

hundred more if the vacant spaces in the galleries were seated. The Duke of Hamilton had thirty pews, containing one hundred and sixty-nine seats, occupied by his tenants and by the colliers connected with his works. The Representatives let ten pews, containing eighty-eight seats; and forty-five pews, containing two hundred and seventy-nine seats, were private property, but paid an annual feu into the church funds. From £20 to £30 per annum was realised from these seats. There were forty-six pews, containing two hundred and seventy-four seats, which paid no feu, being the free property of private individuals; and fourteen pews, containing ninety-nine seats, were the property of the different societies, while some which were the property of private individuals were let at the will of the proprietors at rents varying from 1s. to 4s. per annum. These seats, as will be seen in another place, formed part of the funds of the church.

II.

When the church was opened the minister of Kinneil did duty in both places for about ten years. Bo'ness, therefore, had not a separate and distinct minister until 1648, when John Waughe, A.M., from Lanark, was ordained in the month of November and admitted. He was a student of Edinburgh University. The earlier records of the place contain, as has been seen, many references to Mr. Waughe, and go to show that he was a man of a vigorous mind. In the Presbytery he steadily opposed the "Protestors," and during the Commonwealth was imprisoned for naming the King in his prayers.[1] He married, apparently, as his second wife, Dame Christian Forrester, Lady Grange, widow of Sir James Hamilton of Grange. He demitted his charge in 1670, and would have been denounced with others in 1673 had he not gone to Ireland with his family. He died in Edinburgh, March, 1674, aged about fifty-five, and in the twenty-sixth year of his ministry.

The names of Robert Hunter, A.M., formerly of Dunning,

---

[1] See Scots Fasti.

and John Inglis, A.M., formerly of Hamilton, both appear in 1672 as having been successively in charge here. Presumably they were Episcopal incumbents. Certainly the next two were, for Mr. M'Kenzie says that during Episcopacy the induction of Mr. James Hamilton, in 1678, and also that of Mr. William Thomson, in 1685, are noted in the parish record.

Hamilton was a St. Andrews student, and obtained the degree of A.M. there in July, 1668. He was offered Dalserf in 1677, but he refused, and was afterwards admitted here. Two men were scourged shortly after for committing an assault on him. He died in February, 1685, in the seventh year of his ministry.

William Thomson, A.M., was translated here from Douglas in 1685 as his successor. We find he got into trouble with the Privy Council in 1689 for not reading the Proclamation of the Estates declaring William and Mary King and Queen of Scotland, and for not observing the thanksgiving appointed for 26th April preceding. But we doubt if these offences were committed here, for it looks as if he had been "rabbled out" of the living here in 1687.

On 30th November, 1687, the brethren of the Presbytery of Linlithgow met at Bo'ness, "and having called upon the name of God, they did constitute themselves in a Presbytery." This was probably the first of the regular meetings of the Presbytery after the liberty, and on 7th December they met again at Bo'ness "in order to the settling of Mr. Michael Potter to be minister unto the Presbyterian congregation of the Ness."[2]

Mr. Potter was a student at Edinburgh University, where he graduated A.M. in July, 1663. Before he was "settled" here he had much to suffer. In the early years of Charles II. he would have nothing to do with Episcopacy in any shape or form, refusing to go near a Presbytery which was Episcopalian at least in its form of government.

In 1673, however, he was licensed by the Presbyterian

---

[2] New Stat. A/c., vol. ii.

ministers and ordained by them soon after to the Parish of St. Ninians. We next hear of his election as schoolmaster of Culross by the magistrates of that place, for which action they were summoned before the Privy Council in 1677. He endured much persecution at the rumoured instigation of the Bishop of Dunblane, took refuge in Holland, was afterwards imprisoned in Edinburgh, and finally was carried to the Bass for preaching at conventicles. He was liberated on an Act of Banishment in March, 1685. On toleration being granted to the Presbyterians he joined in forming the Presbytery of Linlithgow, and was duly called here by them and admitted, on 7th December, 1687. Mr. Potter was a member of Assembly, in 1692, and was translated to Dunblane about the same year, having been called to Ecclesmachan also. His son was minister of Kippen, and afterwards became Professor of Divinity in the University of Glasgow.

Mr. Potter's successor, Mr. John Brand, A.M., also an Edinburgh student, does not appear to have been ordained here until 3rd January, 1694. In 1700 he was appointed by the General Assembly with some others to visit Zetland, and, if convenient, Orkney and Caithness. The visit took three months, and both in going and returning he experienced great danger and considerable fatigue. He afterwards published a description of Orkney, Zetland, and Caithness. Mr. Brand, in 1700, married one Elizabeth Mitchell, of the Parish of Canongate, and had a large family. He died in July, 1738, aged seventy, after a long ministry.

William Brand, A.M., who succeeded, was a son of the preceding, and, like his father, a student and graduate of Edinburgh University. He was licensed by the Presbytery in March, 1736; called here on 1st February, 1739; and ordained on 11th April, same year. He died seven years after in his thirty-sixth year.

III.

The next minister was Patrick Baillie (or Pat Baillie, as Jupiter Carlyle, one of his pupils, calls him in his

Autobiography). Carlyle tells us he "gained an ascendant" over him in Euclid, for Baillie had no mathematics and not much science of any kind. He, however, admits that Baillie was a very good Latin scholar, and so expert in the Greek that he taught Professor Drummond's class for a whole winter when the professor was ill. It was through Baillie that Carlyle and some other of Baillie's pupils managed to see the execution of the notorious Wilson in the Grassmarket, which gave rise to the Porteous riot. In describing the firing which that day took place by the Guard under Porteous, Carlyle tells of " one unfortunate lad whom we had displaced " being killed on the stair window by a slug entering his head. Baillie was appointed chaplain to Sir William Maxwell of Calderwood, and licensed by the Presbytery of Hamilton in 1738. He was called to Borrowstounness on 8th May, 1746, doubtless under the patronage of the Hamilton family, ordained on 14th May, 1747, and died on 11th September, 1791, in the forty-fifth year of his ministry. It was during Mr. Baillie's incumbency that the long and famous litigation, in which he and the representatives became involved, with Captain John Ritchie took place. It must have been a considerable trial to the minister. One great relief, at least, he had during that trying period, and that was the writing in 1763 of the biographical sketch of his late elder and friend, John Henderson, shipmaster, which is prefixed to the volume of Henderson's "Divine Meditations and Contemplations," afterwards referred to.

The long ministry of Mr. Baillie was followed by an extremely short one of two years. His successor was John Morton, who was licensed in March, 1781, by the Presbytery of Ayr, and presented here by the Duke[3] in February, 1792. He was ordained in May of the same year, and died in May, 1794.

We next come to the forty years' ministry of Dr. Robert Rennie. In his young days he had an academy at Dumbarton. In 1791 he was licensed by the Presbytery of Cupar, was presented here by the Duke Douglas in October, 1794, and

[3] Douglas, Duke of Hamilton.

ordained in April, 1795. Mr. Rennie had the degree of D.D. conferred on him by the University of Glasgow, in April, 1820. He died on 29th July, 1833, and lies buried near the south-west corner of the North Churchyard. The tombstone can be seen from the pavement on the Church Wynd. He married, in 1809, Jean, eldest daughter of Will Urquhart, Esq., merchant, Glasgow. She died in London in 1851. The family consisted of William, merchant, and John, writer, both in Glasgow. Dr. Rennie's name is not unknown even to the present generation. A few weeks after his settlement here he was called upon by Sir John Sinclair to contribute the Statistical Account of this parish. This he did with conspicuous ability, although handicapped by his very short residence in the district at the time. Throughout these pages we have quoted largely from the doctor's narrative, and the extracts are all of great interest. Like his predecessor, too, he was much in the law Courts with the Representatives, but did not leave off until he emerged triumphant in the House of Lords.

IV.

Mr. Adam Dawson, of Bonnytoun, in his "Rambling Recollections," printed for private circulation in 1868,[4] has several references to the doctor. The latter, he says, affected a fineness in speech and deportment little in keeping with a flock chiefly composed of the roughest mining human materials. In his day the Borrowstounness collier conceived that he had a vested right to a share of all the unprotected produce of the parish, from which even the territories of the manse were not exempted. Seeing one of these worthies helping himself to a portion of the beans growing in his glebe, Dr. Rennie remonstrated with the depredator on the subject. "If you will only wait," said he, "till the beans be ripe, I will give you a peck." "A peck," said the other, with an air of scorn; "go, lad, I'll no' tak' yer bow."

---

[4] Copy in possession of Mr. J. G. B. Henderson, W.S., Linlithgow.

Suffering under a dislocated joint, which baffled the skill of the surgeons, the doctor resorted to one Low at Dunfermline, at that time a celebrated bonesetter, who, it was said, restored the bone to its proper place. "And wha may ye be?" asked Low, after the operation was finished. "I am the Reverend Dr. Rennie, meenister of the Parish of Borrowstounness." "Ay, ay," said he of the bones, nothing daunted by the importance of the enunciation, "a minister wi' grey breeks!"

Yet Rennie was a stringent disciplinarian. It is said that at a periodical examination of the Grammar School of Linlithgow he reproved the rector so sharply in the presence of his pupils for some shortcoming which they had betrayed in the matter of the Catechism that it cost the burgh the services of an otherwise excellent teacher.

The Church Wynd when made went through a portion of the glebe. In the doctor's time a question arose as to the distinctive boundary of the glebe with a collier feuar on the Corbiehall side. The collier won his case, and the minister, it is said, had to pay the expenses out of his own pocket.

On Dr. Rennie's death, Alexander, tenth Duke, as the patron, gave the parishioners the choice of three gentlemen as his successor, namely, the Rev. Kenneth M'Kenzie, from Gorbals Chapel-of-Ease, a Mr. Jackson and a Mr. Campbell. Mr. Campbell, it is said, was profuse in his promises to give "cottar tatties," patches of ground on the glebe where his intended parishioners would be at liberty to cultivate their own little plot. Mr. Jackson was to do "something," he did not say what; while Mr. M'Kenzie made "no promises." Mr. M'Kenzie was elected by a large majority, Mr. Jackson only getting three votes. Mr. M'Kenzie came here in 1834. He was a Highlander and a bachelor. When he died his remains were taken to Glasgow for interment. There are still a number alive in the town who remember the ministry of Mr. M'Kenzie. He preached with black cotton gloves on, in the old style, and was said to be a somewhat dry expositor. He was an antiquarian of considerable acquirements, and his history of the parish as contributed to the New Statistical Account, which we have repeatedly referred to in these pages, is excellent proof of his learning and industry.

V.

In the "Benefice Lectures,"[5] we find the following reference to the Church records of the Parish of Bo'ness:—

I. Records in seven volumes—
    (1) 2nd August, 1694, to 11th July, 1712.
    (2) 15th July, 1712, to 20th August, 1731.
    (3) 27th July, 1742, to 13th March, 1766.
    (4) March, 1766, to March, 1808.
    (5) March, 1808, to January, 1859.
    (6) 7th July, 1867, to 22nd January, 1892.
    (7) 28th March, 1892, to date (1905).

II. Blanks—20th August, 1731, to 27th July, 1742; January, 1859, to 7th July, 1867. This volume entirely awanting. Nothing known of it.

III. All bound in good condition.

In the "Lectures" there is the following concerning the Bo'ness glebe:—

"During the troublous times prior to the Revolution, in 1688, and owing to the annexation of parishes, acres of rich arable and valuable feuing land were lost to the Church. When vacancies in a charge occurred the Church was quietly dispossessed of lands, and, because no claim had been urged for their restitution within the forty subsequent years, these are now beyond the power of recovery.

"A noticeable illustration of this was recently discovered in the case of Bo'ness. The designing of the glebe and its boundaries, as fixed by the Presbytery on the 22nd January, 1650, are clear and explicit. The glebe as thus designed has from time to time been much encroached upon in various ways.

---

[5] By the Rev. Thomas Burns, D.D., Edinburgh, 1905.

The Rev. Kenneth M'Kenzie, Minister of Bo'ness, 1834-1867.
(From a photograph in possession of Mr. John Steele, Bo'ness.)

In particular, while the north boundary is stated to be the sea, the Duke of Hamilton, the only heritor, has gradually taken possession of glebe land along the whole length of the sea boundary, leasing and fencing it as his own, and claiming its minerals. The effect of this is that the present portion of glebe is shut off from the surface of the foreshore, if not also from the minerals. This is a typical instance of the losses the church has sustained. The church of the present day is much the poorer through the depredations of interested parties in years gone by. Now, why was this allowed to take place? In the days of patronage there was a strong temptation on the part of the minister to say nothing when the party responsible for the alienation of Church property happened to be the patron of the living. Indebted to him for promotion, the minister, forgetful of his duty as trustee of the church, was hindered by a sense of personal friendship from resisting insidious encroachments or from seeking the just restoration to the church of the glebe land which by designation in bygone days had belonged to the benefice. Then, as now, encroachments have been made on glebes by the making of new roads and the straightening of fences, oftentimes without protest. And even when protests were made the reply generally given was that the portions shaved off were very small, and nothing of the kind would happen again. But, unfortunately for the church, such encroachments have been frequent, and still continue."

We are not in a position to discuss the complaint we have just quoted, and all we can say is that, if "shaving," and even more than shaving, has taken place on the Bo'ness glebe, a considerable portion of what is left is now well feued, and yields a goodly return.

VI.

Early in the eighteenth century "Dissent" imposed itself, and not without good effect, on the whole on Scottish ecclesiastical life.

The reasons which led up to the "Secession" and the formation of a new body by the Rev. Ebenezer Erskine in December, 1733, were mainly two, viz., the "Marrow" controversy and disputes occasioned by patronage.

There was no congregation here of the Original Secession Church, but there did exist a small body of Cameronians, a thing not to be wondered at in a town where, a century before, the Covenanting spirit had been so prevalent. One of the earliest Seceding churches in Scotland was opened in 1738 at Craigmailing, a few miles south from Linlithgow. For years it served a wide district, stretching from Bo'ness to West Calder, and from Bathgate to Kirkliston. There are now in this same area several churches which claim Craigmailing as their mother. Craigmailen United Free Church in this town is one of these.

The Burgher and Anti-Burgher bodies, which broke up the unity of the Secession in 1747, drew many adherents around them in Bo'ness. The former were attached to the same body at Linlithgow, and had not a meeting-place here until 1795. The latter, however, established themselves first of all in a barn at Little Carriden in September, 1762. Two years later they removed to Bo'ness, having acquired a small property there from the Sea Box, which they made suitable for their purposes. This came to be known as the Easter Meeting-house, and was situated on the site of the present Charlotte Place. Its yard on the north side was used as their burying-ground, and until very recently some tombstones were to be seen there. Two of the parties interred were James Paterson and John Drummond.

VII.

Here are some extracts from the Anti-Burgher minute-book concerning the fitting up of this place and the making of the burying-ground.

The first minute records a meeting at Little Carriden on 23rd September, 1762, "consisting of a part of the united congregation in and about Bo'ness, disjoined from the associate congregation of Craigmealling." Alexander Lang, merchant, was elected preses, and David Christie, surgeon, clerk. Andrew Graham (who was factor to the Hon. Colonel Campbell-Dalrymple of Carriden), John Paris, merchant, and the said Alex. Lang, all elders, were appointed "to speak with Mr. John Ritchie in order to purchase from the Sailors' Box of Bo'ness, whereof he is master, that old house commonly called the Meeting-house."

It was necessary both to collect and spend money for this, so we find an entry under 23rd July, 1763; "Appoints James Marshal to keep the Box as Cashier, to take in the money offered thereto by the Publick, and to expend the same in paying ministers for preaching, and the charges in building the Meeting-house; also David Buchanan and John Cathcart to be key-keepers for the ensuing year, when a committee shall inspect the accompts of said Boxmaster and Keykeepers."

In October following, and still at Little Carriden, it was resolved that the new Meeting-house in course of completion in Bo'ness should be "regulated" as follows:—"The Communion tables to be fixed in the middle of the house 4 feet in breadth. The West end of the house to be seated by Bo'ness people, and the East by those of Carriden, and each party is to put the Communion table in their own end at their own expense. John Paris, Alex. Low, John Cathcart, and Thomas Boyd to apply to the proprietor of the Barn for either taking it off our hands or sufficiently repairing it that it may not be in ruins before we leave it." Money was evidently badly needed in connection with the new place, as in November it is minuted, "The collectors are desired to be very assiduous in gathering in the quotas with speed."

After removal to the new Meeting-house we find the congregation exercised about the use to which the yard to the north might be put. At a meeting on 24th December, 1765, "A vote, after some reasoning, was stated if any burial shall be allowed in this Meeting-house or not, and it was carried in the negative by a great majority." And on 2nd May following we read, "The Meeting agree that the inclosed ground or yard at the back of the Meeting-house be sown with barley and grass seeds for this year till they see how they are to employ it afterwards." By 13th June feeling about it had changed, for we find "It was by a majority of votes agreed that it be used as a burying-place, it being thought to promise most advantage to the congregation in that way. John Paris is appointed to dispose of the grass, &c., that shall be on the yard this year, and give in the money to the congregation."

The following is from a "Sketch of Directions" for the managers regarding the graveyard:—

"A Burial-place, consisting of three layers, or seven foot square, is agreed to be sold for ten shillings, and one layer at five shillings. Every person burying an adult to pay 1/6, a shilling whereof goes to the gravedigger and sixpence to the congregation. And for children 1/2, whereof the gravedigger shall have 8 pence and the congregation 6 pence."

Three years after this it was agreed that a book be given to the clerk and kept by him as a register of the burial-yard describing the length and breadth of the yard; also to have the congregation's decision concerning it recorded therein containing the length, breadth, and price of each burial-place, and the purchaser's name and place in the yard, and of the dues of burials therein, likewise of the money paid, both purchase price and dues.

The minutes, so far as we have observed, contain copies of at least two conveyances of layers. The first, dated 8th June, 1772, is to Ebenezer Thomson, shoemaker, in Borrowstounness. The price paid was 10s., and the ground 7 feet in length, and the same in breadth. The boundaries and situation of the burying-place conveyed are carefully detailed. The next conveyance is to John Paris, who is designed as "Elder in the Associate Congregation of Borrowstounness." It is in the same terms as the other, only the situation of the ground is different.

VIII.

The Anti-Burghers were here some years before they were able to afford a permanent pastor. At Carriden they craved the Associate Presbytery of Edinburgh for "as much supply of sermon that Court can possibly give in conjunction with other vacant congregations; and also the dyet of an actual minister to keep a fast and constitute the Session."

In May, 1765, the members were very anxious to secure the Rev. Richard Jermont, Earlstoun, as their first pastor. They appointed four commissioners to present their petition "and deal warmly with the Presbytery to sustain the call." The Synod, however, did not thing proper to "transport" Mr. Jermont. This was an unfortunate rebuff. A goodly number of probationers preached on trial after this, but no decision was arrived at. Perhaps the members were difficult to please. Whether or not it is clear they were sorely tried at this critical time, as the following extract of 25th November, 1765, shows:—"The Preses, by unanimous consent, enjoyned the whole members of the congregation to set some time apart for supplicating the Throne of Grace for Light and Direction in our present situation that we jointly seek the Lord's Countenance before proceeding to the momentous affair before our hand, vizt., the choice of a pastor."

At last a selection was made, and on 13th August, 1766, the Rev. Thomas Clelland was ordained first minister of the congregation. A minute in July discloses the preparations made for the happy event—"Appoints David Aiken to make a tent against the thirteen day of August, and make it five foot long and four foot wide, and appoints that John Black and John Paris shall provide a scaffold against the ordination, and the tent to stand befor the meeting-house; and the ministers at said ordination to be accomidated by Alex. Lang at the congregation expense."

The tent was really an open-air pulpit and the scaffold a raised platform. Evidently such a large turnout was expected that it was necessary to arrange for the services being held outside instead of inside the meeting-house.

The difficulty of maintaining Mr. Clelland was great, and the minutes during his pastorate reveal many meetings to consider means of making up deficiencies in his stipend. His salary was £40, and although a motion was made to allow £2 more, it "was negatived as impracticable in our present circumstances." Later, "the friendly assistance of the Synod in sending £6 and of the congregation of Denny in giving £6 10s. is gratefully recorded." In August, 1794, pastor and people came to the parting of their ways. We then find this, "The meeting appoint two of their number to wait on our pastor and inform him it would be better for him to demitt than for them to make an application to the Presbytery." When interviewed, however, Mr. Clelland told the deputation "he would lay the state of the congregation before the Presbytery himself without any new representation or petition." In November the Presbytery dissolved his pastoral relations, and at a congregational meeting held thereafter it was agreed that the ministers coming here to afford supply "should be lodged with these members who had the best conveniency for that purpose."

A fixed ministry was not again established for five years, and even then the difficulty in meeting the stipend owing to "the smallness of the numbers who contributed" was very considerable.

At a meeting in June, 1804, we observe that Mr. Carmichael, the new minister, requested the congregation to inform him "at their conveniency whether he might have reason to expect from them the payment of a house rent, say, £5, as asked by him at Whitsunday last year." It is minuted they would have no objections to add £5 or £10 annually more, "but ay and while they were in arrear of stipend (as at present nearly £10) they consider it as impracticable." A year after this Mr. Carmichael intimated that "thro' bodily indisposition he judged it necessary to give in to the first meeting of Presbytery his Demission, and that the congregation should provide accordingly." This minister apparently gave the members much satisfaction, and their conduct towards him at this unfortunate juncture was kindly. We read, "A committee waited on Mr. Carmichael to propose to him to take a voyage for his health, and that the congregation would meantime look out for supply from some of the brethren in the Presbytery, provided he would not give up his charge, but this he absolutely refused." A subscription was then opened for raising a sum of money for him, and this resulted in the sum of twenty guineas being handed him as a donation.

Two more years passed without a pastor. In the meanwhile an effort was being made to raise the stipend to at least £70 per annum, with £5 in name of house rent. This seems strange when we remember their difficulties in raising a smaller stipend. Selection was made in the beginning of 1808 of a Mr. James Thomson, probationer, as minister. A minute relating to his ordination arrangements records, "A proposal was made to open a subscription for defraying the expense of a suit of clothes for Mr. James Thomson." It is not stated whether this proposal was agreed to or not. If it was, no doubt the clerical suit would be given as an act of courtesy and welcome, just as in modern days pulpit robes are presented. We grant that at first sight the circumstances seemed to signify that the young minister was in a state of want. On reflection, however, we have abandoned that idea.

Mr. Thomson was their last pastor. He remained until February, 1812, when he petitioned the Presbytery to be loosed from his charge. The congregation by that time was in a very poor state numerically. Only three minutes appear in the minute-book after this, and from these we gather that some arrangement for sermon was made with the Anti-Burghers of Linlithgow. The charge, anyhow, remained vacant, and the congregation, a mere shadow of its former self, struggled on in a perfunctory way until the amalgamation in 1820.

There is little else to note about the Anti-Burghers, save to show how they dealt with seat-rent defaulters, and built their session-house. As for the first, several people were reported to be "long deficient in their seat rents." It was therefore agreed that every member capable of paying "shall be dealt with in as sharp but prudent a way as possible; and if that will not do, they to be laid before the congregational meeting."

The matter of the session-house emerged after the settlement of the first minister. Frequent meetings were held, and in March, 1769, the congregation having again taken into consideration "the necessity of having a session-house built, agreed by a great majority that one be built at the north-east side of the meeting-house, close to the back thereof, and that the charges thereof be defrayed by a private collection." But the building did not go on for more than a year after that. In June, 1770, the motion was repeated, and again carried, a number of collectors being appointed to collect funds. Five members were also nominated "to be managers of the building, and orders them to get it begun immediately, and with all possible speed get it finished."

The following, some for shorter, others for longer periods, acted as chairmen of the congregation between 1762 and 1812:—Alex. Lang, James Simson, John Paris, John Cathcart, John Jack, James Walker, John Graham, James Ferguson, William Johnston, George Dick, John Anderson (Kinneil Mills), Robert Henderson, Matthew Foord, Andrew Smith, and John Miller.

IX.

Let us now glance at the history of the local Burgher congregation. Although handicapped for many years by the want of a meeting-place in Bo'ness, the Burghers were particularly vigorous, and contained among their members some of the most prominent citizens of that time. In the strong-box of Craigmailen session there is no more interesting document than that which indicates the settlement here of the Burgher congregation. This is a roll-petition of about two yards in length containing over two hundred signatures. The petition itself is short. It is addressed to the Moderator and members of the Associate (or Burgher) session at Linlithgow, and is dated 9th April, 1794. It narrates that the petitioners are members of the Associate congregation of Linlithgow residing in and about Bo'ness; refers to the clamant condition of the place for want of a pure dispensation of the Gospel with which they could join; mentions that numbers of the old, infirm, and young could not attend regularly at Linlithgow, even in the summer, far less in the winter season, considering the badness of the roads; states that they are able to maintain the Gospel by themselves as a distinct congregation, judging from the numbers which had attended the occasional sermons here; and concludes with a crave for disjunction. Annexed to the petition is a docquet by which the petitioners appointed James Morton, Alex. Steell, James Paterson, Eben. Thomson, Robert Brown, James Shaw, William Henderson, Robert Arkley, George Henderson, James Meikle, and Archibald Hardie, their commissioners, or any two or more of them, to present the petition and prosecute the end thereof. This is signed "Alex. Steell, Preses."

A perusal of the two hundred signatures is illuminating. Many of the old Bo'ness surnames appear—Bairds, Browns, Bells, Boags, Gibbs, Hardies, Hendersons, Heggies, Kidds, Marshalls, Meikles, Robertsons, Rennies, Steuarts, Snaddons, Starks, Shaws, and Thomsons; also such family names, to take a few only, still common in the town, as Marget Allen, Isbell Buchan, Margaret Buchanan, Archibald Ballantine, William Baird, Andrew Bennie, Margret Bell, John Brown, William Brown, Robert Brown, Margret Culbreath (now Galbraith), Robert Dalrymple, David Duncon, Jean Drysdelle, James Deas, Richard Grant, John Grant, Eliza Grindlay, John Hamilton, Betty Hamilton, Richard Lumsden, John Marshall, Robert Mitchell, James Miller, John M'Intosh, John Paris, Charles Robertson, John Robertson, John Snaddon, Jean Smith, Katren Stevens, Ann Stewart, John Thomson, and Janet Turnbull. The disjunction craved was granted in due course.

Strong in numbers, with men of activity and business capacity among its members, the newly constituted Burgher congregation appears to have been launched in smooth waters.

Its members may have been enthusiastic and numerous, but their minutes are meagre. The first minute is dated 20th September, 1795, and it is there recorded that the Rev. Michael Garfillan (Gilfillan), Presbytery clerk, ordained James Morton and Henry Stark to the eldership in the forenoon. In the interval of public worship the session was constituted, when, besides the newly-ordained elders, there were present Ebenezer Thomson and James Buchan, who seem to have been elders before. Thomson at any rate had been an Anti-Burgher, but appears to have changed. Buchan was chosen session-clerk. We find nothing of the circumstances attending the choice or appointment of Mr. Harper. There is simply a bald minute, dated 24th August, 1796, which runs—"Which day the Rev. Archibald Harper having been solemnly set apairt to the office of the holy ministry in this congregation, the session met and was constituted by the Rev. Mr. Belfrage."

Brevity was a strong point with Mr. Buchan, for in recording another session meeting on 30th August he simply says—"Being constitute, all members present, spent some time praise and prayer, agreed to meet ordinarily on the first Tuesday of every month, closed with prayer."

The winds and seas very soon arose and raged with great violence for years round the little barque of the Burghers. The situation, however, was faced courageously, and in the long run successfully. All the troubles arose over the erection of the new meeting-house (now St. Mary's Hall). Nisbet, mason, Edinburgh, had the building contract, and from start to finish he gave the greatest annoyance. The building adjoined the northern boundary of the parish minister's glebe, and Nisbet in his operations not only put his materials on the glebe lands, but without permission made a road through them from the north to the south. Just as the foundations were being laid the Rev. Robert Rennie, the parish minister, raised—and no doubt with reason—an action of interdict in the Court of Session against the managers. Fortunately parties met at once and adjusted their differences, and so the first obstacle was removed.

Under the contract with Nisbet the new premises were to be ready for occupancy in August, 1796, but even in the end of September the building was hopelessly incomplete, although he had been paid most of the contract price. The managers were therefore forced to apply to the Sheriff for authority to finish the work themselves at the contractor's expense. This had the effect of making the defaulting tradesman bring the building to a speedy completion. But now came the greatest annoyance of all. Nisbet rendered a large account for extras. Payment was refused, and in 1798 he raised an action for payment in the Court of Session, before Lord Meadowbank. The case was fought by the Congregational Committee, consisting of William Henderson, merchant; Archibald Hardie, baker; James Buchan, merchant; and James Morton, smith. It is of peculiar interest to observe from the papers in the case that the advocate employed for the committee was Francis Jeffrey, afterwards famous as the editor of the *Edinburgh Review*, and latterly raised to the bench as Lord Jeffrey. He was then a young man of twenty-six, and had only been two years at the bar. The case dragged on until the spring of 1799. We have not seen the final judgment—if there was such a thing. But in the preceding July his lordship, in one of his interlocutors, wished the parties "would return to their original dispositions to behave properly and liberally to each other," so that we assume the matter was ultimately compromised by the parties themselves.

In September, 1820, amid much rejoicing in Edinburgh, the Burghers and Anti-Burghers strengthened themselves by a judicious union under the designation of the United Associate Synod. Under this arrangement the provincial bodies, of course, did likewise. So, in December of that year, we find that the whole of the elders of the Anti-Burgher congregation here gave in their accession to Mr. Harper's congregation. The affiliated elders were George Dick, Alexander Aitken, William Duguid, and William Johnston. In the following February the sacrament of the Lord's Supper was dispensed in Mr. Harper's church, when nearly all the former members of the

Anti-Burgher congregation residing in this quarter who had not previously joined Mr. Harper's congregation also gave in their accession. The two congregations were thus united, assembling together for public worship in one place, under the pastoral charge of the same minister, and under the title of the United Associate Congregation.

X.

This was the chief event in the thirty-eight years' ministry of Mr. Harper, if we except the troublesome litigations already referred to. There was some little business trouble, too, in 1832. That year Mr. William Henderson, who had for long acted most zealously as session-clerk, entered into a lengthy correspondence with Mr. Andrew Allan, teacher, Linlithgow, respecting the Easter Meeting-house. The Linlithgow congregation somehow claimed the property, but Mr. Henderson stoutly maintained that both the Anti-Burgher and Burgher Meeting-houses belonged entirely to the United Associate Congregation. Ultimately the Presbytery appears to have taken the matter up, and decided that, when sold, the proceeds were to be divided between Mr. Harper's congregation and the East congregation, Linlithgow. The disputed property was, however, let for fifty-eight years to Messrs. James Shaw, Robert Syme, and James Jamieson. Towards the expiry of that term it was sold, and the present Charlotte Place built upon the site. How the proceeds were disposed of does not appear to be recorded.

Mr. Harper fell into feeble health in the autumn of 1833. In the following February the session agreed, at the request of the Synod, to set apart a certain evening for uniting in prayer to God for the conversion of the world. The minute also states —"An additional reason for engaging in that exercise is the present state of this congregation, our respected pastor being in affliction and having for some time past been unable to perform any ministerial duty." In March it was agreed to apply to the Presbytery for a helper and successor, and also to acquaint Mr. Harper with the views and wishes of the session. The Presbytery then granted moderation in a call for an assistant and successor. Mr. Harper, however, unfortunately died on 5th April, and just on the eve of the election of the Rev. George Hill, late of Warrington. Nevertheless the congregation proceeded to carry out their arrangements, and on the 8th April met and unanimously chose Mr. Hill as Mr. Harper's successor. A call was thereupon made out and signed by sixty-two persons. The Presbytery sustained the call, but Mr. Hill declined, "having received a call from Musselburgh, which he prefers."

Mr. Harper's long connection with Bo'ness is perpetuated to this day. His residence was situated at the back of what is now the Union Bank Buildings in South Street, and the place is still known as Harper's Court.

After Mr. Hill's declinature, further procedure was taken. This resulted in a call to Mr. David Connel, preacher of the Gospel, and his ordination took place on the 13th of January, 1835. His ministry, like that of his predecessor, was comparatively quiet and uneventful, and, curiously enough, it lasted for the like period of thirty-eight years.

Mr. Connel's congregation had a body of managers as well as a session, and the following extract from a congregational meeting held on 28th May, 1838, gives an indication of those in charge of its temporal affairs at that period. Mr. Henry Hardie presided, and the following were appointed managers:— Wm. Henderson, Henry Hardie, John Anderson, James Meikle, George Paterson, Robert Thomson, Wm. Marshall, Andrew Robertson, John Marshall, James Shaw (sen.), James Duncan, James Syme, John Paris, John Hardie, Robert Syme, James Stewart, George Henderson, and James Paterson; Mr. Wm. Henderson, treasurer and convener. The meeting also appointed the following as trustees, viz.:—Messrs. John Anderson, John Hardie, James Meikle, Henry Hardie, Andrew Robertson, Wm. Marshall, John Marshall, James Paterson, George Henderson, and James Shaw, tertius. The meeting authorised Messrs. Wm. Henderson and John Anderson to get legal titles made up to the present church, and also to the Easter Meeting-house, and to do so without delay.

Mr. Wm. Henderson continued to act as session clerk in Mr. Connel's time until the spring of 1844, when he was removed by death. The session minuted the regret which they felt at his death and their gratitude for his long and excellent services, at the same time appointing Mr. James Meikle as his successor. Mr. Meikle had just a few weeks before been "solemnly set apart by prayer and the laying on of the hands of the session to the office of the eldership." He continued to act as session clerk until his death, which occurred suddenly on 5th January, 1853. Mr. Connel himself then acted as interim clerk until October of the following year, when Mr. George Henderson was selected to succeed Mr. Meikle.

In May, 1847, the United, Secession, and Relief Synods met as one in Canonmills, Edinburgh, and assumed the name of the United Presbyterian Church. This was during Mr. Connel's ministry, but we have not observed any notice of the event in the session minutes. There was, of course, no local Relief Church, and therefore no local union, so that might account for the omission.

A session minute of 9th June, 1847, records that James Duncan, an aged member of session, having died since last meeting, they record their sorrow at being deprived of so faithful and useful a fellow-labourer, and express their gratitude to the Head of the Church for having spared him so long among them. It was at this same meeting agreed to record in the minutes certain documents containing two bequests by Mr. Duncan, who was therein designed some time master, afterwards retired commander, R.N. The first was of the sum of £10, which was to be applied towards liquidating the debt affecting the church. The other amounted to £100 sterling, free of duty. It was to be invested by the session, and the interest or proceeds were to be distributed amongst the poor of the church.

XI.

It is unnecessary to recapitulate here the ecclesiastical movements in the Church of Scotland which resulted in the Disruption of 1843 and the formation of the Free Church of Scotland. At that time the Rev. Kenneth MacKenzie was minister of Bo'ness and the Rev. David Fleming minister of Carriden. Both have been described as Moderates of the easy-going type, and as having remained in their comfortable manses to enjoy their easily earned loaves and fishes in peace and safety. Whether their qualities as easy-goers weighed with them or not in their decision we know not, but it is true they did not "come out." Many of the people of both congregations, however, felt it their duty to separate themselves from the Establishment and go into the wilderness with the new body. These people met for divine worship that summer in a yard on the foreshore, used in connection with Mr. Roy's sawmill at the Links. Here, in dry weather, they had the big logs for seats and the blue heavens for roof-tree. In a few months other quarters were found. These were situated in the "Old Barns," in Grangepans, to the east side of Man-o'-war Street, and long since demolished.

To the help of these worthy people came the Rev. Lewis H. Irving, who for conscience' sake had just left his church and manse in the neighbouring Parish of Abercorn. He never became the regular minister of this congregation, but he was instrumental in raising it at first, and superintended its work until a permanent pastor was appointed. Mr. Irving was a man of aristocratic bearing and connections, and his history of the Parish of Abercorn, contributed to the New Statistical Account of Scotland on the eve of his leaving it, still furnishes us with an excellent reflex of his mental qualities and capabilities. He ultimately settled in Falkirk, and devoted his talents and energy to the organisation of the Free Church in this county. Mr. Irving had a taste for drawing and architecture, and this faculty he turned to advantage in drawing plans and making specifications for churches and manses all over the land. The local Free Church Manse is one of the many which he designed, and all his work was done gratuitously. As a preacher he is said to have been a muscular Christian, who at times became vehemently and most alarmingly eloquent. He could speak for an hour on end without notes, and one old Grangepans lady has left her testimony that "she could ha'e sat the hale blessed day and listened to him."

Not until the beginning of 1844 were elders and deacons appointed by the newly formed congregation, and steps taken to build a church. A site was obtained from the Duke of Hamilton—but only on a one-hundred-years lease—at the east end of the Links, and just at the western side of the boundary line between the Parish of Bo'ness and that of Carriden. The new church was neat and commodious. It was not costly, as buildings run nowadays, the total sum spent on its erection being £365 17s. 2d. From time to time, however, during the next sixty-two years it was enlarged, and otherwise much improved.

The foundation-stone of this church was laid on the 20th of August, 1844. Members and their friends walked in procession from their temporary premises in Grangepans to the site at Boundary Street. Here Captain James Hope of Carriden (afterwards Admiral Sir James) delivered an appropriate speech to the audience, and one who heard it has said that the Captain very characteristically expressed himself in nautical language, wishing that they would have a long pull, a strong pull, and a pull altogether.

Beneath the foundation-stone, in a leaden case, were placed copies of the Act of Separation and Deed of Demission, protest by the ministers and elders, copies of the *Witness*, the *Scottish Herald*, and the Edinburgh *Weekly Register*, an almanac, and a list of the office-bearers and managers of the congregation. The stone was then laid by the Captain with Masonic honours. Mr. Irving, as was natural, took a prominent part in the proceedings. He followed the stone-laying with a most impressive speech, and closed the proceedings by fervently imploring the Almighty's benediction on the business of the day.

The first minister of this church was Mr. Alex. P. Dempster. He is said to have been a delicate young man, but possessed good abilities. His ministry lasted for ten years, his death occurring in June, 1854. His successor was Mr. Daniel Wilson, who laboured here with great acceptance for thirty years.

CHAPTER XII.

THE "TRUSTEES FOR THE TWO PENNIES IN THE PINT."

1. The Act of 1744: The first Harbour and Municipal Board: Names of Trustees: Their Powers—2. The first Minute-Book and its Index: The "Overseers" and their Duties—3. Appointment of Officials: Harbour Improvements: Contentions with Local Brewers Begin—4. Trustees Become Alarmed: the Military Sent for: A New and Zealous Officer: "Cask and All"—5. John Henderson, "Shoremaster": Purchase of Boat: Frequent Damage to Piers—6. Brewers' Appeal to Justices: Attempted Compromises—7. Dr. John Roebuck Becomes a Trustee: An Important Letter from Him—8. M'Laren's Law Plea—9. A Diplomatic Move and a Long Letter—10. The Greenland Whale Fishing: The "Peggy" Causes Trouble: A "Scene" at a Meeting—11. Trustees Arrange for Renewal of Act: Additional Powers Wanted—12. Petition to Parliament: The Duke's Tutors Recommend Inclusion of Powers Concerning the "Streets and Avenues."

I.

THE 8th day of May, 1744, saw the beginning of municipal government in Borrowstounness. For some considerable time prior to this the trade of the harbour had increased so much and the burden of its upkeep, which had apparently been borne privately,[1] had become so heavy that the shipmasters and merchants of the port had to seriously deliberate on what course was to be followed for the future. They ultimately decided to apply to Parliament, and received, after a good deal of trouble and anxiety, an Act in the fifteenth year of the reign of George the Second. Under the Act James Main, James Cassels, William Muir, David Stevenson, George Adam, Duncan

[1] Duke William and Duchess Anne in their day obtained power to make a similar levy, but we have seen no evidence of its exaction. The merchants and shipmasters would seem to have themselves contributed.

Facsimile of front page of the first Minute-Book of the "Trustees for the
Two Pennies" containing Minute of Acceptance of Office
by the Trustees and their Signatures.

Glasfurd, Thomas Grindlay, James Glasfurd, and John Drummond, shipmasters; Andrew Cowan, James Tod, Charles Addison, William Shead, John Pearson, and John Walker, merchants, were appointed trustees, and power was given to them to impose " a duty of two pennies Scots, or one-sixth part of a penny sterling (over and above the duty of Excise), upon every pint of ale and beer which should be brewed for sale, brought in, tapped, or sold within the town of Borrowstounness and liberties thereof, in the county of Linlithgow, for the clearing, deepening, rebuilding, repairing, and improving the harbour and piers of Borrowstounness, and also for putting in execution all other the powers given in said Act." The duty was declared to be leviable from the 1st day of June, 1744, and for the term of twenty-five years thereafter. The preamble to the Act narrates that the town was very well situated for carrying on foreign and coasting trade for the benefit of the country thereabouts, and of the town of Borrowstounness in particular, there being many coal and salt works very near to the town. These advantages, it continues, could not be obtained unless the harbour, which was then in a very bad and ruinous condition, were effectually repaired and made commodious. This would require a very considerable sum of money, and the town had no revenues to answer the expense. The inhabitants therefore humbly craved His Majesty to give them authority to levy this imposition or duty. As we have just seen, the request was granted.

This power was renewed by Parliament for other twenty-five years in 1769, and extended with some enlargement of powers over the parish; and the renewal took place again in 1794 for twenty-one years, also with enlarged powers, including the right to exact an anchorage duty of a penny-halfpenny per ton on every ship entering the harbour. We shall deal more fully with these renewals later. Most fortunately the minutes of the trustees have all been preserved. They have been composed and written with the greatest care; the sederunts are all numbered, and each minute-book contains a copious index, so that even to this day it is much easier to find whatever is wanted than in modern minute-books which have no indices at all.

To most of our townspeople, and even, we think, to many of our City Fathers, the existence of these interesting old minutes is unknown.

II.

The first minute-book covers from 8th May, 1744, to 10th August, 1787, a period of forty-three years—the whole of the twenty-five years of the first Act, and nearly the whole of the time of the second Act. The index runs to twelve closely written pages, and is a first-class synopsis of the contents of the volume. Indeed, were it not that the space required cannot be given in our present narrative, we should have reproduced it in full, with some annotations under each entry. Suitable annotations would in effect and with little trouble change its primary character from pure index to useful narrative, and yet every word of the wonderful synopsis would be retained. During the forty-three years embraced in minute-book No. 1 there were 329 sederunts, including not only general meetings of the whole trustees, but of the overseers or county gentlemen appointed under the Acts, and of the Shore, Streets, Water, and other special Committees that were from time to time appointed. Copies of certain mortgages for loans advanced, with various agreements and contracts also appear in the book. There were considerable changes among the trustees as time went on owing to deaths and resignations, but the vacancies were duly filled up after the procedure prescribed by the Act in such cases had been followed. The rule was, that notice of the time and place of meeting for the election of such new trustees should be fixed at or on the Market Cross and on the outside of the church door of the town at least ten days before the meeting.

The 1774 Act, it should be mentioned, consisted of fifteen sections, and nominated certain county gentlemen as "overseers." The duty of these overseers, of whom three made a quorum, was to meet at Borrowstounness on the first

Wednesday in June, 1745, and yearly thereafter, to examine the receipts and disbursements connected with the duty.

The overseers named in the first Act were the Most Noble James Duke of Hamilton and Brandon, the Right Honourable David Earl of Buchan, the Right Honourable John Earl of Stair, the Right Honourable John Earl of Hopetoun, the Right Honourable David Lord Cardross, the Right Honourable Lord Torphichen, the Right Honourable Lord Archibald Hamilton, the Honourable Charles Hope Weir-Hall of Craigie, Esq.; Sir James Cunningham, Bart.; Sir James Dalzell, Bart.; George Dundas of Dundas, Esq.; Alexander Hamilton of Inverwick, Esq.; Thomas Sharp of Houston, Esq.; Alexander Hamilton of Pencaitland, Esq.; John Stewart of Eastbinning, Esq.; Robert Ramsay of Blackcraig, Esq.; George Dundas of Duddingston, Esq.; Andrew Marjoribanks of Marjoribanks, Esq.; Walter Hamilton of West Port, Esq.; James Glan of Longcroft, Esq.; John Gellon of Wallhouse, Esq.; together with the Knight of the Shire of the county of Linlithgow, or any three or more of them.

III.

There were numbers of brewers in the town, at Kinneil, and at Borrowstoun also, and it was this fact that suggested to the promoters of the Act the idea of raising a revenue out of an impost duty on ale and beer.

The trustees from the first had their hands full of new schemes. They also had many contentions with the brewers regarding the exaction of the new duties. There was no standing chairman, the trustees electing one of their number to be preses at each sederunt, and so we find that the work of conducting the meetings was shared by nearly all the members from time to time.

At one of the first meetings it was agreed that the Act of Parliament be "publickly advertised by tuck of drum thorough the town." One George Robertson was appointed officer for convening the trustees to their several meetings, and his allowance for each meeting was twopence sterling, and Thomas Glasfurd, in Bo'ness, was appointed collector of the duty at £15 sterling as a "cellary for said office yearly." Doubts were expressed by the trustees at their very first meeting as to the proper interpretation to be put on certain parts of the Act, and it was resolved "that two of their number should go to Edinburgh and consult ane able lawier with respect to such parts as seem intricate to them." At a later meeting the advice of the "lawier" was read, and the cost thereof—£2 10s. 6d.—ordered to be paid.

It was agreed by a majority to clean and deepen "for the conveniency of shipping coming into the harbour" the east side of the wester key (quay), and two of the trustees were appointed to meet with the masons who were last employed in building at the "keys," and "commune" with them as to the work. In due course these trustees reported that they had "communed" with the masons of "Lymkills" anent building the pier.

The brewers not only refused to pay the collector, but they compeared before the trustees when summoned, and still refused to pay. On 19th July, 1744, they "gave in" a letter to the trustees, in which they intimated that they had unanimously agreed to pay trustees sixpence each boll of malt "grinded at their milns," and in no other shape would they agree unless "stressed." If the impost of two pennies per pint were enforced, the letter continued, they were afraid the whole town would feel the bad consequences thereof. This, by order of the whole brewers in the town, was signed by James Young, William Cunningham, Alexander Taylor, Robert Cram, and Robert Cowan. The trustees unanimously refused the proposal, considering it quite contrary to the Act, and agreed to give each brewer a new summons for another meeting. The brewers were all again charged to make payment, and still refused. The trustees then resolved to "distress" them. Feeling ran so high apparently that no local officer could be persuaded to do this, and the trustees were obliged to send to Edinburgh for a messenger and witnesses. These came on 14th September,

1744, but found all the brewers' doors shut. Thereupon it was agreed by the trustees that "Letters of Opening Doors" should be sent for.

IV.

Things were becoming serious, and John Walker and William Shead, two of the trustees, refused to act any longer. It is evident that there had been many "threatenings against the persons of the several trustees by the brewers." In consequence of this the trustees agreed that Letters of Lawburrows be sent for and executed against the brewers; and, further, that application be made for a party of the military to protect the officers in "distressing" them for payment of their arrears.

Three of the "overseers," Mr. John Gillon of Wallhouse, Andrew Marjoriebanks of Marjoriebanks, and Sir James Dalyell of Binns, met with the brewers and endeavoured to have the dispute adjusted, but things did not improve. James Young, one of the brewers, took out Letters of Lawburrows against James Tod, Andrew Cowan, and Duncan Glasfurd, three of the trustees, and the brewers in the "towns of Borrowstoun and Inveravon suspended the decreets of the trustees against them, alleging that they were not within the libertys and privileges of Bo'ness." All this caused the trustees to engage a James Addison, writer in Edinburgh, to advise them.

John Walkinshaw of Scotstoun and Robert Paterson, merchants, were elected in room of Walker and Shead, resigned.

A new officer was appointed in the person of one George Rodger. The officer's duties had increased very much owing to the disputes with the brewers. The trustees were convened oftener, and he had also to deliver copies of the brewers' charges, and to summon and do everything necessary concerning the brewers. For all this he was to be allowed "therty shillings per annum." Rodger having agreed to the salary and accepted office, the collector was ordered "to pay him 10s. in part, and to take receipt for the same." He appears to have been a zealous officer. A proclamation was made about this time by

"Took of Drum" commissioning any person or persons "whatsomever" that shall see any ale or beer coming into the town without permit from the collector to stop the same, and thereupon give notice to the collector or any of the trustees that the same might be seized. Whoever did so was to be allowed one-half of all such ale. Rodger soon after appointment made a seizure of a cask containing 20 pints of ale brought into the town without paying the duty. The trustees confiscated it for the use of the harbour in terms of the Act, and ordained that it should be "exposed to publick roup after intimation by Took of Drum, and to be set up at 2s. stg., cask and all." It realised 2s. 6d. sterling, the officer receiving one-half and the collector the other for behoof of the harbour.

V.

John Henderson, who had prior to the 1744 Act, been appointed by the shipmasters for taking care of the piers and levying the duties, was granted a commission from the trustees to continue in that capacity under them. His office is described as "shoremaster."

The contract for making additions to the easter pier (not what is now the easter pier, but, as we think, the east side of the wester pier) was with John Miller, John Clark, and John Wilson, masons in Lymkills. It is engrossed in the minute book, and contains a detailed specification of the work. The progress of the masons in preparing the stones was apparently leisurely, and a letter was despatched to see "when they intend to come over and build the said pier, and also to make enquirie concerning boats to bring over the stones."

There appears to have been some difficulty in getting over the materials for building the pier, but it was solved by the trustees purchasing for that purpose an Arbroath boat which was then lying here. It cost £60 sterling, and the shoremaster was authorised to let out or freight the same to any person who might want to freight her to any place at any time when not needed for carrying stones for the pier. After the pier was finished the "ston boat" became unprofitable. It was then exposed to public roup and sale in the house of James Rennie, brewer in Borrowstounness, and bought by Charles Addison at £66 10s.

Great damage was every now and then done by shipping to the west side of the wester pier, and also to other parts of both piers, through shipmasters not securing their vessels as they ought. As a result, the shoremaster was specially instructed to report damage at once, so that the trustees might recover the cost of repairing it from the proper persons, and this order was to be duly intimated to all shipmasters.

George Adam, one of the original trustees, having died, Captain George Walker was unanimously elected in his place. Some time later Robert Paterson, an assumed trustee, having died, and David Stevenson, an original trustee, having refused to act longer, the trustees unanimously elected John Falconer and John Addison, both shipmasters in Bo'ness, in their places.

VI.

The trustees had taken up a firm attitude with the brewers from the beginning, and it was only right they should do so. The duty was the only source of revenue for the maintenance of the town and harbour, and it must also be remembered the trustees had, on the strength of the new impost, undertaken some costly improvements. They therefore insisted on their tax. The brewers were stubborn in their refusals, and ultimately decided to appeal to the Quarter Sessions of the Justices of the Peace for Linlithgow, to be held there on 27th October, 1747, for a final and conclusive judgment in terms of the Act.

Intimation of the appeal was sent to the trustees. The notice ran—"Whereas we the Brewers within the Town of Borness & libertys thereof judging ourselves to be egregiously leised & prejudged by the trustees for the two pennies on the pint of ale or beer brewed or vended by us within the said bounds by them & their clerks daylie distressing us with charges of horning & in consequence thereof threatning us with poinding or imprisonment; & as by Act of Parliament proposing the said impost we are entitled to appeal to the Justices of his Maj^{ies} Peace at their next Quarter Sessions for redress of our grivances :

"Therefor we Alexander Taylor and William Dick, Brewers in Borness, for ourselves and in name of the whole Brewers within the town and priveleges of Bo'ness, doe hereby intimate to you William Anderson, Clerk for the said trustees and collector of the said impost that we have appealled and do hereby appeal to the Justices of the Peace for redress of our grivances to be timeously given unto you and them befor their next Quarter Sessions the 27th curt: and protests you may pretend no ignorance thereof nor insist any further dilligence against us."

They took instruments in the hands of James Clelland, notary public, and the document was dated 9th October, 1747, and signed before George Wood, merchant in Bo'ness, and James Baird, indweller there.

Fully two years before this appeal the trustees, to ease the situation with the brewers, agreed to compromise by offering to take eightpence for each barrel of ale consisting of twelve Scots gallons, and to take bills for the duty. The overseers concurred in the proposal, but it is not very clear whether the brewers accepted. It rather appears that they resented anything whatever in the way of impost, and did all they could, by blank refusal to pay in some cases, and tiresome delay in others, to annoy the trustees. The above appeal seems another instance of their methods. The minutes contain no record of the result, but as we find a continuance of requests to the "deficients" to make up their arrears we may take it that the justices dismissed the appeal. As time wore on the brewers and vintners became reconciled to the tax, and during the last ten years of the Act there was little trouble. The business promptitude of the trustees all through this difficult matter is commendable.

VII.

On 20th September, 1762, the trustees filled three vacancies by the appointment of Dr. John Roebuck, lessee of the coal and salt works at Bo'ness, and John and Robert Cowan, merchants there. All three accepted office, and served the town for many years. The minutes disclose that the doctor, whose character and wonderful career we deal with in another chapter, had given the trustees cause for alarm a year or two before his appointment. On his becoming the Duke's lessee his enterprising energy made itself manifest by his at once commencing operations at the harbour in connection with the north dyke of his proposed "coalfold." The trustees hastily summoned a notary, and protested against such procedure. Despite the protest, the work went on. A deputation of three then called for him, but found he was from home. These gentlemen, however, solemnly warned his manager that if the north dyke was persisted in without giving the trustees an opportunity of talking with Dr. Roebuck they would apply to the Lords of Session for interdict. The threat was not carried out, although the work appears to have proceeded as usual. Two years later we find the doctor interviewing some of the trustees at his house. He then pointed out that he wanted to do the town good; explained that as soon as he got his mine set agoing he would be shipping coal extensively; and that he would help to enlarge the quays and make a basin at the harbour to keep it from silting up. The following letter was received by the trustees a few days after:—

"GENTLEMEN,—Being extremely willing to cultivate and maintain a good correspondence with the inhabitants of Bo'ness, and as far as in my power to promote their interest and accommodation, I take this opportunity to communicate to such of your members, whom I had not the pleasure of seeing at my house on Saturday, that I propose to carry down a waggon road on the west side of the west key and on the east side of the east key for the greater dispatch of vessels coming here to load coals and salt. As in the execution of my design it may be necessary to remove some of the polls on the key for my own accommodation and for the convenience of carts passing up and down the key with merchants' goods, I propose to erect new ones in place of those removed and to plant iron rings by the side of the key in such manner as shall not endanger the key and at the same time secure ships moored thereto. And for the more speedy shipping of coal, and to prevent the same from being a nuisance to the pier, I propose to erect two cranes, but in such a manner as shall be no injury to the pier or inconvenience to the merchants or shipmasters, but occasionally may be used for their benefit.

"Being much concerned for the present state of the harbour, which in a little time must injure, if not ruin, the trade of the town, and understanding from the gentlemen with me on Saturday that the public funds of the town are such as will not allow instantly to remedy the growing evil, I offered to them to advance in the name of the company any sum not exceeding four hundred pounds, free of interest, for executing this laudable and desirable purpose, desiring only to be repaid by receipt of the harbour's revenue after payment of the present debts due thereon, which proposal or promise I still adhere to and oblige myself to perform in case you signify your concurrence therewith.

"I hope, gentlemen, you will consider what I have said as flowing solely from a desire to live in peace and harmony with the gentlemen of Bo'ness, and to contribute as much as in my power to the prosperity of the trade of the town.

"If the whole proposals are agreeable to you I shall be obliged to you if you will enter them in your sederunt book; and, if not, that you would favour me with your answer.—I am, gentlemen, your most humble servant, (signed) JOHN ROEBUCK, for self, and coal company. Kinneil, 14th September, 1762."

All the proposals were agreed to by the trustees, and the worthy doctor, as we have seen, was made a trustee a few days afterwards.

VIII.

We must now refer to one other aspect of a vexed question. Who was liable to pay the duty under the Act? It is disclosed in a law plea of a somewhat trifling character which dragged on for at least six years, and was ultimately settled by arbitration. The process was at the instance of John Crawfurd, tide surveyor here, and John M'Laren, vintner at New Halls,[2] Queensferry, against the trustees. The trustees had seized, because of failure to pay the impost, some small beer and strong ale, which, so far as we can judge, came from M'Laren to Crawfurd for his private consumption. The summons, the trustees said, "seems to insinuate that everybody has free liberty to bring in what quantity of ale or beer they please for the use of private families without being liable to the duty of two pennies in the pint." They considered this clearly against the express words of their Act, and unanimously resolved to defend. Some years later we find the process before the Lords of Session, who had ordered proof to be led as to the practice of other burghs levying a similar impost. Between the time of serving the action and the time we are now speaking of the composition of the local board had considerably changed, and there was now a strong desire, especially among the new members, to have the case settled either by amicable arrangements or arbitration. After a great deal of trouble the latter course was adopted. The methods taken by the trustees to obtain this were somewhat diplomatic, though rather clumsily executed. It was a common custom with the trustees in the conduct of their business to remit correspondence and interviews, not to their clerk, but to those of their number who, by reason of some special aptitude, were regarded as likely to bring the matter in hand to a successful issue. We find, then, that on 19th April, 1763, the trustees resolved to have this "vexacious, tedious, expensive, and troublesome" process brought to a submission, and that two of their number, Messrs.

---

[2] Now the Hawes Inn.

John and Robert Cowan, were desired to write to Mr. M'Laren, in name of the trustees, to see if he would agree to this. They were further instructed to send the letter by express messenger in order to have it safely delivered and to bring back an immediate answer.

IX.

The tenor of the letter is as follows:—

"Bo'ness, 13th April, 1763.—Sir,—At a meeting here yesterday of the trustees for managing the harbour and collecting the impost appropriate for that purpose, they, after conversing with Mr. Crawfurd in the meeting and with his desire and approbation, recommended it to us to write you that they and Mr. Crawfurd will be glad to see you at this place on Saturday first, the 16th curt., to dine with them at the house of Mr. John Bain (Bain was a vintner or spirit merchant, and the trustees had a room or office there at 30s. per annum) at 2 o'clock in order to attempt, by entering into a submission or otherways, the doing away with that tedious, troublesome, and expensive law plea still depending before the Lords, as it has been for many years. It's but very lately that we were called upon to take share of the public business and burden as trustees, but it is much our opinion that if Mr. Crawfurd and the trustees can do this—either away at once among themselves or to submit it—it must save money to the fund here, and also to you and Mr. Crawfurd, as well as much trouble, as we hear it has already been so expensive and vexatious a plea, and tedious, that it has lasted since the commencement of our late war, which is truly shameful, especially when it's considered it may yet last as long. You'll please write us in course that if you decline giving the trustees the meeting they may take their measures accordingly.

"However willing some of them are to have this process ended in an amicable way, yet if you refuse to hearken to reasonable measures they cannot, and must not, drop it, but must see its issue, although at double the expense of money, time, and trouble which it has already cost.

"If we may unasked give you our opinion, it is in assuring you that you shd. gladly embrace this occasion of ending matters.

"This offer is made you merely owing to a dislike that several of our members have to law pleas in general, and this in particular (as it runs away with the public money to pay advocates and writers to defend a petty process in place of masons and barrowmen to defend our harbour from the damage of the sea, &c.), than from any bad state this particular process is in at present as they are by their advocates, &c., encouraged at least as much to persist in it. We say it is therefore our private advice that you should gladly accept the present invitation.—We are, &c.,

(Signed) "JOHN & ROBT. COWAN."

"*P.S.*—In place of sending you this by post, as we intended, we send it to you on purpose, so you'll please to answer it p. the bearer, & let us know if the trustees may positively expect you on Saturday or not."

The dinner never came off, for the messenger returned with a refusal, and the statement that Mr. M'Laren would not move in the matter himself, having left it all in the hands of his agent. As we have said, however, the dispute was ultimately settled by arbitration.

X.

In the sixties of the eighteenth century the Greenland whale fishing had been prosecuted with great briskness by some of the enterprising local merchants, and quite a number of whaling ships belonged to the port. When not in Greenland these vessels lay alongside the piers. With the greatly increased commerce, however, all the available quay space at the harbour was required for regular traders. Therefore we find the trustees on 21st July, 1763, declaring "That the Greenland ships cannot be laid by the sides of the piers during the interval of fishing without great prejudice to the trade of the town by stopping the loading and unloading of other vessels, therefore the trustees have resolved that they shall lie only in the middle of the harbour at equal distances from each pier, and do order John Kidd, havenmaster, to be served with a copy of this their resolution."

Mr. Charles Addison, one of the trustees, and a member of the firm of Charles Addison & Sons, merchants and brewers, owned a Greenland ship called the "Peggy." In September, 1764, she was reported as being "lying in the best part of the harbor which greatly interrupts the loading and unloading of other trading vessels through the winter," and the shoremaster was instructed to tell Mr. Addison to remove her out of the way. This he did, and Mr. Addison's "response" was that he had no answer to give the trustees. They again requested the shoremaster to ask Mr. Addison (who was not present either at this or the previous meeting), before two creditable witnesses, to remove the "Peggy" into the middle of the harbour, "where she was in use to lie in former years," and to report. Mr. Addison found that his colleagues were not to be trifled with, attended the next meeting, and agreed to remove the vessel alongside the "Oswald," on the trustees employing labourers to "throw a ditch" to let her up. They consented. At same meeting Mr. Addison promised to immediately pay up his arrears of the impost duty, which were then considerable. It is possible that Mr. Addison's stubborness in the matter of the "Peggy" was caused by the urgency with which the trustees had been pressing him to clear off his arrears of duty. Be that as it may, an explosion took place at the succeeding sederunt. The shoremaster there reported that he had told Mr. Addison that the ditch was in progress, and desired that he (Addison) might remove the ship as far as he could meantime. In reply, Mr. Addison had refused to remove her until the ditch was completed. Then we find it minuted—"Mr. Charles Addison himself being present at this meeting confirmed the Report of the Shoremaster, and when he also took occasion to treat some of the trustees in a very ungenteel manner. But the trustees being willing to overcome evil with good do hereby order their Shoremaster to throw the proposed ditch with all expedition that no excuse for Mr. Addison may remain."

In the next minute we read—" Charles Addison upon hearing the last Sederunt read, which was wrote after he left the meeting, and finding it contains what he considers to be hurtful to him and such facts as did not happen at said meeting, particularly that he had used some of the trustees at said meeting ungenteely, insisted that this should be altered and the facts insert in the Sederunt of this meeting as they really happened, which request was denied him by the meeting: he therefore hereby protests that the facts be insert in ye Sedt. of this meeting, which are as follows:—

"That he, the said Chas. Addison, in the course of conversation called John Falconer, one of the trustees, a Fool, to which Mr. Falconer answered by calling the said Chas. Addison a Base Rascal, and thereupon the said Chas. Addison took Instruments. The Trustees in answer to this protest have no return to make to it, but adhere to Sed. 185 (where they resolved as we saw, to overcome evil with good & instructed the harbourmaster to carry through the ditch with all expedition) and till called upon in another manner will enter no further upon particulars in relation to this affair."

At the following meeting in October Mr. Addison was not present, but at the next, which was not held until 7th January of the following year (1765), Mr. Addison was not only present, but presided. As nothing more appears in the minutes concerning the disturbing but innocent "Peggy," we hope that during the interval she had been duly moored in the middle of the harbour beside the "Oswald," that the arrears of his dues had been duly squared, and that the unpleasantness between parties had been buried with the passing of the old year.

XI.

Three years prior to the expiry of the first Act the trustees set about applying to Parliament for a renewal of their power to exact the duty of two pennies Scots, and this was granted about two years before the expiry of the original Act. The new Act ran from the 24th day of June, 1767, until the 24th day of June, 1769, and from thence during the term of twenty-five years. It will be noted that the period between 1767 and 1769 was already included in the first Act. The trustees, however, in their second application had asked and received liberty to impose the duty not only in the town and liberties thereof, but in the whole parish. In order then to give the town the advantage of the revenue of the extended area, the Act gave special power to levy the impost over the whole parish between 1767 and 1769, as the twenty-five years of the new Act did not really begin to run until the latter year.

The new Act, while re-enacting almost the whole of the terms of the old one, also gave the trustees some additional powers. The sederunts of the trustees towards the close of the first period disclose their efforts for renewal. They found it of "great consequence" to obtain such, the harbour being again in a ruinous condition, and the funds on hand only sufficient to meet the debts contracted. Dr. Roebuck was asked to immediately see the tutors of the then Duke of Hamilton, and obtain their "approbation and concurrence." He was also to discuss the proposal to get powers to bring fresh water to the town for the benefit thereof and of the shipping. The trustees soon met again "to know what conversation Dr. Roebuck had with the tutors." The doctor reported they were "altogether ready and willing to contribute their utmost endeavours for obtaining the renewal." With regard to the fresh-water proposal, the tutors "thought that this in no respect would be improper."

XII.

At the same meeting Mr. Walkinshaw, Mr. James Main, and Mr. Charles Addison were appointed to meet together and draw up the petition proposed to be presented to Parliament, and also a memorial for the member of Parliament, who was to be charged with the delivery of the petition. Both documents were submitted to the trustees at their next sederunt. Regarding the petition, it is minuted, " The trustees made some little alterations and additions thereon, and now think the same expressed in a pretty natural way: therefore order their clerk to get the same extended by any having a plain hand on large paper in order to be signed: " Messrs. Charles Addison and John Cowan were appointed to wait upon the Hon. Charles Hope Vere with the petition and memorial when extended and signed. But prior to waiting upon this gentleman they were also to wait upon the Duke of Hamilton's Commissioners at Hamilton and get their approbation. A fortnight later the delegates reported they had been at Hamilton, where they were presented to His Grace's tutors, Mr. Muir and Mr. Andrew Steuart. The tutors agreed to the petition, but recommended the trustees to also pray for liberty to apply part of their revenues towards repairing and keeping in good repair the streets of the town and the passages and avenues leading to it.

To this suggestion the trustees agreed. They stipulated, however, that the then acting trustees should be continued in the next Act, with power to name such new members as would make up their number to fifteen, and with full power to choose new trustees in the same way as in the old Act. And to prevent any misunderstanding as to the naming of new trustees, it was resolved to send a letter the next day to the Duke's tutors, " with the names of the present trustees and one more—the present number being only fourteen—for their approbation."

The cost of the deputation of two going to Hamilton was £6 19s. 5d. The expenses of Mr. Hamilton, " our Sollicitor at London " in connection with the renewal, amounted to £278 10s. 8d.

CHAPTER XIII.

THE "TRUSTEES FOR THE TWO PENNIES"—*Continued.*

1. Period of One Hundred Years: The Four Acts Embraced in it—2. The Making of the Harbour Basin: "Slothfull" Masons: £30 Expended on Street Repairs—3. Construction of the Waggon Road and of New Street—4. Petitions from Inhabitants: Providence Road: The Syver Well and Charles Addison's Reclamation of Foreshore—5. Complaints about the Streets: The Rouping of the Street Manure: The Letting of the Bye-ales: Drummond's Imprisonment—6. Throwing Ballast into the Harbour: A Skipper Severely Dealt with —7. Causewaying of the Streets: The Trustees Get a Cart Made: Dr. Rennie's Description of the Town and its Inhabitants—8. The Town in Distress for Want of Water: Schoolyard Engine Water to be Drained off to Basin—9. Funds to be Raised by Subscription: Water to be Brought from the Western Engine: The Water from St. John's Well—10. Herring Curing at the Seaport: Regulations Prepared: Shipbuilding and Details of the Shipping—11. Trustees Decide to Erect a Patent Slip: Mr. Morton's Offer: Subscription Taken and List of Subscribers—12. Trustees Severely Criticised by Public: Their Reply to "Misrepresentations and Unmerited Censure" —13. Copy of Town Accounts for Year Ending 30th May, 1834—14. Trustees their own Sanitary Inspectors: A Candid Report: Mr. Gillespie and the "Sewers, Squalor, and Soot" of Bo'ness—15. An Urgent Appeal to Duke of Hamilton for Assistance: Trouble with People of Borrowstoun and Newtown over Water—16. The Last of the Water Trouble: Various Sources Visited and Reported on: Employment of Mr. William Gale: The Temple Pit Reservoir, Borrowstoun: Capacity of New Supply—17. The Monkland Railway Brought to Kinneil: Proposed Extension to Bo'ness: Opposition of Mr. Goldsmith: His Advisory Letters—18. Summary of Admiralty Report Ordaining Railway Company to make Promenade: Rights in Promenade Bought by Railway Company.

I.

THIS second instalment of early municipal history covers a period of fully one hundred years. It is only possible therefore to indicate the principal schemes undertaken by the trustees

The Old Town Hall.
(By permission of Messrs. F. Johnston & Co., Falkirk.)

See page 323.

during that time. Four Acts are embraced, namely, that of 1769, already referred to, which ran to 1794; one in the latter year which continued the term and enlarged the powers granted under the two previous Acts for the further term of twenty-one years; another in 1816, again continuing the term and enlarging the powers of the other Acts for twenty-five years; and yet another, the largest and most comprehensive of all, not passed until 1843, which was to continue until repealed. It may be mentioned that most of the larger schemes undertaken were duly authorised by these various Acts. The chief feature of the 1816 Act was the power which it gave the trustees to assess and levy from all occupiers of dwelling-houses, shops, and other buildings within the town a rate or duty not exceeding one shilling in the pound upon the rents of such, and to appoint two or more assessors. This was in addition to the usual two pennies in the pint, and was for the purpose of defraying the expenses of lighting, cleaning, and improving the streets and of erecting a town clock. The 1843 Act, again, changed the method of election, stipulated for a qualification on the part of trustees and electors, introduced a declaration when accepting office, and arranged a rotation or period of service. Moreover, as the brewing in the town and neighbourhood had become a thing of the past by that time, the two pennies duty was dropped, and the trustees for the future were known as "the trustees for the town and harbour." Under this Act the number of trustees was to be less than formerly—not fewer than nine and not more than twelve. It also named the first trustees, and these were Robert Bauchop, William Henderson, John Taylor, William Roy, John Hardie, John Anderson, Henry Rymer, James Henry, Henry Hardie, John Henderson, George Paterson, and James Meikle. Their methods were much more modern than those of the old merchants and shipmasters. And while their undertakings were important, yet the records of these do not leave us with the same distinct impression of care and capacity in all their work which those of the "trustees for the two pennies" do. The old trustees were exceedingly fortunate in having gentlemen of great diligence and skill as their clerks. We cannot trace all these, but James Scrimgeour, jun., and David Miln were both in long service under the earlier Acts, while George Henderson served continuously for a quarter of a century. A minute, dated the 4th of December, 1820, records—"The meeting takes this opportunity of expressing their acknowledgments to Mr. George Henderson for his great fidelity, accuracy, and zeal for the interest of the trust for upwards of twenty-five years he has held the office of clerk." Another George Henderson served the Town and Harbour Trustees with much ability for many years, and carried through all the intricate negotiations in connection with the extension of the railway to Bo'ness and other important matters.

II.

Between 1750 and 1780 Borrowstounness was one of the most thriving towns on the east coast, and ranked as the third port in Scotland. This commercial activity is reflected in the minutes, for the trustees were constantly engaged in making every possible improvement at the harbour for traders. Then, as now, the continuous mud silt gave great trouble. But in October, 1762, it was resolved to construct a basin for cleaning the harbour, and in due course the work was carried out by Mr. Robert M'Kell, engineer. A double wall, moated in the heart, was run across between the two piers, enclosing about one-fourth of the harbour at the land side. This contained four sluices. During spring tides these sluices were regularly opened, and shut at full sea when a great body of water was retained. At low water they were opened, and they emptied the basin with so rapid a current that in the course of a few years a great increase to the depth of water in the harbour was made. The basin wall was of similar breadth with the two piers, and gave great accommodation. From it a middle pier, or tongue, as it was called, was also built parallel to the other two, so that the construction of the basin was in every way a great and useful scheme. Additions were afterwards made to the tongue and the piers from time to time as necessity arose. It is minuted on one occasion during the many repairs to the piers that the masons "are very slothfull in performing their day's work." The shoremaster therefore was instructed "to oversee said masons two or three times a day, and if any of them be found idle or neglecting their work to take a note of their names and to report them to the trustees as often as they shall be found that way." At a later date we find the same strict supervision over the same kind of work—" It is agreed that Daniel Drummond, the harbourman, shall work as a labourer with the masons, where he shall be directed during the whole repairs. And if it shall be found that he attends and works faithfully, and takes care to make complaint when the other workmen do not their duty, the trustees mean to make him some little present when the work is finished."

In 1769 it was found necessary to repair the streets, and £30 was allocated thus—£6 on the east pier, and £6 on the west pier, to pave it down to the basin wall; £8 from the church westward; £5 at the east end of the town; and £5 where found necessary. Dr. Roebuck, Robert Hart, and John Pearson were to see that the work was properly executed.

III.

For several months onwards from June, 1772, there is much to be found about the construction of the waggon road. Dr. Roebuck's affairs were in the hands of his trustees, Mansfield, Hunter & Co. They recommenced operations at the coalfield, and John Allenson and John Grieve were their local managers. Evidently some pits on the hill were then opened, and the doctor's trustees wished to have a waggon way down the Wynd and along the shore to the west pier for the shipment of the coal. This presented the town trustees with several excellent opportunities, and they did not fail to seize them. They were, as it is written, "much disposed to accommodate Dr. Roebuck's trustees, so that they might not be obstructed in prosecuting their coalwork business." So they consented to the construction of the waggon way, but upon certain important terms and conditions. One of these was that a new street from the Wynd to the harbour should also be formed. Everything was to be done to the satisfaction of a special committee consisting of John Walkinshaw, Robert Hart, Alexander Buchanan, John Pearson, and John Cowan. The doctor's trustees, of course, were to bear the whole expense, including the paving of the new street with Queensferry stones "by proper bred pavers." It was thought that some of the houses at "Kirkyard Wynd foot" might be damaged in rendering entry to them more inconvenient. For these and all other claims which might arise out of the construction of the new street and the waggon way the town trustees were to be freed, and an agreement in these terms was entered into and carried out. The scheme was beset with difficulties, the chief of which was the crossing of the old street at the foot of the Wynd. Here and elsewhere the waggon way was to be 3 or 4 feet above the street level, and it was to be safely "finished off." The trustees thought that it would end at the head of the west pier, and considerable consternation prevailed when they found Allenson and Grieve proceeding with it down the pier. Such, it was thought, would prove very prejudicial to the trade of the town "by making it impossible for carts carrying down and up goods from passing each other." It was discovered also that each waggon "is to carry about three tons of coal, which is about or near to double the weight that Dr. Roebuck's waggons formerly carried." The matter was adjusted, however, by allowing the railway to proceed, "the trustees of the doctor to stand bound to the town trustees and their successors in office to answer for and make good every damage whatever that might then or in the future be done to the pier in consequence of the railway."

All this was come to after grave deliberation; and the reason for the consent was because "the trustees of the harbour are perfectly disposed to indulge Dr. John Roebuck and his trustees to the utmost of their power consisting with the duty they owe to themselves and the public, being much convinced that the success of the coalliery of this town is perfectly connected with the trade and prosperity thereof."

IV.

Petitions from the inhabitants desiring redress of various grievances were frequent. While the new street was being made the Rev. Mr. Baillie and others craved that the road called Providence leading into the south part of the town "might either be made as it was before, or that the coal managers be ordained to throw a bridge across the waggon way, so that the said Providence Road may be rendered passable as before for leading the grain to the barnyards and other goods to and from the town." Mr. Grieve, on being sent for, agreed, "in presence of the meeting," to execute the bridge forthwith.

Another petition was received representing the ruinous situation of the "Syver Well," and praying that it might be properly repaired and a pump put into it. The trustees consented, and appointed Mr. John Cowan "to write to Mr. Sylby at Edinburgh, or any other proper person, to know at what expense the same can be done, and agree therefor, so as the town may be supplied in this necessary article of life in the most commodious manner." Mr. Sylby's estimate of £4 10s. was accepted, and it was further resolved to have the well built in with large stones.

Shortly after this Charles Addison & Sons craved that a second pump be put in at the Syver well for the purpose of supplying their brewery, the water to be filled with a cask and a cart. The inhabitants petitioned against this, and set forth the inconvenience that would arise to them if a second pump was put in the well for "shipping water in carts." The trustees refused the request, but arranged that a pump should be erected at the Run Well instead. With reference to the Addisons, it is of interest to know that the large property to the north of Market Square, which was burned down in 1911, was built by Charles Addison. His feu charter of the ground was granted by James sixth Duke of Hamilton on the 20th of September, 1752. The narrative runs—" Whereas Charles Addison, merchant in my burgh of Borrowstounness, hath already expended a considerable sum of his own proper money in gaining the area aftermentioned from off the sea (upon which there were never any house or houses built, and which never yielded any rent or profite to me or my predecessors), and in building a strong buttress or bullwork of hewen aceler fenced with many huge stones for the support thereof, and will be farder at a very great expence in building a dwelling-house, office houses, cellors, proper warehouses, and granaries on the said area or shoar of the said Burgh, which works were undertaken and are carrying on by him upon the assurance of his obtaining from me a grant of the said area; Therefor and for his encouragement to compleat so laudable ane undertaking which tends to the advancement of the policy and trade of the said town," and in consideration of his paying a yearly feu-duty and on several other terms and conditions, the reclaimed ground referred to was granted him. The boundaries of the ground so feued are given as the sea on the north; the houses of Mary Wilson on the east; the High Street on the south; and the easter pier and highway leading to the same on the west.

V.

To return to the petitions, another is referred to thus— "The trustees have laid before them a petition from the inhabitants of this town setting forth that the streets are exceedingly dirty and hardly passable, particularly at the easter coalfold opposite to Taylor's pit; also at Margaret Shifton's door, where the water often collects so as to render the passing difficult, and even so as to endanger the health of the inhabitants from colds and disorders in consequence of wett feet." Though they had power under the Act to keep the streets in order and "open the avenues to the town," yet the want of funds prevented their doing so. These funds were, in the first place, to be applied to the improvement of the harbour, and it alone exhausted the whole. In order to give them funds so that the requests in the above and other petitions might be attended to, the trustees resolved to "lett to publick roup" the whole of the street manure of the town. Meantime the collector was instructed to employ a carter and a raker to cart it away. He was also to give notice by the drum on every market day, till 2nd November, 1772, of the intended roup. William Robertson, James Tod, Alexander Buchanan, John Paris, and John Cowan were appointed to make proper regulations "as to the way and manner of carrying off the dung." The roup was adjourned from the 2nd to the 9th, "on account of the badness of the weather." No bidders appeared at the adjourned roup, except Charles Addison, jun., who offered 5s. for the whole for the half-year to Whitsunday. The trustees refused this, but offered to take half a guinea, and Mr. Addison agreed. In course of time this came to be a source of considerable revenue. In 1783 the bye-ales alone were exposed, and John Drummond, as the last and highest bidder, was preferred at the sum of £27 for the year to 1st July, 1784. He failed to pay, and the trustees got decree, and had him imprisoned. Meanwhile he had gone "and declared himself bankrupt on oath, in consequence whereof the Bailies of Linlithgow allowed him an aliment of 7d. per day." His two cautioners attended a meeting, and the trustees, considering the hardship of their situation, agreed to their proposal to pay by two half-yearly instalments, provided they found a sufficient cautioner in a fortnight. Then the minute continues—"As the meeting see no good reason for alimenting John Drummond, they resolve not to do it," and they left it to his cautioners to act in the manner as they saw cause. In after years we find that John Black was almost a regular purchaser of the tack of the bye-ales and also of the street manure, and it would thus seem he had found them profitable concerns.

VI.

To go back a little, we find James Baird, the shoremaster, reporting on the 8th of March, 1773, that Charles Baad, master of the sloop "Venus," had come into the harbour on Saturday with ballast, and, "contrary to the practice of all harbours and of all law," had thrown it out late on Saturday night off the head of the harbour. Baad compeared and denied that he brought in any ballast, upon which the trustees called in John Thomson, workman, and put him on oath. He deponed that he was sent on board to get "a parcell of wands" for Dr. Roebuck & Co.'s coalworks; and that he saw a "parcell of ballast"—about twenty carts and upwards. By mid-day the wands were all taken out of the sloop, and Baad engaged him to come about eight o'clock at night, when it was dark, to assist to throw out his ballast. The sloop had been hauled off about a cable length north of the west pier, and between eight and nine Baad took him off in his small boat. When he got aboard he found Daniel Robertson, carpenter, and Baad's own men busy throwing the ballast overboard. He then commenced to help, and it was all out in about an hour.

Daniel Robertson, being also called in and sworn, corroborated. The trustees found it clearly proven that, contrary to the regulations, Baad had, "when dark, thrown over a considerable quantity of ballast off the mouth of this harbour, to the great hurt and prejudice thereof," and decerned him to pay " Ten pound sterling for this trespass." If he failed to pay, the sloop was to be distressed " by carrying off as many of her sails as when sold will amount to the sum of ten pounds, with all charges of every kind." They had some difficulty in getting the fine, but after taking possession of the sails the money was paid.

VII.

On 9th December, 1776, the trustees had before them a petition signed by William Anderson and James Dalgleish, merchants, and a good many other inhabitants, once more complaining of the great inconvenience that arose from the water lodging at the street opposite to Margaret Main's door at Taylor's "pitt," and praying the trustees to remedy the same by opening a water passage across the street. Mr. Cowan, to relieve the situation, gave leave to lay an open sewer across the timber yard possessed by him opposite to that part of the street complained of, and, as usual, a committee was appointed to see the work done. At the same time, the committee were empowered "to agree with causewaymen or others to execute the necessary work near to Margaret Main's house, and also to repair several broken parts of the street, namely, at Robert Beaton's door—John Mitchell's door—opposite to the Syver Well—opposite to Margaret Shifton's door—near to Mr. Thomson's, watchmaker—near to Widow Mackie's house—near Captain Hunter's house—near Mr. Edward Cowan's house, with several other small broken places of the streets and vennels." Towards the end of the period under review we find in the minutes a "copy of specification for making a cart for taking the fulzie off Bo'ness streets." All the parts are specified carefully, and the wealth of detail given is amusing. The contractor was taken bound to uphold workmanship and material for the space of twelve months after date of furnishing, which was to be within fourteen days after acceptance of estimate. James Meikle, William Marshall, and J. M. Gardner were appointed to get estimates and to accept the best.

Dr. Rennie[1] describes some of the houses about this time as being low and crowded, and bearing the marks of antiquity. For the most part, however, they were clean and commodious. The smoke from the coalworks was a great nuisance, and continually involved the town in a cloud. Houses were blackened with soot, the air impregnated with vapour, and strangers were struck with the disreputable appearance of the place. But these nuisances were being removed from the immediate vicinity to a considerable distance, and more attention was being paid to cleaning the streets. Still, the smoke from the Grange coalworks on the east, the Bo'ness saltpans on the west, and the dust excited by the carts carrying coals to the quays for exportation occasionally inconvenienced the inhabitants. Crowded as the houses might appear to a stranger, no bad consequences were felt. Ordinary diseases were not more frequent here than in other places. In fact, health was enjoyed to a greater degree in and around Bo'ness than in many towns of its size and population. This was

---

[1] Sinclair's Stat. A/c.

accounted for by the fact that the shore was washed by the Forth twice every twenty-four hours. Moreover, the vapours from the saltpans corrected any septic quality in the air. The walks about the town were romantic and inviting; the walks on the quays and on the west beach were at all times dry and pleasant, and greatly fitted to promote health and longevity. Unfortunately, however, tippling houses were too numerous. It was to be seriously regretted that too many people were licensed to vend ardent spirits in every town and village. Such places ensnared the innocent, became the haunts of the idle and dissipated, and ruined annually the health and morals of thousands of mankind. Perhaps if the malt tax were abolished, and an adequate additional tax laid upon British spirits, as in the days of their fathers, malt liquor would be produced to nourish and strengthen instead of whisky, which wasted and enfeebled the constitution; or were Justices of the Peace to limit the number of licences issued by apportioning them to the population of each place and by granting them to persons of a respectable character, a multitude of grievances would be redressed. Writing of the inhabitants, Dr. Rennie states that they were fond of a seafaring life. Many able-bodied seamen from the town were in His Majesty's service, and were distinguished for their sobriety, courage, and loyalty. Adventurers from the town also were to be found in the most distant parts of the globe. On the whole, the inhabitants were in general sober and industrious, and were of most respectable character.

VIII.

The water supply of the town has been a subject which has given much anxiety to the municipal authorities since about the end of the eighteenth century, and has involved the expenditure of very large sums of money. In early days the worry was not that there were no water sources in the neighbourhood. On the contrary, there were natural springs in abundance containing water of an excellent quality. Coal mining operations, however, diverted nearly all these from their original channels. The Act of 1769 gave the trustees power to contract for springs and build reservoirs, but there were no funds. Petitions and complaints were frequently lodged, and in June, 1778, it is minuted—" Almost the whole town is in great distress for want of fresh water, which has of late become exceedingly scarce." It was therefore resolved to get estimates from properly qualified surveyors to bring water to the town through lead pipes, earthen pipes, or through wooden pipes. William Robertson, Alexander Buchanan, and John Cowan were appointed a special committee to get these. The expense, of course, was a great obstacle, for the trustees "did not at all understand that they as trustees were to pay the sum that might be found necessary for bringing water into the town, which they know no way of doing but by a voluntary subscription, with such aid as His Grace the Duke of Hamilton shall please to give." They, however, agreed to pay the expense of such plan if it did not exceed £5 5s., "and to be as much less as they can." But a few years were spent in getting the estimates, and meantime the trustees had to deal with other water affairs. For instance, it was stated at a meeting in September, 1781, that water might be had to supply the town about a hundred yards south of Mr. Main's park, immediately to the south of the town; and a committee consisting of Dr. Roebuck, John Cowan, and some others was appointed to investigate the matter. They did so, and got estimates of what it would cost to bring the said water in an open ditch from near Graham's Dyke down to the meeting-house by way of a trial. The offer of Charles St. Clair or Sinclair was accepted, and the committee was continued to see the work executed. Then, again, the water from the schoolyard engine caused "great damage to sundries," and it was resolved to obtain an estimate "for carrying that water into the bason by a level under the street and by the shortest line." Estimates were produced at next meeting from Charles Sinclair—one for £30 5s. 11d., and the other for £22 5s. 11d. in another way; but the trustees wished to go further into the matter, as it was considered " of some consequence not only as to the convenience, but even as to the health of many of the inhabitants, particularly the younger part, such as school boys, &c., that this hott engine water be carried off in the best and most expeditious manner through and across the streets into the bason or into the sea in the way that shall be reckoned best for the inhabitants in general."

IX.

To bring this about they thought it necessary to appoint a committee consisting of Dr. John Roebuck, James Tod, James Main, James Drummond, and John Cowan, three a quorum, "with power to them to examine, deliberate, and determine on the tract that is reckoned the best." It was further resolved to get a subscription opened for making up two-thirds of the sum wanted, the trustees agreeing to pay the other third. And in case the inhabitants fell short of subscribers for the two-thirds, including what might be given by His Grace the Duke of Hamilton, another meeting of trustees was to be called to consider if they could contribute any more than the one-third.

The trustees met on 8th November, 1781, under the presidency of Dr. Roebuck, to consider the plans, estimates, and surveys for bringing water to the town in lead pipes and in wooden pipes, to be brought from Torneyhill, from St. Johns, and from the Western Engine. The meeting was of opinion that funds could not easily be raised to bring the fresh water from any of those places in leaden pipes, and they were of opinion that wooden pipes would be insufficient. Mr. Charles Sinclair estimated the cost of getting the water brought from the Western Engine in wooden pipes at £187, which was considered reasonable, and they unanimously approved thereof, and agreed to contribute the sum of £30 towards it. Mr. James Drummond was appointed to meet with the water subscribers of the town, and to communicate to them the resolution of the meeting.

An important step in the progress of the water question is recorded in a minute of meeting dated the 9th of December, 1818. There were present Robert Bauchop, John Taylor,

The "Trustees for the Two Pennies"

William Henderson, George Hart, Walter Grindlay, James Tod, Thomas Johnston, John Padon, Andrew Tod, James Johnstone, Ilay Burns, and Thomas Cowan. The committee appointed to superintend the bringing in to the town of the water from St. John's Well then reported that the pipes were now completed to their satisfaction, and that the well at the Cross was also finished. They were glad to say that the supply of water proved to be fully equal to the wants of the inhabitants. The committee also produced the New Shotts Iron Company's accounts, amounting to £218 10s. 4d., of which £38 9s. 4d. was the cost of the new cistern and well at the Cross. This had been found necessary after making trial of a less expensive mode of delivering the water, which, however, did not succeed owing to the very great pressure of water from the reservoir to the town.

X.

Quite unexpectedly the Forth herring fishing, hitherto unknown in this part, was so successful during the season 1794-5 that hopes were entertained that herring curing would be added to the industries of the place. We discover evidences of this in the minutes. The trustees thought that the herring vessels which then occupied the piers should be made to pay a small allowance for the use of these, and also to meet the necessary repairs which carts with a great weight of fish would occasion the buildings. If "little ordinary trade was going forward," they admitted, the use of the piers could be permitted with little inconvenience. But "if trade otherwise was brisk," the herring curing would prove a great obstruction. In this view, it was right the herring vessels should pay a little. At the same time, they wished to do this "so gently as not to make the busses avoid the harbour." The trustees, indeed, were very cautious, "this being the outset of a new business," and they were anxious not to discourage its development. A committee of three was therefore appointed to inquire into the practice and mode of charge in other places where the piers were so used, and to draw up such regulations as appeared to them adequate before the return of the next fishing season. On 3rd August, 1796, a meeting was called to consider the report and draft of proposed regulations of the committee. The regulations consisted of five clauses, "and with a small addition to the sixth and a slight alteration at the commencement of the seventh, unanimously adopted them, and returned their thanks to the committee for the pains bestowed on this subject."

We can only briefly indicate these "Regulations for the curing of herrings at the harbour of Borrowstounness." The persons in charge of all "busses" or herring vessels on entering the harbour were to state whether they meant to cure any of their fish upon the quays. If so, they were to be charged 4d. per ton register for the privilege in addition to the anchorage duty. If no notice was given, and herrings were found on the quays beyond the space of forty-eight hours, they were to be seized and sold, and the proceeds converted to the use of the harbour. If any vessel did not cure to the extent of her full loading, the person in charge, on making testimony of the reason, was to receive a return of such part of the curing dues as the collector thought fit. Those not having vessels, but who might purchase herrings and cure them on the quays, were likewise subjected to the payment of dues, six barrels to be reckoned as equal to a ton register. Very unfortunately the herrings never returned to this part of the Firth in any quantity, and so the careful preparations of the trustees to foster the "new business" and at the same time to increase the harbour revenue proved futile.

Shipbuilding was engaged in on a fairly extensive scale at Borrowstounness from about the middle of the eighteenth to the middle of the nineteenth centuries. Towards the end of the former there were two builders of note—Robert Hart and Thomas Boag, and the vessels built were from 300 to 350 tons burden. The Grays from Kincardine came later, and the last builder on the ground was one Meldrum. He built a ship called the "Ebenezer" and another called the "Isabella."

The shipping[2] belonging to the town at this time consisted

---

[2] See Sinclair's Stat. A/c.

of twenty-five sail, 17 of them being brigantines of from 70 to 170 tons per register. Eight were sloops from 20 to 70 tons per register, and altogether the shipping employed about 170 men and boys. Of the brigantines six were under contract to sail regularly once every fourteen days to and from London. They were all fine vessels, from 147 to 167 tons per register. The remaining eleven brigantines and also one of the sloops were chiefly engaged in the Baltic trade. The other seven sloops were for the canal and coasting.

XI.

We have seen how anxious the trustees always were to improve and extend the trade, and therefore we are not astonished to find that in July, 1781, they saw "of what great utility the having a dry dock properly executed in the bason would be to the trade and commerce of this town." They agreed to meet again in a fortnight "to consider this very essential piece of business," Dr. Roebuck and Mr. Cowan meantime to procure plans and estimates. The proposal, however, fell through, but was not entirely lost sight of. About forty years after it was still thought necessary that either a dry dock or a patent slip be erected for the purpose of repairing ships. After full consideration, the trustees decided to erect a slip, as in their view it would answer the purpose better and cost less money.

On 11th September, 1820, it was reported that a letter had been received from Mr. Thomas Morton, Leith, offering to execute the slip, with all its appendages and necessary excavation and building, for £865. As this sum was not at the disposal of the trustees, they proposed to make a public subscription. Each trustee promised to exert himself to procure the sum required. Mr. Morton was requested to guarantee the work for two years, and to extend the size of the slip so that it might be capable of taking vessels up to 360 tons register. Mr. Morton's offer, however, was not to be accepted until it was seen what subscriptions were obtained. By 4th December the Harbour Committee reported that subscriptions to the amount required had been received, and the meeting accepted Mr. Morton's offer. This slip was the second of the kind he erected in the country.

The following is a copy of the subscription list as recorded in the minutes, with a note of the conditions on which the slip was to be held. It was to be the joint property of the subscribers; the subscriptions were to be paid as soon as the work was completed and fit for use; the rates for the use of the slip were to be fixed by a majority of the subscribers, who were to vote according to their shares of £25 each vote. The Harbour Trustees were to maintain the gate and the basin wall, and the harbourmaster was to take charge of the slip and collect the dues thereof. In consideration of all this and of the money already expended towards the accommodation of the slip, one-half of the revenue arising from it was to form a part of the town's funds after deducting the rent of that part of the premises taken by the trustees from the Duke of Hamilton.

Robt. Bauchop for the Duke of Hamilton,	£105	Brought forward,	£505
Ja. and And. Tod,	50	Alex. Steell,	25
John Padon,	25	Alex. Rowan,	25
Wm. Henderson,	25	John Anderson,	25
Ja. Henry,	25	Rev. Robt. Rennie,	25
Walter Grindlay,	25	John Henderson,	25
Geo. Paterson,	25	J. & C. Green,	25
Geo. Henderson,	25	Henry Rymer,	25
Tobias Mitchell,	25	Mrs. M. per J. Merchant,	25
Jas. Jno. Cadell,	25	Wm. Shairp,	25
James Robertson,	25	Wm. Calder,	25
John Hardie,	25	Robt. Henderson, jun.,	25
James Shaw,	25	John Thomson,	25
Arthur Thomson,	25	Geo. Wallace,	25
Robt. Henderson,	25	Robt. Bauchop,	25
David Thomson,	25	J. P. for Ilay Burns,	25
		Thomas Boag,	25
Over	£505		£905

The slip did not turn out a success, largely owing to the falling fortunes of the seaport about that time. And as the Rev. Dr. Rennie used to say, it certainly proved a slip, for it did not pay any dividend.

XII.

As we have said more than once, the affairs of the town and harbour were well managed. Nevertheless, the actions of the trustees were carefully watched and sometimes severely criticised by various members of the community. This was particularly the case in December, 1825. At a meeting of trustees held on the 12th of that month a long letter or memorial representing certain alleged grievances was submitted. It was subscribed by John Stephens, Peter Petrie, Thomas Boag, Arthur Thomson, Thomas Collins, Robert Boyd, and George Wallace. These parties stated that they had consulted the Sheriff of the county about their grievances, and had been advised by him to apply directly to the Lord Advocate. Before taking this step, however, and in the hope of rendering it unnecessary, they thought it expedient to submit their complaints direct. They hoped the trustees would consider them attentively, and grant what they believed was the general wish of the inhabitants of the town. Shortly put, their grievances were—(1) The want of a sufficient supply of soft water, and the deficiency of wells. As a cause of the deficient water supply, it was stated the diameter of the water pipes was completely inadequate to the consumption of 630 families. Seven years had elapsed without any effectual steps being taken to remedy the evil, and, although the assessment had been increased, they were not aware that it was the intention of the trustees to apply it to this most necessary purpose. (2) The assessment had not been imposed in terms of the Act on proprietors occupying their own houses. (3) That the specific, and consequently the primary, purposes for which the power of assessing was granted by the Act had been totally disregarded, and the intentions of the Legislature for the good of the town entirely frustrated. The last, although perhaps the most direct violation of the statute, was what the complainers were disposed to insist least upon. Lighting the streets and a public clock, however desirable, were not to be compared with that essential necessary of life, an adequate supply of good water. Their request therefore was that the trustees would devote the assessment solely to the supplying of all parts of the town with water, that they would cause pipes of a sufficient size to be laid from St. John's Well to the reservoir, that they would leave a branch pipe at the corner of the school area for the accommodation of the scholars and of nearly thirty families residing in that quarter (a great proportion of whom were old people, and very unable to carry water up the hill), and that they would cause two additional wells to be erected for the benefit of the east and west ends of the town, and adopt such regulations as would prevent any of the water from being carried out of the parish. They concluded by stating that if the trustees refused their requests, they would feel it a duty incumbent on them to resist payment of the assessment, and to seek redress in a higher quarter.

The trustees greatly resented the tone and temper of this memorial, and especially the threat to appeal to the Lord Advocate. Seven very lengthy resolutions were adopted by them by way of reply, and the meeting authorised the clerk to send Mr. Stephens a copy of them for the information of himself and the other complainers. They also ordered two hundred copies to be printed and circulated amongst the inhabitants. The substance of their defence amounted to this—It was quite erroneous to say that the house assessment had been laid on for the special purpose of supplying water. On the contrary, as they specially pointed out, the Act authorising its imposition did not so much as mention the water question. They claimed that they were as much interested as any one could be in the town having a good water supply. Since 1816, they stated, no less than £432 11s. 4d. had been expended for that purpose, being upwards of £100 more than the whole sum yet levied by assessment. They also fully explained their present financial position, and what led up to it, and closed thus:— "The trustees conclude by remarking that they have long suffered in silence the misrepresentations and unmerited censure of those who are more ready to find fault with than to aid them in the service of the public. But now that a formal complaint is made, they deem it only doing justice to themselves to submit this explanation to the candid consideration of the inhabitants at large."

XIII.

The following is a copy of the annual statement of trust funds submitted by Mr. William Henderson for the year ending 30th May, 1834. When we compare this short and simple document with the elaborate annual volume of 80 folio pages which is now its successor we rub our eyes indeed.

Revenue.					Expenditure.				
Received anchorage duty,	£74	12	5		Cash in advance 31st May, 1833,		£103	14	0
„ Street dung,	35	0	0		*Expenses on Harbour—*				
„ Assessment on houses — sum collected,	79	11	0		Paid W. Paton's wages, £28 0 0				
„ Bye-ales impost,	8	3	4½		„ Labourers, Carters, &c., 5 17 9				
	£197	6	9½		£33 17 9				
Cash in advance,	63	10	3½		*Less* Harbour Gates, 0 10 0		33	7	9
					Expenses on Streets—				
					Paid A. Bathgate's wages, £21 13 0				
					„ Cartage of dung, 8 18 4				
					„ Sundries, 0 17 10		31	9	2
					„ Expenses on water,		1	0	11
					Interest on borrowed money—				
					Paid Mrs. Davis, £40 0 0				
					„ Shipmasters Society, 10 0 0				
					„ Shipmasters Box, 10 0 0				
					„ Landsmen's Box, 9 12 0				
					„ W. H., 1 13 5		71	5	5
					„ Mrs. Stewart room's rent, £3 1 6				
					„ Charges on assessment, 3 3 1				
					„ Stationery, posts, and incidents, 0 15 2				
					„ Geo. Henderson's salary, 10 0 0		16	19	9
					„ Wm. Roy in part of his account,		3	0	1
	£260	17	1				£260	17	1

BALANCE ACCOUNT PER LEDGER.

To Mrs. Davies,	£1000 0 0	By assessment on houses and for the balance of this account,	£280 8 7	
,, Society of Shipmasters,	260 0 0	A considerable part of this will not be recovered and should be carried to the General Fund.		
,, Shipmasters' Box,	255 0 0			
,, Landsmen's Box,	249 12 0			
,, Shotts Iron Company—to bear interest from 30th November, 1832,	125 5 2	Bills receivable,	£4 5 0	
,, William Roy,	1 11 4	By General Fund,	1670 5 2½	
,, Cash in advance,	63 10 3½			1674 10 2½
	£1954 18 9½			£1954 18 9½

XIV.

The trustees of the town and harbour were their own sanitary inspectors. Below we give extracts from the report of a special committee, which, along with the Parochial Board, inspected the whole town in October, 1848. Their methods were thorough, and they called a spade a spade. They found the following:—

    Gardner's Land—Horrid.

    King Street—A yard and closed door heaped with filth from the windows and two dunghills.

    Peebles' pigstye—Bad; his cellar ought to have a door or built up.

    Beneficent Society's Land—Bad drain, dunghill, and nuisance.

    Slidry Stane—A noxious drain.

    Wilson's house at Slidry Stane—One continued mass of filth.

    John Marshall's property—Horrid.

    Providence stair—Three dunghills.

    Mrs. Peddie's backdoor—The yard wants paving; two ugly dunghills.

    Robertson's dunghill, &c.—Disgusting.

    Mrs. Wallace complains of two pools in the foundry yard below her bedroom window.

Walker, butcher, kills at his shop, also Stevenson, in his shop.

The Duke of Hamilton's property at the east end of Corbiehall is in a most wretched condition, as the whole of the Duke's property here is, without exception. Would recommend the whole of the Duke's property to be divided into sections, say, of four or five families each.

Nimmo obstructs the pen close with his carts.

Boslem's house ought to be whitewashed.

These things do not make pleasant reading, and with the smoke of the saltpans and coalpits, they undoubtedly combined to give the seaport the unenviable reputation of being a "terribly dirty place." But it would be an entirely unfounded statement to make now. It was, we think, even a bold thing to say in 1879,[3] when Mr. Gillespie wrote about the "sewers, squalor, and soot" of Bo'ness. We may as well hear him out—"Bo'ness, as we have said, is both dull and dirty. Its situation, for one thing, is very low, which militates against its sanitary interests. It is ill-constructed and worse kept; each narrow, crooked street is in a more neglected condition than its neighbour; and the authorities apparently leave everything to the laws of Nature, not thinking it part of their business to make the place clean, healthy, or sweet. The architecture is said to have been once admirably described by an old gentleman with the aid of a decanter and a handful of nutshells thus—'You see this decanter; this is the church.' Then taking the shells and pouring them over the decanter, he said, 'And these are the houses.' Nothing could be truer. There is not one regular street in the town. The poor lieges, too, have the same wretchedly 'reekit' appearance as the place itself. And thus, looking at Bo'ness with its back to the wall, it is strange to think of it as a proud Burgh of Regality. With the exception of the queer-looking old church, it has not a house that would do credit to the humblest clachan." No doubt

---

[3] See Gillespie's "Round About Falkirk."

Bo'ness was at that time in a pretty low way. It was practically stagnant, and grass grew in some of the streets. Mr. Gillespie termed it a condition of comparative indigence. But he was good enough to herald the approach of brighter and better days, in view of the "enterprising and important works being carried out in the extension of the harbour and the construction of a dock."

XV.

We must return, however, to the minutes. There are frequent references throughout these to letters and appeals to His Grace the Duke of Hamilton. We can only mention one, which was in the form of a petition, and the most appealing of all. It was apparently presented at Hamilton by a deputation from the trustees, consisting of John Anderson, Archibald Hunter, Peter Mills, and George Henderson, their clerk. The date of the document is 19th October, 1848, and is signed by Mr. Henderson, "your Grace's faithful and devoted servant." He acquainted His Grace—(1) That the streets in many places were very narrow and wretchedly paved, and susceptible of repair, alteration, and improvement. (2) That the town was most miserably supplied with water in consequence of the mineral workings drawing off the chief supply. Also that the inhabitants were unable to obtain anything like an adequate supply of fresh water for domestic purposes even by standing their turn for hours at the public wells of the town. This annoyance to the inhabitants was the source of many unseemly brawls and disputes. And the want of a copious water supply was clearly standing in the way of the improvement of the sanitary condition of the town. (3) That the authorities and people of the town were without any proper place in which to meet for the discussion and discharge of the town's business, nor was there a hall or public room in which a public meeting of the inhabitants could for any useful purpose be convened.

Coming to financial affairs, Mr. Henderson points out that the trustees were deeply in debt, the arrears of many years.

They had not money to meet the ordinary expenditure required for the town and harbour. They had not the means to pave and improve the streets. They could not afford a better supply of water to the inhabitants, and they could not provide public buildings. In this dilemma they applied to His Grace for assistance. And they respectfully suggested that the case would be met by granting to the town at a merely nominal rent a lease of the Town's Customs and the building called the Town House (part of which is presently used as a county lock-up, a large portion still remaining unoccupied). This favour, he was sure, would go far to enable the trustees to execute the improvements so much required, and would confer a lasting benefit upon the inhabitants.

The Duke was good enough to comply, and he and his factor gave every assistance in connection with the endeavours of the trustees to increase the water supply.

In October, the following year, " the people of Borrowstoun and the inhabitants of Newtown" resented some operations connected with the cutting of deep drains at Borrowstoun, by which the trustees " had every prospect of materially increasing their water supply." They therefore wrote to Mr. Webster, the Duke's factor, to use his influence to stop this interference and to assure the people that the trustees had no intention whatever to deprive the Borrowstoun people of their supply of water. On the contrary, they wished to improve it both for them and the town of Bo'ness. For this purpose they proposed to considerably enlarge the fountain of St. John's Well, which was to be properly enclosed, and a pump put into it for the use of the inhabitants of Borrowstoun.

XVI.

The last phase of the ever-recurring water question which comes within our notice here is by far the most important. From 1846 to 1852 the trustees were almost constantly engaged, sometimes unaided and sometimes with the assistance of experts, in visiting and reporting upon various suggested sources for a new and enlarged supply. They examined two springs in the neighbourhood of Inveravon, the first called Langlands and the second Cold Wells. Both were found highly satisfactory in quality and quantity. No heavy cuttings were required for either. A spring on the lands of Balderstone was also visited, and found suitable in every way. In fact, the committee of inspection unanimously recommended the trustees "to turn their attention to this quarter, being so much nearer to the town, as well as to the pipes which bring the present supply." The method of bringing the water over the hill was by "the plan of a syphon." Mr. Wilson, of Kinneil Ironworks, was next approached for a supply of pit water from the Snab pit. He was quite agreeable to give this. The water was to be filtered, and a pond was to be constructed near the east side of that field above the distillery and south of Mr. Vannan's garden. In the midst of these inquiries the trustees received a letter from James Dunlop, Braehead, with " a short and simple " suggestion. This was that the Dean or Gil Burn,[4] where " a reservoir was formed by Nature capable of containing a quantity of water sufficient to supply in the most complete manner throughout the whole year the inhabitants of Bo'ness. It is excellently suited either for culinary or cleansing purposes, and far superior for the latter purpose to your present supply from St. John's Well." He also pointed out that the quality of the water from the Snab pit was very hard, and very likely would soon become salt or brackish. His suggestion, he ventured to think, was a most useful one, and he hoped the trustees would take the trouble to examine the site. They did so, but considered the plan " quite ridiculous." A resolution was then made to adopt the Snab pit scheme, but it was negatived by a majority of one vote. Mr. Webster, the Duke's factor, took a great interest in the Cold Wells scheme, and obtained estimates for bringing that supply to the town. These amounted to £1000, but the scheme was abandoned as being far beyond the resources of the trustees even with the aid of a public

[4] The Dean Burn was evidently meant, but it appears to have gone under the name of the Gil Burn also.

subscription. The Snab pit water was once more pushed for a while, and Mr. Hall Blyth, C.E., Edinburgh, was engaged. After a time, however, the idea was finally abandoned. The engineer who at last relieved the minds of the trustees, after many visits and the preparation of many specifications, was Mr. William Gale, C.E., Glasgow. He was introduced to the trustees through Mr. Robert Steele, of the Bo'ness Foundry Company. Mr. Gale was stated to be eminently qualified for such an undertaking, and was more employed in bringing water into towns by gravitation than any other engineer in Scotland. The site ultimately fixed on was known as the Temple pit at Borrowstoun. Much interest was taken by the inhabitants in the selection of the site and mode of construction. A public meeting was held, and a special committee of the inhabitants, consisting of William Simpson, James Gray, and Robert Morris, kept in close touch with the movements of the trustees. They especially gave great assistance with the public subscription lists which were opened. These were "not confined to proprietors or any other class, but open to all holding property in or otherwise connected with the town, or having an interest in its welfare, whether residents or not." The resolution to proceed with the Temple pit reservoir was come to at a meeting of trustees held on 14th April, 1852. Those in office at the time appear to have been John Anderson, John Henderson, John Marshall, James Meikle, James Kirkwood, John Taylor, Peter Mills, Henry Rymer, James Jamieson, William Millar, Robert M'Nair, and William Donaldson. The contract was advertised, and fourteen tenders were received, mostly from Glasgow. The joint offer of Allan Henderson and George Gray was accepted at £158 4s. 2½d., being the lowest. Some of the offers were more than double that figure. The work was completed towards the end of the year. Mr. Alexander Gale was inspector, and in a long report made to the trustees in October we find this information:—" As now completed, the reservoir will contain 182·900 cubic feet, or 1,143,100 gallons. Taking the population of the town at 3000, this would keep up a supply of 5 gallons per day for seventy-six days, independent of any supply from St. John's Well or any casual shower that may fall during that time."

XVII.

The establishment of the Kinneil furnaces by Mr. John Wilson, Dundyvan, resulted in the Monkland Railway constructing a single line to Kinneil for goods traffic. It was opened on the 17th of March, 1851, by a trainload from Arden for the ironworks. And it is almost of romantic interest to know that the engine of that train was in charge of Mr. William Thomson, who afterwards became a successful merchant and Provost of the seaport. The extension of the railway to Bo'ness was the next step, but it was a serious thing for the town in one sense, for it meant the probable destruction of the west beach and the Corbiehall foreshore. The trustees were fully alive both to the numerous advantages which the extension of the railway would give, and also to the curtailment of public rights which were involved. Their minutes at this period are full of many interesting items, and contain a lengthy correspondence with the railway company, the Admiralty, and others. A Mr. J. H. Goldsmith appears to have been the people's champion. His letters are dated from Bo'ness, and he writes as if he were a member of the legal profession. But who he was we have been quite unable to discover. On the 13th of January, 1851, he wrote the trustees pointing out "the great and manifest injury which the inhabitants would suffer at the hands of the Slamannan and Bo'ness railway now constructing." These evils, he stated, might have been avoided by compelling the company to carry their railway on arches to its terminus. The west beach and western foreshore were then, we believe, much lower than now, and at the time Mr. Goldsmith wrote it would seem that the railway could easily have been led in as he suggested, on a long viaduct, thus leaving free access to the shore as hitherto through its arches. What, he continues, the inhabitants required, and had a right to demand at the hands

James Watt and his Outhouse at Kinneil.
(From a photograph by David Grant, Bo'ness.)

See page 372.

of the trustees, was their ancient bleaching and bathing ground, and the "freest possible unimpeded ebb and flow of the tide." Should they be unfortunately deprived of these rights compensation by thousands, not hundreds, should be sought for by them and obtained. Was it too late, he asks, to repair past inactivity by immediately sending a deputation to London? He trusted that the ill-advised stipulation for the building of three bridges did not give the power to fill up and make land between the railway and the waggon way. If it did not do so they had a good case, and their present negotiations might be broken off. They thus would have a fair field to begin *de novo*.

It had been resolved by the trustees that their resolution asking for £1000 for servitude rights on the beach should first of all be sent to Mr. Thomas Stevenson,[5] C.E., Edinburgh, to be reported by him to the Admiralty. This produced another letter of protest from Mr. Goldsmith on the 29th of January. At the end he begs to be excused for his hasty and rapidly digested remarks should they be deemed intrusive. The "remarks" consisted principally of the advice that caution was very necessary, and of a re-expression of his opinion that a deputation should be sent to London. The railway company, he says, had been there and told their tale. Why should the trustees not do so also? The telegraph, railway, writers, engineers, and London agents had been put in requisition against them. Why not go and do likewise? The battle was not to the strongest nor the race to the swiftest! "Remember," he concludes, "the fable of the bundle of sticks. United, like you, they were strong—disunited, easily broken and frail!"

By the 3rd of February an agreement had been entered into between the trustees and the railway company. This Mr. Goldsmith had perused, and on finding that it did not exclude the right of the inhabitants to negotiate for compensation for the loss of their beach servitude he once more took up his pen. This time he urged the calling together of the inhabitants. He says, "Had I seen the agreement sooner I should have advised

---

[5] Father of Robert Louis Stevenson.

this course. The agreement is bad law in many particulars." And with these words he disappears from the scene as suddenly and mysteriously as he had entered upon it.

Amongst the other correspondence we find the information that most of the young whales that were then caught in the Firth near Bo'ness were cut up on the beach west from the harbour, and thereafter carted along it to the whale-fishing company's boil house.

XVIII.

The following is a summary of a letter from the Admiralty to the trustees, dated 18th February, which explains the exact position of affairs. It was based upon the careful report of Mr. Stevenson, who on behalf of the Admiralty had inspected the ground and heard the views of parties. It may be mentioned that on that occasion the trustees took the opportunity of mentioning to him that the slag thrown out at Kinneil Ironworks into the Firth had done great injury to the beach, and insisted on his reporting this to the Admiralty:—The railway was to be carried on an embankment from the pier of Bo'ness harbour to the salt pond. This was a distance of 500 yards. Being generally about 100 feet seaward of high water mark the line would clearly be interposed between the shore and the sea. All access by the public to the shore for the purposes of walking, bathing, and drying clothes, and also for carts as hitherto, would thus be cut off. Beyond the site of the railway embankment the foreshore was flat and muddy, and there were one or more jetties there which would be cut off and rendered useless. It would be of little benefit to the inhabitants to have openings or archways under the railway, as immediately outside of the embankment the foreshore was soft mud. The slip of land intervening between the railway and the embankment must be filled up, as otherwise it would become filthy and a nuisance to the town when no longer washed by the sea. Undoubtedly by the construction of the railway the public would be deprived of some advantages and of access to the sea heretofore enjoyed.

The Lords Commissioners of the Admiralty, says the writer in conclusion, could therefore only treat this case in the same manner as a number of others of a like character, namely, that at the embankment, and between the railway and the sea wall for retaining the same, there be laid out and for ever maintained by the company a public way or walk, not less than 300 yards in length and not less than 12 feet wide; that three level crossings, or timber footway crossings, over the railway, not less than 6 feet high, be provided to give the public access to the public way at specified sites; that three flights of steps leading from the public way to the foot of the sea wall of the embankment be provided; and that the necessary culverts or drains across the railway be put in to keep the town dry or clean as heretofore. The parties having landing jetties on the line of the shore to be cut off would require to have others erected outside of the sea face of the railway embankment by the company, with access thereto across the railway. And, lastly, the arch already made under the railway near the salt pond would fall to be maintained by the railway company, along with a proper road leading to the same—a clear headway of 7 feet to be allowed under the arch.

This then explains the origin of the promenade, which was shortly afterwards constructed on the lines just indicated. It existed for a long number of years, and, being the property of the townspeople, was well taken advantage of. The three level crossings were not a success, as they were frequently blocked by long trains of waggons when railway traffic at the harbour began to develop. Several accidents—some of them fatal—occurred, for which the railway company had to pay compensation. The inhabitants therefore were ultimately approached many years ago to sell their rights to the North British Railway Company. After long negotiations it was eventually arranged that in exchange for their rights and privileges they receive £150 per annum for all time. This was then believed to be an advantageous arrangement, and the annual income gradually accumulated and came to form what was known as the Promenade Fund or Common Good. However, in the many changes and re-arrangements made with the railway company in subsequent years, the annual payment seems to have become merged in something else, and the Promenade Fund long ago exhausted in public improvements.

CHAPTER XIV.

THE REPRESENTATIVES OF BO'NESS.

1. Origin of the Body—2. Erection of Parish of Borrowstounness: Manner of Election of Representatives: Their Duties in Early Days—3. Captain John Ritchie and the Reasons for his Action of Declarator—4. Why Manse and Glebe Not Provided—5. The Advocates in the Case: The Contents of the Voluminous Decree: Mr. Ritchie "Gets his Character"—6. His "Violent Measures": His Counsel's Vindication of him—7. The Ritchie Party Demand Production of all Books and Papers of Representatives: Amusing Arguments For and Against—8. The Court Decides who shall in Future Elect the Representatives: Procedure for Calling Annual Meeting: Difficulties over First Meeting—9. Ritchie Unduly Officious: Court finds that Representatives can only Stent for Stipend and Apply their Income for Payment of Stipend Alone—10. The Defenders in the Minister's Declaratory Action for Manse and Glebe—11. What the Lord Ordinary held the Duke should Pay: What the Funds of Representatives Consisted of According to Ritchie and According to Themselves—12. Some of the Productions and their Contents—13. Origin of Division of Churchyard at the Wynd—14. The Tenacity and Stubbornness of the Fight: The "Teazing" of Ritchie: The Appreciation of his Friends—15. Summary of Final Decision of Inner House—16. Fifty Years After: Dr. Rennie's Long Litigation over Disposal of Surplus—17. How Farm of Muirhouse came to Representatives: Result of Dr. Rennie's Appeal to House of Lords: Opinions of the Judges.

I.

IF we except the Sea Box Society, which scarcely comes under the category of a public body, the Representatives of Bo'ness—still in existence, though with a much more formal and circumscribed ambit of government than of old—is the oldest public body in the town. So little does it now bulk in the life of the community that at noon upon the first Wednesday of each year the townsfolk are generally startled by the vigorous pealing of the bell of the Parish Church, to be calmed later, however, by the information that nothing more alarming is happening than their own annual meeting for the election of Representatives.

With the reading of a simple cash statement, the voting of the surplus to the minister, and the annual election, the business is completed, and we hear little or nothing of the Representatives for another year. But stored away in strong safes in a room at the rear of the church is the history of this ancient and one-time very important local body in the form of charters, Acts of Parliament, minute books, and bundle upon bundle of letters, agreements, and other legal documents. How important it was and what part it played in the history of the town during the eighteenth century we shall now endeavour to indicate.

The body arose out of the very unusual circumstances which attended the erection of the first place of worship here, about the year 1638. There was then no Parish of Bo'ness, the parish for the neighbourhood being Kinneil, with a church, manse, and glebe in that village. The inhabitants of Borrowstounness having, as one record has it, "become fairly numerous and wealthy," erected a church at Corbiehall, at their own charges, after consulting the Presbytery. They satisfied the latter about their means of erecting the building, and indicated their hopes of being in time able to raise a permanent fund, the interest of which would go towards the minister's stipend. They were not at once in the position of having a minister of their own, so the minister of Kinneil, for about ten years, did duty in both places of worship.

In 1649 a supplication was made to the Scots Parliament by "the parishioners and inhabitants of the toun and village of Borrowstounness to have the Kirk of Borrowstounness made a kirk by itself, and that the same be divided from ye kirk of Kinneil." The supplication was signed by James Gib, George Allane, John Langlands, and Archibald Falconer; and these parties, while expected to appear themselves before Parliament, were fortified with the power from their constituents "to appoint a procurator to attend the Parliament and present the said supplication." The result was that the Estates "separated and divided the Kirk of Borrowstounness from the Kirk of Kynneil in all time coming whereof it was ance a part, and ordained and declared Grahame's Dyk to bound the same on the south, the sea on the north, Thirlestane on the east, and the castle wall—commonly called Capies Wall—on the west." Then followed an important provision—"Siclik the said estates gives power to those whom the supplicants has chosen to be assisting to the Kirk Session according to Act of Parliament, or some other who shall be nominat by common consent of town and session, to stent yearly every inhabitant and indweller within the said parochin, bounded as said is, according to their abilities for making up the yearly stipend of 800 merks promised and obliged to be payed by the supplicants to the minister and his successors in the said church, and that according to the inhabitants, their abilities, aye and until the annual rent of the supplicants their stock extend to the sum of 800 merks yearly." These are the words of the statute itself, but the supplication of the inhabitants was, "To stent every indweller in our kirk, though they dwell not therein themselves, according to their several abilities, and in order that those who are refractory to do so good a work, and will not give their proportion of the said stipend, may be compelled to bear proportionable burden with the rest."

II.

In 1669, twenty years after the first Act, another change took place in Church affairs. That year the Scots Parliament, on the supplication of Duke William and Duchess Anne of Hamilton, suppressed the Kirk and Parish of Kinneil. Kinneil Parish was then united to Borrowstounness, and the Kirk of the Seaport declared to be the Kirk of the United Parish. The old stipend of Kinneil, together with the 800 merks payable by the inhabitants of Borrowstounness, was appropriated to be the constant stipend in time coming of the minister of the united parish and his successors. A manse and glebe also were appointed to be provided to him by the Duke and Duchess. The old kirk, manse, and glebe of Kinneil fell, under this arrangement, into the policies of Kinneil House. Borrowstounness then became the prevailing name of the united parishes, bounded on the north by the Firth of Forth, on the east by the Parish of Carriden, and on the south and west by the Parish of Linlithgow and the river Avon.

The Representatives for the first hundred years fulfilled many important duties. How the stent or taxation authorised by the 1649 Act was raised, or how that and the other funds of the town were managed until 1672, cannot be traced, the records for that period having been lost. Neither can it be said in what manner the managers or assistants were chosen. From 1672, however, down to 1694 it appears that these persons were annually chosen by a poll of the inhabitants. It was about this time that those elected came to be known as the Representatives, or assistants. They had, in conjunction with the Kirk Session, to impose the stent and to manage it and the other public funds connected with the church and minister's stipend. Out of the moneys received it was their custom to make payment of the 800 merks yearly to the minister, of £6 sterling to the minister for house rent, of 1100 merks yearly salary to the schoolmaster, of 100 merks yearly salary to the treasurer employed in collecting the various branches of the revenue, and also some occasional expenses for the repairs to kirk and kirkyard dykes and schoolhouse.

About the year 1694 the method of poll election was altered by the unanimous consent of the inhabitants. In its place a method was adopted under which the nine retiring Representatives chose others to act with them in electing a third nine. The latter were then presented to the minister as representing the Kirk Session, and the Baron Bailie as representing the inhabitants. On receiving the approbation of these gentlemen they became the managers for the ensuing year. This system of election continued down to 1738, when a slight variation was introduced. A list containing the names of the

Representatives for the preceding year and nine others chosen by them was submitted to the minister and Baron Bailie, who selected therefrom the nine managers for the ensuing year. This continued till about the date of the action after mentioned.

III.

It certainly appears that the management of affairs which were really and truly public, and intended to be so under the 1649 statute, had in course, possibly through indifference on the part of the inhabitants and a spirit of autocracy on the part of the minister and the Baron Bailie, fallen almost entirely into their hands. But there arose in the town a man, clear-headed and exceptionally tenacious, who resolved to end this. This was John Ritchie, master mariner, Box Master of the Sea Box Society. As such he was well aware of the remarkable generosity of the society and its individual members at the time of the building of the church, and later when a permanent fund for the maintenance of the minister was raised. Moreover, he was apparently wholeheartedly devoted to the welfare of the town generally. To clear the air and put matters on a better basis he raised an action in the Court of Session. An expensive and keenly contested litigation followed, in which many hard things were said on both sides. It lasted for eight years, and must have been the chief topic of discourse in the town during that exciting period.

The action was one of declarator, and was raised in the year 1761. It was instituted in the names of John Ritchie, Alexander Thomson, Duncan Stirling, Andrew Fraser, Gabriel Thomson, Robert Nicol, James Kelso, Walter Duncan, Alexander Young, William Shed, William Miller, John Kincaid, Robert Dealls, James Melville, William Burgess, Alexander Cunninghame, John Peacock, John Hardie, James Morgan, and Robert Cram, all shipmasters, sailors, mariners, traders, and inhabitants in the town and village of Borrowstounness and members of the Incorporate Seabox there, against John Cowan, merchant and

Baron Bailie in the said burgh; Mr. Patrick Baillie, minister; Mr. William Logan, precentor; John Addison, merchant; James Main, Thomas Grindlay, Alexander Glassfurd, James Drummond, James Grindlay, James Addison, Charles Addison, John Pearson, merchants; and Thomas Thomson, wright, all elders and members of the Kirk Session, Borrowstounness; and James Main, Thomas Grindlay, Alexander Glassfurd, James Drummond, Duncan Aire, shipmasters; James Scrimgeor, and John Stevenson, merchants; Thomas Johnston, mariner; and James Renny, mason, all assistants to the Kirk Session of Borrowstounness. The pursuers maintained that the assistants to the kirk session were illegally and unwarrantably chosen as being chosen by Baron Bailie Cowan and Mr. Baillie, the minister, instead of by the common consent of the townspeople and the Kirk Session jointly in terms of the Act. It was maintained also that the assistants and session had no power to stent or assess the pursuers or the inhabitants in respect that the funds mortified for church purposes then annually produced the eight hundred merks of stipend necessary. One phase of the stent had proved very obnoxious. Without the slightest warrant, as it seems to us, the Representatives imposed a marriage tax on those newly married. Many submitted to it, as the books of the Sea Box Society show, but the general objection to it was strong. It was more than once mentioned in the course of the case as iniquitous, and it would seem that the contention that it was justified was ultimately departed from. A further contention was that the defenders could not gratuitously gift away any part of the free area of the church without a just and adequate price, and that the heirs and representatives of heritors and portioners of the town ought to be preferred to those whose predecessors did not contribute to the building of the church. Pursuers also objected to a proposal on the part of the defenders to build a second loft above the sailors' loft, which, they said, would incommode the pursuers and their brethren by making their loft a passage or thoroughfare, and would cut off the light from the two windows which were in the area.

IV.

The case was raised before Lord Nisbet. It frequently came before all the Lords by way of appeal on various branches which the Lord Ordinary disposed of as he went along. Finally all the points of Ritchie's case, and of another one by the minister which was conjoined with it, came in their entirety before all the Lords. The decision will be found towards the end of this chapter, but it may be mentioned here that nearly all the things Ritchie contended for were allowed.

While, no doubt, matters required to be cleared up, it cannot after all be said that the Representatives were wilfully guilty of maladministration. Their powers under the 1649 Act were in very general terms, and as circumstances changed with the times it was only natural they should think it within their rights to stent the inhabitants and administer the funds to meet the increasing local expenditure. It would seem, too, that with the death of Duke William in 1694 and Duchess Anne in 1716 the interests of the burgh did not get the attention which the Duke and Duchess had been wont to give them. Some of their successors had long minorities, and during these little expenditure was incurred. At any rate, the feeling locally appears to have been that Baron Bailie Cowan, the chamberlain at Kinneil, was inclined to be over-zealous in the Hamilton interest. Under the 1669 Act, as we have seen, Duke William and Duchess Anne had to provide a manse and glebe for the minister of Bo'ness. This apparently they never did, or were really never requested to do, in the sense contemplated by the Act. A house certainly was originally provided, and accepted by the Representatives as a manse, but the minister would not live in it, whereupon a yearly sum of £6 was granted him for the purpose of providing himself with a house. Thus matters remained somewhat unsatisfactory. It was, of course, all very well during the incumbency of the Rev. John Waugh, the first minister. Mr. Waugh married Lady Hamilton of Grange, and settled there, or at the Dower

House in Grangepans, so there was not, during his ministry, the same necessity for providing a proper manse and glebe. After his death, however, things remained much as they were. Then in time came Ritchie, the fighting captain, and his following, and the management of the Representatives was closely scrutinised and criticised. Mr. Ritchie and his party thought the housing provisions made for the minister quite inadequate, and sharply raised the point as to the liability of the Hamilton family to provide a suitable manse and glebe. Mr. Baillie, the minister, no doubt under the careful advice of his lawyers, appeared to have realised the justice of this argument, for we find that shortly after Ritchie's action against himself and the others was served, he raised a counter-action against the then Duke of Hamilton's tutors and others in the parish to provide a manse and glebe. This action, as the matters involved were analogous on that point at any rate, was ultimately conjoined with Ritchie's.

V.

The counsel engaged in these important and lengthy litigations were men of eminence. For Ritchie there appeared Mr. Thomas Miller,[1] His Majesty's Advocate (afterwards Lord President under the judicial title of Lord Barskimming), Mr. James Dewar, and Mr. Alexander Murray, of Murrayfield; and for the minister, Kirk Session, and assistants, Mr. Alexander Lockhart, Mr. William Wallace, Mr. Robert Bruce, and Mr. John Dalrymple. The Duke of Hamilton's tutors were represented by Mr. Lockhart and Mr. Walter Stewart.

Much of our information for this chapter has been obtained from the decree in Ritchie's case, which was willingly placed at our disposal by the Seabox Society. It consists of seven hundred and eight closely written foolscap pages, and has been carefully bound to ensure its better preservation. The extract was issued on 6th November, 1764, some months after

---

[1] He is one of the characters (Sheriff Miller) in Stevenson's "Catriona."

the final decree was pronounced. Litigation in the Court of Session one hundred and fifty years ago was a very different thing to what it is now, and much less expensive. Procedure was very cumbrous, and oral pleading was not of much account. The causes were conducted chiefly in writing, and there were minutes, representations, answers, replies, duplies, triplies, and memorials without end. Decrees not only contained decisions of the Court, but embodied the contents of the whole pleadings from start to finish. Besides representations and the other papers already indicated, this decree gives the debates of counsel, the orders and judgments of the Lord Ordinary, notes of appeal, and the Inner House judgments on the appealed points. The volume is a valuable local document, for amidst all its legal phraseology it contains facts concerning some of the most interesting and important phases in the history of the community during portions of the seventeenth and eighteenth centuries. These facts, by a lengthy process of winnowing, we have endeavoured to extract from its pages. They are now here recorded in as informal and attractive a style as we could reasonably arrange them.

Mr. Ritchie "got his character" repeatedly from defenders' counsel throughout the case. It was said in Court at the first debate that in raising the action he was actuated by mean, selfish, and spiteful motives. In support of this statement it was explained that Ritchie had demanded a seat in the kirk from the Representatives at a price far below its value, and that demand they did not think it their duty to comply with. Over the refusal Ritchie, it was alleged, had produced "a good deal of bustle and confusion in the town, and among the rest the present process." Sundry of the inhabitants, it was also stated, were much in want of seats, and the Representatives made the proposal to erect a second loft or gallery above the loft or gallery commonly called the sailors' loft. The most considerable and most sensible of the Corporation of Shipmasters and Sailors heartily approved of the proposal, as it appeared to them their loft could suffer no prejudice thereby. Ritchie, however, dissented, and, counsel said, made this an occasion of revenge for the refusal his application for a seat had met with. He was accused of having formed, and in part executed, schemes of profit and power to himself. He had begun by "buzzing in the ears of the common sailors" how affronting it would be to them if they allowed a loft to be put over their heads; that having the good fortune to be well listened to, he got several "turbulent and mobbish meetings" called together, at which some hasty and violent resolutions were entered into. These included authority to carry on litigations in their name, and to use the society's funds for that purpose.

VI.

Most of the shipmasters and the wisest of the sailors opposed these violent measures, and instructed the Box Master to refuse to issue money to Mr. Ritchie for his litigations. This gave rise to Mr. Ritchie forming a scheme to have himself elected Box Master for the ensuing year. His intrigues with the sailors, it was alleged, so far prevailed that a sort of election was made in his favour, although another election was made in favour of the old Box Master. As to the different conclusions of Ritchie's declaratory action, the defending counsel held the poll election was laid aside long ago by consent of all concerned as productive of many wicked and pernicious consequences, and that the then current method, although not a poll election, must still be considered a nomination by common consent of town and session. Counsel further emphatically maintained that the funds laid aside with the object of yielding the eight hundred merks of stipend were not yet able to do so, and that stenting was still just and necessary. He claimed, moreover, that the reparation of the kirk, kirkyard dyke, and schoolhouse, the house rent of the minister, and the salaries of the schoolmaster and treasurer fell first to be deducted. He denied disposing of any of the kirk area gratuitously, and argued at length in favour of his clients' action in making arrangements for erecting a second loft.

Ritchie's senior counsel, the Lord Advocate, replied that

John Anderson.

(From a group photograph taken at the laying of the foundation stone of the Anderson Academy, Bo'ness, 12th June, 1869, within a year of his death.)

See page 386.

the history defenders had been pleased to give of the origin and motives of the process was altogether false and calumnious. Mr. Ritchie had no other motive in joining in the process than to bring the fund appropriated for the minister's stipend under the administration of those in whom it was vested by the Acts, and to put a stop to illegal exactions. Counsel insisted on a fair inquiry into the state of the public funds. He commended the pursuers' action in questioning the right of the minister and Baron Bailie to appoint practically whom they liked as assistants, and begged leave to call such behaviour a direct usurpation, contrary to law and the privileges of the inhabitants. He further submitted to his lordship's judgment whether the pursuers deserved to be treated as mobbers and disturbers of the public peace of the town because they were endeavouring to vindicate the rights of the inhabitants.

To this, defenders' counsel was permitted to reply, and his speech was in an ironical vein. Mr. Ritchie, he said, had been pleased to deny through his counsel all mean and selfish motives and to assume to himself the respectable character of an asserter of the rights and privileges of the people. This, however, was no more than exhibiting the same personage before the Lord Ordinary which he had already with some success put on to the sailors and some of the lowest inhabitants, and thereby procured their concurrence in the process. What his real and true motives were would best appear when the truth of his allegations with respect to the extent of the fund and the pretended mismanagement thereof came to be canvassed.

VII.

The Ritchie party demanded production of the whole books and papers in possession of the Kirk Session, present assistants, and the Baron Bailie relative to the fund in dispute and its application. His lordship was satisfied the request was reasonable, and gave the necessary order, and also called for a state of the stock. Defenders declined to produce the books, but offered excerpts instead, and asked his lordship to reconsider his former decision. The judge, however, was firm, and adhered to his original interlocutor. Defenders then, with marked obstinacy, appealed the point to the whole judges, and they, after lengthy debates and inquiries, decided that excerpts would meet the case, and allowed the pursuers access to the books at Borrowstounness to make notes of what they wished. The arguments for and against producing the books both before the Lord Ordinary and the whole Court are very amusing. Here are some samples. Counsel for the defenders argued that in asking for the books pursuers were only fishing for what discoveries they could make, and his clients could not think it reasonable that a cartload of these books should be transported to Edinburgh and lodged in process, thus exposing them to laceration and other damage. He emphasised the point that they would make a very bulky and voluminous production, and that there would be great difficulty in bringing them to Edinburgh. He also urged they could not conveniently be deprived of their interim use, the administration of the affairs of the community requiring that they should not be allowed out of the town. Later their argumentative fervour increased. An order of this kind for lodging in the hands of the clerk to the process such a multitude of books for upwards of one hundred years back was unprecedented. Moreover, it would impose an intolerable hardship upon the clerks to be burdened with the custody of such a number of books, possibly for years, as there was no saying how long such a process might subsist. They themselves did not think it would be short. Further, they opined none of the clerk's offices could contain half a dozen such productions, and also that the clerks would not be "extremely fond" to take charge of them. Once more they pleaded the books themselves were necessary for "the daillie administration of affairs by the respective communities to which they belong," and that their absence would lead to a "total stagnation of business at Borrowstounness." They also wished to be forgiven for repeating their anxiety about the safety of the books while in Edinburgh—

they might be defaced, or they might be mangled. Ritchie's counsel pooh-poohed this fuss about the books, and went the length of saying that this obstinate refusal to produce them made his clients now firmly believe what they had long conjectured, namely, that these books would expose a certain scene that the defenders would rather wish a veil was thrown over. As to the alleged difficulty of transport to Edinburgh, Mr. Miller ironically said unfortunately his clients were so blind that they could not see the smallest difficulty, the road being good and the distance inconsiderable. As to the total-stagnation-of-business argument, here again they confessed themselves in the dark, for how could it from thence follow that such a thing would happen? Could anything be more easy than to write down the interim occurrences in other books, which could afterwards be transcribed into the ordinary books? They were willing to meet the objections to the removal as far as they reasonably could, and suggested they would be satisfied with having the liberty of inspecting them in Borrowstounness. The offer of excerpts they respectfully declined, as only the strictest examination of the books themselves would be satisfactory.

VIII.

Ritchie in his summons asked, as already hinted, that it be found and declared that the Representatives were illegally chosen, and that the method of choosing in all time coming be by the townspeople and Kirk Session jointly; also that, there being now a sufficient fund for payment of the minister's stipend, the Representatives and Kirk Session had no power to further stent the inhabitants. It is to be noted that the 1649 Act did not specify how the assistants were to be chosen or how many. Lord Nisbet recognised the importance of this part of the dispute, and at once remitted it to the whole Lords. They, on 28th November, 1760, found that the heritors and inhabitants, in conjunction with the minister and Kirk Session, had the sole power of electing their own Representatives or assistants for stenting them if necessary, and for administering the fund already raised by former stents, and that they might "chuse" such competent number of these representatives or assistants as they should think proper. They remitted to the Lord Ordinary to proceed accordingly. The manner, time, and place of calling the inhabitants was then decided by Lord Nisbet. The manner was to be by intimation to be made by the precentor from his desk upon a Sunday two free days at least before the date of meeting; the time of the first meeting was to be any day of the month of December, 1760, or in the following month of January; and he found the proper place "for the meeting of the inhabitants to sitt" to be the church of Borrowstounness. He also found that by the word "inhabitants" none other could be understood than heritors, portioners, householders, and heads of families, or such persons as were liable to be stented in terms of the Act.

The first meeting was held on Wednesday, the 7th day of January, 1761. Soon after the Ritchie party stated that they found two amendments to his lordship's interlocutor absolutely necessary. First, that the election be appointed in all time coming to be held annually on a fixed day, such as the first Wednesday of January yearly; and secondly, that upon the precentor's failing to make intimation the then Box Master to the Sea Box, and his successors in office, should be ordained to do so by causing the officer of the society to go through the town with his bell, and proclaim the meeting of the inhabitants. His lordship granted the amendments craved, the other side having somehow omitted to put in answers. And now another storm in a teacup arose. The minister and the Representatives had been rather badly beaten so far by Ritchie and were in no good humour. They took exception, even after their failure to answer, to the Box Master of the Sea Box having anything to do with the calling of the meeting, and pressed his lordship to reconsider his decision. According to them the emergency intimation would be better made under the authority of the Baron Bailie by beat of drum and the drummer's proclaiming to the inhabitants *viva voce* the place, time, and purpose of the meeting. The Baron Bailie they said, was an officer "cloathed with some kind of authority," but they knew no title which the then boxmaster or his successors in office had to make the intimation.

IX.

Ritchie had recently made the defenders exceedingly wroth by employing notaries to intimate to them personally the terms of the recent judgments in his favour—a course quite unnecessary, and not enjoined upon him in any way by the Court. Further, he had exhibited a dictatorial spirit by demanding the precentor to read a somewhat flamboyant notice prepared by himself calling the meeting ordered by the Court. The precentor, however, refused to make the intimation till he had the liberty of the Baron Bailie, minister, and Kirk Session, and only capitulated after great pressure.

But what perhaps irritated defenders more than all was the attendance in a chaise of Ritchie's agent and his clerk from Edinburgh at the election in the church. This also was quite unnecessary, but it was evidently Ritchie's way of thrusting home his success.

Lord Nisbet adhered to his former interlocutor, and Ritchie remained triumphant.

His lordship had by this time a fair grip of the case. He evidently issued his judgments piecemeal on the points he had fully made up his mind on as the cause proceeded. In the interlocutor adhering to his former opinion about the manner of calling the meeting he dealt another blow to the defenders. There he also found that the Representatives had no power to stent or tax the inhabitants for any other use or purpose than for making up the yearly stipend of 800 merks to the minister; and that they had no power to apply any part of the income to any other purpose than the payment of the stipend; found also that the annual rent or yearly produce of the mortified stock was more than sufficient to meet the 800 merks; and that there was no power to stent or tax the inhabitants except in the case of the failure or decrease of the stock; found, further, that they could not gratuitously gift or give away any part of the area of the church without a just and adequate price, and that all such gifts were void and null; and, lastly, that the pursuers and the other members of the Incorporated Seabox Society had the only right to the sailors' loft in the kirk and to the area above the loft, and that the Kirk Session and Representatives could erect no loft or gallery above the same.

Here was a complete vindication of Ritchie's action; but the defenders, of course, appealed, and continued to fight hopelessly for years.

X.

As it may be interesting to know who, besides the Duke, were involved in the minister's declaratory action for manse and glebe, we may mention the summons ran thus:—
"Mr. Patrick Baillie, minister of the Gospel, at Borrowstounness; James Main, William Muir, shipmasters; Charles Addison, James Grindlay, John Addison, James Addison, and John Pearson, merchants, all elders and members of the Kirk Session of Borrowstounness, for themselves, and in behalf of the said Kirk Session, and also at the instance of John Falconer, Duncan Ayr, Thomas Grindlay, Thomas Johnstone, shipmasters; James Scrimgeour, merchant; Richard Hardie, sailor; James Dobie, Alexander Taylor, and William Aitken, wrights, all present Representatives of the town of Borrowstounness, or assistants to the Kirk Session for making up the yearly stipend to the minister of Borrowstounness, for themselves, and in name of the other inhabitants of the said burgh, against George James, Duke of Hamilton and Brandon, and the other heritors of the United Parish of Kinneil and Borrowstounness, viz., James Thomson, portioner of Borrowstoun; David Hardie, portioner there; Marjory Burnside, relict of the deceased Adam Boyle, merchant in Borrowstounness; and John Boyle, their son; James Thomson, merchant in Edinburgh; Archibald Burgess, maltman in Borrowstounness; John Thomson, wright

and glazier; Robert Cowan, writer; Alexander Buchanan, eldest and only son of the deceast Andrew Buchanan, merchant; Mary Muir, relict of Robert Hay, sailor; James Snedden, sailor; Marjory Wilson, relict of Peter Stephen, shipmaster; James Smith, surgeon; Isobel Black, spouse of James Rannie, mason, and the said James Rannie, for himself and his interest; Adam Boyle, shipmaster; Andrew Cowan, merchant, and one of the Annual Committee of Managers for the Society of Sailors; John Stevenson, merchant; Thomas Dundas, merchant in Linlithgow; Agnes Morton, relict of James Moir, some time Officer of Excise at Linlithgow, and George Moir, residenter in Linlithgow, eldest lawful son of the said James Moir; Isobel Jamieson, spouse to Robert Cram, brewer in Borrowstounness, and the said Robert Cram for himself and his interest; Robert Eglinton, butcher; Sarah Hamilton, daughter of Alexander Hamilton, minister of Stirling; Mr. James Wright, minister at Logie; and also the following persons members of the Committee of Managers for the Society of Sailors in Borrowstounness, proprietors of some acres of land, viz. :—Alexander Hodge, shipmaster; Andrew Mitchell, James Ackie, Robert Baron, junior; and Robert Deas, sailors; as also John Ritchie, shipmaster, for himself and as Boxmaster to the said Society of Sailors, and the other persons aftermentioned, for themselves and either as members of the said committee, as concurring with him, viz. :—Alexander Thomson, Duncan Stirling, Andrew Fraser, Gabriel Thomson, Robert Nicol, James Kelso, Walter Duncan, Alexander Young, William Sked, William Millar, John Kincaid, Robert Dealls, William Burgess, Alexander Cunninghame, John Peacock, and Robert Cram, all shipmasters, sailors, mariners, traders, and inhabitants in the town and village of Borrowstounness, and members of the incorporate Seabox there."

XI.

On 11th February, 1762, Lord Nisbet, having considered the conjoined processes, found the Duke of Hamilton and other heritors of the parish liable in payment of the following items formerly in use to be paid out of the funds:—

(*a*) The house rent payable to the minister for want of a manse.
(*b*) The schoolmaster's and bellman's salary.
(*c*) The expense of repairing the kirk and kirkyard dykes, and decerned against them for payment thereof in all time coming.
(*d*) Assoilzied Ritchie and the other members of the Seabox from the process of declarator at the instance of the minister.

This caused the Duke to appeal to the Inner House, and the case in all its aspects was fought over again. At last, on 10th August, 1764, it was finally decided by the Inner House judges. The decision, which will be found later, upheld, with one or two slight changes, the various judgments of the Lord Ordinary.

It will be appropriate to here refer to the condescendence of the funds belonging to the Representatives which Ritchie, after his investigation of the books, lodged in Court. It was made up thus—

	£	s.	d.
1. The lands of Muirhouse, of 24 bolls victuall and 50 pds. of mining rent yearly,	£200	0	0
2. Mortification bonds granted by the townspeople for the arrears of their seats at the building of the kirk, and amounting to	295	8	4
3. Principal sum of 2800 merks due by the Duke of Hamilton, mortified by the sailors, paying yearly of annual rent	83	6	8
4. The rent of the house called the manse,	40	0	0
5. A tenement of land called the Red House, worth yearly	50	0	0
6. The minister's glebe, worth yearly	133	6	8
7. The seat rents in the body of the church and range,	89	4	0
8. The money arising from ringing the great bell and sale of burying-places, amounting yearly to	60	0	0
Total (Scots),	£951	5	8

This statement bore out Ritchie's contention that the annual income was more than sufficient for the stipend, and that stenting was unnecessary. The minister's answers brought out things differently. He alleged the interest on the mortification bonds was overstated, that the rent of house called the manse should only have been £12 10s., and that the Red House belonged to the Seabox, and ought not to have been included. The only concern the Representatives had with this was that there was one room therein used for a schoolhouse, the Seabox getting the rents of the rest of it. He also argued that the minister's glebe was no part of the stipend fund, and did not fall to be included, and that the seat rents and money arising from the ringing of the great bell and sales of burying-places were so precarious and uncertain that they could not be depended on. A fair statement of the income and expenditure, as he considered it, was then lodged, which showed a yearly income of £56 9s. 5d. sterling, and an expenditure of £61 10s. 9d. sterling. This expenditure did not include anything for the repair of the kirk and kirkyard dykes, and so stenting was still necessary.

The Court, however, was satisfied that Ritchie's statement was fair and warranted, and in the final decision it will be seen that all its items were adopted save Nos. 5 and 6. The first deletion was the Red House, and by agreement of parties this was struck out early in the argument. The second was the sum put in for the glebe, and this deletion would seem to have been quite warranted.

XII.

Some of the productions are interesting. Ritchie's were copies of the two Acts, an inventory of writs lying, it was said, in the charter chest of the town of Borrowstounness, and an extract of the sederunt at the meeting of Representatives held on 7th January, 1761, by order of Lord Nisbet. Among those of the minister was an Act or order in favour of the Representatives, dated 27th April, 1719, by the Bailie of

Regality. It followed on a petition for an authority to stent, and it granted warrant to the Representatives to impose six pennies Scots upon each twenty shillings Scots of house rent, to be paid yearly for the space of four years by the inhabitants. The Duke's productions were numerous, and included an Act and Instrument, dated 22nd January, 1650. This was important, as it disposed of the allegation made that the Duke had not provided a glebe in favour of Mr. John Waugh, the first minister. The Instrument bore that the particular ground therein mentioned "for horse and keys gerse and for glebe, house-stance, and yeards had been mett and designed" to Mr. Waugh and his successors. There were also a number of bonds and title deeds relating to the house originally given by the Duke in lieu of a manse. This house was not considered sufficient for a manse, and the Court ordered the Duke to build a new one. The insinuations in the pleadings that the Hamilton family were trying to get out of their responsibilities were refuted by production of some agreements made between the family and the Representatives, and which, we think, so far justified their fighting the minister and Representatives. They had furnished the glebe, and they explained that the reason why the 1649 Act did not impose the granting of a glebe on the Duke then was that, as a matter of fact, the glebe was really in course of being provided at the time. As to their resistance of the demand for a manse, it was worth while so resisting, seeing they were in possession of an agreement between the Representatives and themselves, wherein a certain house was agreed to be accepted by all parties in lieu of a manse. Doubtless the Court, however, took the view that, when the then incumbent himself raised a process and narrated that he had really no place that he could properly call a good and sufficient manse, he was entitled in law to have it, for they so decreed. Among other points resisted by the Duke's tutors were those that he should be made liable for the maintenance of the kirk, kirkyard dykes, and the schoolmaster's salary. A very spirited fight indeed was here set up for them. It was shown that, after the parishes were re-united, Duke William and Duchess Anne, finding the accommodation of Borrowstounness limited for the two congregations, built an aisle (or, as it is put in the pleadings, "a spacious isle") for themselves and their tenants. At a later date they put in a "gallery for their coalliers." These parts of the building they had always upheld at their own charge, and their successors had continued and would continue to do so. So far as the remainder of the building was concerned, that fell to be upheld by the inhabitants who occupied it through the representatives. One argument sedulously used to make the Duke respond to the demands made on him was, that the annexation of the parish had given his family the following advantages:—(a) They were relieved of the "inconveniency" arising from the Church of Kinneil being situated near the House of Kinneil, where the family sometimes resided; (b) they were relieved of the expense of rebuilding the Church of Kinneil, which was said to be then ruinous; (c) they were assured against any augmentation of stipend which must have been the case had the parishes remained unannexed, as the old stipend in use to be paid to the minister of Kinneil was but 500 merks.

XIII.

Concerning the churchyard and how it came to be divided by a road, in the later pleadings—1762 or thereabouts—we find it stated—There is not now any churchyard within the Barony of Kinneil; the only churchyard within the conjoined parish is that of Borrowstounness, which was purchased by the inhabitants, and which churchyard is divided into two by the high road which passes through the middle of it. The road was made at the desire of the family of Hamilton, for when they lived at Kinneil House their road to Borrowstounness, being frequently interrupted by the tide at a place called Capie's Point, they prevailed on the inhabitants to allow them to "cutt" a road through the churchyard, by which means it was divided into pretty equal parts. Since which time the inhabitants of the Barony of Kinneil were generally buried in the south or upper half of the churchyard, and the inhabitants of Borrowstounness in the north or lower half. But though this was the general practice, many of the inhabitants of the Barony of Kinneil, and among the rest the whole of the Duke of Hamilton's "Coalliers," were buried in the north, as, *vice versa*, there were numbers of the inhabitants of Borrowstounness who were buried on the south side.

It appears also that the Duke was in use to repair the dykes on each side of said road made for the accommodation of himself alone, but never the churchyard dykes. It was said at that time, too, that no person had been buried in the old kirkyard of Kinneil within the memory of man.

In another place in the decree there are references to the old school of Kinneil and the new school of Borrowstounness thus —Before the separation of the town from Kinneil there was a schoolmaster for the Parish of Kinneil, whose salary the Duke paid. Upon Borrowstounness being disjoined and erected into a parish by itself, the inhabitants established a schoolmaster for their own conveniency, to whom they gave a salary of 1000 merks, as it was most inconvenient to send their children to the school of Kinneil, which lay at so great a distance. After the re-annexation of Kinneil to Borrowstounness, the Duke, willing to encourage this town as far as in his power, agreed to drop the school of Kinneil, and transferred the salary as an addition to the schoolmaster of Borrowstounness, and which accordingly he enjoyed at that date.

XIV.

Although not a very pleasant theme, we cannot but revert in closing to the almost wicked tenacity and stubbornness with which the fight was fought to the bitter end. The combination of processes made it all the more bitter. The Duke's agents went most thoroughly into his defence, so much so that poor Ritchie, who really long ago had got from the Lord Ordinary what he was contending for, became heart-sick, and more than once complained that the Duke's tutors were doing all they could to prolong things with the view of tiring him out. The minister and his party also got tired of the repeated representations of the Hamilton agents and the consequent delays. They complained that if the Duke was permitted to go on in that manner multiplying papers it was hard to say when the question would end. Four representations almost on the same point, they said, were without precedent. They bitterly resented this, and frankly admitted they were quite unable to maintain a dispute with so powerful an opponent. The minister himself pleaded he wanted his manse, and had no concern with the dispute between the Duke and the town.

Observations which were far from complimentary were still made by the litigants. The Ritchie party wailed they had "long groaned under the tyranny and arbitrary measures of the minister, Kirk Session, and their assistants." We read also that the Captain's foes even encroached on his family burial-place in the churchyard. For their violent and unwarrantable intrusion in digging up a grave there he sued three persons for £50, and also craved that they be decerned to remove the corpse of Alexander Low's mother interred therein. Of course, he was thought unfeeling and unholy in "wanting the corps of Low's mother raised from her grave." He must have been greatly "teazed," as it is put, on this subject, and towards the end we find some of his opponents "had the audacity," even after the raising of his action about his burying-ground, "to cause interr the body of a cobler in his said burial-place." It is very extraordinary how the feeling against Ritchie was kept up by the defenders. He is described, among other things, as having "a disposition not to be pleased with anything, and to take delight in raising disturbances," and of either "leading or driving" his friends of the Seabox.

But he had his friends, and their pleadings show that they appreciated his "merit, zeal, and activity," and that they were bound in gratitude to him for his generous and public-spirited conduct. In their final tribute they said he was a man of remarkable public spirit, who with some others, in spite of the utmost and united efforts of the minister, Kirk Session, and assistants, brought that process to prevent the inhabitants of Borrowstounness from being oppressed and tyrannised over by a few, and as having had the good fortune to prevail in every conclusion of their declarator.

XV.

In concluding our notes on this long litigation let us briefly summarise the final decision of the Inner House judges on the whole case; they practically on all points upheld the various judgments of Lord Nisbet—

1. The heritors and inhabitants of the town, in conjunction with the minister and Kirk Session, to have sole power of electing their own Representatives.

2. The persons entitled to vote were the heritors, portioners, householders, and heads of families.

3. The annual meetings of the inhabitants for choosing assistants to be held within the church on the first Wednesday of January yearly.

4. The following were found to be the funds falling under the administration of the Representatives, viz.:—Items 1, 2, 3, 4, 7, and 8 of Ritchie's statement of the funds before mentioned.

5. Found assistants and Kirk Session had no power to stent or tax the inhabitants neither then nor in time coming, except in the case of the failure or decrease of the stock or funds.

6. That the rents of the lands of Muirhouse, the annual rents of the bonds, and rents of the seats in the church of Borrowstounness specially appropriated for payment of the said stipend must, in the first place, be applied for that purpose.

7. That the said funds, after payment of the said stipend, must be applied for payment of the repairs of that part of the church possessed by the inhabitants and for keeping the

dykes of the lower churchyard in repair, and that the collector of said funds might be allowed a yearly salary not exceeding £3 sterling.

8. None of the funds under administration of the assistants could be applied by them for repairing the kirkyard dykes of Borrowstounness (except those of the lower churchyard) or for payment of the manse rent and schoolmaster's and bellman's salary.

9. They could not gratuitously gift or give away any part of the area of the said church without a just and adequate price, and that all such gifts should be null and void.

10. That members of the Incorporate Seabox had the only right to the sailors' loft in the kirk and to the area above the loft, and that Representatives could not erect a gallery above the sailors' loft.

11. John Ritchie and the other members of the Seabox entitled to be refunded out of the surplus of said funds, after payment of the stipend and other debts charged thereon, of the sum of £128 16s. 4d., to which their account of expenses was modified and restricted, and of the sum of £73 19s. 1½d. sterling as the expense of extracting the decree. The Representatives ordained to make payment accordingly.

12. That the Representatives were not entitled to take any part of their expenses of the processes out of the funds under the administration.

13. The Duke of Hamilton and his tutors and curators for their interest, and the other heritors of the Parish of Kinneil found liable in payment of the following items formerly in use to have been paid out of said funds:—

    (*a*) The house rent payable to the minister for want of a manse.

    (*b*) The schoolmaster's and bellman's salaries and the expense of repairing the kirk and kirkyard dykes (except that part of the kirk possessed by the inhabitants and the repairing of the dykes of the lower churchyard);

and they were decerned and ordained to make payment thereof in all time coming.

14. The Duke and his tutors and curators for their interest ordained to build a sufficient manse and office houses for the minister of Borrowstounness, and to make payment to the said minister and his successors in office of the sum of £6 sterling yearly in name of manse rent until he furnished the minister with a sufficient manse and office houses.

15. John Ritchie and the other members of the Seabox assoilzied from the whole points and articles of the process of declarator brought at the instance of the minister, Kirk Session, and assistants against them, and declared them quit thereof and free therefrom in all time coming.

XVI.

For fifty years after the long litigation the affairs of the Representatives seem to have gone smoothly. But that body was doomed once again to have a long and expensive law suit. Again the stock which had been appropriated for the stipend fund came in for a critical overhaul. The parties in the former litigation had all passed away, but the fighting spirit had been bequeathed unabated to their successors. The action was raised in the Court of Session in the beginning of the nineteenth century by the Rev. Robert Rennie, minister of the Gospel at Borrowstounness, against James Tod, Alexander Cowan, John Cowan, James Smith, merchants; Alexander Aitken, feuar; John Hardie, baker; and Francis Lindsay, barber, all of Borrowstounness, and as Representatives of the said town. The sums invested to yield the 800 merks had so increased in value that there was annually a considerable surplus over after paying the minister his salary and repairing the church. This surplus the Representatives sought to appropriate for public purposes, one of which was the building of a grammar school. They held that by immemorial usage they had a perfect right to dispose of the surplus as they pleased, provided the minister's stipend and the other expenditure allowed to be made out of the fund by the former decision of the Court were first of all duly met. The minister thought otherwise, maintaining that he and he alone was entitled to the surplus. The case was, in the first instance, brought in the Outer House before Lord Hermand, who decided in favour of the minister. The Representatives appealed to the Inner House, and the judges there reversed the Lord Ordinary's decision, and held that the surplus belonged to the Representatives. The minister then appealed to the House of Lords, and in 1806 was awarded with a unanimous decision finding that he was entitled to the surplus. This decision, of course, was final, and governs the administration of the fund to this day. It can well be imagined what turmoil, contention, and bitterness this second and final litigation caused in the town during the six years of its duration.

The disappointment which the House of Lords' decision caused the Representatives and a large body of the inhabitants was of the keenest kind, judging from the reports and stories of that time which have been handed down in the families of those who had taken a leading part in what they understood to be a fight for the benefit of the community.

So far as we have seen, no personal antipathy to the minister was displayed throughout, although the Representatives fought hard. Their attitude, we think, would be correctly judged by considering it as the expression of an innate belief that—the minister being duly provided for when he got the stipulated 800 merks—the inhabitants of the town were surely the natural and proper parties to benefit by any unexpected surplus from a fund which their forefathers had so spontaneously and unanimously gathered a century and a half before. Their hopes had been raised almost to the point of realisation by the decision of the Inner House. Mr. Rennie, however, was in the position of being able to appeal to the House of Lords, and, as very frequently happens yet, this final tribunal reversed the decision of the Inner House judges and left the minister the gainer.

XVII.

As it was chiefly owing to the increase in the value of the farm of Muirhouse that this litigation arose, let us explain how it came into the possession of the Representatives. During and preceding 1649 the inhabitants had raised a large sum for the "plantation" of a minister. The Seabox Society were particularly generous. They with one consent gave over several bonds which they held in security for money advanced. One was a bond of 2500 merks due to them by the Duke of Hamilton and his heirs, and the other was a bond of 2000 merks lying upon the Muirhouse. The wadset or bond for the latter appears to have been increased at this time to 5000 merks, and James Hamilton of Balderston, the then proprietor of Muirhouse, in granting the new wadset or bond, along with his wife, granted it by arrangement to certain persons "as commissioners for the inhabitants of Borrowstounness and their successors, for the use, utility, and behoof of ane minister of the cure at the Kirk of Borrowstounness." Hamilton of Balderston apparently got into financial trouble, and, not being able to repay his loan, these Commissioners apprised the subjects and became irredeemably vested therein. That, to our mind, is the history of how the Representatives came to possess Muirhouse. All the land in the old Bo'ness Parish belonged to the Duke, save Muirhouse Farm, which was held off the Crown. How did that arise? Evidently when the apprising took place the Rev. John Waugh awakened to business. As we have reason to believe from what we have read of him, his business instincts were strongly developed. Mr. Waugh, apparently, was dissatisfied with the destination in trust in favour of the commissioners. Therefore during the Commonwealth he applied direct to Oliver Cromwell, and received from the Protector a charter in his own absolute right for himself and his successors, ministers of Borrowstounness. Afterwards those entitled to the administration, and who certainly had an interest to take the management into their own hands on account of the assessment which still continued, applied to and obtained from King Charles the Second a charter restoring them the possession and administration. This, then, explains the Crown holding, and at the same time bears out what some of the Representatives at this day like to mention occasionally, namely, that they have in their charter chest a charter from Oliver Cromwell and also one from Charles the Second, with, of course, their respective seals.

Reverting to the House of Lords' decision, the judges took up their stand on the ground that here was a trust, and they referred to and grounded their decision on the documents which in their view clearly constituted the trust. Lord Chancellor Erskine and Lord Eldon both gave opinions. The Chancellor was very strong on the trust argument. He held the Court " could not look off the face of the instruments constituting the trust right." He pointed out that the charter of Charles the Second restoring the lands of Muirhouse to certain trustees and administrators bore expressly to be " for the use and behoof of the minister of the Gospel serving the cure at the Kirk of Borrowstounness," without qualification or limitation, but absolute and unlimited. The Sasine following it was in similar terms. If the parties then in charge of the trust had conceived that they had a right to any surplus after producing the 800 merks, they would, he thought, have qualified the trust on the face of the instruments. With respect to the argument, that the former decree of the Court barred the present case, he found, on looking into the former case, that it was really raised for the purpose of ascertaining what funds were applicable to the payment of the minister's stipend, and that the question of whether the minister had a right to the surplus or not was never discussed. He thought Lord Hermand's judgment in favour of the minister was sound and just, and that in a case of that kind one judge was as competent to form an opinion as several.

We might mention that the Chancellor illustrated his view of the case thus—" If I give an estate to my eldest son as a trustee for a younger brother, and add an obligation on the eldest son to make up the estate to £1000 a year, nothing can show more clearly my intention than that my second son was to possess £1000 a year, and though, perhaps, it might not be in my contemplation that the estate would ever produce so much, yet, if the estate came to be of greater annual value than £1000 a year, could it be said that the eldest son was not still a trustee in that specific estate for his brother?" Upon the whole, he was of opinion the interlocutors of the Court appealed from should be reversed.

Lord Eldon was also clear. "In all human probability," he said, "neither the inhabitants nor the minister at the time thought that the produce of the funds would ever amount to more than 800 merks, but this could never decide the rights of parties. As to the deeds, he thought the fair construction to be drawn from these was that the funds, if not mortified to the minister, were yet appropriated to his use and benefit in terms so clear on the face of the instruments that the Court could not at that distance of time look off these instruments to speculate with regard to the original intention of the parties."

CHAPTER XV.

COAL AND COAL MINING.

1. Local Evidences of Early Mining: Privileges of Miners under 1592 Act: "In-gaun-ee" System: Access Shafts, Ladders, and Spiral Stairs—2. Lawless Behaviour of Miners leads to Act of 1606: Colliers and Salters Enslaved as "Necessary Servants": Sold with Colliery: Partial Emancipation in 1775: Serf System Completely Ended in 1779—3. Agitation for Abolition of Woman and Child Labour in Mines: Royal Comission Appointed to Enquire: The Act of 1842—4. Interesting Local Evidence—5. The Coal and Other Strata in Carriden Parish—6. Bo'ness Coalfield—7. Preston Island and its Coal Mines and Saltpans—8. The Local Coal and Ironstone Mines of Sixty Years Ago—9. Some Mining Calamities: Colliers' Strike: Newtown Families—10. Two Alarming Subsidences.

I.

THE Bo'ness coalfield at one time contained a very large supply of coal, and has been worked more or less extensively since the thirteenth century. Early in that century a tithe of the colliery of Carriden was granted to the monks of Holyrood, and until a few years ago evidences of the workings in those early times were to be found in the old Manse Wood on Carriden shore. At that time the old roads were opened up and modernised in an unsuccessful exploit for coal under the glebe.

In the fifteenth century the Scots Parliament, believing that Scotland was full of precious metals, and hoping to derive a large revenue therefrom, enacted that all mines of such should belong to the King—James I. As the landowners had thus no encouragement to develop their mineral resources, the Act was practically a dead letter, and in 1592—in the reign of James IV.—the Parliament was compelled to modify the old statute to the effect that the Crown was only to get a tenth part as a royalty. This same statute made mention of the hazardous nature of the miners' occupation on account of the evil air of the mines and the danger of the falling of the roofs and other miseries. It therefore exempted the miners from all taxation and other charges both in peace and war. Their families' goods and gear were likewise specially protected. Some have thought that Parliament, even at this early date, was taking a commendably humane interest in the safety and comfort of the miners. Others, again, have asserted that the privileges conferred were meant to act as an inducement to foreigners to settle in this country for the purpose of searching for and working the minerals.

In the early days of mining the fortunate proprietors of land and coal seams under it carried on their own coal works for the most part. Those were still the days of feudalism (though not of slavery, which had died out in the fourteenth century), and vassals and retainers on the estates, quite naturally, turned their hands to the new industry of coal winning. Their wages were paid partly in money, but mainly in produce.

Outcrops were frequently discovered at brae faces, and the coal was originally wrought downwards and inwards from the surface on what was known as the "in-gaun-ee"[1] system. Women, girls, and boys all assisted as bearers by carrying out the coal to the bings, where they stored it until sold.

As time went on the importance of the industry came to be keenly realised by the proprietors of the coal seams. The idea appears to have occurred to them that the shafts, which hitherto had only been sunk for the purpose of ventilation, might be widened, deepened, and used for getting access to the coal lying at greater depths, and also for bringing it to the surface. Thereupon the shafts were rigged out with short wooden ladders resting on crossbeams when the shaft was too deep for one long sloping ladder. Those descending the shaft went down the first short ladder of six or eight rungs, passed along the beam a foot or two, then on to the other ladder, and so on till they completed their dangerous descent. This system

---

[1] In-going eye.

Dr. Roebuck's Tombstone in Carriden Churchyard.

was so difficult and dangerous that the ladders soon came to be replaced by spiral stairs. An old spiral stair shaft was to be seen at the foot of the Back Hill, Corbiehall, about thirty years ago. Though the stairs were safer than the ladders, the toil of the bearers was in no way lessened. Later still the masters introduced the windlass, and subsequently the one-horse gin. The bearers were thus relieved of a part of their burdensome toil, but they still dragged the coal to the pit bottom in primitive hutches without wheels.

II.

Whether it was owing to the privileges given them by the Act of 1592 or to the evil effect which their underground occupation had upon their minds we know not, but, at all events, the colliers as a class suddenly became lawless and greatly given to wilfully setting fire to the collieries from motives of private revenge. Accordingly, Parliament enacted that all who were guilty of "the wicked crime of wilfully setting fire to coalheuchs" should suffer the punishment of treason in their bodies, lands, and goods. This was followed up by an Act in 1606, under which the privileges and exemptions of the colliers were recalled and their freedom very materially curtailed. The colliers, by their foolish behaviour, brought this upon themselves, but pressure was brought to bear on the Legislature by the Earl of Winton, then a favourite at Court, and the largest coalowner and salt manufacturer in Great Britain. By the new Act colliers and salters were enslaved as "necessary servants," and regarded as a pertinent of the lands where they were serving. It is evident that the chief reason for this extreme course was the fear which possessed coalowners, that unless some such compulsory steps were taken there would in future be great difficulty in getting men to undertake so perilous a calling.

Another reason was the increased demand for coal, especially for export. Inducements were held out to the colliers at busy centres in the shape of bounty money. The men were thus drawn to places where the demand was greatest, and many districts were thereby depleted. So the Act decreed that they were bound to remain, and to be practically enslaved at the colliery where they were born. No strange collier could get employment at any coal work without a testimonial from his last employer; and, failing such testimonial, he could be claimed within a year and a day by the master whom he had deserted. Whoever discovered the deserter had to give him back within twenty-four hours under a heavy penalty; and the deserter was punished as a thief—of himself. The Act also gave colliery owners power to apprehend all vagabonds and sturdy beggars and put them to work in the mines. So long as a coal work was in operation on any estate the colliers were not at liberty to leave without the proprietor's consent. They were, in fact, says Mr. Barrowman,[2] attached to the work, formed a valuable adjunct to it, and enhanced the price in the event of a sale. He gives an illustration as late as 1771 where the value of the ownership of forty good colliers, with their wives and children, was estimated to be worth £4000, or £100 each family. Parents bound their children in a formal manner to the work by receiving gifts or arles from the master when they were baptised. Not only were the colliers attached, but by an Act in 1641 other workers engaged in and about coal mines were prohibited from leaving without permission.

Appended to a lease in 1681 of the coal and salt works at Bo'ness in favour of James Cornwall of Bonhard was a list of colliers and bearers delivered to him in terms of the tack. There were thirteen coal hewers, six male bearers (one of whom was reckoned a half), and thirty-one female bearers (seven of whom were reckoned a half each), in all, thirteen coal hewers and thirty-three bearers. These, with one oncost man, the tenant acknowledged to have received and undertook to deliver over at the end of the lease, or an equivalent number.

Under this law of bondage the poor collier and salter lived for nearly one hundred and seventy years, until, in 1775,

---

[2] Lecture, "Scotch Mining and Miners." James Barrowman, Hamilton. Also in "Transactions of Institution of Mining Engineers."

an Act was passed emancipating all who after that date should begin to work as colliers and salters. If working colliers were twenty-one years of age at the time of the Act, they were to be emancipated at the end of seven years. Those between the ages of twenty-one and thirty were to serve ten years longer before gaining freedom. It will thus be seen that the conditions under which freedom was to be given were irksome, and many of the workers accustomed to their conditions failed to take advantage of the Act, and remained serfs until their death. A complete stop, however, was put to the serf system in 1799. It was then enacted that " all the colliers in that part of Great Britain called Scotland who were bound colliers shall be and are hereby declared to be free from their servitude." While the colliers were serfs, they were not slaves, for they received wages, and towards the end of the eighteenth century the conditions of their employment were much improved. Moreover, when coal mining, with the general advance of Scottish commerce, became a more profitable industry, the masters had a difficulty in getting enough men, and increased the wages to induce people to work in the pits.

A great many of the annual fairs or ridings of the miners—and doubtless those of the Newtown, Corbiehall, and Grangepans miners—really originated as a day of rejoicing on the anniversary of their freedom.

III.

The unnatural conditions of life in the mines in those days had a most deplorable effect on the minds of the men, women, and children employed underground. Their miserable existence was pitiable in the extreme. Hugh Miller, alluding to the women who laboured in the pits of Niddry, said he saw in them a type different from any other females in the country. Their mouths were wide open, their lips were thick and projecting, and they resembled in those respects the lowest types of savages in the lowest and most brutalised state.

The women and children acted, as we have seen, as bearers,

and hard and degrading work it was. Before the days of the underground tramway the coal was carried to the pit bottom in creels fastened to their backs, hence the term bearer. Women and girls were preferred to men and boys for such work, as, curiously enough, they could always carry about double the weight a man or boy could scramble out with. The creel was superseded about 1830 by baskets on wheels, and latterly by wooden boxes, which were pushed along the underground railways. The term "bearer" then ceased, and that of "pusher" or "putter" was substituted.

The subject of female labour in mines had, as early as 1793, aroused some attention, but not till 1808 was the matter brought prominently before the public. Mr. Robert Bald, Edinburgh, who took a leading part in the agitation, instanced the case of a married woman in an extensive colliery which he had visited. She came forward to him groaning under an excessive weight of coals, trembling in every limb, and almost unable to keep her knees from sinking under her, and saying, "Oh, sir, this is sair, sair, sair wark. I wish to God that the first woman who tried to bear coals had broken her back, and none would have tried it again."[3]

The public indignation was at length aroused. Mainly through the philanthropic and deeply sympathetic efforts of Lord Ashley (afterwards seventh Earl of Shaftesbury) a Royal Commission was appointed to inquire into the condition of the mining population, and particularly the question of women and child labour in mines. Mr. Barrowman says the report of that Commission in 1812 drew instant and wide attention to the grave evils connected with the employment of women and young persons underground, and a statute was passed in that year prohibiting the employment of females of any age and boys under ten years of age in any mine or colliery. The Act was not regarded by the persons interested with unqualified

---

[3] The last of the East Lothian pitwomen died at Musselburgh in September, 1912, aged 86; and the last in Bo'ness district died in the Newtown six years ago, also at an advanced age.

satisfaction. It threw many females out of an occupation to which they had been accustomed, and they would doubtless take some time to fit themselves into the new state of things. A curious sequel occurred in the Dryden Colliery, Midlothian, where about a score of girls assumed male attire and wrought in this disguise for three months after the Act was passed. They were at length summoned to Court in Edinburgh. On promising not to go below again they were dismissed.[4] In one extensive colliery in the east, at least, the workers petitioned against the bill. Out of the signatures of 122 men and 37 women and girls there were 45 of men and 25 of females marked with a cross (70 out of 159 being unable to write their names), showing in the clearest manner the need there was for a better system of home and school education, and justifying in the most emphatic way the passing of the Act. The successive Acts of Parliament passed since 1842 have tended towards the improvement of the miner and of the conditions in which his work is carried on; and perhaps there is no employment in the country in which the workman is now better safeguarded by legislation.

IV.

A vivid idea of the terrible state of matters which Lord Ashley's Commission was the means of ending is obtained from the evidence taken by the special Commissioners at the various collieries throughout Britain. The Commissioner for Scotland was Mr. R. H. Franks, whose Report contains between four and five hundred examinations.[5] We append the whole of the precognitions taken here about 1840. They make interesting, though somewhat depressing, reading—

James John Cadell.—There are at present employed below ground in our pits about 200 men, women, and children; fully one-third are females. No regulation exists here for the prevention of children working below.

---

[4] See "Tranent and Neighbourhood" (M'Neill), p. 44.
[5] See Report and also Printed Volumes of Evidence, Advocates' Library.

I think the parents are the best judges when to take their children below for assistance, and that it is of consequence for colliers to be trained in early youth to their work. Parents take their children down from eight to ten years of age, males and females.

The colliers are perfectly unbound at this colliery; they have large families, and extremely healthy ones. I believe most of the children can read. There are two schools, at which children can be taught common reading for 2d. per week. There exist no compulsory regulations to enforce colliers paying for their children or sending them to school. Every precaution is taken to avoid accidents; several have occurred, and occasionally happen from parts of the roof and coal coming down on the men; one lad was killed a short time since. The work is carried on about twelve hours per day, and the people come and go as they please.

Archibald Ferguson, eleven years old, putter.—Worked below for four years; pushes father's coal with sister, who is seventeen years of age from wall face to horse road. Pit is very dry and roofs lofty. Sometimes work twelve, and even sixteen hours, as we have to wait our turn for the horse and engine to draw. Never got hurt below. Get oatcake and water, and potatoes and herrings when home. The river which passes through Bo'ness is called the water. Fishes live in the water; has often seen them carted from boats; never caught any. I walk about on the shore and pick up stones or gang in the parks (fields) after the birds.

Janet Barrowman, seventeen years old, putter.—I putt the small coal on Master's (Mr. Cadell's) account. Am paid $2\frac{1}{2}$ each course, and run six courses a day; the carts I run contain $5\frac{1}{2}$ to $7\frac{1}{2}$ cwts. of coal. Father and mother are dead. Have three brothers and five sisters below; two elder brothers, two sisters, and myself live at Grangepans. We have one room in which we all live and sleep. There has been much sickness of late years about the Grange; few have escaped the fever. A short time ago before the death of my parents we were all down, father and all, with low fever for a long time. Mother only escaped who nursed us. Fever is always in the place. (Reads very indifferently.)

The village of Grangepans has been much visited with scarlet fever and scarlatina; the place is nearly level with the Forth, and the houses are very old, ill-ventilated, and the foul water and filth lying about is sufficient to create a pestilence.

Note.—The last paragraph is apparently a comment of the Commissioner's own.

Mary Snedden, fifteen years of age, putter.—I have wrought at Bo'ness pit three months. Should not have "ganged," but brother Robert was killed on the 21st of January last. A piece of the roof fell upon his head, and he died instantly. He was brought home, coffined, and buried in Bo'ness Kirkyard. No one came to inquire about how he was killed; they never do in this place.

Charles Robertson, overseer of the Bo'ness Coal Works.—Since the building of the Newtown the colliers have been more settled as to their place of work, but they still continue to take down very young children, which impedes instruction. Most children can be instructed if the parents please—and fairly so. There are two schools. The one in the Newtown has a well-trained teacher from Bathgate Academy, and one is shortly expected at Grangepans.

Men would do well to let their children remain up till thirteen years old, as they would be more use to them thereafter. No married women now go below; the elder females who are down are single or widows. There are many illegitimate children in the pits that do not get any education.

A man with two strong lads can get his 6s. 6d. a day, fair average wages, as there is no limitation to work.

Rev. Kenneth M'Kenzie, minister of Borrowstounness.—When children once go to work in the collieries they continue at it; and they go as early as eight years of age; but the age is quite uncertain, depending entirely on the convenience, cupidity, or caprice of the parents.

The tendency to remove children too early from school operates to the injury of many in after life. It proves an obstacle to future advancement, and renders the mind much more liable to the influence of prejudice.

With regard to the children employed at the colliery education is at present in a very unsatisfactory state, and will continue so if the matter be allowed to rest with the colliers. A good plan is adopted at some collieries. Every man employed is obliged to pay a small weekly sum for education. A sufficient sum is thus easily raised, and a properly qualified teacher is appointed by the proprietor or master. Individuals are thus constrained to send their children to school who otherwise might be apt to neglect their education. The day and evening school in Bo'ness, Newtown, is specially for the colliery population, but it is not attended; at present the teacher only receives 7s. a week in voluntary fees. The teacher has not been trained. He teaches reading, writing, and arithmetic as well as most adventurers do.

The parochial school is one of the best in Linlithgowshire, but the colliers seldom send their children to it.

V.

Mr. Ellis,[6] writing of Carriden in the eighteenth century, stated that the parish was full of coal, which was of fine quality, and the only fuel then used. It was carried to London, to the northmost parts of Scotland, and to Holland, Germany, and the Baltic. As to price it sold at a higher figure on the hill and to the country people who lived near than any coal in Scotland. Nearly half a century later Mr. Fleming[7] wrote that about 400 yards west of the village of Blackness a bed of calcareous ironstone cropped out on the beach, dipping into the sea in the same direction. When carefully prepared this formed a hydraulic cement of a very superior quality, and in the beginning of the nineteenth century had been actually wrought for that purpose. This stratum was covered with a strong shale, otherwise called blea, varying in thickness from one to

[6] Sinclair's Stat. A/c., *supra*.
[7] New Stat. A/c., *supra*.

twenty feet interspersed with balls of clay ironstone. The alum shale was at one time used in the manufacture of soda, but the work had been discontinued and the premises dismantled.

There were many seams of coal in the parish, some of which had been wrought at their crops or outbursts centuries ago. The coalfield in its western division was supposed to extend across the Forth, and to be connected with the coal formation in the opposite district in the county of Fife. The strata were known to the depth of one hundred and thirty-five fathoms, having been passed by the miners in sinking pits and other operations in the coal mines. The deepest seam then known was the Carsey coal, rising to the north-east along the seashore. This seam and the Smithy seam came out to the surface a short distance to the east of Burnfoot. The Foul coal and Red coal took on to the west of the road leading to Linlithgow. The western Main coal was only in the south-west of the parish, as there was not sufficient cover for this seam to the east and north. This coalfield passed through the south-west boundary of the parish into the Parishes of Borrowstounness and Linlithgow. In approaching the north the dip gradually came round more west; in the middle of the field it was generally north-west. To the east of Burnfoot, after passing the crop of the Carsey coal, no coal was to be found. It was a curious fact that in a district where so many seams of coal occurred whinstone should be found so abundantly. The Irongath Hills consisted of hard whinstone resting in the coal strata; nor did it present itself only in crops on the top of eminences; but it was found in regular seams between, and even in actual contact with the coal. In these hills there was a bed of coal varying from one to eight or ten feet in thickness which had whinstone both for its roof and pavement; and between the Western main coal and the Red coal the seam of whinstone was about seventy feet thick. The fossil remains that have been found in the coal formation consisted of reeds of different kinds. Shells and impressions of leaves were also of more or less frequent occurrence, and on one occasion workmen fell in with a beautiful specimen of that curious extinct genus of fossil plants, the *lepidodendron*. The surface deposits in the west part of the parish near the shore consisted of sea sand and shells resting on blue clay and mud, the clay resting on the coal formation; and in the south-west there was found yellow brick clay, with sand and gravel. Ice-transported boulders that had been met with were often of trap, their weight varying from 3 or 4 cwts. to 4 or 5 tons.

VI

With regard to the coal in the adjoining Parish of Bo'ness, Dr. Rennie[8] has told us that it was wrought here more than three hundred years ago. The depth of the pits in 1796 was about forty-two fathoms. The seam of coal was from ten to twelve feet in thickness, and was nearly exhausted. This was known as the Wester Main Coal Seam. There were various seams—some of them of a superior and others of a very inferior quality. All of them had been wrought in different places and at different times to a great extent, particularly in and about Bo'ness. It was proposed to sink a pit to the west of the town. The depth to the principal seam in this quarter might be about seventy fathoms; but there were several seams at a much less depth. Coal was at that time all worked on the pillar or stoop and room system. The average quantity raised in twelve months for some time before he wrote might be about 44,000 tons. A considerable part of the great coal had been exported at 7s. 9d. per ton. The remainder was disposed of in the coasting trade and in the adjacent country. A great many of the chew coals were carried by contract shipping to the London market at 6s. per ton. What was known as the small coal or panwood was consumed by the salt works, which consisted of sixteen pans, and employed about thirty salters and labourers. The annual quantity of salt made was about 37,000 bushels, which was partly disposed of in the coasting trade. Most of it, however, was for the supply of the country to the south and west of Borrowstounness. The number of colliers, coal-bearers,

[8] Sinclair's Stat. A/c., *supra*.

labourers, and carters employed about the colliery was probably 250.

In 1843 Mr. M'Kenzie[9] wrote that the beds in Bo'ness Parish were all of the coal formation. No coal had in his time been found in this district under the Carsey coal. Even yet it appears to be the lowest of the workable seams. Above the strata in the Snab section, which he referred to in detail, were one or two inferior coal seams which had been partially wrought in former times for the salt pans. And at Craigenbuck, further to the westward, a seam of limestone was also at one time wrought, and afforded an excellent building mortar. The seams of coal about Bo'ness were, generally speaking, of good thickness and excellent quality. The neighbourhood of the Snab (known now as Kinneil Colliery) had been proposed as the most favourable situation for a new winning of the coalfield; and the establishment of a colliery there was expected to be a great advantage to the town.

We have thus endeavoured to indicate in a general way the nature of the geological strata. For those who may desire more detailed data, however, we print in Appendix an illustrative and reliable section of the local coalfield.

VII.

Situated in the Firth to the north of Bo'ness roads is Preston Island, so-called after the Prestons of Valleyfield, to whom it belonged. Looking from Bo'ness it appears to contain a considerable mansion-house, but a closer inspection dispels this impression, and reveals the ruins of the buildings after referred to. A visit to Preston Island, says Mr. Beveridge[10] in one of his interesting volumes, is a very pleasant outing. But let strangers be cautious in straying over it to avoid falling into the open and unguarded coal pit, which is generally full of water. Till the end of the eighteenth century the island

---

[9] New Stat. A/c., *supra*.
[10] Between the Ochils and the Forth (1888), pp. 158-9.

was merely an expanse of green turf at the eastern extremity of the reef known as the Craigmore Rocks, which being within low-water mark all belong to the estate of Low Valleyfield. On Sir Robert Preston succeeding to the property at the beginning of the nineteenth century he conceived the idea of converting this lonely spot into a great centre of trade. The seams of coal which underlie the basin of the Forth were here cropping out at the surface. It therefore seemed quite feasible to undertake the revival of the coal and salt industries which in former days, under the auspices of Sir George Bruce, had made the fortune of Culross and its neighbourhood. Sir Robert had attained to great wealth, partly obtained in trade as the captain of an East Indiaman, partly accumulated by speculation, and partly by marriage with the daughter of a wealthy London citizen. He accordingly erected a large range of buildings on the island, including engine-houses, saltpans, and habitations for colliers and salters. Pits were sunk, fresh water brought from the mainland, and, for a period, a vast industry was carried on. The Forth resounded with the working of the engines, and the loading of vessels with coal went on almost constantly. But, for various reasons, the affair was a losing concern. Ultimately it completely collapsed, leaving the baronet out of pocket to the extent of at least £30,000. Fortunately his means were such that after so great a loss he still remained a man of immense wealth.

After the colliery was stopped the saltpans were let and worked for a considerable period, the last tenant of them adding to his legitimate occupation that of an unlicensed distiller of whisky. Having received a hint, however, that the Revenue officers were upon his track he decamped. Preston Island has since then remained a deserted but singularly picturesque object.

VIII.

The surface of the parish sixty years ago, owing to the coal and ironstone mining, must have presented a busy aspect. Evidences of this are yet to be gathered from the numerous bings of blaes and other refuse still standing in various districts. If we study the matter, moreover, from the old Ordnance maps we find that the place was at one time riddled with shafts and air passages. These shafts, both on the shore in Grangepans and Bo'ness and on the hills above, have been carefully filled up, and the surface as a whole is comparatively secure. All the refuse bings on Grange estate have of late years been removed by the Laird of Grange. Kinneil Colliery Company also are gradually diminishing their old bings.

As we have said in another chapter, Nos. 1, 2, 3, and 4 shore pits, opened by Messrs. John & William Cadell, and also their No. 5 pit, were all abandoned early last century, and remained flooded till 1859.

More than half a century ago, while the shore pits remained drowned, the Grange mining was practically done on the hill—some of it on that estate, and some at the Burn and Mingle pits, taken on lease from Kinneil colliery.

Four of the Grange pits were near the Drum. The Level pit above Bridgeness; the Meldrum pit, at the head of the old incline railway; the Kiln pit, south from it, on east side of the road; and still farther south the Miller pit. The Meldrum pit and the Kiln pit are both now untraceable, having been lately filled up by the present laird, like all the other old pits at Grange, except the Doocot pit at Bridgeness and the Miller pit. Another busy centre was the pit known as the Acre pit, opposite Lochend, near the Muirhouses. Coal and ironstone were both worked here, and a tramway ran down to the incline at the Meldrum pit. Here was a double 3-feet railway leading down to Grangepans, which was constructed by Mr. James John Cadell about 1845. Although the tramway from Lochend along the south side of the Muirhouse road and the incline railway were all in full working order in comparatively recent times, all traces of them are now effectually removed. The incline was finally dismantled about 1890, when a commencement was made with Philpingstone Road.

In the middle of last century there was quite a congeries

of pits in the vicinity of Northbank, which were opened up when Mr. Wilson of Dundyvan leased Kinneil colliery, and began to search for ironstone. Nos. 5, 6, and 7 were all situated near the Red Brae, on the north side of the Borrowstoun and Bonhard road. There was a waggon railway here also. It ran from Kinneil, by way of Newtown, up through the Mingle and Burn pits at Kinglass, and on to No. 7 at Northbank. The empty waggons were taken by small engine right up. Latterly the engine was done away with, and horse haulage was adopted instead. There was also a pit at the top of the Red Brae, known as Duncan's Hole. In fact, the road itself was in olden times called Duncan's Brae.

What was known as the Borrowstoun coalfield included the Mingle and Burn pits, and also the Lothians pit at the east end of the old Row, Newtown.

But there were numerous other pits scattered over the surface of the district—Kinneil colliery, especially in Mr. Wilson's time, having been very extensively worked. It would have at one time fully two dozen pits, and these were chiefly known under a number. The Mingle was No. 1; the Burn, No. 2; Nos. 3 and 4 were north of Bo'mains Farm; Nos. 5, 6, and 7, as already stated, near the Red Brae; No. 8 was Duncan's Hole; No. 9 was the Cousie mine, south of Northbank and east of the Cousie; No. 10 was where the new Burgh Hospital now is; Nos. 11 and 12 were at Bonhard—the former in the field east from the foot of Red Brae and the latter to the east of the Cross roads; No. 13 was below Borrowstoun Farm; No. 14 where the Newtown store now is; and No. 15 west of the present football field at Newtown; No. 16 was in the field east from Richmond House; No. 17, a small pit, to work ironstone at the back of Old Row, Newtown; No. 18 was the Lothians. An important pit at one time was at the Chance, and another south from the Gauze House was called Jessfield. In later times there was what was known as the New Pit on Grange estate, east of the Gauze. Two old pits were the Bailies pit at the head of the Cow Loan, Borrowstoun (sunk about 1830 by Mr. J. J. Cadell, but abandoned because so much whin was found); and the Temple pit, on the lands of Northbank east from the latter pit. There was also the Beat pit, where the new cemetery now is, and the Store pit, near the present store at Furnace Row. Nos. 1 and 2 Snab were in course of being sunk about the period we refer to, the only pit in that neighbourhood being the Gin pit, a little to the east. In the town there were two pits at the foot of the Schoolyard Brae, but although coal was raised they were latterly mainly used for pumping. The condensing engine which James Watt invented and completed at Kinneil was first fitted up at the Burn pit. It was afterwards transferred to the Temple pit, and its large wheel, when in motion, gave the miners much amusement. There are still a number of retired miners of the old school resident about Bo'ness,[11] and it is very entertaining to listen to their intelligent description both of the surface when it was studded with pits and of the various underground workings themselves. In nearly all cases ironstone was wrought, as well as coal, and was calcined at the pithead.

IX.

The mining in all these years has naturally affected both the surface and the underground workings. The surface has in some places been considerably lowered. In other places, where the old stoop and room system was used, before the introduction of the long wall method, the ground is to some extent honeycombed, and holes fall in when the roof gives way over seams not far below the surface. Considering the extent of the mining operations here, the calamities which have befallen the mining population have been comparatively few. The most serious of these occurred at the Store pit at Kinneil and in the Schoolyard pit. Four miners were engaged in driving a mine in the Store pit when the water rushed in upon them from adjoining

---

[11] Among these is Mr. Thomas Hamilton, Borrowstoun, who supplied much of above information concerning the old pits.

W

waste workings, drowning all four. Charles Robertson, foreman, already referred to in this chapter, lost his life along with his son and a nephew in the Schoolyard pit. The three were working at the bottom near the main coal. The day was a stormy one, and the air down below had been diverted in some way, with the result that all three were suffocated. A terrible boiler explosion also occurred here. There were five or six boilers in a row at the pithead. One of them had been under repair, but the water not getting in freely, the boiler became overheated, and burst. One portion landed in the garden at the rear of the Clydesdale Hotel. Strangely enough, the men at the pithead escaped. Bricks and stones from the boiler foundations were sent broadcast with terrific force, and for long distances. A woman and child were passing the old post office in South Street at the time. The woman escaped, but the child, who was by her side, was struck by a brick and killed on the spot.

During the time of Mr. Wilson there was a great miners' strike in the county. Miners from the Redding district in large numbers made a raid on the town bent on plundering Kinneil store for provisions. This and the general excitement caused Mr. Wilson to send to Edinburgh for a detachment of soldiers. In response, a company of cavalry from the 7th Dragoons arrived on the scene, and were billeted at Kinneil and the Snab. Soldiers and miners fraternised freely, and had great ongoings. The officer in charge was a keen sportsman and challenged Mr. Wilson to run his carriage horses against those of the troopers. Several races came off in the Brewlands Park, the scene of many a former horse-racing contest. The soldiers remained for several weeks, and had many an escapade. On one occasion some of them commandeered the town drum and drummed themselves round the streets.

The leading families in the Newtown about seventy years ago were the Hamiltons, Robertsons, Grants, Nisbets, Gibbs, and Sneddens. The Old Row constituted the Newtown of those days, and about one hundred families resided there. It was a strict preserve for the miners and their families, and no lodgers or foreigners were admitted. Bynames were very plentiful, and there were lords, dukes, and earls among them. Peers and Commoners alike resided in the Old Row. Archibald Hamilton and his family represented the lords; Sandy Hamilton, the dukes; and Richard Hamilton, the earls. The Hamiltons of Grangepans are all related to the earls and lords Hamiltons of Newtown. The dukes belong to a separate branch, and are connected with the Robertsons and Sneddens.

X.

Two alarming subsidences have occurred in Bo'ness during the last half-century. They have been described by Mr. Cadell[12] as follows:—

"One Sunday evening about thirty years ago, as a local preacher was addressing a meeting on the subject of the fall of the Tower of Siloam in the Old Town Hall below the Clock Tower, and close to the harbour, the congregation were startled by an uncomfortable feeling as if the floor of the building was subsiding beneath them. No active calamity happened, although a terrible danger was very near, and a kind Providence rewarded the faith of the worshippers and permitted them quietly to leave the building after the close of the service. Next day investigations showed that a huge hole 60 feet deep had formed just under the floor, owing to the giving way of the roof of the Wester Main Waste. In a short time the tower began to sink, so as to necessitate its demolition by the authorities. A small shaft was subsequently sunk to ascertain the nature of the cavity, and many had an opportunity of going down and wandering through the old workings about 50 feet below the surface. The seam was about 10 feet thick, and the old miners had worked it in large square pillars, with beautifully dressed faces and an excellent roof. The surface, however, was so near that the thin roof at places had fallen in, and one of the 'sits' had taken place right under the

---

[12] Coalfields of West Lothian. See Appendix III.

Town Hall. This hole was solidly packed with stone when the Clock Tower was rebuilt.

"On another Sunday evening, 2nd February, 1890, an alarming subsidence took place on the shore end of the old harbour, about 200 feet north of the Clock Tower, and close to the 'tongue' that existed up till then between the east and west piers. The ground gave way under the railway, and when the sea rose the water gushed down like a roaring river, enlarging the aperture, and leaving the rails and sleepers suspended in mid-air. The hole was plugged up with timber, straw, and brushwood, and filled to the surface with ballast and clay. All seemed safe, and heavy trains passed over the place until the 20th of February, when a second and larger subsidence took place, into which the sea at high tide rushed in enormous volumes. It looked as if all the dip workings of the Kinneil Colliery were to be drowned, but so large was the reservoir in the Old Wastes that the tide had not time to fill these up before it was excluded. The hole was securely filled with a foundation of slag blocks, covered with clay and ballast, and it was estimated that 2000 tons of material were swallowed up before the cavity was finally levelled over, in the beginning of March. The seam in these 'sits' had a steep dip westward or north-westward, so that the material slid far down as it was dropped in, and was spread over a much larger area of the waste than if the working had been level. Only a few feet of solid rock had been left between the coal and the bottom of the mud in the harbour, and it is marvellous that the old miners were not drowned out a century ago after their temerity in working the seam so near the outcrop below the foreshore. The water that gained entrance during the last subsidence subsequently found its way down into the Kinneil Company's workings to the west, and for a time entailed heavy pumping there."

CHAPTER XVI.

THE BORROWSTOUNNESS AND GRANGEMOUTH CANAL.

1. Local Disappointment over Selection of Grangemouth as Eastern Termination of Forth and Clyde Canal: Proposal of Merchants and Shipmasters to Make Branch Canal to Bo'ness—2. Failure of First Scheme: Mr. Whitworth Consulted: Extracts from his Report: His Plan and Profile—3. Further Extracts from Report—4. The Estimate—5. Failure of Second Scheme and Its Results.

I.

In what brief references there are in gazetteers and similar works regarding Bo'ness we are almost sure to find this very depressing sentence, "After the opening of the Forth and Clyde Canal its trade gradually declined." And this was only too true. It would be unjust, however, to dismiss the subject with this sorrowful statement. As a matter of fact, no part of our local history deserves to be more carefully recorded and emphasised than the part we have arrived at. We mean the whole circumstances attending the misfortune which was sustained locally through the opening up of the Forth and Clyde Canal and the selection of Grangemouth (or Sealock as it was then called) instead of Borrowstounness as the eastern termination of the canal. We believe heroic, if unsuccessful, attempts were made on the part of the Borrowstounness merchants and shipmasters to have the termination made there. In support it was argued that Sealock, or Grangemouth, was considered by engineers and those capable of judging, as a very unsuitable place for an entry into the firth, vessels of that period having to lie a long time in the roads opposite Sealock waiting for stream tides and suitable winds before they could get in. Borrowstounness, on the other hand, was claimed to be a port possessing great natural advantages, and therefore the proper and more suitable terminus. But Grangemouth was, as we have said, ultimately chosen, much to the disappointment of Bo'ness. We cannot at this distance of time find the true cause of this decision, although local tradition puts it down to the exercise of sinister influences by parties interested in Grangemouth.

The sturdy merchants and shipmasters of the old port did not lie down to this reverse. They clearly foresaw that the Forth and Clyde Canal, when finished, would practically put an end to their trade with Glasgow. Hitherto this had been very extensive, and was carried on by means of packhorses and carriers' carts. It was no rare thing at this time, we have heard, to see in a morning fifty carts of merciant goods start off for Glasgow. In order therefore to avert the impending calamity, what did these plucky residents do? They made one of the boldest strokes that has ever been made in Bo'ness (and we are not forgetting that there have been one or two bold and creditable strokes made in the interests of the town in recent times). They agreed to make a branch from the Great Canal, as it was then called, at Grangemouth to the harbour of Bo'ness, and a company called the Borrowstounness Canal Company was formed. In briefly describing the undertaking Mr. M'Kenzie says—

"Two Acts of Parliament and subscriptions to the amount of £10,000 were obtained. The canal was cut from the river Avon eastward within a mile of the town, and an aqueduct across the Avon was nearly completed; but after an outlay of about £7500 the work was abandoned when not half-finished. The circumstances which prevented the accomplishment of this desirable undertaking need not be stated; but they were, and still are, deeply regretted by the inhabitants of this town, especially on seeing their trade turned into another channel. Much of it passed by the canal direct to Glasgow, and the larger vessels discharged at Grangemouth, which was only a creek of this port, but then became its rival, and was eventually erected into a separate port."

II.

The promoters of this canal of communication certainly undertook a long and tedious task. Evidently money had come in freely at the first, and the work was set well agoing according to a plan laid down by a Mr. Lowrie. Among the enthusiastic promoters were, as might be expected, the members of the Seabox Society, who invested in a number of shares. After executing the work detailed above by Mr. M'Kenzie, and after spending over £7000 of the £10,000 gathered, it was seen that more funds would be needed, as the task had turned out to be a much more difficult one than was at first anticipated. In a brief reference to the reason of the stoppage Mr. Johnston[1] says—

"No doubt want of funds was one of them, but, if local tradition speaketh truth, a portion of the money raised was not expended as it ought to have been, and some associated with the project rendered themselves richer in pocket and poorer in character by their conduct at that time."

Notwithstanding all this, the idea of completing the task was not then abandoned. It was resolved to get a report on the whole proposal from a skilled engineer, as well as an estimate of the probable cost of completing the work, so that more money might be raised. Accordingly, Mr. Robert Whitworth, of Glasgow, under whom the Great Canal was completed, and who was an engineer of great standing, was employed. We have had an opportunity of perusing Mr. Whitworth's report and estimate with accompanying plan.[2] The document is a long one, and it is only here possible to give a few extracts from it.

---

[1] Seabox Records.
[2] In the possession of Mr. J. F. Macaulay.

It is dated Glasgow, 28th December, 1789, is addressed to the company of proprietors of the Borrowstounness Canal, and opens thus—

"Gentlemen,—In obedience to your orders, I have taken the levels and made a survey of the line of the proposed canal from Grangemouth to Borrowstounness, and made a plan and profile of the same. The line laid down upon the plan, which is nearly the same as that laid down by Mr. John Lowrie, is as good a one as can be taken. The level of the reach of the Great Canal above the second lock suits the level of the country very well, as appears by the profile, and from Grangemouth to the river Avon will be exceedingly easy to execute, except at the crossing of the Grange burn, where a small aqueduct will be necessary."

We shall give further extracts later, but these will be more readily understood if we first of all endeavour to describe the plan. In following the description we must remember that there was then no railway in Bo'ness, and therefore no railway stations and sidings either in the neighbourhood of Kinneil or Bo'ness. To begin at Bo'ness—the plan first shows the harbour, then coming westwards a large canal basin is denoted, which if constructed would have taken up the ground, now railway lines, from Masonic Hall and the present passenger station to the bend at West Pier. Along at Corbiehall, somewhere in the vicinity of what was formerly the West End Foundry, now Avon Place, was to be a supply pond. Next to that is shown the "Bucket Pot," near the site of the present slaughter-house. Then on the south side of the proposed canal, and to the westward we think of the present distillery buildings, what was then known as the "West Engine" is indicated. Near to this, on the shore, is Copess or Capie's Point. Still going westward, and evidently near the site of the present Furnace Yard pit, comes a place marked "Castle." This is doubtless the remains of "Castle Lyon," said to have at one time existed in this vicinity. More will be learned of this when we refer to Mr. Whitworth's estimate. The Snab is next clearly shown, with a natural projection pointing north-westwards. In more recent times, of course, this has been projected artificially much further in the same direction by being made up with slag in the days of Kinneil furnaces, and is now known as the Slag Hills. Further west, but a little to the south, comes Kinneil Castle (Kinneil House). Parknook (presumably the present Dykeneuk) is the next point marked, and from here the route of the canal struck away from the roadside and kept along by the Firthside until it came towards the mouth of the Avon. It then diverged to the left, passing the farm steading of Kinneil Kerse on its south side, and from there running to about where the present bridge over the Avon stands, and where an aqueduct for the canal, as we have seen, was at that time partially constructed. We need not follow the plan further, as the Grangemouth territory is not so well known to us. Besides, the route to Grangemouth from the Avon aqueduct was quite easy, as Mr. Whitworth points out, and does not call for remark.

III.

There is a strong dotted line shown on the plan running from Parknook along the present roadside, and then deflecting at the Haining towards the Avon, almost on the same line as the present Grangemouth Road. The part thus indicated was evidently thought to be a more direct and less expensive route than the old one along the shore and through the fields. Mr. Whitworth was asked to survey it, and report on what he thought of its adoption. He took the levels, and reported that, while he considered the canal could have gone that way very well, yet seeing the shore route was fairly on the way to completion, and that a large sum had been spent on it, he could not advise its abandonment.

We must recollect that the road to Polmont was the only road in that neighbourhood at that time, the plan giving no indication of the new road to Grangemouth. As we know, most of the canal from the Snab to the Avon had been excavated when Mr. Whitworth was called in. On his plan therefore the canal line is tinted red and yellow, and there is a note to the effect that those parts shaded yellow were already dug in part; those shaded red were yet to do. Even to this day the big ditch or trench of the canal can quite well be traced on the roadside beyond the Snab, and it is still to be traced in the fields near Kinneil Kerse.

Consider now some further extracts from the report. We add these, because they incidentally describe to us the state of the Snab and Kinneil districts at that period:—

"From the Avon aqueduct to Parknook the canal has been finished for seven feet water; but as it has now to be raised to eight feet, the puddle will want raising on both sides the whole way. The south bank is rather slender, it having been formed with great economy for only seven feet, yet has stood so long to consolidate that it may sustain eight feet without enlarging the base.

"From Parknook to the Snab garden the bank has been a good deal cut away, and will be attended with a good deal of trouble and expense to replace it.

"In passing the Snab there are two ways of doing it. One is round the house and through the offices, which appear to be two pretty good new buildings which would be entirely destroyed. The other is through the garden as represented on the plan and profile. Which of these will be cheaper and more eligible I cannot well say. The latter is more direct and out of the way of the sea. For the present I will suppose the line drawn upon the plan to be adopted and the canal to be finished in the direction already begun to Copess Point, opposite the West Engine.

"From the West Engine to the harbour will require some consideration. There are two ways for it to go. One is through the Salt Works; the other on the outside of the Bucket Pan, which will, of course, take considerable hold of the sea, and will require a strong and high wall to defend it; yet I have no doubt of its being practicable, but will be very expensive."

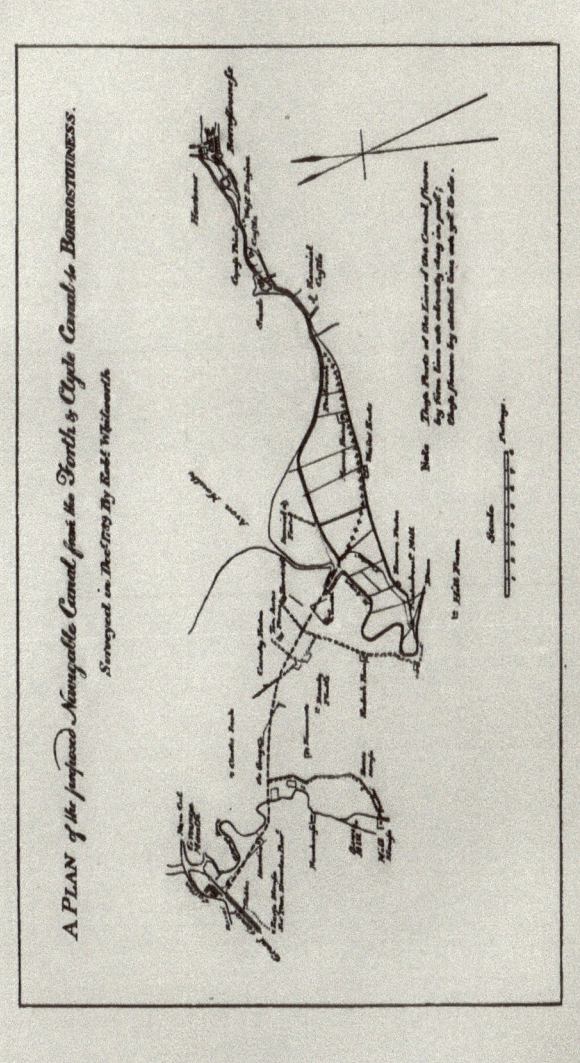

Reduced plan of Borrowstounness and Grangemouth Canal.

(Sketched by J. D. H. Dymock, A.M.Inst.C.E., from Mr. Whitworth's plan lent by Mr. J. F. Macaulay.)

"If there was room to carry it through the Salt Works without taking down some of the principal buildings, and I fear almost destroying the works, it most certainly would be desirable, but I cannot find there is. Indeed, if the worthy proprietor was consenting, perhaps the works that stand in the way might be rebuilt in another place at a less expense than the difference of the two sea walls necessary to defend the canal; but of this I am not certain. I can make no calculation of the line through the Salt Works, therefore for the present I will suppose it to go on the outside of the Bucket Pan, where, I trust, I can be more certain in my calculations."

He also reports minutely on the various sources which would require to be tapped along the route to supply the canal with water, but he was relying also on a fair supply from the Great Canal, as there was always a good deal of water running over the gates of the second lock into the sea.

Mr. Whitworth closes the report by saying—

"If the works be planned and set out with judgment and conducted with economy, I believe the canal may be completed at the following estimate.

"I am,
"With the greatest respect,
"Your very humble servant,
"ROBERT WHITWORTH."

IV.

The estimate, which is divided into sections and carefully detailed, is based on the supposition that the canal be made fifty-four feet wide at top and twenty-seven at bottom, and eight feet deep of water. Digging to be eight and a half feet at the first, as otherwise the canal would soon become too shallow for a vessel drawing eight feet of water to pass freely along.

The following is an interesting example of its terms:—

"To completing the canal (which is in some places part dug) from the west side of the Snab garden to Copess Point, opposite the West Engine. In this part there is a variety of work, as cutting through the whin rock, taking down and rebuilding three hundred and four feet in length of the castle garden wall, completing and continuing Shaw's wall to Copess Point. As one part of this work depends upon another, it cannot well be particularised; the whole, I judge from the best calculations I can make of such an irregular business, may come to about £750."

The total estimate from Grangemouth to the

West Engine was	£10,406	7 6
And from there to the harbour	7,357	2 6
	£17,763	10 0

The latter sum included the cost of proposed lock near the harbour and other expensive items connected with the terminus.

The issue of this report and estimate evidently finished matters. It meant that nearly £20,000 would yet be required—double that originally raised—and this was quite beyond the practical compass of even the most sanguine and enthusiastic of the promoters.

So a great and worthy scheme, originated by worthy men and in a worthy commercial cause, had to be reluctantly abandoned.

V.

Perhaps it should be mentioned here that the townspeople some thirty years before this had met with another great disappointment. This was the strangulation of another big scheme which would, if carried out, have added enormously to the trade and prosperity of the town. It came about thus— The enterprising Dr. Roebuck left his chemical manufactory at Prestonpans, being strongly impressed with the mineral wealth then lying unheeded between the Forth and Clyde, and took a lease of the Duke's coal and salt works here. He was much interested, along with Mr. Cadell, in the improvement and development of the industries of Scotland. As is known, they and others founded the Carron Ironworks in 1759. It is not so generally known, however, that it was their first intention to erect the works in the neighbourhood of Jinkabout Mill, and that the ground was all carefully surveyed for the purpose and found very suitable. But the land, unfortunately, was found to be strictly entailed, and all that could be offered then was a ninety-nine years' lease. This they would not accept, and so were reluctantly compelled to abandon the project so far as Bo'ness was concerned.

Stenhousemuir estate was for sale at the time, so it was purchased forthwith, and upon it were built the Carron Ironworks, whose reputation has been world-wide for a century at least.

To return to the dropping of the canal scheme. Decay in the shipping trade of Borrowstounness did not immediately set in. What with the coal shipments from Kinneil Colliery, under Dr. Roebuck, the local shipbuilding yard, and other industries, the town enjoyed a fair measure of prosperity during the next twenty years. On the 1st December, 1810, however, Grangemouth, which only ranked as an out-station or a creek of Bo'ness, had a Custom-house of its own established, with jurisdiction over Alloa, Stirling, and Kincardine. In that year the total duties drawn at Bo'ness amounted to £30,485 17s. 0½d. Five years later the figures had declined to £3835 6s. 4½d. These figures speak melancholy news for themselves. Grangemouth is a creation of yesterday, so to speak, dating back to 1777 only. It is said to owe its origin to Sir Lawrence Dundas of Kerse, an ancestor of the Earl of Zetland, who was the chief landed proprietor in the district. He called the town into being and patronised it in anticipation of the trade the Forth and Clyde Canal—in which he was also largely interested —was sure to bring to the place.

As a result of the tremendous decrease in the trade of the port, the number of skippers and sailors resident in and about Bo'ness fell away in a marked degree; and we understand the membership roll of the Seabox Society showed a corresponding decrease. For the same reason there occurred a great exodus of well-known and substantial shipowners and merchants, descendants of the men who, when the port began to rise in the seventeenth century, had come from Glasgow and the west, acquired property, and settled here. Among those who went away to settle in Liverpool, Glasgow, and Leith were members of such well-known families as the Grindlays, Hendersons, Cowans, and Mitchells.

CHAPTER XVII.

LOCAL SOCIETIES AND LODGES.

1. Origin of the Seabox: The Bond of Erection: Early Management: Boxmasters and Key-keepers—2. A Sailor Community Indeed: Their Virtues and Business Qualities: The Volume of Extracts Regarding Erection of First Church: Some Quaint Entries—3. Examples of Entries from the Early Cash Books of Seabox: Some of the Boxmasters—4. The Landsmen's or Maltmen's Box: Shipmasters Society Formed: Boxmasters Henderson and Ritchie: The Friendly Society of Shipmasters—5. New Society Avoids Law and Lawyers: The Exodus from the Seaport and Depletion of Societies—6. The United General Seabox: First Office-Bearers: The 250th Anniversary—7. Privileges of Society: The Bellman and James Bennie: Old Custom at Funerals of Poor People—8. Carriden or Grangepans' Seabox: Names of Members: Its Decline and End—9. The Bo'ness Seabox and the Representatives: Issue of Anonymous Pamphlets and Letters—10. An Exciting Meeting of Representatives—11. Origin of the Beneficent Society: An Interesting "Jurnal" of 20 years' Transactions—12. How an Audit was Conducted: Society Passes Resolutions in Favour of Abolition of Slave Traffic—13. Local Freemasons: Lodge Pythagoric and its Old Minute Book.

I.

The local friendly society now known as The United General Seabox of Borrowstounness had its origin in 1634. Among its designations in olden days were "The Ancient Society of Seafaring Men," "The Sea Poor's Box of the Burgh of Borrowstounness," "The Sailors' Society," and "The Sailors' Box Society." Its records are the oldest in the town. Twenty-three years ago a small volume[1] descriptive of the history of the society was issued. It is long out of print. Some of its

---

[1] Records of an ancient Friendly Society, 1890: Thomas Johnston.

members claim that the Borrowstounness Seabox is entitled to rank as Scotland's oldest friendly society, but there is at least one older. We refer to the Shipmasters' Society or Seamen's Box of Aberdeen, whose history was recently published.[2] Their bond of erection is dated 1598, and they, in addition, got a Royal Charter from King James VI., of date 19th February, 1600. This society flourishes at the present day, is still what it originally was, and has for president, vice-president, and treasurer three sea captains. In much of its history it greatly resembles ours, or, perhaps we should say, ours resembles it. It has its "schip," "lockit box," seal, church loft, headquarters, pension roll, and (crowning touch) its flag.

Our bond of erection is dated 3rd January, 1640, but six years before that, the masters and seamen of the port formed themselves into a society for benevolent purposes, and for mutual help in times of need. Indeed, from 1628 money had been contributed by them for such objects. The bond of erection, or, at least, a copy of it, still hangs in the hall of the society, Main Street. In the leisurely and quaint style of the Scots legal documents of the period it fully describes the objects of the society, and brings its subscribers under specific obligations and penalties. It was prepared by John Ronnald, "Notar Public Clerk in Borrowistounnes," and is signed by John Langlands, Geo. Allan, John Gibb, Richard Falconer, and over one hundred and twenty others. That in itself shows how well-off we were for skippers and mariners in those days.

The revenue, according to the bond, was to be derived from contributions out of wages on their return from each voyage. Contribution was to be made also for each vessel belonging to or taking its name from the town. A visitation of the box was to be made every quarter in the year by the masters who happened to be at home, with consent of as many sailors as the masters thought expedient to take with them on these occasions. At every visitation the box and two keys thereof were to be delivered to such men and for such a term as the

---

[2] The Shipmaster Society or The Seamen's Box of Aberdeen : Alexander Clark, 1911.

master-visitors should think most suitable. The money collected was to be distributed for the relief of distressed persons, but primarily of such mariners as were sufferers through age, infirmity, or accident. Such relief was only to be given with the consent of two or three masters who should happen to be at home, and in no other way. And it was lastly stipulated that, whatever person or persons thereafter whom it should "pleas the Lord to bles and plaice as maisteris of ane Schippe within the towne," that master should be obliged to subscribe and consent to and obey the terms of the bond in all points.

The Seabox was carried on for the succeeding hundred years with great success. As it owed its origin to the enterprise of the local skippers, they naturally had the chief share in its management. This was very simple, yet thorough. During its early years there is no reference to a Boxmaster, operations being apparently left to the two key-keepers and such masters as were available. In time, however, mention is made of the Boxmaster, who is clearly esteemed the chief official, his principal colleagues being the two key-keepers. There is nothing at first in the nature of a minute book, the cash book serving the double purpose of keeping a record of the intromissions and the appointment of the Boxmaster and two key-keepers from time to time. Docquets setting forth the quarterly and other examinations of the books also appear. Their "depursements," as they were called, were kept in a separate volume, and were few for a long time. In fact, the idea seems first of all to have been to collect a substantial fund. When they got this—and, as the contributions were substantial, they soon succeeded—they commenced to lend out sums on bills to local merchants, to the Duke, and to the trustees for the town and harbour. They at the same time made up the pension rolls regularly, paid goodly sums, chiefly to widows of mariners, and gave relief of various kinds. Towards the end of the seventeenth century we find an annual docquet certifying the examination of the book, a second appointing or re-appointing the Boxmaster, and a third and larger one giving the changes made in the pension roll and amount of the pensions, along with an instruction to

x

the Boxmaster to give effect to the changes during the ensuing year. These things were done at the annual general meeting, and the docquets were signed by all the skippers and mariners present. The box is still in existence, though now unused. It is in truth a "strong box," and has locks of a very peculiar and complicated kind.

II.

A glance over the earlier books and papers of the society shows that, two centuries ago, the town was practically given over to shipping in a quiet, leisurely way. Many of the shipmasters were owners of their own craft, and most of the crews were composed of local men, whose outstanding qualities were godliness, thrift, and broad human sympathy Our skippers and sailors, as has been fitly said, were a really superior and meritorious body of men; they displayed great intelligence, zeal, and discretion in the management of their affairs; they looked at life and all its responsibilities from an earnest point of view, and were deeply and conscientiously imbued with the national religious spirit of the time. We were then a sailor community indeed, with all the picturesque romance, all the quiet tragedy of the sea in and around us. Much, nay, nearly all, of this has during the intervening years given place to a more materialistic atmosphere. Yea, the port has greatly changed its features, and the people their characteristics.

One of the most interesting records belonging to the Sea-box is a volume of extracts from its books from 1633 to 1652, compiled by the late John Anderson, regarding the voluntary erection of the Church at Corbiehall. These not only contain "Ane Declaration of the names of those individuals who contributed to the building and what they did bestow," but also a declaration of the names of those who "payed to the plantation of the Minister and what they gave, which did begin the 10 January, 1648." The society itself contributed handsomely towards the building of the church and the provision of the minister's stipend, as will be found in the chapter on the

Representatives. Two things were very close to the hearts of these old seafarers—religion and education—and we must ever gratefully remember their generosity in the furtherance of these causes.

Every item in the volume just referred to is entered with conscientious detail. Among those dealing with the "depursing" of the voluntary contributions we find—

> 1636.—To William Anderson to go to Leith to buy the Jeasts to the Kirk Laft.
>> To Patrick Glen in compleat payt. for the ground of the Church and yard.
>> To Peter Steven for an corball of oak to be the cross-tree in the Bell-house for the hanging of the Bell.
>> For upbearing of some timber from the seaside to the Church.
>> To John Anderson, Slater, in earnest when he agreed for slating of the Church.
>> To William Anderson, who concludes his account for binding of the roof.
>> To the Skipper who brought up the last thousand sklaits, upon the 7 July, for the freight thereof.
> 1638.—To John Anderson for thigging of the porch and laying on the rigging stone, which concludes him of all his wants that ever he can crave of the said work.

It was the custom in Scotland in these days to allow workmen drink money or drink itself, apparently as a part of their wages. Accordingly, we find entries such as these—

> In drink silver to the skipper's men for bringing west the timber from the pier to the Church in a "flott."
> For an free lunch to the Wrights and others when the roof was set up.
> In drink silver to the slater's men.
> For the Slater's ale, which was every Saturday night allowed to them a quart.

> To the Slaters when they closed the porch, and that in closing silver.

After the building of the church the loft and stair leading thereto were erected for the accommodation of the "skipperis and marineris." Here are one or two more entries:—

> To Alex Scott and his wife for serving the masons the time they were building the stair, for the space of 26 days.
> To John Anderson's man in drink money.
> To Janet Russel for Ale to the Masons the time they wrought the stair.
> To William Reding three days "shooling," at lyme.
> To bread and drink to the gentlemen's men for lime carrying.

In 1653 a good deal of legal work was entailed by the foreclosing of Balderston's Bond over Muirhouse, and we find these entries:—

> Spent with the Writers in Linlithgow.
> Sum spent in Linlithgow when we received Comprisement.
> Sum for home bringing the papers out of Edinburgh.
> Sum for the charges of the Minister, two days in my house.
> Sum for a boy to go twice to Edinburgh.
> Sum for horse hire, horse meat, and boy's meat.
> Sum of charges spent with Writers in Linlithgow.
> Sum for a boy to go to Linlithgow with a letter for some papers.

III.

Let us now take a few examples of the wording of entries from the earlier cash-books of the Seabox itself:—

1635.
July 28.—Putt in by James Wilsone for a Holland voyage.
Oct. 14.—In the name of God putt in be Richard Falkoner for ane Rotterdam voyage.

Local Societies and Lodges

1637.
April 16.—Paid in to the Box and that for a London voyage by John Gibb.
July 25.—Paid in to the Box for ane Ostend voyage by Alex. Hardie.

Here are further entries in later years:—

1755.
July 29.—Recd. from Capt. James Crawford as a compliment to the poor. He was Commander of the "Thistle" to Greenland.
July 30.—Paid in by Alex. Hardie, a voyage with James Glasfurd.
Aug. 16.—Received from Robt. Nicole, a Greenland voyage with the "Peggy."
Received from James Hardie, a Greenland voyage with the "Peggy."
Paid in by James Hutton, a Greenland voyage with the "Thistle."

The following are examples of the "depursements":—

1635.
June 20.—Given out of Box to ane distressed person be consent of George Allan.
1643.—Paid to several distressed persons at sundry and divers times.
Paid to the Clerk John Ronald for the writing ane Band.
Depursit to pay Ministers stipand.
Nov. 19.—Lent for Band to My Ladie Marquis Hammiltonne (£1666 13s. 4d.).
Sent to Holland with Alex. Allan in venture of licht money to doe according to his best power.
1647.—Given to 5 poore Frenchmen of St. Maloos taken by the Ostenders.
1648.—Item for mending the glass of ye Sailors' Laft in the Ness Kirk ye 6 of February 1648.

1649.—Given to a distressed Seaman robbed by Irish Men of Warre to help him to his friends.
Payit to Margot Speiris four and half Boll of Maill.
Payit for Jeane Ritchie's maill.
1658.—To John Hardie to buy him his bannit and shune be order.

1661.
April 4.—Given to Allan Robertsone for mending the Seamen's Laft door.

1702.
Sept. 11.—To James Kidd, mariner in this place, in great distress by order.
Oct. 5.—To William Gray, prisoner from Dunkirk, being a seaman belonging to Dublin by order.
Oct. 13.—To a distressed gentlewoman by order.

1703.
Jan. 11.—To ane poor Seaman wanting ane hand by order.
March 16.—Spent at putting in March stones at the land.
July 29.—Payd to Andrew Wilson for getting out horning & caption upon George Gib's Band & inhibition against John Gib.
Sept. 20.—Payd ane shipbroken Sailor by order.
Oct. 2.—Payd a shipbroken man of Pettenweem by order.
Oct. 12.—For answering the Head Court for Meldrum's house.
Nov. 8.—To a distressed man and his wife by order.
Dec. 6.—To John Burns a broken seaman by order.

1704.
Feb. 7.—To shipbroken Dutchman by order.
Debursed by Richard Durie for the Mort Cloathes.
Aug. 5.—For ridling and souring of two bags of lyme.
Sept. 2.—Paid workmen their drink money and 4 hours in Hugh Monteiths.
Dec. 3.—John Young and his wyff for ane year's feu deutie from Martinmas 1703 till Martinmas 1704 for the Meeting house.

1705.
April 21.—To tuo shipbroken men who had come from Rotterdam both belonging to Dublin by order.
May 8.—For answering at the Head Court for Meldrum's house.
Nov. 7.—To 3 Seamen taken by the French.
Nov. 19.—To John Saxum a broken seaman by order.

1738.
Jan. 4.—Payd for a new Register Book.
Jan. 5.—Payd to Clerk Wilson for Bonds and other writings.

1748.
April 7.—Given to James Cambell taken by the Algerians in a vessel called the "Swallow"; after three years' slavery was re-taken by a Maltese ship of war.

1749.
April 11.—To William M'Phearson and two others whose tongues were cut out by the Turks of Algiers; all three in melancholy case.

1753.
Sept. 20.—By cash given to a dumb sailor having his tongue cut out by the Algerines; attested by the Consul of Leghorn.

There are hundreds upon hundreds of entries throughout the books similar in nature to those just instanced. The credit entries are interesting as showing the names of the various skippers and mariners belonging to the port, and the different places, home and foreign, with which they traded. As for the debit entries, they show the extent and variety of the society's benefactions.

It has been impossible to trace the names of the various Boxmasters of the society, but those whose names occur most frequently are Richard Dawling, James Falconer, James Cassils, and in later years John Henderson and John Ritchie.

The books, especially between the years 1660 and 1678,

were written with great care. Each page was headed with the year "anno   ," and at the end of each year the writer finished up with a benediction of his own, to this effect, "And so much for the year   ."

Among the numerous docquets in the book we find the following:—

"All being comptit & reckoned togidder the 24 of Jan., 1646, the money being putt in ane Pourse and sealled with wax, it did extend to the soume of £479 11s. 2d. (Scots)." This is then signed by James Gibb, Richard Falconer, and five others.

IV.

By the middle of the seventeenth century Borrowstounness contained quite a thriving community of brewers, maltsters, and traders, and in August, 1659, they, in emulation of their seafaring friends, started a Landsmen's Box or Maltmen's Box. For two hundred years this society continued to exist, and did much benevolent work. Ultimately, as we shall see, it was incorporated with the old Seabox. The cash and sederunt books of the Landsmen's Box are now in the possession of the Seabox Society. There is nothing in them calling for special comment. To return to the affairs of the Seabox, we find that evidences are to be found in the year 1733 of a general slackness in the management, which gave rise to dissatisfaction and discontent. New and more exacting rules were therefore adopted, and as the original bond of erection could not be found, a fresh bond was prepared, and signed. Evidently the old bond was discovered later, as there is now no trace of the new one. Doubtless it would be promptly destroyed on the recovery of the original. Dissatisfaction still remained, and in 1738 there occurred the first secession from the ranks by the establishment of the Shipmasters' Society. It is said to have been successful, but all its books and papers, save a sederunt book commencing in August, 1775, are amissing.

The Seabox still continued to have trouble over the

enforcement of its rules, and a hypercritical spirit became very manifest. From November, 1755, onwards we discover frequent references in the minutes to the Ritchie litigation. Dissension was rife, because the shipmasters and the sailors formed themselves into two distinct parties. The critical point was reached over the annual election of the Boxmaster. This office had for long been held by John Henderson, who was of a quiet and non-contentious disposition, yet a sagacious and capable officer. The go-ahead Ritchie, however, had designs on the office. There was the Ritchie party, composed chiefly of sailors, and the anti-Ritchie party of shipmasters and some others. Feeling ran high, contests were keen, and ultimately the fighting captain achieved his purpose, and supplanted Mr. Henderson as Boxmaster. We are not much surprised therefore to find that a second secession from the ranks took place in 1756. The new and rival organisation was called "The Friendly Society of Shipmasters," and was established by a large number of the anti-Ritchie shipmasters. The new body flourished for more than a century, and acquired considerable property. It was, along with the older Shipmasters' Society, finally amalgamated with the General Seabox in 1863. Few of its records have been preserved, but we learn that James Main was its first treasurer, and that its management was in the hands of a committee of ten shipmasters.

V.

The litigious spirit of Ritchie and the result of a law suit in which he had involved the Seabox over the Boxmastership appear to have been taken as a warning by the new body. Accordingly, as Mr. Johnston humorously says, they resolved to have nothing to do in future with gentlemen of the legal profession. This is borne out by the terms of the following special rule:—

"To avoid all manner of law suits or other litigious disputes that may arise among the members concerning the direction of affairs of this friendly and charitable society, and to prevent the burdening the public fund or stock with fruitless and unnecessary expense, it is hereby specially provided, covenanted, and agreed to, that if any differences shall hereafter at any time arise amongst any of the members in relation to any part of the whole premises, the same shall be referred to the final determination of two neutral men to be mutually chosen, and in case of variance to an oversman to be named by the said arbiters, and that the expense of the said submission and decreet to pass thereon shall not be paid out of the public fund, but by the disputants themselves, as the arbiters shall think fit; and if, notwithstanding of this special provision, any member or number of members shall hereafter take upon them to commence any law suit contrary to the plain meaning and intention of this clause such member or members shall forfeit all right, title, and interest that he or they might otherwise have as members of this friendly society."

Among those who were called in as arbiters were the Rev. Patrick Bennett, minister of Polmont, and the Rev. Patrick Baillie, minister of Bo'ness, and the rule seems to have operated very smoothly and successfully.

All three societies flourished for years, and particularly so between 1750 and 1790, when the port attained to the height of its prosperity. But a great change was in store for them. This occurred in the earlier part of the nineteenth century through the opening of the Forth and Clyde Canal, and the consequent depression of trade in Bo'ness. A native who died nearly fifty years ago has left on record that he remembered seeing the sailors of the port walking in procession to the number of four hundred. With the falling fortunes of the place, however, came the exodus of the principal shipowners, shipmasters, and sailors, and the membership of the local friendly societies was very greatly reduced. About 1820 we find Mr. John Anderson appointed treasurer of the Seabox, and by this time its membership consisted of three. He prepared a new set of rules, but Mr. James Grandison, one of the remaining members, complained to the county justices. They, in March, 1823, cancelled Mr. Anderson's rules, and appointed Mr. Grandison, "the only member of the society at present resident in Bo'ness, along with James Heggie, the officer, now a pensioner on the funds thereof," and the Rev. Dr. Rennie, and other local gentlemen to meet and make choice of proper officers in terms of the original articles. These met on 10th July, when James Grandison was appointed preses; Walter Grinlay, treasurer; Ilay Burns, notary public, clerk; and James Heggie, officer. The meeting recommended these officers to frame new rules, and submit them to the justices for approval. This was done, and in 1824 Mr. Anderson became clerk, and a few years later treasurer.

VI.

In 1857 an agreement was arrived at whereby the Seabox Society and the Landsmen's Society amalgamated under the common title of "The United General Seabox." To the new concern the Landsmen's Society transferred stock to the amount of £1051 7s. 4d., consisting mostly of bonds and Gas Company shares. The office-bearers then appointed were Alexander Blair, preses; James Paterson, clerk; John Anderson, treasurer; Peter Liston, first key-keeper; Robert Campbell, second key-keeper; Alexander Wallace, first trustee; David Paterson, second trustee; F. Mackie, third trustee; John Johnston, jun., officer. Rules were prepared, and the society duly registered. Six years after, the Shipmasters' Society and the Friendly Society of Shipmasters were also incorporated with the Seabox. At that time the membership of the Seabox was twenty-seven; that of the Shipmasters' Society eight; and of the Friendly Society of Shipmasters ten. Several of the latter were also members of the Seabox. The funds now, as the result of the amalgamations, amounted to £6000, and once more new rules were necessitated. The chief of these provided members with an allowance in sickness and infirmity until sixty years of age; a payment to shipwrecked members; funeral money at the death of a member or his wife or widow; an annuity to members above sixty years of age and to widows and children. Another important regulation was that not until the expiry of twenty years were the members of the three other societies to be put on a complete equality with those of the original Seabox. Since 1857 the following have occupied the office of preses:—Captain Alexander Blair, 1857-1864; Mr. Alexander Wallace, 1864-1870; Mr. William Miller, 1870-1872; and Mr. William Thomson, 1872-1911. On 31st December, 1884, the members celebrated the two hundred and fiftieth anniversary of the founding of the society.

While the charm and romance of the old seaport no longer encircle the Seabox Society, the present body is quite a thriving institution. Its capital has now reached nearly £10,000, and the annual income £700. A large part of this capital consists of house property, new and old, yielding a fair return. Its three oldest members are Messrs. John White, William Thomson, and William Miller.

VII.

In times past the Seabox had several important privileges. They had the right of charging dues for planks and barrows used for loading and discharging vessels; and for every boat which came into the harbour with fish. They had also the right of appointing the town bellman, and of supplying him with a bell, but how the right originated there is nothing to show. The former of these rights was given up about forty-five years ago; but the latter was only relinquished in 1897, when the Town Council took over the duty. The Seabox possess a model frigate named the "Muirhouse," which hangs in the sailors' loft in the parish Church. It was on view at the Scottish Exhibition of National History, Art, and Industry in Glasgow, 1911. The bronze handbell belonging to the society was also exhibited at same time. It has a ship stamped upon it, and the motto of the society, "Verbum Domini Manet Aeternum." Around the outer edge is the inscription, "This bell belongs to the Seamen's Box of Borrowstounness, 1647." In connection with the office of bellman, Mr. Grandison, while occupying the position of treasurer, had to deal strictly with an infringement of the society's rights in this respect. One James Bennie, "a stout, young man, residing in Bo'ness," had commenced business on his own account as a public crier, using a horn when making his public intimations. This was resented by the Seabox, who maintained that they had the sole privilege of appointing a bellman. It had been the invariable practice of the society to appoint its own officer, generally an old seaman unable to go to sea, but quite fitted for the duties. Bennie's opposition considerably affected the perquisites of the officer, and Mr. Grandison put the whole facts and circumstances before the county justices. Bennie was notified to lodge answers, but evidently gave up his opposition, as nothing further appears in the records.

Another aspect of this bell-ringing falls to be noted.[3] At the burials of the poor people here a custom almost obsolete in other parts of Scotland was, we believe, continued into the nineteenth century. The beadle perambulated the streets with a bell and intimated the death of the individual in the following language:—" All brethren and sisters I let ye to wit there is a brother departed at the pleasure of the Almighty" (here he lifts his hat) "called . . . All those that come to the burial come at . . . o'clock. The corpse is at . . ." He also walked before the corpse to the churchyard ringing his bell.

VIII.

The seafarers belonging to Carriden—and there were a goodly number one hundred and fifty years ago—also had a Seabox Society. Its designation as disclosed in their articles was "The Society of Mariners or Seabox of Carriden or Grangepans." Instituted about the end of the eighteenth century, it was similar in objects to that of Bo'ness, although it never really reached a very flourishing state. Progress from

---

[3] Sinclair's Stat. Ac., Vol. xviii.

the first was very slow, and to induce an increased membership its articles and rules of government were revised by a Quarter Sessions of the Peace held at Linlithgow on 5th May, 1807. The society came to an end ten years after this, owing to the diminishing number of masters and seamen in Carriden.

One of its interesting relics is a model ship, which hung for long years in the west loft of the old Church of Carriden at Cuffabouts, and is now to be found in the new church there. The United General Seabox possess one of its minute books (1777-1818). Admissions were few and far between. Here are the names of some of its members:—David Cumming, Charles Wood, John Graham, John Chapman, William Bruce, Robert Taylor, William Hodge, George Ritchie, John Duncan, James Boyd, Patrick Boyd, William Smith, Alexander Ritchie, John Nelson, George Boage, William Thomson, David Cumming, jun., James Drummond, James Campbell, John Hamilton, William Campbell, James Henderson, and Duncan Corbett. Lists of the widow pensioners also appear. In 1768 James Boyd was its master and William Smith its treasurer. That year the "stock" of the Box consisted of a tenement of houses in Grangepans possessed by three tenants; cash in the hands of James Hutton & Co., Leith; certain acres of ground called Peasehill; and cash in the hands of William Baxter, merchant in Grangepans. In February, 1804, George Boag was elected preses and Alexander Bisset, "schoolmaster of Carriden," was appointed clerk "to manage the business of the society according to their rules, and to have £1 yearly for his trouble." Their late Boxmaster, James Boyd, having died, and things not having been left to their satisfaction, it was agreed to peacewarn his widow "from her house in the Boxland, and to let the same to Alex. Bissett, present clerk, for the term of fifteen years at the yearly rental of £6 sterling."

In the course of a few years Mr. Bisset, at his own special request, was relieved of the tenancy, and recompensed for the improvements he had effected on the ground. Little else is to be gleaned from the books, except that when a small bond was repaid the money was ordered to be disposed of in the "national stocks."

The Seabox likewise possess the old Carriden Box itself, and the mortcloth used at the funerals of its members. The box is constructed of strong wood securely bound with iron. Inside the lid Mr. John Anderson affixed a coffin lid bearing the following inscription:—"This box is presented by John Anderson, merchant, Bo'ness (for near 40 years past treasurer of the General Sea Box, Bo'ness), to the General Sea Box, Borrowstounness. It is all that remains of the Sea Box of Carriden, a very old institution, which, when it fell into few hands, was plundered, and it is a singular fact that few of the plunderers died a natural death—a warning to others to avoid such conduct. Bo'ness, 4th Feb., 1856."

We have a feeling that this story of the plundering and the fate of the plunderers is exaggerated. No doubt it would be handed down to Mr. Anderson, and in its frequent tellings had come to be looked upon as the incontrovertible truth. In any event, it afforded Mr. Anderson an excellent opportunity to "wag a moraleesin heid."

IX.

The Bo'ness Seabox were long involved in disputes with the Representatives. We have dealt with these at length in another chapter; but we desire to refer briefly to three important public manifestos bearing on its closing stages, copies of which are preserved among the papers of the society. They take us back exactly a century, when one of the many bitter controversies over the management of the church funds raged in the town. There was then no local press, and the controversialists resorted to the issue of pamphlets and anonymous letters printed in Falkirk.

The first of the prints emanated from a public meeting held at the Hamilton Arms Inn on 18th December, 1812. It was in the nature of a summons to the inhabitants to attend the annual meeting on the first Wednesday of 1813 "for the purpose of choosing their Representatives." There had evidently crept into the management a distinct church element bent on securing the greatest possible surplus for the minister even at the cost of allowing the church to fall into disrepair.

Very pertinently the public were reminded of the decision of the Court in the Ritchie litigation. The minister and Kirk Session, it was then held, had only a voice, along with others, in the choice of Representatives, and that, when chosen, these had the sole management. It was stated that the interest of the minister was directly opposed to that of the town, and the inhabitants were exhorted to continue to themselves their right of management by securing an independence on the part of their Representatives; to disappoint the underhand and interested designs of any who would oppose a just election; and to hold out to censure and scorn any who to serve their own sinister motives would wantonly distract the peace of the community by depriving its members of their lawful rights.

The reply took the form of an eight-page pamphlet, signed by "An Independent Inhabitant and Friend of the Town." It alleged maladministration on the part of the representatives of the previous year, and sought to justify the action of driving them from the helm of affairs. As a result of this removal, the writer stated that the church, which had been neglected previously, had been put in order without any dispute or interference on the part of the minister and session. Further improvements were still in view, and the minister had at his own expense instituted a free school. The assurance is then given that there was not the remotest intention on the part of the minister and session to wrest the administration of the funds from the town, far less to allow the church to go into decay. Finally, an invitation was extended to "the heritors, portioners, householders, and heads of families" to exercise their lawful rights at the ensuing election.

As a counterblast to the above, "A Townsman," on 30th January, 1813, issued a fly-leaf circular, in course of which the following passage occurs:—"Since the decision in the House of Peers, no objection can be made to the destination

Captain Donald Potter, R.N.

(Photograph by Eric Jamieson, Bo'ness, taken by permission from an oil painting in the possession of Mr. Alex. Galbraith, Upper Kinneil.)

See page 380.

of the surplus; it is the law of the country. But the right of the inhabitants to the management of these funds is equally well-established; and the primary purpose of the trust is the maintenance of the house of worship in proper order."

X.

Answering an allegation of extravagance levelled against the former Representatives, the writer says, "Men acting for the public to the best of their judgment and without remuneration are at least entitled to decent treatment; but if their conduct be indeed wanton and unprincipled and their proceedings unwarrantable and malicious, can they not be made amenable to 'a Court of justice?' But no—nothing could in this case be done, but by a highly reprehensible mode of procedure, and a formidable muster of colliers to drive these maladministrators from the helm of affairs. A bold stroke, truly worthy of those who projected and executed it! And setting decency and all regard to character aside, a free school is to become subservient to the management of church funds, and the continuance of it is stated to depend entirely on this new management being supported by the public!!! It is no disgrace to a man to be poor or to stand in need of such a benefit to his children, but is he therefore to sacrifice his conscientious ideas of right and wrong, and tempted and allured by a charitable institution to debase his mind by giving his vote to what he may secretly consider a bad cause!! When a solemn appeal is reflected upon, who would have expected such an exposition? Is this charity on a proper principle? Is it not hateful to God? Refer to the fate of Ananias and Sapphira, and reflect on the fatal consequences of an appearance of giving all to the Lord while a part is retained to be appropriated to selfish, interested purposes."

Such, then, are a few specimens of public letter writing in Bo'ness a hundred years ago. There was great bitterness on both sides, and much personal abuse, but we have refrained from reproducing many lurid paragraphs.

Y

There was one other time of excitement fifty years later, judging from a minute of meeting of the Representatives, dated 5th January, 1853—"A very great number of the inhabitants attended, and likewise assembled along with them several members of the Kirk Session, all for the purpose of electing their Representatives. A considerable number of parties from neighbouring parishes and minors and others not liable to be stented, and having no votes, also attended the meeting. Mr. James Dunlop, teacher, was clerk. Mr. John Marshall, corn merchant, and Mr. Robert Steele, of the Borrowstounness Iron Foundry, were both nominated and seconded for the chair." Mr. Steele's election appeared to have been the more regular, in respect that his supporters were mostly qualified electors. However, "Mr. Marshall and Mr. Steele both took the chair, and sat for a time together." Mr. Marshall's supporters then sought to go into the question of who really had the support of the qualified electors, when "a tremendous uproar and tumult arose in the church, in the midst of which Mr. James Meikle, an heritor and elector present, expired. Mr. Anderson here implored for peace, and protested that the church should be cleared of parties not entitled to vote, and that the business should not be farther proceeded with till quiet was restored. During the uproar Mr. Marshall several times went out and in to the precentor's desk, the place appointed for the chairman, and at last finally abandoned it to its occupant, Mr. Robert Steele, the duly elected chairman of the meeting."

What a contrast to the mechanical regularity which now prevails at these meetings!

XI.

The societies above described were not the only local organisations for assisting the necessitous in sickness and distress. During the latter part of the eighteenth century there had been a benefit society called the Trades Society, but for some reason unknown it was not successful. On the 18th of May, 1781, certain late members of this body met in the house of Mr. James Scotland, merchant, for the purpose of uniting together in a new society, under the title of "The Beneficent Society in Borrowstounness." The proposal, as recorded in the first minute, reads thus—

"And for that purpose each of us should lay into one common stock or fund the proportion each of us received at the dissolution of the foresaid Trades Society, which, with a small triffle added to it, makes two pounds sterling for each person to pay in order to rease a fund for the supply of ourselves or others well-disposed persons in distress that may choose to join with us in said scheme, as also for the supply of the widows and children of such: which proposals being unanimously agreed to, and the said monie paid, a copie of Articles prepaired by John Jack was then read as rules proposed for the regulation thereof." The rules are not engrossed in the minute book or "Jurnal book," as it is headed, but copies were immediately printed. Those present were John Black, John Jack, Hendry Simmers, William Reid, Arthur Melvil, James O'Concher, James Scotland, William Miller, James Matthew, Alexander Shaw, William Cunning, Walter Anderson, and Alexander Wilson, all residenters in Bo'ness. John Black was elected president and John Jack secretary, and both held office for many years.

A perusal of the first minute book, with which alone it is possible for us to deal, and that very briefly, makes interesting reading. It extends from May, 1781 to 1800, and contains 407 sederunts, all most methodically written and rubriced. At the first meeting it was mentioned that the Box of the Trades Society had been sold at its dissolution for 10s. 6d., and it was agreed to purchase same at said money, "which was done accordingly, and paid out of the entry money, and the remainder lodged in the Box." The funds then amounted to £25 9s. 6d. Thirty-nine appeared to be the age-limit for admission. All the members of the original society, however, on paying £2, were admitted as free members, independent of age. The entry money was 10s., but as several persons over age wished to enter they were admitted on condition either of paying £2, or 10s., together with weekly dues for every week over thirty-nine years of age from the time of application. At the third sederunt we find the meeting "orders John Jack to provide two books, with three quairs of good, clean paper in each, the one for a waste minute book and the other for a correct Jurnall Book of the minutes of this society, and to be each half-bound in folio." In the early stages, meetings were held fortnightly to collect dues; then after a time every four weeks. These dues seem to have varied from 1s. to 3s. per week. The society was very strict about exacting them, and when any member failed to pay he was fined unless he could give a reason satisfactory to the committee. Such fines went into the general fund, but not so those imposed for any dereliction of duty, such as contumacy of the clerk and unsatisfactory absence of the Boxmaster or key-keepers. These officers were fined 2d., and in some cases 4d., which was always spent for the "good of the house" in which the meeting was held.[4] Here is an example from a minute—"It being found that our clerk was not only absent last meeting, but had the key along with him, and business being thereby stoped throu want of both box and books, therefor its agreed the clerk pay a fine of fourpence, and said fine spent for the benefite of the house we meet in, which fine was paid and spent accordingly."

XII.

The society was very successful from the first, and the minutes disclose the frequent admission of members. In addition to those present at the first meeting, we find the following names among its early members:—George Wills, Robert Drysdell, James Foot, James Baird, John Foot, flesher; David Brown, barber; Geo. Dick, shoemaker; and James Adam, tide waiter. The clerk at this time writes the name of the town thus—"Bo^{rst}ness." For long, numbers of the members refused the benefit to which they were entitled, "as seeing that by the goodness of Providence they were not in necessitous circumstances it should be left for those who were

---

[4] The Society varied its place of meeting—the house of——, *i.e.*, alehouse.

so." Here is a specific case—"Mairon Pibbles, spouse to Henry Simmers, having died, the officer handed the husband £1 for funeral expenses." Simmers appeared at next meeting, and "returned thanks to this society for their beneficent rememberance of him in the late dispensation of Providence he was vizeted with by sending on that ocation one pound str., and although he aknolodges said money to be his due according to the rules of this society, yett as he is convinced this fund was errected and desined for the relife only of such members or there concerns as are realy in straitened circumstances; and, as he has reason to acknowledge the kindness of Providence that this is not at present the case with him, he thankfully returns the said one pound in order that it may be applyed where real necessity calls for it."

When the society was small the members depended upon ordinary report as to sickness or death moneys to be paid. Afterwards two inspectors were appointed at the annual meeting, whose duty it was to report upon any necessitous cases.

The surplus funds were invested locally at 5 per cent., mainly on personal bond backed by cautioners. As these accumulated and the local demand for money was small, we find the clerk intimating that he "had wrote" to Messrs. Ramsay & Co. and to Sir William Forbes & Co., bankers, Edinburgh, for their terms for money deposited. After receiving the replies the society decided to accept the terms offered by Ramsay & Co.

We would call special attention to the methods of the Auditing Committee, which were nothing if not thorough. Sederunt No. 407, 4th February, 1800, Thomas Collins preses, reads—

"At a Meeting of Committee of Examinators and the Council, inspected the books of the Society by adding the columns of monthly dues in a perpendicular and horizontal direction, and found them right; then compared their totals with the sums in the waste book and journal, and found them to agree; again compared every article of income and expenditure in the journal with the sums in the cash account; and lastly inspected and approved the balance proof sheet."

There is one other matter which we cannot omit. About 1792 Great Britain, as we know, was roused to indignation by the revelations of William Wilberforce and others as to the cruelties connected with the slave traffic in America and the British West Indian possessions. Following the example of other similar societies throughout the kingdom, the members of the Beneficent Society held a special general meeting on the subject in the Mason Lodge, under the presidency of Robert Drysdell. While not presuming to petition the Legislature, the members considered it right to declare and publish in the leading newspapers in Edinburgh, Glasgow, and London their denunciation of the slave traffic. They objected to it as cruel, immoral, and unjust. Cruel in separating husband and wife, parents and children, brothers and sisters; immoral in exposing them promiscuously for sale like cattle; and as rendering callous and hardened the mariners who were employed in capturing and transporting them. They finally approved of the conduct of all those members of Parliament who had so long and steadily laboured for the abolition of slavery in the British Dominions. The local meeting was large and enthusiastic; the resolutions, which were six in number, were, after a full discussion, voted on one by one, and unanimously carried.

The Beneficent Society, like the Seabox, has a worthy history, but a much less chequered career. It still exists, owns several valuable properties, has a capital of £4600, and a yearly income of over £300. Members in sickness and infirmity get an allowance until sixty-five years of age. A payment in name of funeral money is also made on the deaths of members or their wives. Annuities to widows and children and to members above sixty-five years of age are likewise provided. The present membership stands at fifty.

XIII.

There is in the possession of Masonic Lodge Douglas (409), Bo'ness, an old minute book which gives us one or two peeps into the social life of the town during the latter half of the eighteenth century. This minute book belonged to the local lodge of Freemasons which existed here at that time, but which became extinct. It was known as the "Pythagoric," evidently named after Pythagoras, the celebrated Greek philosopher, who in his day formed, among other things, a select and secret brotherhood. Unfortunately, the minute book is not very complete, a great many of the earlier pages being awanting. Lodge Douglas, however, is to be congratulated on having it even as it is, for it was at one time, we believe, in possession of Grand Lodge. The "Pythagoric" stood as No. 90 on the roll of Grand Lodge.

The first minute appearing in the volume is dated 27th December, 1768, and the last 21st December, 1789. Glancing over the names appearing from time to time, we find many old friends—names that frequently appear in the minutes of the Town Trustees and other local bodies, *i.e.*, Charles Addison, James Addison, Dr. J. Short, Dr. John Roebuck and his brother Benjamin, and others. The membership does not seem to have been very large. The minute just referred to bears a record of the Festival of St. John and the election of office-bearers. There was a good attendance of brethren. A great number of visiting brethren also attended. Convened at Brother Bain's, they marched in procession to the lodge with "flamboys," and to the music of a French horn. That evening Charles Addison was elected R.W.M. for the year.

The work of the lodge was carried on very thoroughly and with great credit. The fortnightly meetings usually ended in harmony. On one occasion, in May, 1770, Brothers Buck, Stable, and Wilkinson, comedians, honoured the lodge with a visit. That evening the brethren, out of courtesy to their visitors, appointed a night when they should assemble in the Town Hall, in regalia, to see the performances by their friends of two farces called "The Citizen" and "Miss in Her Teens."

The brethren resolved in one case to have a ball, "in order to entertain our fair, lovely, and amiable sisters, who are always willing and ready to oblige the brethren and to compensate in some measure for their being debarred the knowledge of our mysteries." And afterwards this entertainment seems to have occurred almost annually. The minutes are carefully written, even to always taking due note of the closing harmony. The accounts of the harmony, however, are by no means stereotyped, the secretary apparently taking a pride in varying his phraseology. The following are a few examples:—

"The brethren enjoyed themselves with as great pleasure and satisfaction that a summer night could admit."

"Assumed an agreeable cheerfulness without the least mixture of reserve."

"The hilarity was kept up with the singing of songs and expression of sentiments of brotherly love."

"Much friendship was displayed on every countenance."

"They enjoyed themselves with every pleasure peculiar to the craft."

"With great joy for the welfare of Masonry."

"Peace and harmony concluded the evening."

"Brothers Macdonald and Hardy entertained the brethren with the violin and bagpipe"!

We find one motion so popular that the brethren "expressed their approbation with innumerable shouts of joy," and to another their assent was signified by "an universal clap." Truly the Pythagoreans were a jovial and hearty set.

But they could be stern and strict, for we find them assembled on the 9th April, 1771, under the mastership of James Addison, "on account of a Brother, who, on the morning of the 7th inst., was guilty of attempting to murder Henry Ballnevis, a Tidesman, by stabbing him with a knife as he lay sleeping in bed on board the 'Elizabeth and Jean' at Borrowstounness." The master, we read, in a very suitable speech on the occasion, observed that the expulsion of the Brother was the only means in their power for maintaining the honour of Masonry and preserving the peace and concord of the lodge. The offender's expulsion was thereupon unanimously agreed to. The meeting thereafter ordered him to be divested of all (lodge) clothing and banished from the sacred walls of the lodge; and the secretary was instructed to send a note of the resolution to Grand Lodge for their attention, which was done.

CHAPTER XVIII.

EMINENT NATIVES AND RESIDENTS.

1. John Henderson: his Wonderful Career—2. How the "Meditations" were Published—3. Colonel James Gardiner—4. William Wishart, 12th Principal, Edinburgh University: William Wishart secundus—5. Dr. John Roebuck: the Gravestone in Carriden Churchyard—6. James Watt and his Experiments at Kinneil—7. Some of his Engines—8. Professor Dugald Stewart: his Character and Achievements—9. Life at Kinneil: Mrs. Stewart and her daughter—10. Captain Donald Potter of the Royal Navy—11. Principal Baird: a Distinguished and Useful Career—12. Henry Bell: the "Comet" in Bo'ness—13. Robert Burns, D.D.—14. John Anderson—15. A Humorous Genealogy and Character Sketch—16. Admirals Sir George and Sir James Hope: Sir John Lees—17. James Brunton Stephens.

I.

It has been truly said that biography is the most pleasant and profitable of all reading. So we offer no apology for including in these pages a few brief biographical sketches of eminent men who have been born in, or identified with, Kinneil, Carriden, or Borrowstounness.

JOHN HENDERSON, SHIPMASTER (b. 1686, d. 1758).

John Henderson was born at Borrowstounness on the 25th of May, 1686, and was the son of Richard Henderson, merchant and factor there, and Christian Waldy, his wife. The mother was remarkable for her piety, and did all in her power to train up her son in the paths of religion and virtue. John appeared to have a "good genius," and his parents proposed to give him a liberal education. He was, however, severely whipped by his master for a fault of which he had not been guilty, and refused to go any more to school. In after years he deeply regretted this. At fourteen he went to sea, serving his apprenticeship with Captain Alexander Stark. Two years after, he had the misfortune to lose the sight of an eye by a fall into a ship's hold. Having completed his apprenticeship, he sailed for several years in foreign vessels or in ships of war and privateers. He was thus brought much into contact with loose and dissolute company, and to this he fell a victim. But he soon saw the error of his ways, and in early manhood became intensely religious. His Bible was his constant companion. Well acquainted with its precepts, he could upon all occasions quote passages to the point with great facility. And when he intended to make a present to an intimate friend he always selected a Bible. Once in time of war he was taken by the enemy and stripped of all his clothes. He patiently bore that loss, but when a Spaniard took his Bible and attempted to throw it into the fire, saying that it was "not good," he ran and snatched it from him, saying it was "good," and the Spaniard stood mute. Henderson rose to the position of master of a merchant ship; and when delivered from peril— for his dangers were many—he expressed his most grateful sense of the Divine goodness. When at sea or lying in harbour he employed what leisure time he had in meditating and writing on religious topics.

When obliged, through bodily indisposition, to give over going to sea he returned to his native town and filled the offices of "shoremaster," or harbourmaster, and also Boxmaster to the Seabox. The duties of these he discharged with great fidelity and exactness "in obedience to the commands and from a regard to the authority of his God." Indeed, he put conscience into every duty which God or man commanded. He was for many years a member of the Kirk Session of Bo'ness Parish Church, and the Rev. Mr. Baillie testifies that he was careful and diligent in the duties of his office, and always showed a suitable concern for the interest of religion and success of the Gospel. Referring to the regularity of Mr. Henderson's attendance on the public ordinances, he says that in so doing John Henderson plainly showed that he waited on them as the ordinances of Christ, and depended upon Him, and not on the dispensers of them. Nor did he ever allow himself to be carried about with every wind of doctrine. So amiable were the tabernacles of God unto him that he could not be restrained from attending them, even when suffering from great bodily weakness. His son-in-law writes that his regard for the Lord's Day was twofold—first, as a commemoration of the work of redemption as finished, and, secondly, as being always particularly refreshing to himself. The manner of his observing the Sabbath in his family was "pretty singular." His ordinary method was to "convocate" his family four times to praise God, read a portion of His word, and call upon His name in prayer—once in the morning, then betwixt sermons, soon after them, and again at night. Besides this he used to retire to his closet at least seven times to worship God in secret. And that he might be the more capacitated to perform these duties with vivacity and spirit he did eat none from morning until night, when his natural strength of body began to fail, and even then he did eat but sparingly.

It has been written of him that he was a loving and affectionate husband, a tender and indulgent parent, and at vast pains to have his offspring rightly instructed in the principles of Christianity. But he never ceased, through fondness, to correct vice when it took place and reprove folly when it appeared. It pleased God to exercise him throughout his life in a variety of afflictions, including the loss of children and grandchildren, "and several other very distressing scenes of life." All these he endured with the greatest patience and submission to the will of God, never murmuring or repining even under the heaviest afflictions. In the month of May, 1758, he went to Edinburgh to see his daughter and her husband. A few days afterwards he was seized with what was called an iliac passion, the pain of which he endured with the greatest calmness and serenity. When under this trouble his daughter asked him if he still adhered to what he had formerly believed concerning the way of salvation by Jesus Christ. To which he answered, "I know no other way; I desire no other way; I will seek no other way; I despise all other ways."

And the last words he uttered were these, "My Lord and my God." He died in the seventy-second year of his age. "Mark the perfect man," quotes Mr. Baillie, "and behold the upright, for the end of that man is peace."

II.

We regret we cannot fill in the mental picture of this devout old shipmaster as we would have liked, but we have learned enough to regard his life and character as worthy of remembrance. When old John Henderson kept his numerous journals and diaries he had no idea that any of their contents would ever be published. After his death his daughter and her husband showed his papers to several persons of judgment and piety. They were of opinion that, though not so accurate as those written by persons having greater educational advantages, a published selection might, by the blessing of God, be of great use to many. His writings in their view contained plain evidences of their author having been taught the reality of religion by the Holy Spirit, and also demonstrated that true Christians might have clear views of its doctrines and duties though deprived of the advantages of human learning. They thought it wise, also, to show how one who was so many years abroad, and when at home was engaged in a variety of worldly business, employed his leisure hours and carefully redeemed the time. And they particularly hoped that such a volume would be of especial use to sailors and all those who knew and were acquainted with Mr. Henderson when alive. Acting on this advice, therefore, Mr. and Mrs. Thomson published the "Meditations."

"The memory of Mr. John Henderson, shipmaster," wrote Mr. M'Kenzie,[1] "is held in high estimation in this place. He was a man of singular humility, benevolence, and piety,

[1] New Stat. A/c., *supra*.

spending much of his time in divine meditations, which he was in the habit of committing to writing, 'to keep his heart from wandering and fixt upon divine and spiritual subjects.' The selection[2] from these published after his death forms a composition remarkable for the regularity of its structure, and for the simplicity, spirituality, and fervour of its devotional sentiments."

The book was published in March, 1763, and a copy lies in the Mitchell Library, Glasgow. It consists of 412 pages, and contains meditations, soliloquies, prayers, and spiritual poetry. The "Meditations" were edited by his son-in-law, Mr. James Thomson, merchant in Edinburgh, and following his preface is a short account of the author by the Rev. Pat. Baillie, minister of Borrowstounness.

III.

Colonel James Gardiner (b. 1687, d. 1745).

Built into a wall at Burnfoot, Carriden, is a tablet with this inscription—

> To the memory of Colonel James Gardiner, born here January 10th, 1687; mortally wounded at the Battle of Prestonpans, September 21st, 1745.
>
> A brave soldier and a devout Christian.
>
> "I have fought a good fight, I have kept the faith."— Tim. iv. 7.

Readers of Scott will remember that Colonel Gardiner was Edward Waverley's commanding officer. The reverence which Waverley gave to his chief, the horror with which he witnessed his death, and the unavailing efforts he made to get near to help him when cut down by the Highlanders, form part of the graphic description of the battle.

His pious character recalls Hedley Vicars and Chinese Gordon.

---

[2] "Divine Meditations and Contemplations in prose and verse on some of the most important and interesting doctrines of Christianity."

Colonel Gardiner.

(From a photograph by Eric Jamieson, Bo'ness, taken by permission from an oil painting in possession of Mr. S. B. Hog of Newliston.)

Philip Doddridge, the famous divine and hymn-writer, was on terms of the closest intimacy with Gardiner, and about two years after Prestonpans he wrote Gardiner's biography. There he gives a vivid and lengthened account of his friend's spiritual experiences. Jupiter Carlyle, also, in his autobiography gives frequent glimpses of him. Thus abundant material is at the disposal of any one who wishes to make the acquaintance of this brave and pious soldier. Doddridge is evidently in doubt as to the year of his birth, as he gives 1687-8, but the tablet at Carriden has 1687.

Gardiner's father was Captain Patrick Gardiner,[3] of the family of Torwood Head, and his mother Mary Hodge, of the family of Gladsmuir. The Captain served in the Army in the time of William and Queen Anne, and died with the British forces in Germany shortly after the battle of Hochset.

The son, afterwards Colonel Gardiner, was educated at the Grammar School of Linlithgow. He served as a cadet very early, and at fourteen years of age obtained an ensign's commission in a Scots regiment in the Dutch service, in which he continued till 1702, when he received an ensign's commission from Queen Anne. At the battle of Ramillies, where he specially distinguished himself, he was wounded and taken prisoner, but was soon after exchanged. We are told that at this battle, while calling to his men to advance, a bullet passed into his mouth, which, without beating out any of his teeth or touching the forepart of his tongue, went through his neck. The young officer, like so many of the wounded engaged with the Duke of Marlborough's army, was left on the field unattended, and lay there all night, not knowing what his fate might be. His suspicions at first were that he had swallowed the bullet, but he afterwards made the discovery that there was a hole in the back of his neck, through which it must have passed. In the morning the French came to plunder the slain, and one of them was on the point of applying his sword to the

---

[3] Burnfoot came into the possession of Florence or Lourance Gairdner, "bailie in Grangepans" in 1647 who afterwards disponed it to Patrick Gairdner.

breast of the young officer when an attendant of the plunderers, taking the injured lad by his dress for a Frenchman, interposed, and said, "Do not kill that poor child." He was given some stimulant, and carried to a convent in the neighbourhood, where he was cured in a few months. He served with distinction in the other famous battles fought by the Duke of Marlborough, and rose to the rank of colonel of a new regiment of Dragoons.

As a young man he was what would now be called fast; but he was at all times so bright and cheerful that he was known as the "happy rake." His remarkable conversion occurred when waiting till twelve o'clock on a Sunday night to keep a certain appointment. To while away the time he took up a book which his mother had placed in his portmanteau. This was "The Christian Soldier; or Heaven Taken by Storm." The result was that he forgot his appointment, and became converted. Nor was the change either fanatical or temporary. Gardiner was still as careful, active, and obedient a soldier as ever, but now he tried in his private life to avoid even the appearance of evil. He was specially anxious to appear pleasant and cheerful lest his associates might be led to think that religion fostered a gloomy, forbidding, and austere disposition. At the same time, he set himself sternly against infidelity and licentiousness.

The circumstances connected with Colonel Gardiner's death at the Battle of Prestonpans are very tragic, and have been frequently treated in history and fiction. The brutality connected with his death cannot be excused and scarcely palliated by the ignorance of his assailants. By all who knew him—military friend or foe—his death was deplored.

IV.

WILLIAM WISHART, TWELFTH PRINCIPAL OF THE UNIVERSITY OF EDINBURGH, 1716-1729.

Mr. Wishart was a son of the last minister of Kinneil. There is no available evidence as to date and place of birth, but it is highly probable that it was Kinneil.[4] The eldest son, afterwards Sir George, entered the Army, and ultimately acquired the estate of Cliftonhall, Ratho; the next, afterwards, Sir James, of Little Chelsea, was a Rear-Admiral in the Royal Navy, and died in 1723; and the third became one of the ministers of Edinburgh and Principal of the University.

William Wishart[5] succeeded the great William Carstares in the Principalship, and it is thought that the latter recommended him to the Town Council, with whom the appointment lay. William graduated at Edinburgh in 1676, and afterwards proceeded to Utrecht to study theology. Like his father, he had to suffer imprisonment, for on his return from Holland (1684) he was imprisoned by the Privy Council in the "Iron House" on the charge of denying the King's authority. He was released the next year under bond, with caution of 5000 merks, to appear when called. He then became minister of South Leith (it will be recalled that his father also was minister in Leith after the suppression of Kinneil), and afterwards of the Tron Church. Wishart was five times Moderator of the General Assembly, and has been described as " a good, kind, grave, honest, and pious man, a sweet, serious, and affectionate preacher whose life and conversation being of a piece with his preaching made almost all who knew him personal friends." Two volumes of his sermons were published. His career as Principal seems to have been uneventful.

We may mention here also that on the 10th November, 1736, the Edinburgh Town Council proceeded to elect to the fifteenth Principalship William Wishart secundus, son of the above. The induction, however, was postponed till November of the next year, a charge of heresy evidently barring the way. When called to be Principal he also received a call from New Greyfriars. The Edinburgh Presbytery interposed and objected to the doctrine of some sermons published by him

[4] See "Scott's Fasti."
[5] See Principal Sir Alexander Grant's "History of the University of Edinburgh."

while minister of a Dissenting congregation in London, in which he had maintained "that true religion is influenced by higher motives than self-love." After a keen debate the General Assembly absolved Wishart from heresy, and he entered upon his charges. He is said to have been more of a scholar and man of letters than his father, and of an original turn of mind, adopting a different style of preaching from that formerly in vogue. He was less stiff and formal, dealt more with moral considerations, and used more simple and, at the same time, more literary language. His first act as Principal was to start a library fund for the University. He also made an attempt to improve the system of graduation in Arts by demanding literary theses from the graduates. The Principal took a great interest in the more promising of the students, constantly visited the junior classes, and used all means in his power to improve scholarship in the University.[6]

V.

Dr. John Roebuck (b. 1718, d. 1794).

John Roebuck was born in Sheffield, where his father was a manufacturer of cutlery. He possessed a most inventive turn of mind; studied chemistry and medicine at Edinburgh; obtained the degree of M.D. from Leyden University in 1742; established a chemical laboratory at Birmingham; invented methods of refining precious metals and several improvements in processes for the production of chemicals, including the manufacture of sulphuric acid, at Prestonpans, in 1749, where he was in partnership with Mr. Samuel Garbett, another Englishman.

In 1759, he, along with his brothers, Thomas, Ebenezer, and Benjamin, William Cadell, sen., William Cadell, jun., and Samuel Garbett, founded the Carron Ironworks, which at one time were the most celebrated in Europe. His connection with Borrowstounness began about the same time when he became the lessee of the Duke's coal mines and saltpans, and took up

---

[6] Grant's History, *supra*.

residence at Kinneil House. The history of his partnership with James Watt, the part which he played in the government of the town, and the unfortunate collapse of all his plans are elsewhere referred to. In 1773 the doctor, owing to his financial misfortunes here, had not only to give up his interest in Watt's patent, but had also to sever his connection with the Carron Company. His spirit and business enterprise, however, were undaunted, and, in 1784, we find him founding the Bo'ness Pottery. He died here in 1794, and was buried in Carriden Churchyard.

From the various works which he projected, all of a practical nature; from his generous and kindly treatment of James Watt, and his keen desire to promote the interests of the inhabitants of Bo'ness, we readily conclude that, in ability and real goodness, he was far above the average man. This is attested by the monument to his memory which his friends erected over his grave. The inscription is in Latin, but we give below a translation[7]—

> Underneath this tombstone rests
> no ordinary man,
> John Roebuck, M.D.,
> who, of gentle birth and of liberal education, applied his mind to almost all the liberal arts. Though he made the practice of medicine his chief work in his public capacity to the great advantage of his fellow-citizens, yet he did not permit his inventive and tireless brain to rest satisfied with that, but cultivated a great number of recondite and abstruse sciences, among which were chemistry and metallurgy. These he expounded and adapted to human needs with a wonderful fertility of genius and a high degree of painstaking labour; whence not a few of all those delightful works and pleasing structures which decorate our world, and by their utility conduce to both public and private well-being he either devised or promoted. Of these

---

[7] By Mr. C. A. Malcolm, S.S.C. Library, Edinburgh, and Mr. James Mill, M.A., Lecturer, Edinburgh University.

the magnificent work at the mouth of the Carron is his own invention.

In extent of friendship and of gentleness he was surpassing great, and, though harassed by adversity or deluded by hope and weighed down by so many of our griefs, he yet could assuage these by his skill in the arts of the muses or in the delights of the country.

For most learned conversation and gracious familiarity no other was more welcome or more pleasant on account of his varied and profound learning, his merry games, and sparkling wit and humour. And, above all, on account of the uprightness, benevolence, and good fellowship in his character.

Bewailed by his family and missed by all good men, he died on the Ides [*i.e.*, 15th] of July.

A.D. 1794, aged 76,

in the arms of his wife, and with his children around him.

This monument—such as it is—the affection of friends has erected.

VI.

JAMES WATT (b. 1736, d. 1819).[8]

The name and fame of this celebrated natural philosopher and civil engineer are so well known that they require little mention here. He was born in Greenock, but Glasgow and Birmingham were the chief centres of his labours. Bo'ness, however, has a right to claim more than a passing interest in his early endeavours to improve the steam engine. He had been struggling as a mathematical instrument maker to the University of Glasgow when his friend Professor Black spoke of him to Dr. Roebuck, who was engaged sinking coal pits. Roebuck had been time and again thwarted in his attempt to reach the coal by inrushes of water, his Newcomen engine having proved practically useless. Therefore, when Dr. Black

---

[8] See also Smile's "Lives of the Engineers," vol. v., Boulton & Watt.

informed him of this ingenious young mechanic in Glasgow who had invented a steam engine capable of working with a greater power, speed, and economy, Roebuck immediately entered into correspondence with Watt. Roebuck was at first sceptical as to the principle of Watt's engine, and induced him to revert to the old principle, with some modifications. Against his convictions Watt tried a series of experiments, but abandoned them as hopeless, Roebuck being also convinced of his error. Up to this time Watt and Roebuck had not met, but in September, 1765, Roebuck urged him to come with Dr. Black to Kinneil House and fully discuss the subject of the engine. Watt wrote to say that he was physically unable for the journey to Kinneil, but would try to meet him on a certain day at the works at Carron, in which the doctor had an interest. Even this, however, had to be postponed. Roebuck then wrote urging Watt to press forward his invention with all speed, "whether you pursue it as a philosopher or as a man of business." In accordance with this urgent appeal, Watt forwarded to Roebuck the working drawings of a covered cylinder and piston, to be cast at the Carron Works. This cylinder, however, when completed, was ill bored, and had to be laid aside as useless. The piston rod was made in Glasgow, under his own supervision, and when finished he was afraid to forward it on a common cart lest the workpeople should see it, and so it was sent in a box to Carron in the month of July, 1766.

This secrecy was necessary to prevent his idea being appropriated by others. Roebuck was so confident of Watt's success that in 1767 he undertook to give him £1000 to pay the debts already incurred, to enable Watt to continue his experiments, and to patent the engine. Roebuck's return was to be two-thirds of the property in the invention. Early in 1768 Watt made a new and larger model, with a cylinder of seven or eight inches diameter, but by an unforeseen misfortune "the mercury found its way into the cylinder and played the devil with the solder. This throws us back at least three days, and is very vexatious, especially as it happened in spite of the precaution I had taken to prevent it." Disregarding the renewed demands of the impatient Roebuck to meet and talk the matter over, Watt proceeded to patch up his damaged engine. In a month's time he succeeded, and then rode triumphantly to Kinneil House, where his words to Roebuck were, "I sincerely wish you joy of this successful result, and I hope it will make some return for the obligations I owe you."

The model was so satisfactory that it was at once determined to take out a patent for the engine, and Watt journeyed to Berwick, where he obtained a provisional protection. It had been originally intended to build the engine in "the little town of Borrowstounness." For the sake of privacy, however, Watt fixed upon an outhouse in a small enclosure to the south of Kinneil House, where an abundant supply of water could be obtained from the Gil burn. The materials required were brought here from Glasgow and Carron, and a few workmen were placed at his disposal. The cylinder—of eighteen inches diameter and five feet stroke—was cast at Carron. Progress was slow and the mechanics clumsy. Watt was occasionally compelled to be absent on other business, and on his return he usually found the men at a standstill. As the engine neared completion his anxiety kept him sleepless at nights, for his fears were more than equal to his hopes. He was easily cast down by little obstructions, and especially discouraged by unforeseen expense. About six months after its commencement the new engine, on which he had expended so much labour, anxiety, and ingenuity, was completed. But its success was far from decided. Watt himself declared it to be a clumsy job. He was grievously depressed by his want of success, and he had serious thoughts of giving up the thing altogether. Before abandoning it, however, the engine was again thoroughly overhauled, many improvements were effected, and a new trial made of its powers. But this did not prove more successful than the earlier one had been. "You cannot conceive," he wrote to Small, "how mortified I am with this disappointment. It is a damned thing for a man to have his all hanging by a single string. If I had the wherewithal to pay the loss, I don't think I should so much fear a failure; but I cannot bear the thought of other people becoming losers by my schemes, and I have the happy disposition of always painting the worst." Bound therefore by honour not less than by interest, he summoned up his courage and went on anew. In the principles of his engine he continued to have confidence, and believed that, could mechanics be found who would be capable of accurately executing its several parts, success was certain. By this time Roebuck was becoming embarrassed with debts and involved in various difficulties. The pits were drowned with water, which no existing machinery could pump out, and ruin threatened to overtake him before Watt's engine could come to his help. The doctor had sunk in his coal works his own fortune and part of that of his relations, and was thus unable to defray the expense of taking out the patent and otherwise fulfilling his engagement with the inventor. In his distress Watt appealed to Dr. Black for assistance, and a loan was forthcoming; but, of course, this only left him deeper in debt, without any clear prospect of ultimate relief. No wonder that he should, after his apparently fruitless labour, have expressed to Small his belief that, "Of all things in life, there is nothing more foolish than inventing." The unhappy state of his mind may be further inferred from his lamentation expressed in a letter to the same friend on the 31st of January, 1770—" To-day I enter the thirty-fifth year of my life, and I think I have hardly yet done thirty-five pence worth of good to the world; but I cannot help it." By the death, also, of his wife, who cheered him greatly in his labours, an unfortunate combination of circumstances seemed to overwhelm him. No further progress had yet been made with his steam engine, which, indeed, he almost cursed as the cause of his misfortunes. Dr. Roebuck's embarrassments now reached their climax. He had fought against the water until he could fight no more, and was at last delivered into the hands of his creditors, a ruined man. His share in Watt's invention was then transferred to Matthew Boulton, of Birmingham.

VII.

This was the turning-point for Watt. Birmingham was an excellent trade centre, and within it were to be found experienced mechanics. The firm of Boulton, Watt & Co. was formed in 1774, and Watt's success was thenceforward ensured.

Although Roebuck had to give in, there is no doubt that Watt was so much indebted to him at the beginning that, without his aid and encouragement, he would never have gone on. Robinson says, "I remember Mrs. Roebuck remarking one evening, 'Jamie is a queer lad, and without the doctor his invention would have been lost, but Dr. Roebuck won't let it perish.'"

Watt's connection with Kinneil and Bo'ness must have lasted a number of years. There are many stories concerning his engines,[9] probably mostly experimental, which were in use at the local pits. These, no doubt, were in operation, and attained a considerable degree of success before he removed to Birmingham, but too late to be of any practical assistance to his partner Roebuck. Of the engine at Taylor's pit the workmen could only say that it was the fastest one they ever saw. From its size, and owing to its being placed in a small timber-house, the colliers called it the "box bed." The one at the Temple pit was known as Watt's spinning wheel. The cylinder of his engine at the Schoolyard pit lay there for many years. It was in the end purchased by Bo'ness Gas Company, in whose possession it now is. The outhouse at Kinneil in which Watt constructed his first engine and conducted his many experiments still remains, but it is in a dilapidated condition. Undoubtedly Watt's mental endowments were great, but he was called upon to suffer disappointment after disappointment and bitter reverses of fortune. His courage, force of character, and mechanical genius ultimately carried him towards complete success, so that he retired with a handsome fortune.

---

[9] One at the Burn pit (afterwards transferred to the Temple pit), Taylor's pit, and the Schoolyard pit.

VIII.

DUGALD STEWART (b. 1753, d. 1828), PROFESSOR OF MORAL PHILOSOPHY IN THE EDINBURGH UNIVERSITY.

After relinquishing the duties of his Chair in 1809 this eminent Scotsman retired to Kinneil House, which his friend the Duke of Hamilton had placed at his disposal. Here he spent the twenty remaining years of his life in philosophical study. From Kinneil he dated his *Philosophical Essays*, in 1810, the second volume of the *Elements*, in 1813; the first part of the *Dissertation*, in 1821, and the second part in 1826; and, finally, in 1828, the *Philosophy of the Active and Moral Powers*, a work which he completed a few weeks before the close of his life.

Dugald Stewart was born in the precincts of Edinburgh University, where his father, the Professor of Mathematics, resided. He studied at the University there, but after a time was attracted to Glasgow University, like a good many others, by the fame of Professor Reid, who occupied the Chair of Moral Philosophy. At the age of nineteen he was accepted by the Senatus as his father's substitute during the latter's illness, and returned to Edinburgh. Two years later he was appointed assistant and successor. With three days' preparation he, in 1778, undertook the work of the Chair of Moral Philosophy when Adam Ferguson made his visit to America. In 1785, the year of his father's death, he exchanged Chairs with Ferguson. It was a happy exchange for Stewart. He was so versatile that he could, at a moment's notice, occupy any Chair in the University, and there is no doubt that as Professor of Mathematics he discharged the duties with distinction. But his reading, his studies, and the natural bent of his mind peculiarly fitted him to be the popular exponent of Dr. Reid's commonsense philosophy. His fame became so great that he drew young men of family and fortune to attend his classes. He was in the habit of boarding students, and it has been said that noblemen did not grudge £400 for the privilege of having their sons admitted to Professor

Stewart's charming home. Among those who attended his class were the young men who afterwards became Lord Palmerston, Lord John Russell, Lord Brougham, Lord Cockburn, and Lord Jeffrey.[10]

Lord Cockburn has left us some very vivid and sympathetic recollections of Stewart as a lecturer, and of the influence he exercised over his students. Entrance to Dugald Stewart's class was, he says, the great era in the progress of young men's minds. To him his lectures were like the opening of the heavens. He felt that he had a soul; and the professor's noble views, unfolded in glorious sentences, elevated him into a higher world. Stewart, he affirms, was one of the greatest of didactic orators, and had he lived in ancient times his memory would have descended to us as that of one of the finest of the old eloquent sages. Flourishing, however, in an age which required all the dignity of morals to counteract the tendencies of physical pursuits and political convulsions, he had exalted the character of his country and of his generation. Without genius or even originality of talent, his intellectual character was marked by calm thought and great soundness. His training in mathematics may have corrected the reasoning, but it never chilled the warmth of his moral demonstrations.

All Stewart's powers were exalted by an unimpeachable personal character, devotion to the science he taught, an exquisite taste, an imagination imbued with poetry and oratory, liberality of opinion, and the highest morality. His retiral made a deep and melancholy impression on his students and on all those interested in the welfare of mental philosophy.

In his earlier years Mr. Stewart had resided at Catrine House. Catrine, originally the country-house of his maternal grandfather, and there he met and entertained the poet Burns. This friendship was renewed on the poet's visit to Edinburgh.

His biographer[11] has told us that Mr. Stewart's time at Kinneil was almost exclusively devoted to his literary labours.

---

[10] See Cockburn's "Memorials."
[11] "Memoirs of Dugald Stewart." By John Veitch. (Vol. i. of Sir Wm. Hamilton's edition of Stewart's works.)

Dugald Stewart.
By permission from "Scottish Men of Letters in the XVIII. Century," by H. Grey Graham (Black).

He, however, relieved these by friendly intercourse, and by the calls of those strangers whom the lustre of his name led to pay a passing visit to Kinneil. Among his friends was Sir David Wilkie, the painter. He was always in search of subjects for his pictures, and Mr. Stewart found for him in an old farmhouse in the neighbourhood the cradle chimney introduced into the "Penny Wedding." Other friendly visitors at Kinneil included Lord Palmerston and Earl Russell. A detailed account of the life and writings of his father, which abounded in anecdotes and notices of the many distinguished men with whom he was on terms of intimacy, was prepared by Mr. Stewart's son. Most unfortunately this memoir and the greater part of the professor's correspondence and journals were unwittingly destroyed by the son in a fit of mental aberration brought on by a sunstroke. Little record, then, is left of his long and interesting occupancy of Kinneil. In 1822 he was struck with paralysis. The attack affected his power of utterance and deprived him of the use of his right hand. Happily, it neither impaired any of the faculties of his mind nor the characteristic vigour and activity of his understanding. It, however, prevented him from using his pen, and Mrs. Stewart became his amanuensis. From a letter written by her to a friend in 1824 we find that Mr. Stewart's health was as good as they could possibly hope after the severe attack three years previously, and that he walked between two and three hours every day.

In 1828 Mr. and Mrs. Stewart went to Edinburgh on a brief visit to their friend Mrs. Lindsay, No. 5 Ainslie Place. Here Mr. Stewart was seized with a fresh shock of paralysis, and died on 11th June. He was buried in the Canongate Churchyard. A monument to his memory, erected by his friends and admirers, stands upon the Calton Hill.

Mr. Stewart was twice married. His first wife was Helen, daughter of Neil Bannatyne, Glasgow, and the marriage took place in 1783, after a long courtship. She died in 1787, leaving an only child, Matthew, on whom his father centred all his affections. He in time entered the Army, and rose to distinction. The professor's second wife was Helen d'Arcy Cranstoun, third daughter of the Hon. George Cranstoun, youngest son of William, fifth Lord Cranstoun. This marriage took place in 1790. Mrs. Stewart, we are told,[12] was a lady of high accomplishments and fascinating manner—uniting with vivacity and humour depth and tenderness of feeling. She sympathised warmly with the tastes and pursuits of her husband, and so great was his regard for her judgment and taste that he was in the habit of submitting to her criticism whatever he wrote. Mrs. Stewart also held a high place among the writers of Scottish song. She died in 1838. There were two children of this marriage—a son, George, a youth of great promise, whose death, in 1809, occasioned the deepest affliction to his parents, and led to Mr. Stewart's retirement from professorial duty—and a daughter, Maria d'Arcy, who survived her father and mother, and died in 1846. Miss Stewart was endeared to a very extensive circle of friends by the charms of a mind of great vigour and rich culture, manners the most fascinating, and a heart full of warmth, tenderness, and affection.

Mrs. and Miss Stewart were the last occupants of Kinneil House, and their departure after the professor's death was much regretted by every inhabitant of the parish. The active benevolence of the family was extensive, and was long and gratefully remembered.

X.

Donald Potter (b. 1756, d. . . .).

In one of the privately enclosed burial-places alongside the east wall of the lower churchyard lie the mortal remains of Donald Potter, captain of the Royal Navy. This is almost all that can be gathered of this worthy, for the lettering on the memorial tablet is so eaten away as to be indecipherable. On the top of the stone there is still to be seen a splintered

---

[12] Memoirs, *supra*.

cannon ball hooped with iron. Beneath are carved a crown and an anchor.

Donald Potter was a native of the parish of Livingstone, in this county. His father was James Potter, and his mother Katherine Mitchell. At an early age he joined the Royal Navy, and by good conduct, gallant deeds, and long and efficient service rose to an important position. He specially distinguished himself under Admiral Howe in his crushing defeat of the French fleet off Brest on the 1st of June, 1794. In October, 1809, Potter received a commission as lieutenant of His Majesty's ship the "Bellona," and in February, 1811, was appointed to the same position on board the "Princess." Much to his regret he had to retire about 1814, when he settled in Borrowstounness, where he had some relatives. Upon the mantelpiece of his sitting-room he kept an interesting relic of the famous battle in the shape of a cannon ball. On every recurrence of "the glorious first of June" he had the ball gaily decorated with ribbons, and, dressing himself in his full naval uniform, paraded the town. Thus arrayed he would call at various inns to drink to the memory of his old admiral and success to the British Navy. In 1829—some years before his death—the date of which is not now ascertainable—he appears to have purchased his burial-place, erected his headstone, and left instructions for the fixing of his much-prized curio upon it after his death. The following year—November, 1830—he was appointed to the rank and title of a commander in His Majesty's Fleet (retired). He was then seventy-four, and from all accounts lived for some years afterwards.

Mr. William Thomson, of Upper Kinneil, was one of the captain's intimate friends. To Mr. Thomson he left the portrait (a photograph of which we reproduce) and his sword and pistols. Mr. William Miller received other relics from a grand-nephew of Potter's many years ago. Among these are a miniature of the captain painted on ivory, and his three commissions, two of which bear the signature of Lord Palmerston.

XI.

GEORGE HUSBAND BAIRD, EIGHTEENTH PRINCIPAL OF EDINBURGH UNIVERSITY (b. 1761, d. 1840).

This distinguished divine was born in 1761 in a now-demolished house attached to the holding of Bowes, in the hollow to the west of Inveravon farm-house, in the Parish of Borrowstounness. His father, James Baird, while a considerable proprietor in the county of Stirling, at that time rented this farm from the Duke of Hamilton. Young Baird received the rudiments of his education at the Parish School of Borrowstounness. Upon his father removing to the property of Manuel the boy was sent to the Grammar School at Linlithgow. It has been said of him that as a schoolboy he was more plodding, persevering, and well-mannered than brilliant. In his thirteenth year he was entered as a student in Humanity at Edinburgh University. There he speedily evoked favourable notice because of his devotion to his classwork and the progress which he made. In 1793 he succeeded Principal Robertson in the Principalship at the early age of thirty-three. Baird had married the eldest daughter of Lord Provost Elder, who had paramount influence in the Council, and exercised it for the election of his youthful and untried son-in-law. We believe it used to be jocularly said that his chief claim to the Principalship was as "Husband" of the Lord Provost's daughter. Nevertheless the appointment turned out well, although he was at a distinct disadvantage in succeeding a man of high literary fame like Principal Robertson. Baird held the Principalship for the long period of forty-seven years, saw the students increase from 1000 to 2000, new University buildings erected, the professoriate augmented, and great developments in other ways. He lived through many long strifes and litigations, and died leaving the Senatus still at war. He was one of the ministers of the High Church of Edinburgh.

But Baird did most excellent work,[13] and made a lasting

---

[13] See "Dictionary National Biography."

name for himself outside the University. Towards the close of his life he threw his whole soul into a scheme for the education of the poor in the Highlands and Islands of Scotland. He submitted his proposals to the General Assembly in May, 1824, advancing them with great ability and earnestness. Next year the Assembly gave its sanction to the scheme, and it was launched most auspiciously. So intense was his interest in this work that in his sixty-seventh year, although in enfeebled health, he traversed the entire Highlands of Argyll, the west of Inverness, and Ross, and the Western Islands from Lewis to Kintyre. The following year he visited the Northern Highlands and the Orkneys and Shetlands. Through his influence Dr. Andrew Bell, of Madras, bequeathed £5000 for education in the Highlands of Scotland. In 1832 the thanks of the General Assembly were conveyed to him by the illustrious Dr. Chalmers, then in the zenith of his oratorical powers. He died at his family property at Manuel, and is buried in Muiravonside Churchyard.

XII.

HENRY BELL (b. 1767, d. 1830).

At the ruins of Torphichen Old Mill, on the banks of the river Avon, about six miles from Bo'ness, there was unveiled, on a blustery afternoon in November, 1911, a tablet bearing the following inscription:—

Henry Bell,
Pioneer of Steamship Navigation in Europe.
Born in the Old Mill House near this spot, 1767 A.D.
Died at Helensburgh, 1830 A.D.

The tablet, which is of Aberdeen granite, is placed in the centre of the old gable, the only remaining part of the original structure. It bears a representation of the "Comet," showing how the funnel of the ship was also used as a mast.

This worthy son of Linlithgowshire had an interesting

connection with our seaport. For many years shipbuilding was extensively carried on at Bo'ness. A great many of the vessels were built for Greenock merchants for the West India trade. The business was owned by Messrs. Shaw & Hart, and with them Henry Bell, when about nineteen years of age, found employment. It is said that when here his attention was directed for the first time towards the idea of the propulsion of ships by steam. His connection with Bo'ness extended over a period of two years, after which he settled in Glasgow. For a number of years pressure of business kept him from pursuing his idea of propelling ships by steam. At length he designed, engined, and launched the "Comet" on the Clyde in 1812. The little vessel was herself in Bo'ness in 1813, and the event was one indelibly imprinted on the memories of that generation. She probably came down from the canal at Grangemouth, and when first seen was thought to be on fire.

Bell, it seems, had sent her round to the yard of his old masters to be overhauled. When she resumed her sailings several local gentlemen took advantage of the first trip by steamboat from Bo'ness to Leith. Her speed was six miles an hour, and the single fare 7s. 6d.

The Bell family have been well known in and intimately identified with the Linlithgow district for many centuries. Some of the older members were burgesses of the burgh, and many of them were engaged in the millwright industry in the district. They were also tenants of Torphichen Mill, Carribber Mill, and Kinneil Mill. Another family of Bells were owners of Avontown, and were connected at different times with the ministerial and legal professions, one of them having been town-clerk of Linlithgow.

XIII.

Robert Burns, D.D. (b. 1789, d. 1869).

In his notes of Bo'ness Parish, Mr. M'Kenzie[14] says, "A considerable number of clergymen might be mentioned as

---

[14] New Stat. A/c., *supra*.

connected with this parish by birth or residence. One family has produced four clergymen of the Church of Scotland, all of distinguished excellence, though, perhaps, the editor of the last edition of 'Wodrow's Church History' is best known to fame." The family referred to was that of John Burns, surveyor of Customs, Bo'ness. His four distinguished sons were the ministers of Kilsyth, Monkton, and Tweedsmuir, and the subject of this sketch.

Robert[15] was born at Bo'ness in 1789, educated at the University of Edinburgh, licensed as a probationer of the Church of Scotland in 1810, and ordained minister of the Low Church, Paisley, in 1811. He was a man of great energy and activity, a popular preacher, a laborious worker in his parish and town, a strenuous supporter of the evangelical party in the Church, and one of the foremost opponents of lay patronage. In 1815, impressed with the spiritual wants of his countrymen in the Colonies, he helped to form a Colonial Society for supplying them with ministers, and of this society he continued the mainspring for fifteen years. Joining the Free Church in 1843, he was sent by the General Assembly in 1844 to the United States to cultivate fraternal relations with the Churches there. In 1845 he accepted an invitation to be minister of Knox's Church, Toronto, in which charge he remained till 1856, when he was appointed Professor of Church History and Apologetics in Knox's College. Burns took a most lively interest in his work, moving about with great activity over the whole colony, and becoming acquainted with almost every congregation. Before the Disruption he edited a new edition of Wodrow's "History of the Sufferings of the Church of Scotland from the Restoration to the Revolution," in four volumes, contributing a life of the author; and for three years—1838-1840—he edited and contributed many papers to the "Edinburgh Christian Instructor." He also wrote a life of Stevenson Macgill, D.D., 1842. There is a memoir of Dr. Burns by his son, Robert F. Burns, D.D., of Halifax, Nova Scotia; see also "Disruption

---

[15] See "Dictionary National Biography."

Worthies," and notice by his nephew, J. C. Burns, D.D., Kirkliston.

XIV.

JOHN ANDERSON (b. 1794, d. 1870).

John Anderson was known in his day and generation as "the King of Bo'ness," and his name has been perpetuated in the Anderson Trust, the Anderson Academy, and the Anderson Buildings. He was the only son of John Anderson, teacher, Bo'ness, and of Jean Paterson, his spouse, and was born and lived all his days in the seaport. Possessing shrewd business capacity, he in time became merchant, shipowner, and, later in life, agent for the Royal Bank of Scotland. He conducted his businesses with ability and success, and rose to considerable influence in the place. In addition, he was connected officially for many years with the local friendly societies, and devised many schemes for their improvement. Mr. Anderson was a man of strong will and tenacity of purpose, and left his mark on every project with which he was associated.

Always fully alive to business possibilities, he, to meet the increase in the population which followed the establishment of Kinneil Furnaces, converted his extensive cellarages in Potter's Close (now demolished) into dwelling-houses. The consequent growth of the town at this time, coupled with a renewal of the Greenland whale-fishing, led to a great period of prosperity, in which he, as its principal merchant, almost enjoyed a monopoly. He owned the whalers "Success," "Alfred," and "Jean," and had a large share in the boiling-house at the top of the Wynd. On the formation of Bo'ness Gas Company, in 1842, he was appointed its first chairman. To use a common phrase, Mr. Anderson was very lucky. He did not, however, concentrate all his powers upon self-aggrandisement. In him the poor of the town had a good friend during his lifetime, and by his will he provided pensions to deserving persons. Interested all his life in education, he advanced its cause by erecting and endowing the Academy which bears his name. The foundation-stone of this building was made the occasion of a great Masonic demonstration on the 12th of June, 1869. Another function in which, a decade before, he played a prominent part was the visit of the eleventh Duke of Hamilton and his wife, Princess Marie of Baden. They were received in great style by Mr. Anderson, and entertained to cake and wine on board the Greenland ship. Their Graces afterwards proceeded to the Town House, and there gave a handsome donation towards the erection of the Clock Tower.

Mr. Anderson died on 14th April, 1870, and was buried beside his father, mother, and sister Margaret in the lower churchyard at the Wynd. This burial-place is covered by a large, flat stone bearing some appreciative words concerning his mother and sister. The former is described as "active, cheerful, and constantly occupied," and as having "sought pleasure nowhere and found happiness and content everywhere." Of the latter he says, "Active in her habit, kindly in her disposition, she was a sister highly to be prized."

Some years ago Mr. Anderson's trustees, who had been instructed to renew and keep the family tombstones in order, resolved to erect a new monument to his memory in the cemetery, as the lower churchyard was now practically abandoned. So, upon Saturday, 24th December, 1904, Mr. William Thomson of Seamore, one of the original trustees, performed the ceremony of unveiling a handsome granite block, suitably inscribed, which stands near the main entrance to the new cemetery.

XV.

Below we reproduce a somewhat humorous, but, we believe, quite accurate genealogy and character sketch of Mr. Anderson, which is prefixed to a presentation volume of the poetical works of Robert Burns (London, 1828), in the possession of Masonic Lodge Douglas. It refers to Mr. Anderson's initiation into Lodge No. 17, Ancient Brazen, Linlithgow, which apparently met at Bo'ness for the purpose. The volume was presented by

Mr. Anderson, and, either out of compliment to him or at his own desire (but, in either event, with his knowledge and consent), the chronicle we refer to was prefixed.

Here is what the scribe has written—

"1. And in the days of the Kings called George and William and of Queen Victoria, mighty Sovereigns of Scotland, there dwelt in the ancient town of Bo'ness a virtuous man called John, of the tribe of Anderson.

"2. Now, the genealogy of this John of Bo'ness is as follows:—There was a pious man called John the Preacher, of the tribe of Anderson, who took unto himself Agnes, the daughter of Bryson. [This is evidently his grandfather, who was a Burgher minister at Elsrickle, near Biggar.]

"3. And she bore him a son, John, who waxed strong in knowledge, and in process of time taught the people many things out of the law and the prophets. [This was his father.]

"4. And John, the teacher, took unto himself an excellent wife, called Jane, of the tribe of Paterson, whose ancient progenitors were mighty rulers in Italy in the latter days of the Cæsars and the Apostles, and hence is derived their Roman name of 'Pater' and 'filius'—father-son, now Paterson.

"5. And this daughter of the tribe of Pater bore unto the teacher, John of Bo'ness, and also Agnes, who married Robert, of the tribe of White, who is a dealer in things that are hard in the royal city of London, and Margaret, a fair maiden of good understanding, and much esteemed and respected by all who knew her.

"And John of Bo'ness is a man that deals in all kinds of merchandise. He 'takes heed to his ways,' as reminded by the wise men of old and the prophets, therefore he has gold and silver and menservants and maidservants, and also divers ships that go far off for riches, even unto the borders of the Holy Land. Moreover, this merchant was much respected for his wisdom and for his upright ways. Wherefore he was made a ruler among the people,[16] who bowed down their heads before him when he sat in the judgment seat; and his good name went abroad, so that there was none like unto him in Bo'ness for skill in shipping."

The chronicle then concludes by recording Mr. Anderson's initiation on the 14th of September, 1849.

XVI.

ADMIRAL SIR GEORGE JOHNSTONE HOPE, K.C.B. (b. 1767, d. 1818).

We have elsewhere dealt with the Hope family in connection with their ownership of Carriden estate. The notable careers of the two admirals, however, claim some mention.

Sir George was the eldest son by the third marriage of the Hon. Charles Hope Vere, and fifth child of his father, who was the second son of the first Earl of Hopetoun. He entered the Navy at the age of fifteen, and after passing through the usual gradations attained the rank of captain in 1793, and that of rear-admiral in 1811.[17] During the interval he had commanded successively the "Romulus," "Alcmene," and "Leda" frigates, and the "Majestic," "Theseus," and "Defence," seventy-fours. At the battle of Trafalgar he was present in the latter vessel. He served as captain of the Baltic fleet from 1808 to 1811. In 1812 he went to the Admiralty, and the following year held the chief command in the Baltic. In the end of the same year he returned to the Admiralty, where he remained as confidential adviser to the First Lord till his death on 2nd May, 1818.

---

[16] He was made a Justice of the Peace and along with two other Justices held Courts here.
[17] "Scottish Nation," vol. ii., p. 496.

He was a very distinguished officer, and highly appreciated in the service for his exemplary discipline, his decision, promptitude, and bravery, and his veneration for religion.

ADMIRAL SIR JAMES HOPE, K.C.B. (b. 1808, d. 1881).

James Hope was a child of ten when his father, Admiral Sir George, died. His youth therefore was spent under the direction of his mother and of his father's trustees. Anxious to follow in his father's footsteps, he entered the Navy, and had an equally distinguished career. He has been described by one who served under him abroad as a brave gentleman and a good-hearted soul, and this is borne out by all who knew him in this neighbourhood. When in command of the "Firebrand" he opened the passage of the Parana, in the River Plate by cutting the chain at Obligado in 1845. He was Commander-in-Chief in China, and brought about the capture of Peking. On two occasions he was seriously wounded. The first was during the attack on the Peiho forts in 1859. He was directing operations from the bridge of the "Plover" when a shell struck the funnel chainstay. A fragment glanced off, and, striking Hope, became deeply embedded in the muscles of his thigh. This entirely disabled him for four months. His recovery was very slow, and he was lame ever afterwards. The ship's surgeon was able, after some trouble, to extract the splinter; and a photograph of it is preserved, with a note giving full particulars of the occurrence. The second occasion was near Taeping. Hope, because of his disabled condition, was directing movements from a sedan chair, and was in consultation with the French Admiral. A shell from the guns of the enemy struck the latter under the chin and decapitated him. Hope himself was violently thrown from his seat, and his old wound reopened. He was gallantly rescued by the late Tom Grant, of Bo'ness, who was all through this campaign with the Admiral. In later years his old chief succeeded in getting Grant a pension, although he had scarcely completed his twenty-one years' service.

The late Tom Thomson, of Carriden, another old naval man,

Admiral Sir James Hope.
(From a photograph in possession of Mrs. James Kidd, Carriden.)

was with Hope while on the "Majestic" when she was with
the fleet in the Baltic under Sir Charles Napier. Hope
was an out-and-out Scot, and in his younger days agitated for
the introduction into the Navy of a Scotch uniform, especially
the Balmoral bonnet. The experiment was tried, but given
up as unsuitable.

He took great interest in his men on or off duty, and
arranged many private theatricals on the main deck for their
amusement, taking a special delight in the presentation of
"Rob Roy" and other Scottish pieces. Thomson spoke
highly of his discipline and the thoroughness with which he
instructed and drilled his men.

After the Pekin Treaty, in 1862, Admiral Hope was engaged
as an adviser at the Admiralty. He afterwards resigned his
command, and went into retirement. For some time he lived
in London, and afterwards settled at Carriden. In conjunction
with Lady Hope he associated himself in his later years with
many religious and philanthropic movements in the district.
He bought up some of the old properties in the Muirhouses, and
remodelled and rebuilt the village, including the old school and
schoolhouse. He was twice married, but had no family. The
Admiral died in Carriden House, and was buried in the north-
west corner of the churchyard at Cuffabouts. A cable from
one of his old ships surrounds the grave. His tombstone bears
the inscription, "Sir James Hope, G.C.B., Grand Commander
of the Bath, Admiral of the Fleet. Born 8th March 1808;
died 8th June, 1881."

The late Sir John Lees, private secretary to the Marquis of
Townshend when Lord Lieutenant of Ireland, and who afterwards
filled the office of Secretary to the Post Office in Dublin, was
in his youth brought up, Mr. Fleming says, in Carriden parish.
He was eminently successful in life, and afforded a memorable
example of the distinguished place in society to which the careful
cultivation and judicious application of superior talents may
raise their possessor. He was created a baronet on the 21st
June, 1804.[18]

---

[18] New Stat. A/c., Carriden.

XVII.

JAMES BRUNTON STEPHENS (b. 1835, d. 1902).[1]

To Bo'ness belongs the honour of being the birthplace of James Brunton Stephens, the poet of the Australian Commonwealth. His father was John Stephens, who filled the office of parochial schoolmaster of Borrowstounness from 1808 to 1845 with much dignity and ability. The school and schoolhouse were then situated in what is now known as George Place. James was born in August, 1835. His early education was received from his father, and among his schoolmates were John Marshall and John Blair, who became well-known doctors, the first in Crieff, and the latter in Melbourne, Australia. On completing his school education he proceeded to Edinburgh University. In all his classes he secured an honourable place, but abandoned his course without taking a degree. He was tempted away from the mere diploma by an offer to become a travelling tutor, and with the son of a wealthy gentleman he travelled for three years to Paris, Italy, Egypt, Turkey, Asia Minor, Palestine, and Sicily. On returning to Scotland he became an assistant master in Greenock Academy. In 1866, his health having given way, he was advised to emigrate to Australia. Arriving in Queensland, he obtained a tutorship in an up-country station, and spent several years in learning the sports and occupations of the bush. During this time he wrote "Convict Once," his best poem, and later "The Godolphin Arabian," a humorous and racy account of the sire of modern thoroughbreds. In 1874 Mr. Stephens received an appointment as a teacher under the Department of Public Instruction in Brisbane. Here he began to contribute to the local Press, and in 1876 won a prize of £100 offered by the *Queenslander* for the best novelette. At this period he married and settled in one of the Brisbane suburbs. In 1880 he published a volume of miscellaneous poems containing many humorous pieces that strongly appealed to the public. Mr. Stephens latterly filled the position of Chief Clerk in the

---

[1] See also "The Poets and Poetry of Linlithgowshire" (1896). A. M. Bisset.

Colonial Secretary's Office at Brisbane, and was greatly esteemed for his geniality and wit. He was very Australian in the selection of his themes, his inspiration being found in his immediate surroundings. Among the humorous poets of Australia he held a first place, but, like Hood, he could be serious on occasion. In this vein he was equally successful. He was keenly alive to the importance of uniting all the Australian States, and in 1877 his poem, "The Dominion of Australia," did a great deal to stimulate flagging interest in federation. On the 1st of January, 1901, he published a poem in the *Argus* entitled "Fulfilment," which was dedicated, by special permission, to Her Majesty Queen Victoria.

In June ef the following year Mr. Stephens died in his sixty-seventh year, and was survived by his widow, a son, and four daughters.

CHAPTER XIX.

CONCLUSION.

1. Borrowstounness a Plague-infested Town in 1645: Special Committee to Prevent Spread of Pestilence: Their Powers and Regulations: Erection of "Gallases" by Magistrates of Linlithgow: An Outspoken Skipper Gets into Trouble: Customs Revenue, 1654: Proposed Bridge over the Avon, 1696—2. Defoe's Visit to and Description of the Town, c. 1726: Jacobite Soldiers on Borrowstoun Muir, 1745: Their Depredations: Visit of the Poet Burns, 1787, and his Impressions—3. Population of Parish between 1755 and 1841: Longevity of Inhabitants: History of Custom House: Shipping Returns to Admiralty for 1847 and 1848: Grain Trade—4. Tambouring and Silk-spinning: The Greenland Whale-fishing: The Whaling Vessels and their Officers: Sailing and Home-coming of the Fleet Described: The Boiling House at the Wynd: The Fire: End of the Industry: 5. Bo'ness Pottery: Its Various Owners: The Ware Produced: Extent of the Works: Character and Customs of Potters—6. The Soapwork, Flaxdressing Factories, The First Iron Foundry: Links Sawmill and Woodyard, Ropework: The Distillery: The Kinneil Furnaces: The Snab and Newtown Rows: Kinneil Band: Carriden Band—7. The Carting Trade: Tolls and Tollbars—8. Educational: Schools and Schoolmasters in Carriden—9. Those of Bo'ness: The Notorious Henry Gudge: Kinneil School—10. The Care of the Poor: Interesting Facts and Figures: The Resurrectionists — 11. The Cholera Outbreaks: Carriden Board of Health: Its Instructions to the Inspectors—12. Foreshore Reclamation Schemes: Formation of Local Company of Volunteers, 1859: The Burgh Seal and Motto.

I.

In this chapter we conclude by gathering up a number of historical facts which lie scattered throughout the three centuries embraced by the present narrative.

Conclusion

Notwithstanding every precaution Borrowstounness became a plague-infected town in 1645. So much so that the Scottish Parliament[1] appointed a Special Committee to prevent the spread of the pestilence. Many persons succumbed; and because the seaport was then the resort of many people from Linlithgow, Falkirk, and other places the danger of the plague spreading throughout the country was considerable. Full power was given to the Earl of Linlithgow, Lord Bargany, Sir Robert Drummond of Midhope, John Hamilton of Kinglass, John Hamilton, chamberlain of Kinneil; the Provost and Bailies of Linlithgow, and others, or any three of them to meet at Linlithgow, or any other place, at such times as were necessary to cause Borrowstounness to be visited and inspected, and to do everything requisite. Strict "bounds" were prescribed the people of the Ness, and they were specially enjoined "not to come furth thereof without their order under the pain of death." It may be mentioned that these Commissioners had power, should any person disobey their commands, "to cause shoot and kill them." The Provost of Linlithgow, and in his absence any of the bailies, was to be convener of the rest "upon emergent occasion." But the people of the infected seaport did not respect either the commands in the Act or the regulations of the Committee, and the magistrates of Linlithgow considered that an "emergent occasion" had arisen, for we find[2] that they "ordaint the Maister of Wark to erect twa gallases—ane at the East Port, the other at the Wast Port, and gar hang thereon all persons coming frae Borrowstounness and seeking to enter the town." No doubt this summary procedure had a restraining effect on the defiant spirits from the Ness, and we do not expect it would be necessary to adorn either of the "gallases" with any victims. On the recommendation of the Committee, Parliament at a later stage ordained that a collection be made in the shires of Linlithgow and Stirling for the sufferers in Borrowstounness.

---

[1] See Scots Acts.
[2] Dawson's "Rambling Recollections."

In the troublous times of the Civil War, which resulted in the beheading of King Charles I. and of his loyal henchman, the first Duke of Hamilton, one local shipmaster got into trouble for speaking his mind. The matter came fully before the Kirk Session, and also the Estates in Edinburgh. The latter body[3] found it "cleirlie provine that John Watt, skipper, had uttered some disgraceful speeches against certain of the ministers of this kingdom, affirming that they had been accessory to the death of the King." Watt was ordained to pay £100 Scots to the Kirk Session of Borrowstounness; and "the chairges of the witnesses" who went to Edinburgh and were examined about the speeches uttered by him were to be "payt them aff the first end of the said hundreth punds." Watt was also ordained to acknowledge and confess before the congregation of Borrowstounness that he was "a lier" in uttering them; also to find a surety who would become bound with him that he would never do the like again. A perusal of the old Scots Acts reveals, among other things, that the Parliament in 1655 fixed the salaries of the officers of Customs and Excise, and it is incidentally mentioned that the receipts for these branches of revenue for October, November, and December, 1654, were estimated at £382 0s. 4¼d.; also that in 1701 it considered a "petition of the poor seamen of Borrowstounness who served in the Scots frigate commanded by Captain Edward Burd for payment and relief from the cess imposed on the town and for redress for wrongs committed by William Cochrane of Ferguslie"; and, further, that in 1706 an address against the Union was signed and submitted by several of the inhabitants. But perhaps the most interesting thing to be found is the authority which the Parliament granted in 1696 "for the building of a bridge at Borrowstounness over the Avon and a wall enclosing the road to it through the grounds of the Earl of Arran," and it also fixed the bridge toll. This proposal emanated from the seaport during its first period of commercial

---

[3] See Scots Acts.

prosperity. At that time a very large quantity of the imports were taken by pack horses to the west. The only suitable road was by way of Linlithgow, and this involved the payment of Customs dues to that town. The new bridge, it was thought, would avoid these, and also give a more direct means of communication with the west. The Burgh of Linlithgow protested against the scheme, and apparently some of the inhabitants of Borrowstounness also petitioned against it. Whether the funds were not forthcoming, we know not, but the proposal was not carried into effect.

II.

We must not omit to chronicle that one of the earliest descriptions of the Ness is from the pen of Defoe, celebrated as an English pamphleteer and politician, but more known to fame as the author of "Robinson Crusoe" (1719). His first visit to Scotland occurred in the year 1706, and lasted for twelve months. He was then on a mission to promote the Parliamentary Union of the two countries. In after years he was frequently in Edinburgh, and his impressions of it and the other Scottish towns which he visited are recorded in his "Tour Through Great Britain" (1724-26). In this volume he writes, "Borrowstounness consists only of one straggling street, which is extended along the shore close to the water. It has been, and still is, a town of the greatest trade to Holland and France of any in Scotland, except Leith; but it suffers very much of late by the Dutch trade being carried on so much by way of England. However, if the Glasgow merchants would settle a trade to Holland and Hamburgh in the firth by bringing their foreign goods by land to Alloa, and exporting them from thence, as they proposed some time ago, 'tis very likely the Borrowstounness men would come into business again; for, as they have the most shipping, so they are the best seamen in the firth, and are very good pilots for the coast of Holland, the Baltic, and the coast of Norway."

During the Jacobite Rebellion of 1745 a portion of the

Pretender's army on its way to the east country encamped three nights on the Common or Muir, which lay to the south of the thriving village of Borrowstoun. The village had a considerable population of weavers, brewers, and agricultural labourers. In fact, it is said that it contained four breweries about that time. The Highlanders during their sojourn there made free, like Mr. Wemmick, with everything portable. When remonstrated with by the irate villagers for plundering their fowls, meal, milk, and butter, the soldiers offered the consolation that they would bring them "a braw new King." Many of the inhabitants were so alarmed at the wanton depredations that they buried their valuables in their gardens. Instructions and warrants had been sent on different occasions through the Custom-house here to the Sheriff of Linlithgow, the magistrates of South Queensferry, and the bailie of Borrowstounness regarding suspected persons and ships. The Custom-house then contained a number of broad-sword blades and cutlasses, which formed part of a shipment from Germany. So when here the rebels conceived the idea of plundering the building, because they were very indifferently provided with arms. On the Sunday morning they marched down, with their pipers in full play, to the east end of North Street, where the Custom-house was then situated, and succeeded in carrying off some of the weapons and other articles. The morning after their departure from Borrowstounness a small silver box, shaped like a heart, was found on the Muir by the great-grandfather of James Paris, Deanforth, in whose possession it now is. The workmanship is chaste, and in the centre of the lid there is a fine Scotch pebble. The curiosity looks like an old-fashioned snuffbox, although the opinion has been expressed that it had probably been used for holding consecrated wafers. In considering this view it is useful to remember that many of the Prince's followers consisted of Roman Catholic Highlanders, who, though rude and turbulent, were devoted to the ceremonial rites of their religion.

In August, 1787, the poet Burns left Edinburgh on a tour to the Highlands in company with his friend Nicol, one of the masters of the High School of Edinburgh. They first journeyed to Linlithgow, then to Bo'ness, and from there to Falkirk and Carron. His diary contains this entry, "Pleasant view of Dunfermline and the rest of the fertile coast of Fife as we go down to that dirty, ugly place, Borrowstounness; see a horse race, and call on a friend of Mr. Nicol's, a Bailie Cowan, of whom I know too little to attempt his portrait." Mr. Cowan was the Duke's baron-bailie. He lived for a time in the old mansion-house of Gauze, and later at Seaview. It would seem that he was in the latter house at the time of the poet's call. In front of it there was then a fine stretch of open shore ground, upon which horse racing often took place, and it was doubtless from the bailie's house that Burns watched the sport. From his references to the view of Dunfermline and the dirtiness of Borrowstounness it is thought that Burns travelled from Linlithgow by the easter road, and came along to Seaview through Grangepans and Bo'ness. The place apparently damped his poetic ardour, for he did not leave any effusion upon a window pane or elsewhere. By the time he arrived at Carron the muse had returned. The visit to the famous ironworks was made on a Sunday, and admission was refused. Whereupon on a window pane of an old inn near by he scratched—

"We cam' na here to view your warks
In hopes to be mair wise,
But only, lest we gang to hell,
It may be nae surprise;
But when we tirl'd at your door,
Your porter dought na hear us;
Sae may, should we to hell's yetts come,
Your billy Satan sair us."

To this a Mr. Benson, at that time employed at the works, and the father-in-law of Symington, the inventor of steam navigation, penned the following reply:—

"If you came here to see our works,
You should have been more civil,
Than to give a fictitious name
In hopes to cheat the Devil.

Six days a week to you and all
We think it very well;
The other, if you go to church,
May keep you out of hell."

III.

The following figures[4] regarding the population of the Parish of Borrowstounness are noteworthy:—

In 1755 it was	2668
In 1795, town, 2613; county, 565,	3178
In 1801, exclusive of 214 seamen,	2790
In 1811, exclusive of 184 seamen,	2768
In 1821, exclusive of 158 seamen,	3018
In 1831,	2809
In 1841,	2347

A table compiled with much care from the register of deaths for a period of twenty-five years immediately preceding 1834 shows the number of deaths was 1342. During that time 167 persons died between sixty and seventy years of age; 227 between seventy and eighty; 119 between eighty and ninety; and 11 upwards of ninety. The town, in fact, was remarkable for the healthiness and longevity of its inhabitants.

Subjoined is a list[5] of the local mechanics in 1796, exclusive of journeymen and apprentices—

Bakers,	11	Masons and Slaters,	3
Barbers,	5	Tailors,	10
Blacksmiths,	7	Shoemakers,	15
Butchers,	3	Weavers,	6
Clock and Watchmakers,	2	Joiners, Glaziers, Cart-	
Coopers,	3	wrights, &c.,	15

Also one surgeon, one writer, one brewery in the town, and one distillery in the parish.

The Custom-house was removed here from Blackness

---

[4] New Stat. A/c., vol. II.
[5] Sinclair's Stat. A/c.

Conclusion

through the influence of the Hamilton family; and the first ledger of the "Port of Borrowstoun Ness" commences on 26th December, 1707. About the year 1796 Grangemouth, South Queensferry, North Queensferry, St. Davids, Inverkeithing, Limekilns, Torry, and Culross were all attached to the Custom-house here. The annual revenue received, excluding these creeks, averaged £4000; and the salt duty amounted to about £3000. Altogether the number of officers employed in the Custom-house business was forty-four. On the 1st December, 1810, Grangemouth was erected into a separate port. Thereafter the area of Bo'ness district and the staff employed were gradually reduced. In 1845 there was one collector, one comptroller, and one tide-waiter, and eight others at the creeks still remaining part of the establishment. Now, the port and district of Borrowstounness includes the Firth of Forth from the right bank of the river Avon to the left bank of Cramond Water and midway to the stream. The establishment consists of a collector and eight officers.

The following returns for two years were sent to the Admiralty from Bo'ness:—

1847.	Ships.	Tons.	
Arrivals under 50 tons,	323	15,076	} coasting.
,, above 50 ,,	212	11,600	
,, under 50 ,,	10	1,210	} foreign.
,, above 50 ,,	12	685	
	557	28,571	Total.

Exports, outwards,	4,000 tons coals, coasting.	
,, ,,	500 ,, ,, foreign.	
Grain, inwards, -	3,500 qrs.,	} coasting.
,, outwards, -	700 ,,	
,, ,, -	6,600 ,, foreign.	
Pig iron, - -	1,500 tons, coasting.	
,, - -	2,000 ,, foreign	
Timber, - -	304 loads from foreign.	

1B

1848.	Ships.	Tons.	
Arrivals under 50 tons,	396	16,820	} coasting.
,, above 50 ,,	195	27,222	
,, under 50 ,,	9	2,047	} foreign.
,, above 50 ,,	8	708	
	608	46,797	Total.

Coals, outwards, -	5,000 tons, coasting.	
,, ,, -	600 ,, foreign.	
Grain, inwards, -	3,000 qrs.,	} coasting
,, outwards -	500 ,,	
,, inwards, -	500 ,, foreign.	
Pig iron, outwards,	25,000 tons, coasting.	
,, ,, -	3,000 ,, foreign.	
Timber, - -	350 loads.	

The corn trade, both British and foreign, was very considerable. There were three large granaries and some smaller ones in 1796, with accommodation for upwards of 15,000 bolls. Any rooms which were in repair in the old Town House at this time were also used as granaries.

IV.

Some mention must now be made of local industries and manufactures other than coal mining, salt making, and shipbuilding, which have already been considered. Many of the women in the town and the country around earned a comfortable subsistence in the early years of last century by tambouring and spinning silk. The latter was spun from the waste of Spittalfields' manufacture, which was sent by sea from London to agents here. They afterwards returned the yarn to be manufactured into stockings, epaulets, and other things. Tambour work was extensively employed for the decoration of large surfaces of muslin for curtains and similar purposes. Much work was done for the West Indies, consisting principally of light, fancy goods. Many a single woman and many a widow depended solely on tambouring for their living.

What was known as the "long strike" occurred about seventy

Henry Bell.

See page 383.

years ago. The dispute was between the laird of Grange and his miners, and the stoppage lasted six months. At that time Mr. Cadell was heard to say, and with some little force, "If it had not been for the wives of the miners tambouring the men would have given in long since." It was fine work, and some of the colliers' wives and those of the sailors were dexterous hands at it. They could make as much as 2s. 6d. per day at the frame. All the light these workers had at nights was got from a collier's lamp placed in the middle of a saucer, and great were the fears of the women folks lest the lamp was upset on the frame. In time pattern weaving was brought to resemble tambour work so closely that it largely superseded it, and the old frames were finally laid aside.

About the middle of the last century the Greenland whale fishing was taken up locally for the second time, and developed to a much greater extent than before. There are only a very few alive now who remember this period. Still we occasionally hear of the narratives of the old sailors and harpooners concerning their trips to Greenland and Iceland, and their perilous encounters in these Arctic regions. The port was the home of many well-known whaling ships, notably the "Success." The popular refrain with the Bo'ness people applicable to this vessel was, "We'll go in lucky Jock Tamson's ship to the catching of the whale." Besides the "Success" there were the "Home Castle," the "Rattler" (Captain Stoddart), the "Juno" (Captain Lyle), the "Larkins" (Captain Muirhead), the "Alfred" (Captain William Walker), and the "Jean" (Captain John Walker). The officers on board the "Jean" were William White, Alexander Donaldson, John M'Kenzie, and John Grant. A line coiler was paid at the rate of £2 19s. per month. Each whaler carried a crew of fifty, and was away many months at a time. The men during the whaling were required to man the small boats which set out with their harpooners to the capture of the whales. Sometimes their prize would be so large as to require six small boats fully manned to tow it to the whaling ship. The harpooners were looked upon with great pride by their comrades.

Occasionally they suffered a galling experience when they failed to hit their mark, or when, after doing so, the line broke and the whale got away. Harpooner J. M'Kenzie, of the "Jean," had once an experience of the latter nature which had a curious sequel forty years afterwards. The "Terra Nova," of Dundee, captured a whale in which his harpoon was found. The harpoon bore the name of the maker, William Cummings, blacksmith, Kinneil, and the year 1853. It was handed over by the owner of the "Terra Nova" to the Dundee Museum. The late John Smart Jeffrey, Bo'ness, succeeded in getting the harpoon on loan, and exhibited it here for a month. Before returning it he had a facsimile cast for preservation.

There were always great ongoings attached to the sailing of the whalers, and particularly the "Jean." Women came down from the mills at Linlithgow, and sailors' wives and sweethearts were all on the quay. The sailors generally had a new rig-out of canvas trousers and jumper and blue bonnets with double ribbons. Before sailing, cannon were loaded, and whenever the sails were set the ships sailed away amidst cheers and the booming of the cannon, which made the town shake. The cannon used on board for the whaling were made by the Carron Company, and were about half the size of the field-piece now mounted in Victoria Park. About eight months later the return of the sailors was anxiously looked for, as much by the townspeople as by their own friends. The first intimation the inhabitants received of their homecoming was the boom of cannon, which rent the air, as the whalers sailed up the Firth. The whole population again turned out to welcome them, and for weeks after their arrival the sailors entertained their friends and acquaintances with long stories of their sufferings and hairbreadth escapes on the ice. We can quite understand that the sailors had to overcome many hardships, and not the least of these was scurvy. This was caused by their having to live so long upon salt meat.

There were two boiling-houses in the town, where the oil was boiled and made ready for sale. Latterly the principal one was at the top of the Wynd. Many of the whaling sailors were employed here during the off-season. There were two large copper pans from 15 to 20 feet long and 12 or 14 feet broad. These were sunk in the ground, and fired from below. The blubber was kept at boiling heat, and constantly stirred by two men until the whole oil was boiled out. It was then run off through the large taps in each boiler into casks. All refuse was carted away to the seashore. The men who saw to the tanks and the boiling of the oil were the harpooners. The boiling-house was owned by a company of seven gentlemen, some of them local and some of them from Edinburgh, with John Anderson as its leading spirit. A great fire occurred in the premises nearly sixty years ago. No one knew the cause of the outbreak. It was discovered at nine o'clock at night, and raged with great fury until midnight. As it happened, there was a large quantity of oil in barrels in the building. At considerable risk a good many of these were rolled out into the Wynd and through into the manse grounds by the gate opposite. The burning oil streamed down the Wynd, and caused much consternation. Nothing could be done to save the place, as there was no water available. Indeed, at this time it could scarcely be had for domestic purposes. The premises were gutted, but were shortly afterwards reconstructed on similar lines. A new copper boiler, 12 feet by 6 feet, was fitted up in the north-west corner of the building, and several cast-metal coolers put in on the north side. Whaling, however, soon came to prove unremunerative, and was given up by Mr. Anderson. The "Jean" was turned into a merchant trader, and was lost in the Baltic; and shortly after Mr. Anderson's death, in September, 1870, the plant and furnishings at the boiling-house were sold by auction.

V.

As already stated, the indefatigable Dr. Roebuck, in the year 1784, established the pottery in which for the next century was conducted one of the most important local industries. This gave Bo'ness a very wide reputation for the manufacture of many useful kinds of pottery ware, and it also created a new class of workers in the town. The manufacture of hardware is still continued on an extensive scale in two large new potteries in Grangepans. But the old Bo'ness Pottery, with which we are now to deal, was finally closed, and the works sold fourteen years ago. The pottery passed through the hands of a number of proprietors after Dr. Roebuck. Among these were Shaw & Son, with Robert Sym as managing partner; the Cummings, James Jamieson & Co., and latterly John Marshall & Co. A hundred years ago it employed forty persons, including men, boys, and girls. The clay for the stoneware was imported from Devonshire, but the clay for the earthenware was found in the parish. Cream-coloured and white stoneware, plain and painted and brown earthenware were the articles principally manufactured. Seventy years ago the buildings consisted of two kilns on the south side of the Main Street and two on the north. These employed from eight to ten kilnmen. The pottery buildings and kilns occupied all the available space on the north, for the tide then came far up into what is now reclaimed ground. In Mr. Jamieson's time the business was greatly extended, and printers and transferers were imported from Staffordshire. On his death the business was found to be insolvent, and the Redding Coal Company, who were the principal creditors, took possession for a time. Ultimately a settlement was arranged, and the works were sold to Mr. Marshall, who retained the old manager. Under the new proprietor the business flourished. Ground was rapidly reclaimed, the material for this purpose being carted from the Schoolyard pit. As the ground was filled in, kilns and workshops were added. Mr. Marshall was enterprising, and introduced machinery in every department. Almost every variety of stone and earthenware was now manufactured.

The potters in the days of the Cummings were less respectable in character than what they afterwards became. They had not much reputation for good behaviour and sobriety, as is illustrated by the following story:—A deformed woman, belonging to the town, was unfortunate in not getting a husband, and her somewhat chastened solace on the subject was, "I

Conclusion 407

daursay I'll just hae tae tak' a potter yet." Drinking bouts were frequent within the premises, and at times the main gate had to be locked to prevent drink being taken in. This led to strategy on the part of the potters within. Sometimes, with the aid of accomplices outside, bottles were pulled up to the windows by cords. At others it was smuggled in in a water can. The pottery boys also were often despatched for liquor in many a secret and curious way. But this debauchery was in time rooted out of the works. Mr. Marshall did everything in his power to encourage intellectual and moral culture in his workpeople. As an evidence of this he gave his support to a reading-room and other facilities for the cultivation of the mind. This was established in the house of William Cummings, and was confined to potters. It was carried on for many years with great success. The contribution was one penny per week. Mr. Marshall assumed William M'Nay as a partner, and he likewise took a keen interest both in work and workpeople. The place therefore continued to prosper for many years. At length its trade sadly declined, and the works were ultimately closed.

The potters formed a conspicuous part of the Annual Fair Procession of a past generation, and even down to thirty years ago. The men made a fine display, dressed in white trousers, white apron tied with blue ribbon, and black coat and tall hat. They carried specimens of their ware in the shape of model ships and model kilns, and there was also a brave display of Union Jacks and ships' flags. The first passenger train to leave the town, more than fifty years ago, it is noteworthy, carried the potters on their first excursion.

In the Scottish Exhibition, Glasgow, of 1911, several specimens of the ware manufactured in Bo'ness Pottery in its early days were on view.

VI.

During the eighteenth century a soapwork and two considerable manufactories for dressing flax flourished in the town. They are defunct long ago. The soapwork was situated in the vicinity of the present Albert Buildings. It was owned by John Taylor, who was known as "Saepy Taylor." It employed six men, and paid annually to the Government about £3000 in duty. For the first fifty or sixty years of the same century Borrowstounness was a great mart for Dutch goods of all kinds, particularly flax and flax seed. Very large quantities were imported both for dressing and selling rough. But as the manufactures of this country advanced so as to increase the demand for Dutch flax, the traders and manufacturers in other places imported direct into their own ports, and in consequence the trade here declined.

What we believe was the first of the many ironfoundries to be found in the town in the nineteenth century was started about the year 1836. It was originally carried on under the firm-name of Steele, Miller & Company, and afterwards came to be known as the Bo'ness Foundry Company, which is still its designation. The founder of the firm was Robert Steele, who prior to settling in Bo'ness was a traveller for the Shotts Iron Company. Miller was a moulder to trade, and he was assisted in the practical work by James Shaw. It also gave employment to several other workmen, and for many years a considerable business was carried on.

At the east end of the town there existed about the same time an extensive bonded woodyard, as well as an open woodyard on the Links. Connected with them, and driven by steam, was a sawmill containing both circular and vertical saws, and a very ingenious and efficient planing machine. The same steam engine moved machinery for preparing bone manure. This sawmill and woodyard are still in existence, but on a much larger scale. On the south side of the Links there was also a ropework on a small scale, but the ropemaking was abandoned over twenty years ago.

The Bo'ness Distillery, at the west end of the town, has been in existence for nearly a century. Writing in 1845, the Rev. Mr. M'Kenzie described it as an extensive establishment even then. The revenue paid to Government, he says, including malt duty, was sometimes considerably over £300 per week. It was at that time working on a limited scale, producing only spirit of superior quality. For a time it was owned by the firm of Tod, Padon & Vannan, and afterwards by A. & R. Vannan. In 1874 it was purchased from them by James Calder. It is now the property of James Calder & Co., Limited, and with its attendant manufactories of by-products is a very large concern indeed. We learn from recent figures that there is a weekly output of 50 tons of yeast, 25,000 gallons of spirits, and 300 tons of grains for cattle feeding; also that the duty last year on the firm's production amounted to £1,000,000 sterling.

With the collapse of the local canal scheme the seaport fell on evil times. The return of better days, however, was heralded in 1843 by the starting of Kinneil furnaces by John Wilson of Dundyvan. He was an ironmaster of repute in the west, and his proposal to exploit the ironstone in this district was hailed with delight. Had Dr. Roebuck but realised the value of these seams when he was lessee of the colliery he might have been saved all his financial troubles and losses. The furnaces were four in number, and were situated on the high ground about a mile west from the town. For many years, when in full swing, they were a commanding feature in the landscape, especially in the night. The iron at that time was melted with the hot-air process, and the tops of the furnaces were open. Great columns of flame sprang towards the heavens, lighting up the Firth and the surrounding district for miles. Bo'ness was then poorly lighted, and it is said that the glare materially assisted to illumine the dark places of the town.

Mr. Wilson, who when here lived in the Dean, had the reputation of being an excellent business man and most approachable. He was a Liberal in politics, and contested the county against Lord Lincoln, the Conservative. Wilson was no speaker, but the election was keenly fought, and he only lost the seat by seven votes.

One of the managers for John Wilson & Co. at Kinneil was

Mr. John Begg, a grand-nephew of the poet Burns. He lived at the Dean for many years, and took an active share in the government of the town. After his death, in 1878, the manufacture of coke was established on an extensive scale. Eventually the ironworks were closed down, and have since fallen into decay. The remains of the furnaces and coke ovens are still to be seen. It should be stated that the erection of the furnaces led to the building of the Snab or Kinneil Rows for the accommodation of the miners and other workers employed. This contract was in the hands of James Brand, and its execution caused considerable stir about the place in several employments. The Newtown Rows on the Linlithgow Road were also built about the same time, largely by William Donaldson, mason. Another thing connected, in a sense, with the furnaces was the institution of Kinneil Reed Band on the 30th of June, 1858, the inaugural meeting being held in the Old Schoolroom at Newtown. All the members were connected with Mr. Wilson's ironworks, hence the reason of the name. On the roll of original members were eight of the name of Sneddon, six Robertsons, two Grants, and two Campbells. On Christmas Eve, 1858, in response to an invitation from Captain William Wilson, the band proceeded to his residence at the Dean. They played in their best style, and the captain expressed himself as highly pleased with their performance, and entertained them to supper. Bo'ness and Carriden Band was instituted in the same year. Its members, again, were mostly connected with the Grange Colliery. This band has made a great name for itself, and has perhaps been more conspicuously successful as a musical combination than any band in Scotland.

VII.

Reference to the furnaces and the Snab Rows brings us to the carting trade, which before the coming of the railway was an important branch of local industry. Mr. Wilson brought the railway to Kinneil, but for half a dozen years prior to that there was abundance of work for the carting contractor driving the parrot coal from the pits to the quay and the iron from the furnaces. The iron was known to be carted to the quay at as low a charge as 9d. per ton, although the ordinary rate was 1s. It was shipped to the Continent. The leading carters in the town at that time where William Kinloch, the Edinburgh carrier, and James Johnston, the Glasgow carrier, and James Gray. Thomas Thomson and his father, in Grangepans, also did a large share of that work, and, while the Thomsons had the honour of carting away the first pig-iron turned out at Kinneil, their principal work was in carting the barley which arrived by boat from the north for the distilleries of Glenmavis, at Bathgate, and of St. Magdalen at Linlithgow. They also carted stones to Linlithgow Bridge from Bo'ness for the formation of the arches in the viaduct there prior to the opening of the Edinburgh and Glasgow railway. The Bo'ness Pottery also afforded them considerable trade. Most of the ware there manufactured was carted to Edinburgh. On the return journey the carts brought back rags, which were used for chemical purposes by Robert W. Hughes in what was known as the Secret Work at the Links.

Allied to the carting trade is the subject of the tolls and toll bars. There was supposed to be a distance of six miles between each toll, but the miles appear to have been short in those days. To begin with, there was the Carriden toll at the foot of the brae, where the toll-house can still be seen. The next was on the Queensferry Road at the Binns west gate, and known as the Merrilees toll. Further east was the Hopetoun Wood toll, just at the present hamlet of Woodend. At Kirkliston there was another, and going west towards Linlithgow was the Maitlands toll at St. Magdalen's Distillery. On the Linlithgow and Queensferry Road was the Boroughmuir toll, and on the road between Linlithgow and Bo'ness was the Borrowstoun toll. An important toll in the west was the Snab toll, which was situated a few yards to the east of the present entrance to Snab House. These tolls were under the control of the Justices and Commissioners of Supply for the county. They were put up to auction every year, and knocked down to the highest bidder. Many of the tolls were licensed, which raised their value, and as high as £500 has been known to be given for the lease of one of them for a year. Borrowstoun toll was licensed, and the thirsty Newtown miners had methods of their own for getting a supply there early on the Sunday mornings. This and the Snab toll were the two best in the district. They always let at the highest rates, because the traffic through them was exceptionally heavy. Merchandise for the west all went towards Grangemouth for shipment through the Forth and Clyde Canal. In addition, the farm traffic was considerable. After the opening of the Edinburgh and Glasgow railway a big traffic was done to and from Bo'ness by way of Borrowstoun toll. The receipts from the tolls must have yielded large sums, as the tariffs were fairly high. A scale of charges was approved by the Justices, and exhibited at each toll bar. The keeper could not demand more than the stipulated rates, but was free to make special terms, and take less from regular customers. The approved scale exacted 6d. for a horse and loaded cart. If the cart returned empty no further charge was made, but if loaded the sixpence charge was again imposed. One of the lessees of Borrowstoun toll was a Waterloo veteran, named James Bruce. He was badly wounded in the battle, and lay on the plains of Waterloo for three days and three nights. At length he was picked up and cared for, and although he had been frightfully slashed about the shoulders and other parts of his body by the swords of the Frenchmen, he ultimately recovered, and was able to return to this country. He also got a bullet in his arm, which was extracted after his death, and kept as a curiosity by his son. Bruce kept the toll at Borrowstoun for a long time, coming there from the Woodside toll, on the Bathgate Road. The tolls were abolished on the passing of the Roads and Bridges Act in 1878.

VIII.

Only very fragmentary information can be recorded concerning the educational affairs of the district. Had it

Conclusion

embraced a University or even a Burgh or Grammar School[6] there would doubtless have been much of interest to relate. As it is, we are confined to four kinds of schools—the Kirk Session Schools, the Parish Schools under the Act of 1803, the Private Schools, and the Secession Schools. The old Parish School of Carriden was situated at the Muirhouses, the title to it being dated 1636. In 1804 we find one Alexander Bisset referred to as the schoolmaster at Carriden, and twelve years later there are references to Samuel Dalrymple as the schoolmaster. There must have been others prior to these, but we have not traced them. We have seen[7] the record of a meeting held at Carriden on the 7th May, 1829, for the purpose of fixing the schoolmaster's salary, in terms of the statute, for the twenty-five years following Martinmas, 1828. It was then resolved that the salary should be the maximum one (£34 4s. 4d.), with the allowance of two bolls of meal in lieu of a garden until such should be provided for him. At the same time it was agreed that the school fees be as follows:—

For Reading English,	2s. 6d.	per quarter.
For English and Writing,	3s.	per quarter.
For English, Writing, and Arithmetic,	3s. 6d.	per quarter.
For Reading English, Writing, Arithmetic, and English Grammar,	4s.	per quarter.
For Latin, along with the other branches above mentioned,	5s.	per quarter.

And for any higher branches of education the fees were to be according to agreement between the teacher and pupils.

The last of the old parish schoolmasters was Adam B. Dorward. He was an excellent teacher, and during his later years served under the School Board in the new school near Carriden toll. Half a century ago the first wife of Admiral Sir James Hope established a school in what is now known

---
[6] See Scottish Education. J. Kerr, LL.D., 1910.
[7] Minutes of Heritors of Carriden.

as the West Lodge at Carriden. This was successfully conducted for many years. In paragraphs ten and eleven of our first Appendix will be found some interesting information by Mr. Dundas about the "pettie" or private schools in Carriden. We are in a position to supplement these somewhat. A school which occupied an important place in Carriden from the early part of last century onwards was the Grange Works School. Most of the children connected with the Grange Colliery and saltworks were sent here, the school fees being deducted from the wages of the employees. This school was situated on the north side of the Main Street near the east end of Grangepans. The building is still standing, and is yet known as the Old School. A salt girnel or cellar occupied the ground floor. The whole of the second floor was utilised as a schoolroom; and the top storey was used as the schoolmaster's house. One of the early schoolmasters here was a Mr. Blair, who prior to coming to Grangepans had been in service at Hopetoun House. His school was attended by nearly one hundred scholars, and his advanced pupils assisted him in teaching the younger children. Blair was succeeded by a weaver from Bathgate named Wardrop. But the most eminent of all the masters in that school was Thomas Dickson, who in his early years had been educated for the ministry. He was painstaking and conscientious, and his abilities attracted to the Grangepans School many of the children of the well-to-do merchants in Bo'ness. Many of his pupils achieved great success in after life, and several of them followed in his steps professionally. Among these were William Wallace Dunlop, who became headmaster of Daniel Stewart's College, Edinburgh; the late Alexander Shand, the successor of the second John Stephens, Bo'ness, and afterwards one of the Established Church ministers of Greenock; and William Anderson, late Rector of Dumbarton Academy.

IX.

With regard to Borrowstounness there were five schools in the town and parish in 1796, and all well attended. The

Conclusion 415

parish schoolmaster commonly employed an assistant, and had generally from eighty to ninety scholars. He had a salary of 200 merks Scots (£11 2s. 2¼d.), besides the perquisites of his office as session clerk. The fees then paid were—

English and Writing, per quarter,	£0 2 6
Latin or French,	0 5 0
Arithmetic and other branches of Mathematics,	0 3 6
Navigation or Book-keeping, per course,	1 1 0

We find that on 7th November, 1803,[8] the amount of schoolmaster's salary in Bo'ness Parish was fixed at 400 merks Scots per annum, and that was to continue to be the salary payable for and during the period of twenty-five years, from and after the passing of the Act.

It was at same time determined that a commodious house for a school be provided, with a dwelling-house for the residence of the schoolmaster, and a portion of ground for a garden. A scale of fees was likewise fixed at this meeting. This minute was subscribed by Dr. Rennie, the minister, before these witnesses—George Hart, shipbuilder, and John Taylor, baker, in Bor-ness.

This school was, we understand, the first in the Presbytery built under the 1803 Act. It was erected at what is now known as George Place, and contained more than the legal accommodation. The schoolrooms were on the ground floor, and the schoolmaster's house, which had a separate entrance to the west, was upstairs. The garden ground was rather deficient in size, and an equivalent in money was given. So far as we can gather, John Stephens, who had been schoolmaster under the old system, was retained under the new Act, and his whole service extended over a period of fifty years.

In December, 1808, Mr. Stephens petitioned the heritor and minister, pointing out that the fees fixed in November, 1803, were "too low in general, and not equal to the fees

---

[8] Minutes of the Heritor and Minister of Bo'ness.

paid in almost every town in Scotland." He therefore requested that they be increased and made more in keeping with those towns of "similar size and respectability over the kingdom," and the request was acceded to. The following are the scales of 1803 and 1809:—

1803—English, per quarter, - - - - 2s. 6d.
    English and Writing, per quarter, - - 3s. 6d.
    English, English Grammar, and Writing
        per quarter, - - - - - 4s.
    Arithmetic, per quarter, - - - - 5s.
    Arithmetic and English Grammar, per
        quarter, - - - - - - 5s. 6d.
    Practical Mathematics, per agreement.
    Book-keeping, - - - - - a guinea
    Latin, per quarter, - - - - 6s.
    French, per quarter, - - - - 6s.

1809—English Reading, per quarter, - - 3s. 6d.
    English and Writing, - - - - 4s. 6d.
    English Grammar and Writing, - - 5s.
    Arithmetic, with English Grammar and
        Writing, per quarter, - - - 6s.
    Latin and Greek, per quarter, - - - 7s.
    Practical Mathematics, per quarter, - 7s. 6d.
    Book-keeping, per quarter, - - - 7s. 6d.

In 1845 there were ten schools in the parish, only one of which was a parochial school. The others we will refer to later. Early this year Mr. Stephens died, and in March John Stephens, his son, then parochial schoolmaster in East Kilbride, was appointed as his successor. He died in 1865, and on 19th April Alexander Shand, then a teacher in Newington Academy, was elected to the vacancy. His father was cashier at Kinneil, and he himself, as we have seen, was educated at Mr. Dickson's school in Grangepans. Mr. Shand resigned in 1868 to prosecute his studies for the ministry. Among the favoured applicants for the position at this time were William Thomson Brown,

Rector of the Grammar School, Dunfermline, and Adam B. Dorward, Carriden. Mr. Brown was finally chosen, and at the time of his retiral, upwards of twenty years ago, was headmaster of Bo'ness Public School. Among the masters of the many private schools were James Adams, who taught in the Big House at Newtown, and John Arnot, whose premises occupied the site of the present Infant School. Arnot taught navigation, and many of his pupils became captains in the merchant service.

One of the local teachers of this period achieved an unenviable notoriety. We refer to Henry Gudge, whose school was situated at the rear of the present Co-operative Store in South Street. The story of his downfall is well known to the older generation. He lived in Corbiehall, where he had some property, which, it is said, was transferred to John Anderson in settlement of some debt. Gudge became despondent over the transaction and intemperate in his habits. He worked himself into the belief that he had been wronged, and decided to have his money back. There was no bank in Bo'ness then, and he knew that Mr. Anderson was in the habit of sending money to Falkirk by a boy who was Gudge's nephew. One Saturday the dominie lay in wait for the boy about a mile and a half from Bo'ness, and, on meeting him, directed his attention to a hare in a field. While the boy went in chase of the hare, real or imaginary, Gudge got possession of the money bag, containing about £300, and absconded to Edinburgh. Mr. Anderson offered a reward of £25 for information leading to the arrest of Gudge. The advertisement was seen by a girl living in Edinburgh, who was a native of Grangepans, and had attended Gudge's school. She kept her eyes open, and one day saw him enter a public-house in Bristo Street, and informed Detective M'Levy. M'Levy took Gudge into custody, and found £180 of the money concealed in three ginger beer bottles found in his pockets. Gudge was transported to Tasmania for twenty years. Towards the expiry of the period he showed a desire, from letters which came to Bo'ness, to return to his native country, but he died in Van Diemen's Land in 1859.[9]

We should mention that in 1845 there was a school at the farm town of Upper Kinneil, supported by the tenantry, for the convenience of children in the barony. The schoolmaster got a small salary, and the Duke provided him with a schoolhouse so that he might make his school fees moderate. About this period the teacher was James Rutherford, a big man, but very lame. He was a good, all-round scholar, and was often employed in land measuring. Among other things he taught basketmaking. The reeds and willows were gathered in the district by the pupils, many of whom became expert basketmakers.

The Dissenters supported a school for many years. This and the other schools in the town were not endowed, and many of them were taught by females.

X.

Both in Bo'ness and Carriden the care of the poor was a subject which received most sympathetic and generous treatment. Even at the present day it could not be more carefully and usefully handled. We need make no reference to the administration of the poor funds in Carriden, for that is done very fully by Mr. Dundas.[10] The minutes of Carriden heritors also, it should be said, contain most carefully compiled lists of the poor there, and full annual statements of poor funds. In Bo'ness the poor were numerous. The funds for their support included weekly collections at the church door, rent of property purchased with poor funds saved, the interest of legacies, and mortcloth dues. The amount received from the last was trifling, because the county parishioners and the different corporations in the town, such as the Sailors and Maltmen, kept mortcloths of their own, and received the emoluments. In 1796 the pensioners who got regular supply

---
[9] See Detective M'Levy's "Curiosities of Crime."
[10] See Appendix I., paragraphs 8 and 9.

numbered thirty-six. Occasional supplies upon proper recommendations were often granted to such persons as were reduced to temporary distress. Upon any pressing emergency, wrote Dr. Rennie, the liberality of the opulent part of the inhabitants was exemplary. These people, he also says, were well-bred, hospitable, and public-spirited.

A severe winter was experienced about 1795, and nearly £60 sterling was collected and distributed in a most judicious manner by a committee of gentlemen in the town. Begging was common, but it was explained that the paupers who went about from house to house were, for the most part, from other parishes. We have elsewhere referred to the method of managing the poor funds of Kinneil. The average receipts and expenditure of the poor funds for Bo'ness for the three years ending 1837 were as follows:—Income—Church door collections, £45 2s. 6d.; rent of landed property, £32 8s.; interest of bond, legacy, mortcloth dues, and proclamations, £37 18s. 7d.; total, £115 9s. 1d. The total expenditure, however, came to £225 0s. 1d., and the deficiency of £109 11s. had to be made up by the Duke of Hamilton. There was in 1845, and still is, we believe, an association of ladies for the purpose of supplying the poor with clothes, meal, and coals in the winter. The farmers generously aided in this work by carting the coals gratuitously. There was also a Bible and Education Society, in the support and management of which Churchmen and Dissenters united. From its annual contributions about twenty-five poor children received a plain education. And the Scriptures, the Shorter Catechism, and school books were supplied to the poor gratuitously or at reduced prices.

The whole interesting history of the poor funds of Bo'ness was recently reviewed in an action of declarator at the instance of the Parish Council,[11] and as a result the body now known as Bo'ness Parish Trust was formed.

We now refer to a more gruesome subject. Until some

---

[11] Bo'ness and Carriden Parish Council against Kirk Session of Bo'ness, 2 F., pp. 661-670.

twenty years ago there stood at the gate of the South Churchyard, at the Wynd, a small watch-house. This was used for the purpose of sheltering the watchmen during the raids of the "Resurrectionists" in the first quarter of last century, when corpses were stolen for anatomical and other purposes. Every householder had to take his turn in the watch-house, or find a substitute. It was usual to watch for at least a sufficient time for the body to be considerably decomposed. Some of the local worthies made a profession of watching, and they were paid for their services at the rate of 1s. per night. In addition, parties employing them invariably provided bread and porter for supper. It was no unusual thing therefore for miners on their way to work in the early morning to find certain of these watchers hanging over the churchyard wall suffering from a more potent influence than the want of sleep.

XI.

There were two serious outbreaks of cholera here last century. The first occurred in 1831, and the second about twenty years later. The second outbreak was especially deadly, and it was not an unusual thing to meet a friend in good health the previous night and to learn of his or her death the following morning. Many well-known people of that day had fatal seizures. These included Mrs. Hill, wife of Mr. George Hill, watchmaker; Mrs. Campbell, of the Green Tree Tavern; Robert Grimstone, her brother; Matthew Faulds, West Bog; and Peter Thom, of the East Bog. We understand the churchyard on the shore at Corbiehall was necessitated because of the havoc which this outbreak caused among the inhabitants.

We have not seen any records bearing on these outbreaks so far as concerns Bo'ness. One of the minute books of the heritors of Carriden, however, contains the "Minutes of the proceedings of the Board of Health instituted in the Parish of Carriden to adopt precautionary measures against the threatened invasion of the pestilential disease, usually denominated Asiatic or epidemic cholera morbus." The first of these is dated Carriden

Church, 20th December, 1831, and contains this introduction—
"A disease of the most malignant description, and formerly unknown in Europe, originating in Asia, and taking its course through Russia and other countries in a westerly direction, having begun to make its ravages in some of the southern parts of our island, a public meeting of the inhabitants of the parish was called on the previous Sabbath from the pulpit to adopt measures for the purpose of preventing, if possible, by human means, the communication of such disease by infection, and of mitigating its virulence if, unfortunately, the malady should come among us."

A local Board of Health was then instituted, having Mr. James John Cadell of Grange as president and the Rev. David Fleming as secretary. Power was given them to convene the Board as circumstances required. Mr. Fleming stated that, in consequence of an urgent recommendation which he had felt it to be his duty to give the people from the pulpit, a good deal of attention had been paid by them to the cleaning, whitewashing, and ventilating of their houses. He also read an extract from a letter from Mr. James Hope of Carriden, then in London, recommending the instant adoption of strong measures to ward off, if possible, the threatened evil. Mr. Hope had sent the sum of £20 for the purpose of providing warm clothing for the poor, and this the minister had been endeavouring to disburse to the best of his judgment. The parish was then divided into seven districts, each under the inspection of three or four persons.

The following rules were adopted as instructions to the inspectors, and recommended to be duly enforced by them upon the parishioners:—

1. No private dunghills to be allowed nearer the dwelling-house than 12 feet.
2. All pigstyes to be removed from dwelling-houses to a convenient distance, and to be kept regularly clean.
3. All rabbits to be removed from dwelling-houses, and all other animals to be recommended to be removed,

except the usual domestic animals, such as dogs and cats.

4. All dung to be removed when equal in quantity to a cart-load, and all householders to clear once a week immediately before their own dwellings.

5. The inspectors to meet in a week to give in their report, and thereafter the Board to meet once a fortnight on Tuesdays in the Session-house at twelve o'clock noon.

On the 27th December the inspectors reported, for the most part, that everything was "in a tolerable condition of cleanliness, with the exception of John Black's keeping a sow." This he was required to remove. Dr. Cowan reported that the fever was abating, but the inspectors were urged to continue their efforts to remove all existing nuisances. Subscriptions to the amount of £54 are detailed in February, 1832, and lists of those relieved. The quantities of flannel and blankets, meal and potatoes given out are also detailed from time to time.

Towards the end of the year the dread disease was greatly mitigated. This, in a great measure, was due to the excellent services of Dr. Cowan and to the thorough methods of the local Health Board.

When the disease was stamped out the doctor submitted an interesting tabular view of all the cases, giving name, age, date of the seizure, date of death or recovery. In it we find the smallest number of hours from time of seizure till death, 11; greatest, 95; average, 33. He also stated that the patients who died were all, with one exception, in a state of collapse, no pulsation of the heart being perceptible. The exception was not in a state of collapse—the patient had recovered, but rose too soon, and this caused a fatal return of the malady.

We have not observed any record of the second outbreak having extended to Carriden. As we have said, it was very bad in Bo'ness, so more than likely Carriden was seriously affected also.

XII.

In modern days the important subject of foreshore reclamation is at last receiving great attention. Here, however, we had a practical illustration of it on Kinneil estate in the time of the first Lord Hamilton, who, as we have seen,[12] made extensive reclamations from 1474 onwards. Mr. Cadell in his recent work[13] evidently unconsciously refers to these when he says—"A portion of the Carse of Kinneil, on the Duke of Hamilton's estate, has been reclaimed long ago by a low dyke faced on the outside with stone. The land inside the bank is a few feet below the level of high water at spring tides; but this is a very old intake, the record of which I have not been able to discover." Reference to his foreshore reclamation map confirms our impression. Those who wish to study this very practical and far-reaching subject will find the whole matter fully discussed in two of Mr. Cadell's chapters. The methods employed in his own extensive reclamations are also described. We can do no more here than quote what was written on the subject to the two Statistical Accounts in 1796 and 1845 respectively.

Dr. Rennie states—"It is highly probable that all the low ground in the parish was formerly part of the bed of the river Forth. This opinion easily gains assent, because immediately at the bottom of the bank, far from the shore, and far above the level of the present spring tides, shells, particularly oyster shells, are to be seen in several places in great quantities. At low water, above two thousand acres, opposite to the parish, are left dry. It is said that a Dutch company offered for a lease of ninety-nine years to fence off the sea from the acres with a dyke to prepare them for the purposes of agriculture, which would have been a vast accession to the carse grounds of the parish. But the project failed, and a large extent of ground remains useless, showing its face twice every twenty-four hours to reproach the fastidiousness and indolence of mankind." Mr.

---
[12] p. 26.
[13] "The Story of the Forth," p. 227.

M'Kenzie referred to the same subject thus—"Between Bo'ness harbour and the mouth of the Avon about one thousand acres of a muddy surface are exposed at low water. These, if reclaimed from the sea for agricultural purposes, would be a valuable addition to the Carse of Kinneil. This part of the frith is becoming shallower, owing to the accumulation of mud brought down by the Avon and Carron, and especially by the Forth, and the beach is assuming more of a fluviatic character. Sir Robert Sibbald says, 'These shallows have the name of the Lady's Scaup.' The Dutch did offer some time ago to make all that scaup good arable ground and meadow, and to make harbours and towns there in convenient places upon certain conditions, which were not accepted."

Towards the end of the year 1859 the inhabitants of Borrowstounness were summoned by tuck of drum to assemble at the Old Town Hall to take into consideration the formation of a company of Volunteers. Captain William Wilson, of Kinneil, a son of Mr. John Wilson, and a captain in the 2nd Lanark Militia, was called upon to preside. On the platform with him were the Rev. Kenneth M'Kenzie, Provost Hardie, Linlithgow; John Vannan, distiller; John Stephens secundus, parish schoolmaster; Patrick Turnbull, factor to the Duke of Hamilton; John Begg, manager, Kinneil; and Dr. Murray. The Rev. Mr. M'Kenzie, who sported a scarlet vest as a badge of patriotism, delivered a powerful oration on the duties of the citizens of a free country, concluding with a stirring appeal to come forward at once and enrol. As a result of this no fewer than one hundred patriotic and sturdy fellows from Bo'ness and Carriden enrolled before the meeting was closed. The swearing-in of the company took place at Kinneil House on 1st June, 1860. Sheriff Kay officiated, and was accompanied by many of the gentry of the county. The day was observed as a holiday in Bo'ness, and crowds of people assembled to witness the interesting ceremony. As showing the enthusiasm of the members it need only be said that those whose occupations prevented them from attending drill in the evenings turned out at five o'clock in the morning. At that period the Government did nothing except supply the rifles. The county gentlemen came to the rescue, and paid for the accoutrements. The salary of the drill instructor had to be paid by the members of the company, who had to bear the cost of their own uniforms besides. The price of each uniform was £2 15s. This and the 10s. 6d. per man for the instructor the Volunteers bore cheerfully. Latterly the Government became alive to their duty, and increased their grant. But it was not until they made the full grant that drill went on in a proper way and the interest increased.

A memorable event in the history of the Volunteer movement was the great Scottish Review of 7th August, 1860, in which 22,000 Volunteers took part in Holyrood Park. The Bo'ness men were taken by steamer to Leith, and marched up to Lochrin, where they were attached to the Breadalbane Highlanders.

Among the few who now remain of the originally enrolled company are Captain William Miller, V.D., and Corporal James Paris.

When Borowstounness began to officially adopt a seal and motto we have not precisely ascertained. It is almost certain, however, that it was not much more than fifty years ago. They are described by the late Marquis of Bute[14] —

On the waves of the sea a three-masted ship in full sail to sinister.

The seal on which these arms appear is in a general way taken from that of the Seabox Society. When both are closely examined, however, a number of differences are seen. The society's seal has the three-masted ship on the waves and turned to sinister, but the sails are in this case furled. There is also *in chief a lion rampant*, which latter upon the old bell of the society, dated 1647, is represented as *passant*. The origin of the lion cannot be satisfactorily accounted for. As for the motto, "*Sine metu,*" this, again, is a departure from that of the Seabox Society, which was, as we have elsewhere stated, "*Verbum Domini manet in æternum.*"

---

[14] See "The Arms of the Baronial and Police Burghs of Scotland," 1903, pp. 70-71.

APPENDICES.

APPENDIX I.

"THE PARISH OF CARRIDEN 200 YEARS AGO."

(Being a lecture delivered in 1900 by the Rev. William Dundas, B.D., Minister of the Parish, and reprinted here by his kind permission.)

1. Period covered: Earlier records amissing—2. Forgotten places: Miners, Seafarers, and Saltmakers; The Piers at Causewayfoot and Burnfoot—3. The old seats of population: Forgotten place-names: List of common surnames—4. Functions of Kirk Session: They restrict sale of drink, deal with overcrowding, and birch bad boys—5. Old Church at Carriden House described: Trouble over the Elders' seat—6. William Young the beadle receives various "rebukes"—7. Administration of Church Ordinances: Marriage banns, Baptism, and the Sacrament—8. The Kirk Session and the Poor—9. Revenue from mortcloth dues: More help for the poor—10. The Old Parish School at Muirhouses: Deed of gift, 1636: The "pettie" schools: The Schoolmaster and "Doctor": Trouble with John Currie—11. Kirk Session control of "pettie" schools: Visitation of schools and examination of scholars—12. Concern of Kirk Session for the religious condition of people: Regulations against "randie beggars": The need for "testificats"—13. Illustrations of the variety of offences dealt with by Session—14. The "black stoole" of repentance: The procedure adopted here—15. Session deals strictly with those speaking lightly of it and the elders—16. James Kid of Burnfoot and his "proud, irreverent manner": Other quarrels of husbands and wives—17. The many faults of Elspeth Sleigh: Her misdeeds denounced from pulpit: The Soldiers at Blackness and "debaucherie"—18. The "jougs": Two vagabond boys called the Pods: Methods of Elders to enforce church attendance—19. Strict observance of the Sabbath, Fast, and Thanksgiving Days.

1.

There are no books—whether they deal with the story of the people in pure history or seek to depict their social life in the novel—that half so vividly paint for us the life of the common people as the old Kirk Session records in Scotland. The following therefore is an endeavour to give from these a picture of life in the Parish of Carriden two hundred years ago. This period has been chosen because it takes us back to the Revolution Settlement and its many changes, when the Kirk Session obtained almost sole power in everything concerning parish life, and we shall thus see not only how that power was used, but we shall also find a fulness and freshness about the proceedings which need not be looked for afterwards. Alas! the Kirk Session records before this date have disappeared. During the Covenanting times an Episcopalian minister was, of course, intruded into the parish. At the Revolution the "curate," as he was called, was speedily "rabbled out" by the parishioners, who, like the great mass of Scottish people, had never really adopted

Episcopacy. The curate—a Mr. Park—took the records with him when "rabbled" out of the manse. The Session made strenuous efforts to recover them. But Mrs. Park at least had powerful friends—notably Major Cornwall, then Laird of Bonhard; so although the session "ordained Duncan Allan and James Waldie to deal with Bonhard to persuade Mrs. Park to cause her husband deliver the church register, &c.," no effect was produced.

II.

Great changes take place in two hundred years. Even the very face of the country alters. There are, of course, but hints of this in the records. But these hints leave a vivid impression. Where will you find "the sands of Bridgeness Point" or the Muir pointed to in Muiredge and Muirhouses. And there is no loch now at Lochend or elsewhere. One of the most familiar terms in the records is the "Waterside," a term now never employed, so great is the change. Again, there were then four principal means of employment—agriculture, coal mining, seafaring, and saltmaking. Agriculture occupied relatively much the same position it holds now, although the people of those days would have been less astonished at the apparition of the enemy of all mankind than at the sight of the modern "reaper and binder" at work. Coal mining was carried on at Kinglass, Bonhard, and Grange. But the miners were serfs, and women and their creels took the place of engines and hutches.

Bridgeness Harbour has taken the place of the piers at Causewayfoot (or Cuffabouts) and Burnfoot; and the Seamen's Loft is now at best but a name of the past, like the seamen who sat in it and formed, perhaps, the most important part of the inhabitants. We have now but two or three sailor parishioners, and none of those notable master mariners and owners who once had the parish as their home and made it more intimate with Holland than with Edinburgh. And the last of the salters has vanished with the saltpans in Grangepans. But salt-making hereabouts was in those days no small matter. An old parishioner informed us that a minister of Muiravonside told him that in his remembrance the site of the present manse and the lower glebe were nothing but "a rickle of dauners and a plane tree." Indeed, along no small part of the shore of the parish saltpans were then continually busy. There were the Grange Pans, the Bonhard Pans, erected and wrought in connection with Bonhard pits, and Carris Pans occupying continuously more than half the seaward limit of the parish.

III.

There have been great changes, too, in the seats of population in the parish. A collection was to be made and collectors were appointed. Here are their districts—Binns Bounds, Bonhard and Northbank, Grange and Bridgeness, Kinglass, Muirhouses and Cuffabouts, Muiredge, and Little Carriden. Two collectors were

Old Church and Churchyard of Carriden.

appointed to each district, save Grange and Bridgeness, which had three, and Muirhouses and Cuffabouts, which had also three. Blackness was, of course, included in Binns Bounds. Kinglass was evidently the most populous part of the parish. Little Carriden—which lay opposite Muirhouses and embraced the upper part of the present glebe—and Muiredge have disappeared altogether. Then we have the now strange names of Ryehill, Doghillock, Kingsfield, Cotohonhill (Cowdenhill), where there was a fair on the 1st of May. It is of interest, too, in this connection to compare surnames. It would take too long to give a complete list if it were available, as it must be remembered that only the names of the very good—the session and the witnesses—and the very bad—illdoers of various kinds—are mentioned. But take the following:—Bryce, Bisset, Barclay, Butcher, Bishop, Barrie, Cramb, Cathcart, Cockburn, Crookston, Cowie, Caldhouse, Carfin, Clunie, Casilis, Davie, Falconer, Frank, Graham, Gilchrist, Glass, Hart, Hutcheson, Hosie, Innes, Keir, Knight, Leask, Lamb, Lyall, Mathieson, Meiklejohn, M'Conochie, M'Rowan, Moutray, M'Lean, Mosie, M'Elfrish, Moodie, Pye, Paton, Piggins, Page, Richmond, Smeaton, Shade, Spittal, Tulloch, Umphray, Wood, Younger.

IV.

In practice if not in theory the position of the Kirk Session was at this time autocratic. It exercised all the functions of the various bodies which in our time carry on the local government of a parish. It did a good deal else besides. Like the Town Council, it dealt with money found. "Ordained William Young to have ane half-crown contended for betwixt him and the deceased James Ewing." Like the sanitary authority, it dealt with overcrowding. "Ordained David Cathcart to speak to Mount Lothian to build new houses to his coal grieves in Kinglass that some families might not lye together in a very little room like so many beasts." To a certain extent it dealt with the sale of drink. It shut up or restricted the sale of strong drink in public-houses on the Sabbath, while its members were in the habit of going round the parish and enforcing early closing on Saturday nights, "seeing that nothing was drunk after eight at night." Thus they were certainly more thorough than the present licensing authorities, and doubtless their methods were more effective than those now prevailing. In regard to even civil offences the session did birch bad boys, and it was continually dealing with offenders against civil law and handing them over to the magistrates for punishment.

V.

The church then stood in the old churchyard in front of Carriden House. It had two "lofts," the seamen's and the colliers', "the Grange Isle" and the ordinary oblong floor space. The floor was of clay. It was unheated. It was not regularly seated. People applied for leave to put in a seat, and the session, if they saw fit, assigned them a certain portion of the floor space for that purpose.

"The indwellers in Thirlestane petitioning for a large seat in the west end of the church are permitted to put in one—that part being vacant."

The elders had a seat of their own next the pulpit; and, strange to say, that seat was looked upon as most desirable. It is possible that it was hidden from the minister's eye by the pulpit. One of the very first minutes tells that a lock was put on it. But that was not enough. Ere long a woman had to be reproved for "meddling with the elders' seat," and then there came a long dispute regarding the seat with John Campbell—not in this matter alone—a sad stumbling-block in the session's path. Campbell took possession of the elders' seat, and after much debate the session appointed "James Wilson and the session clerk to go up to Linlithgow to Sebastian Henderson, procurator to the Sheriff Court there, and to inform him in all points the right which the session has to that seat, which John Campbell wrongouslie and contentiouslie possesses; that the session built the same for the use of the elders, and that the said Campbell has another seat in another part of the church which his predecessors built, and to order him in the session's name to represent the same before the Sheriff." Following this Campbell offered a compromise which was satisfactory to the procurator but not to the session. The matter had to go back to Court again. Ere it could be dealt with, however, the minister died, and there is no further record. Some of the seats at anyrate were movable, for we find that "David Cunningham is appointed to reprove William Young, beadle, for suffering people to go into the church and take out seats."

VI.

It may be remarked that this is not the only reproof that William Young got. He was rebuked for tolling the bell for funerals without receiving the fee for so doing. He was also called into the session and "challenged of several things against him: First, that he made not the graves deep enough, to which he answered that he made them as deep as ordinary; secondly, that he should not break ground (make graves) on the Sabbath Day. Answered that he could not help that in respect that the ground did not stand. If a grave were opened the day before it would fall all in before the morrow, which put him to as much trouble as if he were to break the ground on the Sabbath. He was ordered by all means possible to help it and to see if it could be foreborne."

Another of the beadle's offences was the ringing of the bell too soon on the examination (catechising) day.

The church does not seem to have been either wind or watertight on several occasions. "It was ordained that any of the elders that goe to Linlithgow to know what the sclatter means in not pursuing the sclating of Carriden Kirk, being engaged by the heritors so to do a pretty while ago." And again the session "appoints the clerk to show Bonhard or his lady that the Earl of Buchan and his lady complained much of a window which is not glazed which doth much harm; and desyre them to glaze it." And the session-house, "the minister's

Sabbath Day's retiring chamber," as it is quaintly termed, was very frequently in bad repair.

VII.

Notices of the administration of Church ordinances are often interesting And first as to baptism. It was "ordained John Anderson to employ some wright to make a seat opposite the beadle's seat so that they may hold up their children to be baptised." If no father could be found for a child, or if the father refused to present his child, then another man had to be found to present the child and engage to see it brought up at school.

Proclamation of the banns of marriage was then on three successive Sundays. On one occasion proclamation was stopped by a woman before completion. She was asked to give willingly to the poor for this breach of Church law. She refused, however, and was forthwith ordered to pay two rix dollars to the poor's box, "with certification that if she did not her goods would be poinded." If after the banns were fully published no marriage took place, the parties became guilty of "mocking the kirk," and were fined a rix dollar each. "James Allan reported his enquiries regarding the backgoing of the marriage betwixt James Duncan and Mary Smeale, told that each laid the wyte on the other. They were appointed to pay a rix dollar each for the use of the poor for mocking the kirk." By an Act of Session in July, 1695, marriage out of church was not solemnised unless a rix dollar was given for the poor, and this Act was renewed in February, 1704.

In those times the Sacrament of the Lord's Supper was celebrated even less frequently than now. But this defect was made up for in some measure by the habit of receiving of all celebrations of the Sacraments in neighbouring parishes. And it was not only held that by baptism we become members of the Church, but also that all who had come to the years of discretion, were free from scandal and lived a religious life, had a right to sit at the Lord's Table. Of their qualifications, however, the session were judges, and their warrant was the leaden token of admission to the Communion. "The Sacrament of the Lord's Supper being to be celebrate at Mid-Calder, Sabbath next, appoint such who are known to be prayers and keepers of family worship to have testificats for receiving tokens there."

At the very beginning the session "ordained that none were to be buried between sermons, especially in the summer time." While a little later it was ordained that the bell for lifting was not to be rung by the beadle within one hour before or half an hour after public service—the week-day service for exposition of Scripture.

VIII.

The Kirk Session were the Parish Council of those days, and undertook the sole charge of the poor. They paid for the education of poor children at school; they gave the beadle payment for digging graves for the poor, and the wright payment for making their coffins. The beadle received six pence Scots (a halfpenny of our money) per grave, and the wright forty shillings Scots (three shillings and fourpence of our money) for six "mort coffins." A poor woman complained that she had no clothes to go to church in, and an elder was appointed to buy her a coat and jacket. Two sailors from the parish had been taken and made slaves to the Turks. The elders began a collection for their ransom, and appealed for fuller help to the Presbytery of Linlithgow. They took collections so that poor "lads o' pairts" from the parish might attend the University. They helped "broken," *i.e.*, shipwrecked seamen—"Ordained James Wilson to give forty shillings to a poor Virginia man broken at sea, to help him to Newcastle." The session found a minister's widow in great destitution, and they gave her twelve shillings. They made a collection for the sufferers by the great fire at the Canongate Head, Edinburgh, and by the fire at Queensferry. They made a collection also for Kinkell Harbour.

The sums quoted are always in Scots money, in which £1 is equal to twenty pence sterling, one shilling to one penny sterling, and one penny one-twelfth of a penny sterling. There are thus £12 Scots in £1 sterling.

How did the session provide even for the ordinary necessities of the poor, especially at a time when there was much poverty? They had the ordinary church collections, and if there was special need they had special collections. They relied also on the fees exacted for the performance of all duties of an ecclesiastical character. We are told that the baptisms in Mr. Park's time, under Episcopacy, were first 14s., afterwards 6s., now 18s; marriages 50s.—30s. for the poor, 14s. for the schoolmaster, and 7s. for the beadle. The session appoints now "the schoolmaster to have the marriages 40s., whereof 16s. might be given to the poor, 4s. to the doctor—assistant schoolmaster—6s. 8d. to the beadle, the rest he might keep to himself."

There were also payments for proclamation of banns, and various fines.

IX.

But the principal source of revenue from dues was, it would seem, dues charged for the use of the mortcloth. These dues were at first £3 for the mortcloth and 30s. for the little mortcloth. In 1693 materials for a new mortcloth were brought by one of the elders from Edinburgh, and £40 in all were spent on these and its making up. The session gave the use of the mortcloth without charge to those unable to pay. But two matters connected with the mortcloth produced much worry. The seamen got a mortcloth of their own. As a very serious diminution of their revenues would have taken place if it were used, the session remitted the matter to the Presbytery. The dispute went on, and we find it recorded that "James Hart, Duncan Allan, and James Wilson are to speak to their respective masters to see if they will join with the session in interposing their authority for warranding the beadle not to open the kirkyard gate nor make a grave to any who shall have the seamen's mortcloth till they pay into the Eleemosynar (the keeper of the mortcloth) 20s. for the meikle and 10s. for the little mortcloth; as also the said elders to commune with the seamen anent the same." A compromise seems to have been arranged, in all probability on these terms. The second matter remained a source of constant trouble. People who got the use of the mortcloth would not pay the dues. It was ordained that the keeper of the mortcloth give it to no one until he either receive payment or ample security. And finally the clerk was instructed to give a written order to Thomas Knox, constable, "for calling for money for the mortcloths from such as owes for the use of them." But even this was not enough, so the session fell back on the last resource of all creditors, and handed the dues over to a lawyer to collect.

Dues were also charged for the erection of headstones. These, too, got into arrear. But a more summary method regarding them could be and was taken. The people who had erected headstones were severally informed that "if they did not pay five merks at once their headstanes would be cast over the church dyke."

Before passing from the subject of the care of the poor, we notice one or two curious examples of the session's action in this respect. "It was ordained anent one William Hardie, a poor, sick man, the session orders a chopin of honey, with such materials as are prescribed by doctors to be put with it to be given to him," while they gave a woman "a rix dollar to help to pay the doctor for cutting off her finger." And they paid £3 to another doctor for endeavouring "to cure a woman with a distemper," *i.e.*, insane.

The sum obtained from the collections, fines, dues (other than mortcloth dues), amounted from July, 1695, to July, 1696, to £561 12s.; while the amount spent on the poor in the same period was £533 17s. 2d., leaving a balance of £27 14s. 10d. For the mortcloth there was received during the same period £202 9s., and from this fund there was spent £44 18s., leaving a balance of £157 10s. 6d. The mortcloth fund accumulated, and was lent out at 5 per cent.

X.

After the Church comes the School. The old Parish School stood on the vacant triangular bit of ground at the Muirhouses in the angle between the Linlithgow and Miller Pit roads. A copy of the deed of gift of this ground by Hamilton of Grange, in 1636, still exists. Besides this school there were a number of "pettie" schools which were seemingly but rooms in the houses of the teachers. That the Kirk Session had great zeal for education, and that they adopted the most thorough-going methods in order to secure the efficient instruction of the children of the parish is amply proved by the records. Over all schools they exercised the very strictest supervision, discharging all the functions of the School Board, save that they asked no yearly contributions from rates, and even to a certain extent taking the place of the Education Department. There was constant friction between the "pettie" schools and the parish school, and this friction must have been one of the session's trials. That there may be impartial judgment in this matter, it is well to remember that the parish schoolmaster was also the session clerk.

The parish schoolmaster was nominally appointed by the session and heritors—virtually by the session only. He was paid his salary by the heritors. This salary, however, required to be augmented by fees. To the schoolmaster an assistant, who was termed "the doctor in the school," was granted by the session, who paid for his services the salary of £24 Scots (£2 sterling), and assigned him a share of certain dues. It is interesting to follow the story of one of those "doctors" under the Kirk Session—John Currie. Three years after his appointment it was ordained that "Duncan Allan and William Halliday intimate to the doctor of the school not to be found reading his own book in school when he ought to wait on the teaching of the children, which if he be found to do the session will take notice of it."

Apparently John Currie did not receive this monition in the spirit of meekness, for in September—the reproof had been administered in February—a minute reads—"It being complained by the schoolmaster that one John Currie, who was doctor to the public school, had deserted the said schoole and had gethered a schoole at Grangepans to the great prejudice of the public schoole, David Jamieson and Alexander Duncan are ordered to goe in the session's name and discharge him from keeping the said schoole, and to take the books from the children and to put them out of doors; and certifie the said Currie that, if he offer again to convene, the session will refer him to the magistrate." At the next meeting of session "Alexander Duncan and David Jamieson reported their diligence in obeying the session's appointment in discharging John Currie his keeping of schoole, and their putting forth the children; but that he had since convened his schoole, and said he would keep it whether the minister and session would or not. The session therefore referred it to the Laird of Bonhard, Baylie of the Regalitie of Borrowstounness, to take such cause with him as accords, which the said Laird of Bonhard did in every point to the satisfaction of the session." Good fortune, however, came to John Currie. He was offered the appointment to a school by the Kirk Session of Borrowstounness Parish. But he could not accept it, could not, indeed, it would appear, live in that parish till he got a certificate of good character from the Parish of Carriden. This gave the session their advantage, and they knew how to use it. "John Currie, compearing, and craving a testificat to Borrowstounness, was refused the samen till he gave it under his hand that he should receive no children from this Parish of Carriden to Borrowstounness, where he had a call to be a schoolmaster, and to get two of the representatives there as caution for him to the effect above mentioned."

XI.

The Kirk Session had thorough control over the pettie schools. They visited and examined them frequently. But these schools acted to the prejudice of the public school, in their opinion. For example, we are told that "One William Ross, at Blackness, was discharged from keeping schoole in prejudice of the public school." Then it was found that children, though the elders deemed they should, would not leave the pettie schools and attend the public school. Elders were, for instance, appointed to "visit David Cathcart's schoole and write down the names of such as were able to come to the public schoole, and to testify to him that if he put not them away speedily the session would close his schoole altogether." David Cathcart was an elder, and he seems to have laid this matter so to heart that he no longer sat in session. The master of another of the pettie schools was offered the post of doctor in succession to Currie—partly in order that his own school at Bonhard might be shut by his acceptance. He would not accept, however, "and the session passed from their offer and ordained him to leave the parish."

Grangepans was specially guarded against pettie schools. One minute "appoints Robert Jamieson and James Wilson to goe discharge Sarah Small, in Grangepans, she not having the session's allowance conform to the order of Presbytery." In this case the session's action was amply upheld by future events. Sarah Small appears again in the record in quite another connection. "Sarah Small and Margaret Robertson, dilated for fighting and flyting, were ordered to be summoned against the next day." Next day "Margaret Robertson cited and compearing, denyed it, but told that Sarah Small strake her on the face, rave the toy off her head, and dang her to the ground, and did cast a dauner in at her door. Sarah Small, compearing, denyes all that Robertson said of her, and complains that the said Robertson called her a witch thief." Witnesses were called, who proved conclusively that each was guilty of what the other alleged against her, and even of more besides.

The session took care that the teachers of the pettie schools should at any rate know something about their duties. Here is an example of several cases of the kind that might be quoted—"John Hart and William Bryce to visit Jean Donaldson's school and take notice and tryall of her if she can teach the children by syllabling the words."

As we have said, the Kirk Session was the School Board of those old days. And no School Board now discharges its duties so thoroughly as did the Kirk Session of Carriden in the end of the seventeenth century. It frequently ordained certain of its number—never including the minister, however, for some reason we could not discover—to visit and examine the schools. These elders reported the results of their visits and examinations, and frequently commented very favourably on "the children's proficiency and the schoolmaster's diligence." They brought no unfavourable reports—at least, no such reports are recorded. The elders were the School Board officer themselves. A very common appointment was that all or some of them should go round the parish and press the parents to send their children to school. In cases in which this had no effect, parents were summoned before the session and rebuked, while a promise was extracted that they "would have a care in future to send their children to school." When smart children were discovered, they had prizes assigned them for their encouragement in learning. At little cost, far too little cost, good educational work was done in Scotland of those old days, and she was then first of nations in the matter of education. Though one of the elders and the schoolmaster had to make and mend the seats, that did not prevent children in the public school of Carriden getting such an education as enabled them to proceed straight to the University of Edinburgh.

XII.

In its control of the general affairs of the parish and its influence on the life of the people, the Kirk Session owed its power to its ecclesiastical position, to the favour for Presbyterianism, to the strong religious feeling that prevailed—a feeling that had been largely augmented by the persecutions of the Covenanting times. Besides, there was no other authority to do the work which greatly needed doing. The session was a compact body, of the people and constantly among the people; there were no Dissenters; and if there were any Episcopalians they had to be very quiet, while no Roman Catholic dared profess his faith.

The great concern of the session was the religious condition of the people. But we cannot separate religion from daily life and morality—the widespread ramifications of moral questions brought the Kirk Session as a Court, to which was committed the spiritual rule of the parish, into contact with every phase of the life of its people. And it was felt to have power even beyond that which belonged to it as a Court of the Church. If the Church of Scotland no longer made and unmade kings, its support was more a necessity to the civil power than was the favour of the civil power to the Church.

We must remember the times were still most unsettled, and that although the great mass of the people were peaceable and orderly, there was a large roving population of evil habits and bad character.

The session were possessed by the idea that by all means the parish must be preserved from the presence, influence, and contamination of this most undesirable element. And, further, it was impossible for them to allow "randie beggars," as they termed them, to settle in the parish and become a burden on the liberality of its people, who were frequently taxed to the utmost to provide for their own poor.

It would seem from the numberless notices dealing with the matter that almost the greatest trouble the session had was the "resetting"—not for a night or a short time, but through the letting to them of rooms and houses—of these "undesirables." Doubtless there was considerable weight in the pecuniary benefits they must have received, and fear of the consequences of refusal, while the sympathy of the poor with the poor would have effect. Still, one cannot help wondering why many of the people persisted in sheltering these wanderers, especially as most lamentable misfortunes befel some of them through so doing, and the wrath of the Kirk Session was not a thing to be despised. Now the session summon a man for resetting randie beggars. Then they appeal to Sir Walter Seaton of Northbank to "extrude randie beggars" out of his houses. Judgment of extrusion was passed on one Margaret Falconer, who is termed not only a "randie beggar" but also "an intolerable fiery scold." But Margaret refused to vacate. The session appealed to the Laird of Bonhard; he was the resident magistrate and she tenanted one of his houses. Bonhard, however, though usually very ready to carry out the session's behests, gave in this case, for some reason or other, the ambiguous answer that "he would think about the extruding of Margaret Falconer." On another occasion, to give one more instance, Bonhard was asked to "extrude one Alexander Taylor out of the parish as being a person unworthy of any Christian society." Again, several elders were appointed to "speak to the resetters of those thieves at the Muiredge." And at last a general intimation was made that "no one was to set houses to such as could not maintain themselves and had not a testificat."

The "testificat" played a very important part indeed in parish life. No one was allowed to remain in the parish—if the session could help it—save he or she brought a testificat from the last parish lived in, stating that he or she had removed from it "free from all public scandal." Bonhard was an Episcopalian, and did not attend the Parish Church, but had a chaplain of his own. Powerful though he was, and greatly though the session were indebted to him, they at once demanded the production of Bonhard's chaplain's testificat. Bonhard's servants had also to produce testificats, as had those of Carriden House. "Two gentlemen lately come to the parish" were forthwith waited upon by the elders and asked for their testificats. If these were not forthcoming, those whose houses were occupied by persons not possessing them, or in whose service they were, were at once commanded to turn them out or dismiss them. This command was not always promptly obeyed. One woman told the session that "she would keep her woman servant from the north whether the session would or no." The session replied that a testificat must be produced or she herself would be dealt with. This was enough. Even when produced, testificats were not always approved. Either they were not free from ambiguity or the persons were not properly vouched for. On the other hand, when people leaving the parish sought testificats they were not always granted. To a woman who asked one the reply was given that it would not be granted "till she had first purged herself of that scandal of fighting with her neighbours." The desire to be rid of an undesirable parishioner was not so strong as the determination to enforce righteous punishment and to support general principles of government. Thus the power of the testificat was twofold. No one who had entered the parish could remain in it without producing one. No one intending to leave the parish dared depart without obtaining one. It is instructive to note that at one session meeting testificats were granted to parishioners going to Holland, Flanders, and Ireland. Inquisition, demand, and threats could not bring testificats from all nor secure the expulsion of all who could not produce them. When these means failed, the session drew up what is termed "a list of vagabonds and others not having testificats," and gave it to Bonhard that he might proceed according to civil law. But no more than the session was Bonhard successful. However, the session then agreed to "ask Bonhard to grant a general warrand to Thomas Knox, constable, for answering the minister and session in any business they may have to doe with at any time." This was granted. Thomas, in obedience to instructions, set about ordering all not having testificats out of the parish. On more than one occasion we find Thomas Knox asks and receives "something for his pains" from the session. Testificats were demanded from those who came from Bo'ness, and we are tempted to think that no love was lost on that parish when we read that the session appointed one of the elders "to goe and advise that woman who came from Borrowstounness to goe out of the parish."

XIII.

The eyes of the session were everywhere, and, like a famous professor, what they did not know of parish life (and deal with, too) was not knowledge. A man was summoned "for falsifying a deed of write." And a man had to appear for "committing a ryot in the house of William Halliday," one of the elders. William Bryce was appointed "to challenge John Twell for not being more vigorous in obeying the Laird of Bonhard's commands and the session's orders." George Walker was told that "the session was much displeased he should keep a woman that scolds her neighbours and otherwise miscarries." A man was summoned for having produced "bad blood" between himself and a neighbour by taking that neighbour's house "over his head." Elspeth Waldie was reproved for "haunting a trooper's company," and William Robertson's sister for "singing profane songs on the Coal Hill." "William Halliday, dilating that he had been informed anent some that had been too late on Saturday night, is ordered to see who they were and report next day." Again, "John Waldie dilated Patrick M'Carter and John Miller for goeing through the towne of Bonhard on Mundayes night with drawn knives in their hands and saying they would defy all the towne." These men were then summoned. Miller compeared, M'Carter didn't, and was summoned a second time. Miller denied the charges against him. He was asked why he had a "naked knife." He answered "it was to cut his ain craigcloth, because he was like to be choked therewith by people that fell upon him." At another meeting M'Carter compeared and answered "that he stroke at them that were struggling with John Miller." He denied he was drunk, but confessed he drew a knife "because it behoved him to do so when others came out with grapes against him."

James White's wife is reproved "for playing at the cards and entertaining strangers too late on Saturday night." John Burnet and James Henderson, in Northbank, are reproved for their foolish jesting and offering to sell and buy the said Henderson's wife. And the session permitted no tyranny. "James Hart and James Allan are appointed to reprove John Main and his wife for their too much severitie and insulting over the workmen of Grange Works." The session tendered its warmest thanks to William Waldie, factor to Bonhard, for whipping the miners for cursing and swearing. A woman was severely rebuked for calling her neighbour "a Cameronian jade"—a term of obloquy that tells its own tale of the bitterness of ecclesiastical disputes. David Callender was rebuked for his idleness in running away from his work. Again, "Elspeth Dick, in Grange, having presented a complaint before the session wherein she complains that James Henderson and others have, to her reproach and abuse of her good name, made some base rymes which they had in write, and that the coal grieves had the double thereof, and therefore craved that the session would take notice thereof and suppress the samen. The session recommend it to John Hardie and James Brown to reprove these persons and to call for such papers from them, and burn those papers, and withal to certifie them that if they be found to spread or sing such papers or reproachful songs of her or any else, they will be proceeded against by the session."

A report reached the session that a master had beaten his servant most severely, and that the man had died in the field shortly after. They set themselves to inquire into the matter at once. A boy stole clothes from a neighbour's house. He had to appear before the session and sustain a sharp rebuke, while he was threatened with much worse things should he offend again. And Elspeth Cumming was dilated "for going aboord from Grangepans to a ship with ale to the sojers her alone and staying with them some time." The matter was referred to the Baylie of Grangepans[1] to imprison her for some space.

XIV.

If the offence reported upon—dilated, as it was styled—was slight, the session simply informed the delinquent if he did not amend "the session would take notice of him"—a threat terrible enough. The session, as a regular Court summoned by their officer, accused parties before them. If they deemed that the matter was not a grave scandal, and the party appeared and made a full confession, with profession of determination to amend, then it ended with a "sessional rebuke" and "a certification to carry himself warily for the future or he would have to suffer public rebuke." If the offence was really of a scandalous character, then a public rebuke was administered

---

[1] The Baron Bailie of Grange Estate.

It consisted in sitting on the "black stoole" of repentance before the congregation on three successive Sabbaths. Frequently, and more frequently as time went on, offenders did not appear when summoned. But, according to the form of process which is still the law of the Church and of the land, nothing could be done until they were summoned three times.

The form of process was therefore gone through, the session taking care when appointing the officer to make the third citation to appoint also two elders to give warning personally of the consequences of disobedience to the third summons. This third citation was seldom disobeyed, and when disregarded, the parties usually took the precaution of removing themselves from the parish.

When the form of process had been completed and there was still no compearance, the parties were straightway declared from the pulpit to be contumacious and disobedient, and were suspended from all Church privileges. But if they had not left the parish, the matter, as a rule, never ended there. Sometimes they were passed on to the Laird of Bonhard to be imprisoned or fined. In one place we read, "It was reported that the Laird of Bonhard, in obedience to the session's reference to him, had imprisoned William Crookston, who had now given all securitie to conform himself to the session's demands." And again we find that when a man was cited and did not compear, "the session referred it to the Baylie of Borrowstounness to cause his officer apprehend and secure him till he find caution to answer the session when called." Sometimes suspected parties would not confess. For them there was frequently a sharp remedy. Such a case occurred, and "it was referred to the Baylie of Borrowstounness to cast them into prison till they confessed their presumed adultery." From time to time a list of scandalous and disobedient persons was sent to the Justices of the Peace, that those who would not satisfy ecclesiastical demands might feel the force of the power temporal. And on one or two occasions the Justices wrote and asked the session for such a list. For instance, "A letter from the Clerk to the Justices of the Peace direct to the minister and session was read desiring that the session give up all the fornicators and other delinquents in the parish against Tuesday next." As an effect of these conjoined measures few remained long in the parish who had been declared scandalous and disobedient without humbly coming forward to crave the removal of their censure and to promise to sit obediently on the "black stoole."

We sometimes wonder if the behaviour of all those who thus sat in open confession was always to edification. Certainly it was not in a case reported to us and vouched for by an eye-witness in another Parish Church. In this church the session insisted that the penitent should put on a white sheet. The particular delinquent on this occasion, during one of the long prayers, to the great edification of the congregation, who were "standing glowering about them, as usual," adroitly slipped the sheet off her shoulders and placed it gently on those of one of the elders who was standing near with bowed head and shut eyes.

XV.

Let us look at the Kirk Session in all its plenitude of power as it is pictured in the language regarding itself. They were not in office after the Revolution six months before an elder dilated a woman for cursing the minister and session. "Whereupon she was ordained to sit upon the stoole and receave a public rebuke for these things the first Lord's Day, with a certification that if she did not sit thereupon she would be declared scandalous and disobedient. But she not sitting upon the stoole, was declared scandalous and disobedient, the whole session assenting." On another occasion an elder, in the course of his visitation, was stigmatised by a woman as "an auld doited ——." Not long after another woman was cited before the session for calling an elder "a slave and ane hypocrite rascal." Two elders were "ordained to go to Eupham Brown, spouse to John Wilson, coal hewer, and sharply rebuke her for her un-Christian expressions regarding William Halliday, and for opening her mouth against other elders, and show that if she be found in the like fault the session would proceed against her severely."

Here is a case of bold bearing before the session as a Court. William Hosie, cited and compearing, being asked why he should have taken in another man's wife to his house, he being alone, and that it was very scandalous, did irreverently and un-Christianly make answer, saying, "By his faith, he did no hurt or harm by keeping house with that woman for his servant." Being rebuked for his rash and irreverent carriage in swearing in face of the minister and session, answered again, "By his faith he did not evil; he behoved to keep a servant," adding that none within the parish could prove scandal upon him. He being put forth during the session's deliberations, it was concluded to refer him to the civil magistrate. And being called in, it was told him that he behoved "to be ane of a most wicked and flagitious practice, which was clearly evident by that his base and un-Christian bearing in the face of a reverent minister and session, which he ought to look upon as a Court of Christ." He was told he would be given up to the civil magistrate; hereupon he left the parish and he was referred to the Sheriff-Depute of Linlithgow. The following extract gives us a realistic picture of a woman of independent mind and unrestrained tongue:—"Isabel Anderson dilated for not frequenting the kirk and for scolding, and for saying she cared neither for minister nor session, and for saying the elders were lying in whoredom, and for bidding her neighbours—(the rest must be unmentioned)—was summoned against the next day."

XVI.

The case of James Kid is so good a picture of life and of the session and its difficulties that we give it in full—"The session appoints William Bryce and James Brown to goe forthwith and reprove James

Kid, at Burnfoot, for abusing his wife and striking her, and to certifie to him that the session will not suffer any such base carriage in him or any other, but will give him up and over to the Justices of the Peace." At next meeting "the elders reported their speaking to James Kid, who took their reproof indifferently satisfying; promised to give obedience to the session; also promised for the future to carry more calmly upon condition that his wife do not at any time provoke him by contradicting him in such and such things as he warns her not to meddle with him therein." The session's dealings with Mr. Kid were not allowed to end there. Exactly a year after we find "James Kid cited and compearing, was told that the session had dealt very kindly with him in their forbearing him, whereas he had, after four or five times summoning, never compeared, but added to all others his miscarriages contumacie. To which he, in proud, irreverent manner, not dis-covering his head, answered that he had sent word he could not win. Was challenged why he strake and beat to the ground the church officer. Denyed he strake him to the ground, but said why was the kirk officer meddling with his ground which he had paid for. Was told that that ground was none of his. Answered, by his faith, it was his, and he would make it appear soe to be. Was challenged for frequent beating and abusing his wife. He stiffly denyed, but said she carryed like a beast to him, and put it to the session to prove it. Being urged to tell whether he strake her: answered the session must prove it; and again answered by his faith he would be wronged by none, for he was a credit to his name, and would quit the life before he would be wronged by any. The session dismisses him and refers him to the Baylie of Borrowstounness."

The quarrels of husbands and wives have been subjects of animadversion since the world began, and they crop up at almost every meeting. One woman is reported to "weep late and air, and that her husband shuts her out when he can get no peace with her din." Even the following is found—"Ordains John Anderson and George Muphray to reprove. John Robertson, elder, and his wife for their scolding and drunkenness."

Here is a one-act drama of married life, with all the stock characters which leaves nothing to be desired in the energy of its actors—

"Witnesses in regard to the fighting one with another of David Callender, his wife, mother-in-law, and others testified: That Callender's wife came to John Miller's door when he himself and his wife were in bed, desiring him for God's sake to come and help, for her husband would kill both her and her brother; and that when he and his wife, Elspeth Dick, rose and went with the said Callender's wife and had come to his mother-in-law's house, they saw the said Callender sitting and swearing, and that when the said Callender went forth, his own wife, his mother-in-law, and others took up stanes and did cast at him and fell in his hair, and Callender's wife did always bid, 'Kill the dog and rive him all in bitts,' and that his mother-in-law swore by her soul she would have amends on the dog to-morrow." These parties did not appear, and were referred to the magistrate.

We are afraid part at least of the following could be paralleled at the present day. Witnesses in another case declared "that John Fairney, being drunk, did fall asleep, but that one Katharine Paton, coming into his wife's house, would have him awakened to drink more. His wife offering to hinder the bringing in of any more drink, he swore he would have ale, and would drink with Paton. That he swore he would ding out his wife's harns, and that he took up a rung or cudgell and did beat his wife, and did strike her five or six times."

In another case a man confessed that "he did give his wife a buffet, but that if he did not do so he could have no life with her. He did regrate it, professed sorrow, and besought the minister and session to take some effectual means for her bettering."

XVII.

Here is seemingly a hard case—

"Alexander Nimmo and Elspeth Sleigh, his wife, cited, the man only compearing. Interrogated how it came that he a man designing good should be found to disagree with his wife to the scandal and reproach of religion: Answered that he was very sorry that ever it should have been his sad lot to be so, which he asserted was far against his mind. But it was his sad misfortune to be yoked with a wife that crossed him daily in many ways, but particularly in these things—that she will not frequent ordinances either in coming to the kirk on the Sabbath or the examine on a week day, and that she is a great scold, a great curser and swearer by the name of God, and that she will not join with him in family exercise to worship God: that upon his reproving several her miscarriages and exhorting her to carry otherwayes, she arose in a furious manner as one distracted, and strake at him, and took him by the throat, and had almost choaked him; and he, in his own relief and defence, shutting her from him, she fell and bled a little, upon which she cried and clamoured more. He did earnestly beg and entreat that the session would take some effectual way, as in their wisdom they thought most convenient, whereby to bring her to carry in some ways more soberly."

It all ended with the denunciation of her misdeeds from the pulpit before the congregation.

The appearance of such faults as cursing and swearing are, like the "cursing of one Jean Hog," "frequent and ordinary." Once a man gave the ingenious excuse for a fall into this sin that at the time he "was almost brained by a fall in the coalpit." It would not be to edification to cite examples of the oaths employed, even although they were frequently both vigorous and graphic. And, of course, there are other sins that must be allowed to pass without notice, which are yet frequently enough in evidence. Drunkenness, too, would seem to have been very rife, and Sunday drinking is specially noted.

Soldiers were a sad trouble to the session in many ways. There was a garrison at Blackness and a camp at Balderston. Thus it came to pass that "James Anderson is ordered to complain to the Governors of Blackness and Balderston regarding the debaucherie in Jean Grant's house with the soldiers." Other elders were ordered to "rebuke the coalbearers for haunting the camp at Balderston as casting themselves in a fountain of filthiness." Also, "Some soldiers having been found drunk at or about the Murrays on Sabbath last, the session refers to William Halliday and Arthur Pollock to enquire who they were and where they got the drink."

The relations of neighbours with each other had frequently to be dealt with. It was the frequent endeavour of the session to have them "at peace and charity with each other." Two elders are appointed "to goe and cause William Ellis and James Savage's wife shake hands." Very frequently neighbours are summoned before the session for "fighting and flyting" with each other. As, for example, it was reported that "Agnes Mitchell declared she would be Marion M'Cunn's death or she hers, while Marion had called Agnes a drunken jade"—and they were cited to appear. A woman was summoned for praying that her neighbour "might have a sad and cold armful of her husband."

Barbara M'Vey is summoned for calling a man "an ill-faured thief" and his wife a witch. She had been taking a lapful of dung out of this man's yard when his wife came out and stopped her procedure. Upon this the expressions complained of were employed. Barbara was referred to the Justices of the Peace.

XVIII.

For scolds like this woman there was a peculiar form of punishment, the "jougs" or scold's bridle, examples of which are still preserved, attached in some cases to the gates of the Parish Churches. In Carriden they were not the peculiar adornment of the fair sex alone, and a good supply must have been in existence judging by the following:—

"Appoints a recommendation to Walter and Alexander Moodie, coal grieves, and John Main, oversman to the works of Grange, that they put such of the workpeople or bearers under their charge whom they hear or know to be banners, cursers, swearers, or scolders, in the jougs, and cause them to stand therein such quantitie of time to the terror of others, their doing of which the minister and session will take as good service done to God and His Church." This recommendation was accepted and obeyed to the session's satisfaction.

"Hooligans" were found even in those days. But they met with a summary and effective method of treatment. "Appoints James Wilson and Archibald Nimmo to speak to Edward Hodge and John Craig, skippers, anent two vagabond boys called the Pods, because of their idleness in the place, refusing to work, although they might be employed about the coal-works, and for their lewd, cursed life and practice, and their giving a bad example to the children of the place, to see if they will take them away over sea and let them goe to any who can make use of them."

The session had much to do in order to enforce the due observance of their religious duties by the people of the parish. There were two services in the church every Lord's Day. Then there were, besides, the weekly "Exercise"—a week-day exposition of Scripture, and the "Examine" or catechising, held in the various districts of the parish in turns. At all these the people, "not being let or hindered," were expected to attend. On one occasion a general catechising by the elders was ordered—"It was recommended to all the elders in their respective quarters to pose the people with these queries at the taking up of the names to the examine—(1) If they have a Bible; (2) If they read a part thereof each night; (3) If they have a catechism; (4) If they pray with their families; (5) Whether they keep their children at school; (6) Whether they have been examined formerly, and how oft; (7) If there be any wants testificats, to call for them."

The session set themselves to enforce attendance at the church and at the "Examine." Let us point out some of their methods and give some examples of their action. First of all it was ordained that the elders go through now Blackness, then Northbank, then Grangepans on the following Lord's Day and note those who were unnecessarily absent from church. Following on this comes this appointment, 3rd March, 1696—"The session, from this time forth till summer be over, appoints the elder with his colleague who collects this Sabbath to goe through the several quarters of the parish, especially the Waterside, at the next Sabbath after the collection, and notice who may be absent from sermon needlesslie, or who are vaging in the fields or found tippling and drinking." On 26th March following Alexander Duncan reported that "he was through the parish on Sabbath last, and found nothing but closed doors." And again, not long afterwards, it was resolved that the elders should go through the parish now and then on Sabbath and see who were out of the kirk. About a year after there was a specific appointment to John Anderson and James Brown to go through the parish next Sabbath "to observe if they find any debaucherie and to see if they find any absent from church without sufficient ground." With regard to individual examples of "not keeping the kirk" or "not haunting the kirk," as it was indifferently styled, we have a man who was told that "if he came not next Sabbath he will be declared scandalous and disobedient," and another who is summoned for striking his wife and not keeping the kirk. Again, a man is summoned "for setting his house to a man who keeps not the kirk," while "Doghillock" was referred to the Sheriff "for his constant withdrawing from ordinances, his drinking, playing at cartes, mocking at religion and religious persons, a night vager, and others." But even when people attended church their behaviour evidently sometimes left something to be desired. For example, during sermon one day there was a regular fight in the kirk loft, in which there was reported afterwards "great effusion of blood."

XIX.

Strict observance of the Sabbath, Fast, and Thanksgiving Days was enforced, and those who did not attend "the dyett" of examination in their district were summoned and rebuked. "Doghillock," a very great offender, yoked his cart on the Thanksgiving Day, and was referred to the Sheriff. John Humphray was ordained to speak to John Anderson "against this grievance for not giving kindling coals to the salters, so that they are forced to keep fire at the pans on the Lord's Day, notwithstanding (as they say) their master allows them." There are frequent rebukes for shearing and working on the Fast Day. Elders were appointed to speak to Walton about some of his family pulling lint on the Fast Day. Helen Annieson was summoned "for setting plants on the Fast Day." She said she did not know it was a sin, and also added that "if she had known it would have been offensive to the minister and session she would not have done it."

Offences against the keeping of the Sabbath are still more numerous than even those against the keeping of the Fast Day. "It was reported to the session that many of the men employed about the coal works of Grange were working all the day on Sabbath last, and that even the cart-horses were employed carting bricks and other materials to a fire engine, which had given universal offence, as it could not be construed a work of necessity, nor a work that could be finished in one day, or attended with any other loss than every man in a Christian congregation must sustain by not being allowed to oblige their servants and horses to work on the Lord's Day, and thereby loses their labour every seventh day of the week, and must against their will delay till Munday what they could wish to do on the Lord's Day. . . . The session, having considered the matter, agreed to summon these people to compear on Sabbath first after worship to hear what reasons they can give for what seems a contempt of the Christian laws both of God and of the country." This was in 1772.

Three women went aboard a ship lying off Grangepans on a Sunday to visit the sailors, and had to appear before the session and give "satisfaction" before the congregation. A man was "advised" by the session "not to sell drink on the Sabbath, excessively or otherwise," on pain of being reported to the Governor of Blackness. William Halliday was appointed to reprove a woman "for taking in her green kale to the pot on Sabbath." In connection with brewing, it was ordained that no one was to begin "masking" after 12 noon on Saturday. Isabel Herrick was forbidden to beg at the kirk style on Sabbath, and William Bryce was appointed to "tell John Tarbet, officer, to read what public papers he is appointed to read at the kirk style and not the kirk door." These, of course, do not strictly refer to breaches of the Sabbath, and are only mentioned in this connection. And it was agreed that "intimation be made that noe masters of families" (the phrase is both characteristic and suitable) "suffer their children or servants to vage either in time of divine service or before or after sermon." It was appointed that "any elder in his respective quarters should notice if they see any children playing or others vaging on the Sabbath day. James Hart and Robert Johnston are appointed to rebuke Henry Anderson for selling ale and milk on the Sabbath Day and for not keeping the kirk."

"It is recommended to John Anderson and William Halliday to take notice of those who after sermon gethers at the Braeheads and other places breaking the Sabbath, and to report." Robert Johnstone and John Waldie were appointed to "reprove people in the Muiredge who suffer their child to goe forth to play in companies on the Sabbath afternoon."

We have numerous examples which prove that the parish churches in many cases were at this time of very small size. Taking into account the fact that the Parish Church was the only place of worship, how did it accommodate all the people if these drastic methods were as successful as one would suppose they must have been? Or, after all, was there a great deal of non-churchgoing in spite of despotic authority and its most rigorous employment?

We have striven to give some idea of the story told by the Kirk Session records of those far-off times. We must leave you to point your own moral, draw your own conclusions, and make your own criticisms. Be it remembered, however, in our reflections that the times were sadly out of joint and discipline greatly needed; and, above all, that the people who were nurtured under such a règime as that of the Scottish Kirk Session are the people who have made the name of Scotland great, and to no nation do Scottish people yield in love of liberty and freedom, explain the matter how we may.

Note.—In this lecture Mr. Dundas also dealt with the cases of Witchcraft and Superstition in the Parish revealed in the Records. These, however, have with his consent been incorporated in the text of the chapter on Witchcraft.

APPENDIX II.

THE HOUSE OF HAMILTON.[1]

Nos. 1 and 6-14 of the undernoted are more particularly referred to in Chapter II.

1. Walter Fitz-Gilbert—Walter, the Son of Gilbert.

2. David Fitz-Walter Fitz-Gilbert succeeded his father probably before 1346, and carried on main line of Hamilton. David was one of the Barons

[1] See Scots Peerage, vol. iv., pp. 339-397.

in the Parliament of Scotland when the succession to the Crown was settled on John, Earl of Carrick, and his successors. His seal is reported to be still attached, and around the shield are the words—"Sigill David Filii Walteri." Date of death indefinite.

3. David Hamilton, his son and heir, is said to be the first of the family who formally took the surname. He was alive in 1381, but date of death indefinite. One of his sons was the ancestor of the Hamiltons of Bathgate.

4. John, or as he became Sir John of Cadzow, succeeded his father before 1392. Three years after he granted the lands of Bawdriston or Balderston to Adam Forrester of Corstorphine.

5. James Hamilton of Cadzow is named son and heir to his father, Sir John, in a writ in 1397 granting him the lands of Kinneil. Died before 1440.

6. James Hamilton, the eldest son succeeded, and was first to take prominent place in Scottish history. Became the first Lord Hamilton.

7. James, second Lord Hamilton and first Earl of Arran, son of the preceding by the Princess Mary. A Regent during part of minority of James V. Died about 1529.

8. James, second Earl of Arran, succeeded his father while a minor. Governor of Scotland during minority of Queen Mary. Duchy of Chatelherault in France granted the Earl. Died, Hamilton, 1574 or 1575.

9. John, afterwards first Marquis of Hamilton, third son of preceding. Advanced in Royal favour. Advised the King, James VI., in all matters of sport. A staunch Protestant. Died, April, 1604.

10. James, second Marquis, succeeded his father at 15. Attended King James VI. on his visit to Scotland, 1617. Created a Peer of England and a Knight of the Garter. Died suddenly at Whitehall, March, 1625.

11. James, third Marquis and first Duke. Succeeded father at age of 19. Became intimate with Charles I. Sent by King to put down disturbances over Laud's Service Book. Executed at Westminster, 1649.

12. William, second Duke, brother of the preceding. Mortally wounded at Battle of Worcester, 1657.

13. Anne, Duchess of Hamilton in her own right, succeeded her uncle. Married William, Earl of Selkirk. King Charles II. bestowed on William the courtesy title of Duke of Hamilton for life. The Duke and Duchess did much to extend and develop Bo'ness.

14. James, Earl of Arran, fourth Duke of Hamilton, eldest son of Duchess Anne and Duke William, succeeded five years after his father's death, which occurred in April, 1694, his mother not conveying the titles and lands to him till then. He was then forty-one. Duchess Anne long survived her husband, and even outlived her son by four years. James had an eventful career. He was created Duke of Brandon, and was killed in the celebrated duel with Lord Mohun in 1712.

15. James, fifth Duke of Hamilton and second Duke of Brandon, succeeded his father when about ten years of age. He was three times married. He died, aged forty, in March, 1743.

16. James, sixth Duke of Hamilton, succeeded his father at the age of nineteen. In 1755 he received the Order of the Thistle from George II. He died in England, January, 1758.

17. James George, seventh Duke of Hamilton, succeeded at the age of three. In 1761, by the death of Archibald, Duke of Douglas, the young Duke became the male representative and chief of the House of Douglas. His guardians asserted his right to the Douglas and Angus estates, and this led to the well-known "Douglas Cause." The House of Lords, however, in February, 1769, decided in favour of Mr. Douglas, son of Lady Jane Douglas or Stewart, sister of the Duke of Douglas. The young Duke of Hamilton died the same year, at the age of fourteen.

18. Douglas, brother of the preceding, succeeded as 8th Duke at the age of thirteen. He had as a tutor Dr. John Moore, father of Sir John Moore, the hero of Corunna. The Duke came of age in 1777, and raised a regiment of foot, the 82nd, which distinguished itself in the American War. He put forward the claim that he was entitled to be summoned to Parliament as the Duke of Brandon, and the claim was upheld. Was invested with the Order of the Thistle in 1786. He died at Hamilton, 2nd August, 1799, without issue, and was succeeded by his uncle. The Duke was married in 1778 to Elizabeth Anne, daughter of Peter Burrell, of Beckenham in Kent. It was Douglas who presented the Rev. Robert Rennie with the living of Bo'ness parish. It would seem to be this Duke, who, shortly after his marriage, presented to the town what Dr. Rennie describes as the elegant building, said to be an exact model of Inveraray House, at the head of the harbour. The ground floor was intended for a prison, the second floor for a court room, and the attic storey for a school. The original intention was not carried out, and the building was in 1795 going to ruin. Any rooms in repair were at that time being used as granaries. If the original intention with respect to the use of the building had been carried out, the Doctor says the house would have been highly useful and ornamental to the place. The building collapsed nearly thirty years ago, owing to the mineral workings below. Its tower, however, remained, but was taken down about 1889. A shaft was then opened beside it and material taken down to build up a secure foundation. Thereafter the tower was rebuilt, and still stands securely. At the front is a panel containing the Hamilton coat of arms.

19. Archibald, ninth Duke of Hamilton, uncle of the preceding, succeeded at the age of fifty-nine. He inherited large estates in England both from his mother and his grandmother. Before succeeding to the Dukedom he was for a time M.P. for the county of Lancaster. He died in England 16th February, 1819, and was buried at Lancaster beside his wife, who died before he succeeded to the dukedom. She was the fifth daughter of the sixth Earl of Galloway by his second marriage. They had two sons and three daughters. The sons were Alexander, who succeeded as tenth Duke, and Archibald, for long M.P. for Lanark—an eloquent speaker and a strong opponent of the Administration of Pitt. He exerted himself greatly in the cause of burgh reforms, and died unmarried in 1827.

20. Alexander, tenth Duke, succeeded his father when 52 years of age. He was fond of the fine arts, and spent several years on the Continent in their study. Like his father, he was for a time a Member of Parliament. In 1806, however, he was called to the House of Lords under the title, Baron Dutton. He was named Ambassador to Russia, but resigned office on a change of Ministry. Nevertheless, he travelled largely in Russia and Poland. He died in August, 1852, at the age of 85. The Duke married his cousin, second daughter and co-heir of William Beckford, Font Hill, Gifford, Wiltshire. They had a son, who succeeded, and a daughter Susan.

21. William Alexander Anthony Archibald, eleventh Duke of Hamilton, born February, 1811, succeeded at the age of 41, and died in Paris in July, 1863. In 1843, he married the Princess Mary of Baden, youngest daughter of the reigning Grand Duke of Baden, and the cousin of the late Emperor Napoleon III. They had issue, two sons and one daughter.

The volume of the marriage celebrations of Duke William and the Princess Marie has a few references to Kinneil. There was a great gathering and procession at Hamilton of all the tenantry. Kinneil tenants joined the procession at Larkhall, but no names are given. The battalions from the different parishes in which the Ducal Estates were situated were marshalled and each placed under a Leader. The tenants from each parish wore a distinguishing plant in their hats. Each Leader carried a flag on which was inscribed the name of his parish in gold letters. Kinneil men all wore a sprig of holly in their hats, and they were led by Robert Rutherford, Esq. This gentleman, it would seem, was the Mr. Rutherford, W.S., Edinburgh, who was the Edinburgh agent for the Estate at that time. The tenants were all on horse-back—1500 horsemen altogether. Over 2500 were entertained to dinner in different halls in Hamilton. There was a deal of speech-making, but there is no reference to any orator from Kinneil. The Duke, however, specially thanked the Kinneil men for their presence.

22. William Alexander Louis Stephen, the elder son of the preceding, succeeded as twelfth Duke in 1863 at the age of 18. He was maintained and confirmed by the Emperor Napoleon III. in the title of Duc de Chatelherault in France, 20th April, 1864. He died in 1895, aged 50. The Duke was well-known in sporting and racing circles. He married, in 1873, Mary Montague, eldest daughter of the seventh Duke of Manchester. They had a daughter, Mary Louise, of Brodick Castle, Arran. She was married on 14th June, 1906, to James, the Marquis of Graham, eldest son of the Duke of Montrose.

There were great festivities and rejoicings at Hamilton and elsewhere on the Ducal estate on the coming of age of the twelfth Duke, which occurred 3 years after his succession. These also have been preserved in an interesting volume. His mother, the Princess Marie, Duchess of Hamilton, was held in great affection and esteem, and shared conspicuously in the enthusiastic congratulations. The day of the great event was Monday,

Appendix II. 453

12th March, 1866. Bo'ness held high holiday, and the town was gaily ornamented at various parts with flags. In the afternoon a dinner took place in the Town Hall at which the tenantry, with the gentry of the neighbourhood and the Harbour Trustees of Bo'ness were present. About 100 gentlemen sat down to dinner, during which a band of music performed. The chair was occupied by Mr. Turnbull, Kinneil, supported by James Webster, Esq., Staneacre, Hamilton; the Rev. Mr. Mackenzie and others. Mr. John Begg, Kinneil Ironworks, and Mr. Alexander Kirkwood, farmer, Hainings, discharged the duties of croupiers.

The health of the young Duke was proposed in eulogistic terms by the chairman, and was received by the company with the utmost enthusiasm and drank with all the honours. The Rev. Mr. Mackenzie proposed the health of Her Highness the Duchess of Hamilton. The toast met with a warm and enthusiastic reception.

The foresters and workmen on the estate were entertained to a supper and ball at Kinneil House, while £32 was given to be distributed among the poor. The sum of £15 was given the "old residenters" of Bo'ness, and £5 to the band.

23. Alfred Douglas, thirteenth Duke, son of Captain Charles Henry Douglas Hamilton, R.N., succeeded his kinsman, the preceding Duke, at the age of 33, having been born 6th March, 1862. He is the premier peer of Scotland, heir-male of the House of Douglas, Hereditary Keeper of Holyrood House; late Lieutenant R.N.; claims the Dukedom of Chatelherault. On 4th December, 1901, His Grace married Miss Nina Poore, youngest daughter of Major Robert J. Poore, Wilts. The heir to the Dukedom, the Marquis of Douglas and Clydesdale, was born 3rd February, 1903. There are several other children. In the autumn of 1903 the Duke and Duchess and the infant Marquis of Douglas and Clydesdale paid a private visit to Kinneil House, and there met and entertained their agricultural tenantry. On 17th July, 1908, however, they paid their first public visit to the town, and were presented by the Town Council with an address of welcome. They were most heartily received. The visit coincided with the Annual Children's Festival and the Crowning of the School Queen, Her Grace the Duchess performing the latter ceremony. That same day they entertained the members of the Town Council and representatives of the local public bodies at luncheon in Kinneil house.

In 1911 the Duchess graciously gifted to the town of Bo'ness a Nurses' Home.

The Arms of the Hamilton Family (as recorded in the Lyon Register) are :—

> *Quarterly.*—1st and 4th Grand Quarters Counter-quartered, 1st and 4th, Gules, Three Cinquefoils Ermine; 2nd and 3rd Argent, a Lymphad Sable Sails Furled Proper Flagged Gules; 2nd and 3rd Grand Quarters, Argent, a Man's Heart Gules Ensigned with an Imperial Crown Proper, on a Chief Azure of Three Stars of the First.

Crests.—1st, on a Ducal Coronet an Oak-tree Fructed and Penetrated Transversely in the Main Stem by a Frame Saw Proper, the Frame Or for Hamilton; 2nd, on a Chapeau Gules turned up Ermine a Salamander in Flames Proper, for Douglas.

Supporters.—Two Antelopes Argent, Armed, Gorged, with a Ducal Coronet, Chained and Unguled Or.

Mottoes.—Through: Jamais Arrière.

APPENDIX III.

The following Table may be considered an approximately correct statement of the general section of the Bo'ness Coalfield. It is compiled by Henry M. Cadell, Esq., B.Sc., F.R.S.E., of Grange, and is to be found in a contribution by him on "The Carboniferous Limestone Coalfields of West Lothian," published in vol. xxii., 1901-1902, of the Transactions of The Institution of Mining Engineers.

GENERAL SECTION OF THE BO'NESS COALFIELD.

	Thickness of Strata.	Depth from Surface.	Thickness of Divisions.
MILLSTONE GRIT.			
Upper Division of Limestone Measures.	Feet.	Feet.	Feet.
Craigenbuck or Levenseat Limestone, forming the base of the Millstone Grit, Strata, chiefly sandstones and beds of fireclay, about	300	300	700
Dykeneuk or Calmy Limestone,	...	...	
Strata, including a few thin coal seams, beds of volcanic rock and thick sandstone,	400	700	
Middle or Coal-bearing Division of Limestone Measures.			
Index Limestone 2 to 3 feet,	3	703	
Strata, including two beds of trap, 60 feet thick,	130	833	
Splint Coal Seam, 2½ to 3 feet,	3	836	
Strata,	47	883	
Corbiehall Coal Seam, 2 to 3 feet,	3	886	
Strata, with one thin coal seam,	60	946	
Upper Ironstone and Seven-feet Coal Seam, with ribs of stone,	10	956	950
Strata, with four thin coal seams,	50	1006	
Trap, forming two beds, varying in thickness,	120	1126	
Wester Main Coal Seam or Shales, 12 feet thick in places,	30	1156	
Trap, in one thick bed averaging about	86	1242	

Appendix III.

MILLSTONE GRIT.	Thickness of Strata.	Depth from Surface.	Thickness of Divisions.
Middle or Coal-bearing Division of Limestone Measures.	Feet.	Feet.	Feet.
Wandering Coal Seam variable in thickness or shales,	10	1252	⎫
Trap, in three beds, with strata between,	85	1337	
Strata, generally sandstone,	32	1369	
Red Coal Seam 2½ to 3½ feet,	3	1372	
Strata, including the fireclay coal seam, 1½ feet,	97	1469	
Lower Ironstone, Parrot, and Six-feet Coal Seam, variable in thickness with blaes bands,	20	1489	950
Strata,	38	1527	
Easter Main Coal Seam, 3 to 4½ feet thick,	4	1531	
Strata, with bed of intrusive trap, very variable in thickness and position,	100	1631	
Smithy Coal Seam, 2½ to 3½ feet thick,	3	1634	
Strata,	15	1649	
Carsey Coal Seam, 12 to 20 inches thick,	1	1650	⎭
Lower Division of Limestone Measures.			
Strata, with two thin coal seams,	70	1720	⎫
Carriden Limestone, 2 feet 7 inches thick,	3	1723	
Strata,	97	1820	
Limestone (Hosie Limestone), 3 feet thick,	3	1823	350
Strata, with thin limestone and coal seam, say	177	2000	
Lower or Hurlet Limestone,	...	...	⎭

In the section above recorded the average total thickness of workable coal is as follows:—

	Feet.	Inches.
Splint Coal Seam,	3	0
Corbiehall Coal Seam,	2	6
Seven-feet Coal Seam,	4	6
Wester Main Coal Seam (where present), say,	8	0
Red Coal Seam,	3	0
Parrot and Craw Coal Seam above the Lower Ironstone Seam,	2	0
Six-feet Coal Seam,	5	0
Easter Main Coal Seam,	4	0
Smithy Coal Seam,	3	0
	35	0

APPENDIX IV.

Place-Names of the District.

Compiled from the "Place-Names of Scotland," of the Rev. J. B. Johnston, B.D., Falkirk, and other sources, with the assistance of Mr. George M'Currach, Bo'ness, and the whole kindly revised by Mr. Johnston.

ABBREVIATIONS.

G.	Gaelic.	Sc. — Lowland Scots.
W.	Welsh.	O.N. — Old Norse.
A.S.	Anglo-Saxon.	The figures refer to year.
Eng.	English.	Prob. — Probably.

Name.	Situation and Description.	Derivation.
Avon,	River which forms western boundary of parish. Well fitted for purposes of machinery. Falls of considerable height may be found and there is plenty of water.	G. *Abhuinn* (pron. aoun) water, river.
Bridgeness,	Old "town" near the haven of that name on Grange Estate. The Roman tablet must have been a conspicuous object on this ness as it stood on a rocky promontory.	No bridge here. O.N. *Bryggja næs*, "cape of the landing stage." It does not mean "bridge." Old spelling Brigneese.
Borrowstoun,	Old village on Linlithgow Road a mile from Bo'ness.	Dr. Rennie says: Probably "the town of the borough" as being in the vicinity of Linlithgow (2½ miles distant) the county town in the neighbourhood; "Burrowstoun," i.e., a regular municipal borough is found as a common Sc. word from 15th century, and it is found in Eng. as early as c. 1200. Anciently spelt Burwardston sometimes, but it cannot be regarded as authentic here.
Borrowstounness,	Forth seaport, 18 miles west of Leith.	Derived from Borrowstoun and Ness, which signifies a point of land projecting into the sea.

Appendix IV.

Name.	Situation and Description.	Derivation.
Bonhard,	An old mansion on eminence east of Erngath Hills.	G. *Bon-a-h'àird*, at the end of the height.
Brewlands,	A park in Kinneil policies.	Brewing was carried on in old village of Kinneil near or in this field; or the field containing some heights or ridges, the derivation might be from broo = brow.
Binns,	Estate adjoining Carriden on the east, 4 miles from Linlithgow.	G. *Beinn* = hill. The Eng. plur s. often suffixes itself to a Gaelic name.
Barrel Brae,	Now part of Victoria Park; braes above Thirlestane.	A natural spring here, and a barrel was kept beneath as a receptacle. The new fountain is in the same vicinity though not fed by the natural spring.
Blackness,	Castle on shore at east end of Carriden Parish.	In 1200 spelt Blackenis.
Bonnytoun,	An estate lying to the south of the Erngath Hills.	In 16th century charters the form of "Bondington" occurs. This is A.S. *bondan tun*, "village or farm of the householder or husbandman." We find it in 1451 already Bonyntone.
Bog— East and West,	Roads leading from Main Street to Braehead uniting at Charlotte Place, from whence the road is known as the Bog.	Self-explanatory: swamp or marsh. In the steeper parts of this hill are still to be found evidences of spring water. Not as some think from name of an individual.
Corbiehall,	District between Railway Station and Distillery and immediately below the 50-foot bank.	Corbie, Sc. for raven, crow. Somewhat uncertain here.
Cowdenhill,	Old "town" between Grangepans and Bridgeness beside a rocky knoll.	G. *Caol dùn*, narrow hill.
Carriden,	Now eastern part of combined parish of Bo'ness and Carriden.	Gildas in 560 spells it Cair Eden. Welsh Triads, *Caer Eiddyn* = fort on the slope or hillside. W. *Caer*, G. *Cathair* (pronounced Kar) a fort; and W. *eiddyn*, G. *eadunn*, genitive, *eadainn*, "a hill slope." There is no doubt about this.
Cuffabouts,	Old "town" on the shore near Carriden Toll.	Corruption of some form not found. Spelling, 17th Century, Cuffabout.

Name.	Situation and Description.	Derivation.
Causewayfoot,	In same vicinity.	This was the termination of the old mineral roadway or causeway from Bonhard mines on the hill; there was an old landing-place on the shore here.
Castleloan,	On Kinneil Estate.	Prob. loan or avenue either to Castle Lyon, the Dower House of Lady Margaret, only daughter of John Lyon, seventh Lord Glamis, and widow of John, first Marquis of Hamilton, at one time in the vicinity of the present Furnace Yard pit; or the loan to Kinneil Palace or Castle.
Coalgate,	Originally a narrow road from the high ground above into Bo'ness by way of present Schoolyard Brae.	Coal + Sc. gate = way. The whole roadway from top to bottom was known as the Coalgate. *See* School Brae.
Drum,	Farm on high ridge South of Grange House.	(*. Druim*, L. *Dorsum*, the back; hence a hillridge.
Dean,	Burn in Kinneil Estate in a rocky den.	Eng. a valley or glen, generally deep and wooded. Cognate with O.E. Denn or Den, a cave or lurking place.
Forth,	Estuary or Firth.	Prob. in its present form from Norse Fjord—a firth, but the name Forth is older than Norse days; see *Place-Names of Scotland*, s. v.
Grange,	Estate to East of Bo'ness.	Farm; probably originally the Grange or Farm of the Monks who had their domicile on opposite shore near Culross, and who possessed these lands.
Grangepans,	Village to east of Borrowstounness and in vicinity of Grange Estate.	Grange + pans—the Saltpans belonging to Grange.
Gauze,	Farm in a hollow to the south of Bo'ness.	Derivation uncertain. Old spelling *Gawes*. Either Sc. *gaw*, slit or opening made in a pond or loch to drain it off; or else *gall*, spelt in Sc. *gaw*, a bare spot in a field; *Gaw* also old Sc. for a whinstone dyke, and whinstone crops out at the spot.

Appendix IV.

Name.	Situation and Description.	Derivation.
Grahamsdyke,	District on topmost ridge above town along which the Roman wall or Grims or Graham's dyke was situated.	The legend is that "Grime," nephew to Eugenius, King of the Scots, with his troops, broke through the wall a few miles west of Falkirk, and that his name was afterwards given to the wall. This is very improbable however; Grims dyke is a name all over. Grim may be translated as goblin or bogy's ditch.
Gil burn,	In Kinneil Estate in a rocky bed.	Icelandic *Gil* = ravine + burn, known also as the kirk-burn.
Inveravon,	Farm at west-end of old parish of Kinneil.	At the mouth or estuary. G. *inbhir*, mouth of river or confluence; G. *Abhuinn*; W. *Afon*, a river, a stream.
Kinningars,	Level field to east of Grange House, with wooded bank on south-side.	Very likely *Cunningar* = a warren, in Scots Act of Parliament, James I. A.S. or Mid-Eng. *conin, cunning-garth*; "rabbit enclosure." Old spelling, Cunninghare.
Kinglass,	A farm to south-east of Gauze farm.	G. *Cinn glais*, "at the head of the stream." There is a small burn in the vicinity.
Kinneil,	Old parish to west of Bo'ness. *See* text.	In 1250 Kinel; for other old spellings, *see* text. Bede in 720 speaks of a Pennel-tun at the end of the Roman wall, which the Picts called Peanfahel, or modernised Pennvael. W. for "head" or "end of the wall." The addition to Nennius *c*. 1150 calls this Cenail.
Lochend,	West of Muirhouses at junction of Old Kirk Road and Miller Pit Road.	Self-explanatory, a Loch having at one time existed west of this.
Muirhouse Farm,	Situated on west side of Linlithgow Road on south side of Flints Brae.	The farm lands were at one time part of Kinneil Muir; therefore House on the Muir.
Muirhouses,	A village in Carriden parish east of Lochend Cottages.	Early spellings, Murehous, Muirhouse, also Murrayes. Possibly G. *Mor uisg*, big water; but this is far from certain.

Name.	Situation and Description.	Derivation.
Northbank,	West of Bonhard and on the northern slope of Erngath Hills.	Self explanatory.
Newtown,	Village on road to Linlithgow, between Bo'ness and Borrowstoun.	Self-explanatory: 99 years lease taken by Kinneil Co. early last century and new Colliers' rows erected in addition to "Old Row."
Panbraes,	Ridge above Corbiehall, with road on top.	The Duke's salt pans were on the shore ground immediately below these braes. Coal is said to have been worked for the pans at then brae-faces and was known as "pan-wood."
Philpingstone,	Part of Grange Estate formerly known as Grange Philpingstone.	Old spellings, Phipenstane, Philpewstoun, see text chap. ix.
Providence Brae,	Footway from West Partings to the upper parts of West End. The Anderson Academy stands on the east side of it.	There is a congeries of very old and very small houses in this district, and in older times these were frequented as hiding places from frequent local raids of the press-gang. The district thus came to be known as Providence.
Stacks,	On hill, west from Blackness; a farm.	O.N. *Stak* or G. *Stac* = a cliff. Cognate with Eng. stock.
Schoolyard Brae or Sliddery Stane,	Road to Braehead from west-end of South Street. It was originally a continuation of the Coalgate and known for long as such.	There was a school in the Red House, and the entrance to it, which was the same as that to Mr. White's present joiner's shop, was known as the School Brae and so described in local title deeds. Mr. Steele's property is described as bounded on the east by the Coalgate. The Sliddery Stane was a large flat boulder lying on surface near present crossing at Stewart Avenue.
Thirlestane,	West-end of Grangepans.	Possibly derived from Lord Thirlestane who, in the sixteenth century, had a liferent of the Barony of Carriden.
Vennel,	Formerly a foot passage between North and South Streets, where Market Street now is.	An alley or lane. Fr. Venalle.

Appendix IV.

Name.	Situation and Description.	Derivation.
Voluntary Stairs,	West Partings; at foot of Providence Brae.	These led from the town up Providence to the Burgher or Voluntary Church at the top of the Brae, built about 1795.
Walton,	Farm in southern part of Carriden Estate on road to Queensferry.	*See* text: There is a well here: Well + toun. Not from town on Roman Wall.
Woolston,	Croft between Walton and Champany.	Local family of the name of Wolf. So originally " Wolf's town."

There are a number of old place-names in the district, which are now forgotten, inasmuch as the places themselves have practically disappeared. In the old titles of Carriden we find Wester Carriden, Corscobie Baulk, Peasehill, Catcraig, Ryehill, Westfield, Corsehill, The Green of Bonhard, Haining Craig, Muirrigging, Grange Muir, Muirsyde, Muiredge, Linmouth, Linnora, the Old Water Gang, the Little Goat, St. John's Bank. Craiginnour really meant, we think, Craigmore Rock in the neighbourhood of Preston Island in the Forth. Kinneil titles two or three hundred years ago also reveal a number of names and places now never heard of. There are references to Brokenbook, Greenhook, and Crockatwheelmiln; Kirklands pertaining to the Vicar of Kinneil; lands called the Bucklands also pertaining to him; the Kirkburn; Kilslaid or Kilsland; Croftangrie, at west part of town of Kinneil; Forresters land and the Muirepark of Kinneil; lands of Cruikitwell, Westwood, Gibbesbank, Rowstland, and Meggistre. An acre of ground in the Ness was described as the "Smiddieheuch."

APPENDIX V.

BOTANICAL NOTES.

From the narrative of Rev. Kenneth M'Kenzie, contributed in April, 1843, to New Stat. Account, vol. ii., pp. 123-127 :—

Mr. M'Kenzie explains in a note that the following article on the botany of the district was compiled by Mr. James C. Bauchop (a son of the factor at Kinneil). Mr. Bauchop submitted specimens of nearly all the fungi to the Rev. Mr. Berkeley, then the best authority on the subject in this country, and this gentleman confirmed or determined the names of the species.

Bo'ness parish, although of limited extent, exhibits rather a numerous flora, including a large proportion of the whole plants of Linlithgowshire, some of which appear to be confined within its limits.

On taking a general view of the botany of the county there is not perhaps much, excluding the Cryptogamia, which has not been found in the rich neighbouring district of Edinburgh; while many of the more interesting plants of the coast disappear westward, and those of the higher range of the Pentlands are not met with on the less elevated hills of Linlithgowshire. Partaking, however, of the same advantage of situation upon the Frith of Forth (an arm of the sea, it may be observed, which, besides being remarkable for the many rare plants found on its shores, would seem by its influence upon the climate and scenery to enrich the botany of the whole valley of Forth); possessing also the important requisite of every variety of soil this county is far from being deficient in a botanical point of view. If the observation be directed to that part of it which comprehends the parish of Bo'ness, although promising in its general features, it would scarcely be expected on a more particular inspection to be the best locality for plants. The maritime species which, as said before, gradually diminish in numbers as the shore of the Frith is traced upwards will be seen, on reaching this, to have almost entirely disappeared owing to the great accumulation of mud and perhaps, also, the diminished saltness of the water. Besides this, there is no ground sufficiently elevated for producing the plants of high situations. The flora of the parish is thus so far wanting in variety. There are, however, certain favourable circumstances which account for the large number of plants, on the whole, to be met with. The scenery is finely diversified with woods and plantations which shelter in abundance their peculiar species. The river Avon also, forming the boundary on the west, appears to have brought down the rarer plants which are found in ascending its higher course. The deep rocky dens at Tod's Mill accordingly abound with such, and *Scirpus sylvaticus*, *Melica nutans*, *Chrysosplenium alternifolium*, *Eupatorium cannabinum*, *Trollius europæus;* and plants by no means commonly met with may there be gathered in abundance, if the romantic beauty of the scene, as the river winds amidst its steep and wooded banks, may allow the eye to rest upon the humbler vegetation around. The flowering fern, *Osmunda regalis*, is also seen in this spot but does not extend higher up; although frequent enough on the west coast it appears in Scotland to shun the sharper breezes of the east; and the station just mentioned is probably the nearest to Edinburgh. *Tortula rigida* a small species of moss, which is chiefly confined to the south of England, also grows abundantly by the river side at Inneravon. The presence of these two plants, especially the fern, seems to indicate a certain approach to a western climate, or is owing to the highly sheltered situation. The flowering fern becomes more frequent in Stirlingshire.

Among the few maritime plants within the bounds may be mentioned *Scirpus maritimus* and *Aster tripolium* which are seen in the summer months plentifully covering the brackish marshes below Kinneil. The aster is not a rare plant and is mentioned chiefly because it was found in the same place by Sibbald nearly 180 years ago, and what is more deserving of notice as connected with the gradual changes which take place in estuaries, he also observed growing on the shore *Thalictrum minus* and *Arundo arenaria*, a strictly maritime plant, well known to bind the loose sand of the seashore, neither of which is now to be seen; a circumstance of some importance as it confirms the supposition derived from other observations that there has been a great increase of the sleeches since Sibbald's time. In some spots even there has been a change from a comparatively sandy to a muddy beach. On searching the shore eastward the same plants do not begin to appear for several miles until the shore changes its character.

The natural copse wood of Kinneil, the only one in the county, affords, as might be expected, some rather peculiar plants, among which may be reckoned *Betonica officinalis*, very rare in this part of Scotland, and *Habenaria albida*, for which it is a singular station, that being a plant of hilly pastures. It is chiefly in this wood that the additions to the Scottish Cryptogamia were found, and which will afterwards be specified. *Geranium phocum*, *Listera Nidus-Avis*, *Arum maculatum* are a few of the rarer flowering plants to be met with in the woods. In regard to the comparative prevalence of natural orders, the *Graminiæ* are the most numerous in species, the *Orchidiæ* somewhat deficient. The common reed fills the ditches and wet places of the carse lands. *Poa aquatica* and *Festuca elatior* grasses of highly nutritive properties are abundant by the side of the Avon.

Of the Cryptogamia, the Musci are not uninteresting. *Hypnum murale* and *Tortula revoluta* are frequent in old stone walls about Kinneil. *Tetraphis Browniana* and *Jungermannia furcata* occur in fruit; the latter very rare in the Dean plantation. *Dicranum flexuosum* covers the entire bank at Tod's Mill in abundant fructification. *Hypnum piliferum* is common, but not in fruit, although it may be obtained in that state about Hopetoun Woods in the parish of Abercorn.

Of the Lichenes and Algæ there is nothing particular to be said. The marine are very scarce from the nature of the beach. The Fungi now remain to be noticed, which, as they have not been so extensively investigated in Scotland as other plants may on that account be expected to afford greater novelties. The agarics are particularly numerous. In this parish two localities for these may be distinguished as abounding in kinds of generally different forms and qualities. In the rich old pastures of Kinneil those of fragile and delicate appearance often dissolving in decay may be looked for, while the surrounding woods and plantations harbour the larger species, which are usually acrid or tufted. Among the latter *Agaricus Piperatus*, *Volemum*, *Flexuosus*, *Vellereus*, *Adustus*, although not generally common, are abundant under Kinneil copse. Of the former A. Sowerbei, a curious species, may be mentioned as growing on the bank by the shore. The following list of Fungi of different genera, gathered in the woods immediately around Kinneil, are allowed to be additions to the Scottish flora; the first nine are likewise quite new to Britain. The names are chiefly those of Fries and Berkeley.

Several species, apparently undescribed, were met with; but, as they have not yet been sufficiently examined it is not judged proper to publish them in this place. Although Fungi are obscure plants, and little regarded, the subjoined list may be useful as a guide to those who attend to such things in other parts of the country, besides appearing necessary to complete this botanical view:—

Agaricus saccharinus.
,, *algidus.*
Arcyria fusca.
Stemonitis typhoides.
Didymium costatum.
,, *clavus.*
Diderma lepidota.
Cribraria fulva.
,, *argillacea.*
Agaricus albo-brunnius.
,, fulvus.
,, columbetta.
,, foetens.
,, fumosus.
,, blennius.
,, grammopodius.
,, butyraceus.
,, camptophyllus.
,, glyciosmus.
,, capillaris.
,, depluens.
,, racemosus.
,, pterigenus.

Agaricus sericellus.
,, rhodopolius.
,, reticulatus.
,, sowerbei.
,, varius.
,, sanguineus.
,, radicosus.
,, collinitus.
,, plumosus.
,, erinaceus.
,, medius.
,, iris.
Cantharellus sinuosus.
,, fissilis.
Merulius pallens.
Hydnum ochraceum.
,, udum.
Pistillaria quisquiliaris.
Didymium cinereum.
,, farinaceum.
Doratomyces neesii corda.
Diochia elegans.

As the various species of Fungi are more generally distributed in temperate regions to which they are chiefly confined than plants of higher rank, owing perhaps to their greater simplicity of structure, it is very probable that all of the above might be found throughout Britain wherever these circumstances chiefly required for the production of the order, shade, and moisture exist. The Fungi of the continent, indeed, are in a great many cases identical with those of this country. To this law of comparatively general distribution there are, however, exceptions, and some of the species appear to be very local, their diffusion depending upon causes which are not understood. There is also a peculiarity connected with the stations of Fungi: while some species are equally constant to these as the higher tribes of plants, there are others very uncertain in this respect, disappearing for a succession of seasons together, seemingly without any relation to the more obvious influence of moist weather. The causes of this would appear to be obscure as the plants themselves, but the fact probably points to a field of investigation in some measure peculiar to them, although in regard to the more general views of botanical geography they may have less claim upon the attention.

The following is a general list of a few more of the rarer plants:—

Hippuris vulgaris.	Jungermannia polyganthos.
Veronica montana.	Marchantia conica.
Viburnum opulus.	*Fungi.*
Fedia olitoria.	Agaricus ceraceus.
Aira cristata.	,, confluens.
Milium effusum.	,, clavus.
Festuca bromoides.	,, scaber.
Sagina maritima.	,, mutabilis.
Adoxa moschatellina.	,, titubans.
Origanum vulgare.	,, vaginatus.
Hieracium umbellatum.	,, fuliginosus.
Carex curta.	,, flaccidus.
Musci, &c., in fruit.	,, parasiticus.
Gymnostomum Heimii.	,, cochleatus.
Didymodon trifarum.	Cantharellus cornucopioides.
,, heteromallum.	,, lutescens.
Orthotricum diaphinum.	Radulum orbicura.
Hookeria lucens.	Calocera viscosa.
Hypnum complanatum.	Helvella elastica.
Grimmia tricophylla.	Leotia lubrica.
Hypnum alopecurum.	Pezeza macropus.
Brium legulatum.	Physarum sinuosum.
,, rostratum.	Geoglossum cucullatum.
Jungermannia crenulata.	

APPENDIX VI.

TABLE OF MODERN INFORMATION COMPILED FROM OFFICIAL SOURCES.

I.

Population of Bo'ness Burgh at 1911 census, including
84 shipping, - - - - - - - 10,862
Parish Landward, - - - - - - 3,172
                                                    ——
                                                 14,034

Acreage of Burgh, 515. The Burgh Boundaries were extended in 1894, and an Interlocutor, dated 15th May that year, by the Sheriff of the County defines them in detail. Roughly, they are the sea on the North; Kinningars Park on the East; Grahamsdyke, Chance, and part of Dean

466 Borrowstounness and District

Road on the South; and on the West the western boundary of the Cemetery; then Westwards, skirting Kinneil Schoolhouse and through to Dean Burn; then North-west, passing entrance to Kinneil Station, and from thence seawards.

Assessable Valuation—		
Burgh,		£41,759
Parish,		63,856
Railways and Canals,		10,460

Combined Total Assessment in Burgh, 7/6·52 per £1.

The following show details of the assessments for the year ending 15th May, 1913 :—

	Owners.	Occupiers.
Burgh Rates,	1s. 9¾d.	2s. 9¼d.
Parish Rates,	1s. 7d.	1s. 7⅝d.
County Rates,	3¼d.	1d.

Before imposing the parish rates a 20 per cent. deduction is made on the rentals of all lands and heritages, and a 35 per cent. deduction on railways.

PUBLIC BODIES, SCHOOLS, AND CHURCHES.

Town Council (Police Burgh) consisting of Provost, Two Bailies, Dean of Guild, and Eight Councillors—Twelve in all. Town Council Committees—Finance, Water, Lighting, Streets and Cleansing, Slaughterhouse, Public Health, Sewers and Drains, Fire Brigade, Burgh Property, Public Parks, Fair Committee, Town Hall Management, Assessment Appeals, Old Age Pensions; also Public Library Committee, consisting of Ten Town Council Representatives, and Ten House-holders' Representatives.

Local Licensing Court.—Three Members of Town Council. *Burgh Officials.*—Town Clerk, Burgh Chamberlain, Burgh Surveyor and Sanitary Inspector, Medical Officer, Medical Superintendent of Burgh Hospital, Matron, Collector of Rates, and Burgh Procurator Fiscal.

Police Establishment.—One Inspector, One Sergeant, and Ten Constables. Chief Police Station at Corbiehall. District Stations at Grangepans and Richmond.

School Board.—Nine Members. *Officials.*—Clerk, Treasurer, Compulsory Officer, and Master of Works.

Schools.—*Nine*—namely Bo'ness Academy (Higher Grade), Bo'ness Public, Bo'ness Infant, Grange Public, Kinneil Public, Borrowstoun Public, Carriden, Blackness, and St. Mary's.

Staff.—5 Head-masters, 4 Head-mistresses, 12 Male Assistants, 49 Female Assistants. Staff pay-bill for 1912 (exclusive of St. Mary's Voluntary School), Day, £7315; Evening, £304; Total, £7619. Number of children on Roll, 3000.

Appendix VI.

Parish Council.—Thirteen Members with Cemetery Board and Landward Committee (5). *Officials.*—Inspector of Poor, Clerk to Council and Cemetery Board, Registrar for Bo'ness Parish, with separate Registrar for ecclesiastical parish of Carriden.

Other public Boards comprise Anderson Educational Bequest; Anderson Trust; Bo'ness and District Nursing Association; Carriden and District Nursing Association. There is also a Nursing Association connected with Kinneil Colliery.

Churches.—Bo'ness Parish Church; Carriden Parish Church; Craigmailen U.F. Church; St. Andrew's U.F. Church; St. Catharine's Episcopal Church; St. Mary's Roman Catholic Church; Bo'ness Baptist Church; branch of the Scottish Coast Mission, and Salvation Army Corps. There are various other religious organisations.

II.

Harbour and Dock.—Dock opened in 1881. Extent, $7\frac{1}{2}$ acres; cost £200,000. Harbour and quays rebuilt and extended, and area increased from $2\frac{1}{2}$ to $5\frac{1}{2}$ acres. Extent of Dock quayage, 2400 feet; Harbour quayage, 1900 feet.

Town's interest in Harbour and Dock undertaking transferred to North British Railway Company in 1900. Dock and Harbour are furnished throughout with hydraulic machinery of the most modern description. The Engine House is situated at the east end of the Dock, and there are also 3 accumulators in other places.

Coal Hoists.—These number four, three of which were recently replaced by Tannett, Walker & Co., Ltd., Leeds. No. 1, situated on the north side, is the newest and largest, and has a lifting capacity of 35 tons; Nos. 3 and 4, on the east side, have each a capacity of 30 tons, and are fitted with high levels.

Cranes.—There were originally six portable hydraulic cranes for discharging purposes, but there are now sixteen. Twelve are at the Dock and four at the west pier of the Harbour. Six were erected in 1912 by Tannett, Walker & Co., Ltd., and the average capacity of 14 of the cranes is 30 cwts., whilst 1 is of 3 tons capacity and another of 2 tons capacity.

Borrowstounness and District

Port Trade Returns.—The following tables contain some interesting figures:—

	1907.		1911.		1912.	
I.—*Foreign Trade.*	No.	Tons.	No.	Tons.	No.	Tons.
Vessels in with Cargo—Steam,	165	114,809	157	115,489	163	116,166
,, ,, Sail,	141	28,375	94	18,135	59	13,137
,, in Ballast—Steam,	361	231,775	270	183,842	253	168,606
,, ,, Sail,	24	3,695	51	4,905	32	3,401
Total Freight Inward,	691	378,654	572	322,371	507	301,310
Vessels out with Cargo—Steam,	541	328,744	428	283,943	417	266,138
,, ,, Sail,	197	35,603	134	19,828	98	16,326
,, in Ballast,—Steam,	1	1,110	8	7,726	7	5,905
,, ,, Sail,	—	—	—	—	1	389
Total Freight Out,	739	365,457	570	311,497	523	288,758
II.—*Coasting Trade.*						
Vessels in with Cargo,	142	39,742	113	30,814	112	31,635
,, in Ballast,	374	71,753	358	92,208	353	103,890
Vessels out with Cargo,	462	80,894	463	105,897	458	107,354
,, in Ballast,	96	41,473	109	40,059	103	49,630

Total value of Imports.

1907,	£317,449
1911,	318,729
1912,	360,836

Pitwood Imported.

	Loads.	Value.
1910,	196,976	£235,032
1911,	203,577	250,280
1912,	207,231	295,387

Coal Statistics.

	Exported.	Shipped Coastwise.
	Tons.	Tons.
1907,	708,852	91,304
1908,	629,101	108,122
1909,	573,778	151,627
1910,	632,292	187,629
1911,	591,704	158,167
1912,	569,260	161,517

Note.—This does not include Bunker Coals.

Staff.—Harbour Master; Deputy Harbour Master, four dock gatemen, Collector of Dock and Harbour dues.

There are also 8 registered Pilots.

H.M. Customs and Excise.—Customs staff consists of Collector and eight officers. Excise staff, Surveyor and eight officers.

Appendix VI.

Post Office Staff.—1 Postmaster, 5 Sorting Clerks and Telegraphists, 1 Telephonist, 8 Postmen, and 3 Telegraph Messengers.

Banks.—Royal Bank of Scotland; Clydesdale Bank, Ltd.; Union Bank of Scotland, Ltd.; The Bank of Scotland.

Solicitors, 6; Doctors, 4.

Newspapers.—*Bo'ness Journal*, Market Square. *The Linlithgowshire Gazette, Falkirk Herald,* and *West Lothian Courier* also have branch offices in the town.

Shipbrokers, Coal Exporters, Pitwood Importers, and Shipping Agents, 9.

Consulates for Denmark, Germany, Norway, the Netherlands, Russia, and Sweden.

Licensed Premises.—Hotels, 2; Public Houses, 16; Licensed Grocers, including one Porter and Ale only, 11.

Farms.—There are 25 farms in the district—1 on Grange Estate, 3 on Carriden, and the others on Kinneil Estate.

III.[1]

Factories within Burgh at 31st December, 1912.—Bakers, 2; Foundries, 3; Sawmills, 2; Engineers, 2; Potteries, 2; Ship-breaking yard, 1; Gas Works, 1; Aerated Water Works, 1; Chemical Manure Works, 1; Distillery (including departments for methylated spirit, extract of malt, and extraction of oil), 1; Laundry, 1; Coal Pits, 5 (2 belonging to Bridgeness Coal Co., 3 to Kinneil Coal Co., Carriden Coal Co. are at present sinking one within the Burgh. Their other pit is at Carriden.

Pit Prop Yards (which in nearly all cases are equipped with Sawmills), 6.

Shops Act, 1912.—Shops on register at 31st December, 1912. Bakers, 9; Bootmakers, 9; Butchers, 14; Chemists, 4; Confectioners, 17; Cycle Agents, 3; Drapers, 18; Fishmongers, 2; Fruiterers, 9; Grocers, 22; Ironmongers, 3; Jewellers, 3; Painters, 3; Restaurants, 5; Stationers, 3; Tobacconists and Stationers, 5; Miscellaneous, 12.

Workshops on register at 31st December, 1912. Tailors, 8; Dressmakers, 6; Bakers, 4; Bootmakers, 9; Plumbers, 6; Cycle Repairers, 3; Watchmakers, 3; Joiners, 6; total, 45.

Water Supply and Water Works.—Carribber Reservoir. Completed 5th June, 1879; cost, £1,715; capacity, 16,000,000 gallons. It was deepened and enlarged in 1887 at a cost of £4,500. Capacity then increased to 25,441,419 gallons. Gathering ground 250 acres. Bomains Service Reservoir. Completed on 10th June, 1884, at cost of £2,000; area 6

---

[1] The information in this paragraph has been kindly compiled by Mr. John Louden, Burgh Surveyor.

acres; capacity 16,112,719 gallons. Lochcote Reservoir. Completed 5th June, 1900; catchment area = 600 acres; total cost, £30,000; cost of Reservoir alone, £14,000, or £70 per million gallons; capacity of Reservoir, 200,500,000 gallons. Trade consumpt in Burgh in 1900 = 51,460,000 gallons. Trade consumpt in Burgh in 1912 = 114,793,000. Average annual trade consumpt during past five years = 127,754,000. Domestic consumpt per head per day for domestic purposes = 35 gallons. Consumpt per head per day for trade purposes, 25 gallons. Supply for street watering, latrines, &c., per head per day, ·33 gallons. For all purposes, 60·33 gallons per head per day. Some years ago a scheme of filtration was adopted and a filter house erected at the North West End of Bomains Reservoir. The pattern of filters adopted was Bell's Mechanical Filters, of which eight batteries, costing £3000, were installed capable of filtering 1½ million gallons in 24 hours. The remainder of the scheme, which when finished cost £5,000, included the laying of an 8-inch pipe from the filter-house to convey a supply of unfiltered water solely for works purposes, and the laying of several service pipes within the Burgh.

Note.—The cost of filtration inclusive of upkeep, working expenses, and repayments is 4d. per head per 1000 of the population.

Electricity Works.—Capital borrowed, £37,000.

Year	Quantity generated in P.T. Units.	Quantity Sold.				Total Quantity Accounted for.	Total Maximum Demanded.
		Public Lamps.	By Contract.	Private Consumers by Meter.	Total Sold.		
1906	140,453	62,661	10,013	32,417	105,091	125,366	116 K.W.
1909	429,491	85,371	12,000	257,058	354,429	413,429	220 K.W.
1912	820,441	103,701	471,236	134,087	709,024	758,851	295·8 K.W.

Death rate in the Burgh during 1912 from all causes = 15·00 per 1,000 of population.

Birth Rate = 33·9 per 1,000 of population.

Average death rate during the past five years = 15·68 per 1,000 of population.

Average birth rate during the past five years = 33·60 per 1,000 of population.

Average deaths under one year per 1,000 births during the past five years = 122·4.

Cleansing Staff.—Foreman, 6 Scavengers, 6 Carters, 6 Horses and Carts.

INDEX.

INDEX.

ACCOUNTS, copy town, for year ending 30th May, 1834, 263
Anderson, John, 386
Anne, Duchess, 79, 105, 450
Antonine's Wall, 3
Arbitrations, interesting, 106

BAILLIE, Rev. Patrick, 204
Baird, George Husband (Prin. Edin. Univ., 1761-1840), 382
Bell, Henry, 383
Beneficent Society, 355
Binns, The, 12, 197, 457
Blackader, Rev. John, 130
Blackness, 1, 14, 15, 56, 457
Boiling House, 404
Bo'ness in the early days, 19
—— Coalfield, 306, 316, 454
—— Kirk of, 40, 105
—— Old Town Hall, 323
—— Parish, 40, 163, 276
—— Pottery, 405
—— Schools and Schoolmasters, 414, 466
—— Seal and Coat of Arms, 425
—— and Carriden Band (formation of), 410
Bonhard, 11, 457
Borrowstoun Muir, 398
—— Village, 11, 20, 456
Borrowstounness, as a Burgh of Barony, 56
—— objections by Linlithgow thereto, 56, 79
—— as a Burgh of Regality, 78
—— Constitution of Burgh of Regality, 79
—— Charter to Duchess Anne, 79
—— Opening ceremonies of Regality Court, 79
—— Regality Court Book, 78
—— Register of Deeds, 94
—— Roll of heritors, tenants, and vassals, 81
—— Burgh Tolbooth, 80, 115
—— Martyrs, 123

Borrowstounness Old Churchyard, 295, 420
—— Old Roadways, 77
—— Shipmaster's Will and Testament, 104
Botanical notes, 461
Brand, Rev. John, A.M., 204
Brand, Rev. William, 204
Bridgeness, 11, 456
—— Furnaces, 162
Burghers and anti-Burghers, 210
Burns, Robert (the poet) at Bo'ness, 399
Burns, Robert, D.D., 384

CADELLS of Grange, 152
Cadell, William, of Haddington, 152
—— William, secundus, 152
—— William, tertius, 153, 158
—— —— John, 153
—— —— James John, 160
—— William Archibald, 160
—— Henry, 162
—— Henry Moubray, 162
—— Crest, 162
Campbell, Sir Colin, 11
Capies Wall, 47
Carron Iron Company, 153
Carting Trade, 410
Carriden, 1, 54, 58, 80, 113, 119, 163, 457
—— House, 9, 11, 166
—— Boundaries of Parish, 163
—— Estate and its Owners, 164
—— Old Church and Churchyard, 167, 179, 431
—— New Church and Churchyard, 170
—— Riots re Burial at, 172
—— Kirk Session Functions, 431
—— Kirk Session Records, 431
—— Old Church Road, 177, 186
—— Lord President Hope and, 179
—— Hope, Admiral Sir George of, 179
—— Hope, Admiral James of, 186
—— Maxwell, William of, 176

1 G

Index

Carriden, Maxwell, William (2), 177
—— Ministers of, 193
—— Binns House and General Dalyell, and his Scots Greys, 197
—— Anti-Burghers, 210
—— Witches, Trial of, 119
—— Schools and Schoolmasters, 412, 435, 466
—— Coal, 314
Cholera Outbreaks, 420
Chance Pit, Litigation with Grange Colliery, 156
Churches. *See* Ecclesiastical
Clenging of Vessels, 74
Coal, Discovery of in District, 22
—— Restrictions on Exportation, 60
—— and Coal Mining, 305
—— Regulation of Supply and Charges, 65
—— and Ironstone Mines, 318
Connel, Rev. David, 221
Cornwalls of Bonhard, 11, 13
Covenanters, 34, 37, 38, 39, 123
—— The National Covenant, 123
—— The Solemn League and Covenant, 125
—— Borrowstounness Martyrs, 127
—— Seaport, a Haunt for Fugitives, 126
—— Persecution of Rev. Mr. Wishart, 128
—— Blackader, Rev. John, 130
—— Cargill, Rev. Donald, 132
—— Cuthell, William, 143
—— Gouger, William, 143
—— Hamilton, Rev. James, 133
—— Hamilton, Sir Robert, 133
—— Stewart, Archibald, 132, 137
—— Harvie, Marion, 132, 136, 138
Cowdenhill, 11, 457
Cromwell, 19, 37, 65
Cruming, Patrick, of Carriden, 54
Cuffabouts, 11, 170, 457
Custom House, History of, 400
Cuthell, William (Martyr), 143

DALYELL, General, of Binns, 197
Defoe's visit to Bo'ness, 397
Dempster, Rev. A. P., 225
Distillery, 408
Drummond, John, imprisonment of, 251

Duguid, James (of Muirhouses) and Old Church Road at Carriden, 187
Duncanson, Roger (Coalmaster), 60

EASTER Wellacres Field, 5
Ecclesiastical history, 200
—— First Parish Church, 201
—— Ministers of Borrowstounness, (1648-1746), 202
—— Burghers, 210, 216
—— Anti-Burghers and their pastors, 210
—— Formation of Free Church, 223
—— Secession Church, 210
—— United Associate Synod, 219
—— Rev. Arch. Harper, Burgher Minister, 1796-1820, Minister United Associate Congregation, (1820-1834), 218
—— Rev. David Connel, 221
—— Free Church Ministers, 223
—— Sailors' loft action *re*, 290
Educational, 412

FISH, Thirlage of and regulation for sale of, 95, 96
Flax dressing, 407
Foreshore, Reclamation of, 249, 423
Forrester, Dame Christian, 150
Forth and Clyde Canal, 325

GARDINER, Colonel James, 366
Gauze (Gawes) House, 11, 458
"Gibbites," 133, 144
Gil-burn, 263, 459
Gouger, William (Martyr), 143
Graham's Dyke, 3, 459
Grain-trade, 401
Grange Estate, early History, 147
—— Old House, Description of, 147
—— Hamiltons of, 148
—— Cadells of, 152
—— Coal Company, 154
—— Salt Pans, 161
—— Lady, Action against James Riddell, of Kinglassie, 67
Grangepans, 11, 161, 458
Greenland Whale Fishing, 239, 403

HAMILTON, House of, 23
—— Family, 449

Index

Hamilton, Rev. James, 133, 203
—— Sir Robert (Martyr), 133
Harbour, Formation of Basin, 246
—— Erection of Slip, 259
Harper, Rev. Archibald, 218
Harvie, Marion (Martyr), 132, 136, 138
Henderson, John, Shoremaster, 232, 362
Herring Fishing, 257
Hope, Admiral George J., K.C.B., 389
Hope, Admiral Sir James, 390
Hunter, Rev. Robert, A.M., 202

"IN-GAUN-EE" System. *See* Coal Mining
Industries—
  Brewing, 229
  Carting, 410
  Coal, 305
  Distilling, 408
  Flax Dressing, 407
  Furnaces, 270, 409
  Grain, 401
  Herring Fishing, 257
  Ironstone, 318
  Iron Foundries, 408
  Oil, 404
  Potteries, 405
  Saltmaking, 22, 54, 55, 161
  Shipbuilding, 258
  Soap, 407
  Tambouring and Silk Spinning, 402
  Whale Fishing, 239, 403
Inglis, Rev. John, A.M., 203
Inveravon Castle, 26
Iron Foundries, 408
Irving, Rev. Lewis H., 223

JAMES VI., First Visit to Scotland, 57
Jacobite Soldiers at Borrowstoun, 397

KINGLASSIE (Coal Works), 67
Kinglass, 459
Kinningars, 459
Kinneil, 1, 6, 10, 26, 27, 29, 35, 37, 54, 58, 80, 459
—— Barony of, 24, 38, 77, 95

Kinneil Church, 48, 66, 201
—— Furnaces, 270, 409
—— House, description of, 44
—— Ministers of, 51
—— Mercat Cross, 55
—— and General Monk, 65
—— Village, 47
—— Railway, first to, 270
—— Reed Band (formation of), 410
—— Roman Coffins found near, 9
—— Nether, 5
—— Upper, 9

LAUGHING Hill, 8
Linlithgow, objections to B. being erected into a Burgh of Barony, 56
—— Magistrates in trouble, 73

M'KENZIE, Rev. Kenneth, 207
Marches, Perambulation of, 99
Martyrs, 17, 126
Melville, Andrew, 17
Miller or Miller's Pit, 159
Mining (see under coal)
—— calamities, 321
Modern information, 465
Muirhouses (Murrayes), 11, 459
Municipal, beginning of local Board, 226
—— Act of 1744, 226
—— First "trustees for the two pennies in the pint," and their duties, 226
—— What the first Minute Book (1744-1787) discloses, 228
—— New Act (1767-69, 1794), 242
—— Second period of local municipal history (1769-1869), 244
—— New powers, 245
—— Dirty Streets, 250
—— What the Second Minute Book discloses, 256

NATIVES, Eminent, 362
Newtown Families, 322
Northbank House, 11, 12

PAIRK, Rev. John, Carriden, 133
Place Names of District, 456

Index

Plague, (1625-35-45), 61, 71, 75, 395
Poor, Care of, 418
Population of Parish between 1755 and 1841, 400
Potter, Donald, R. N., 380
Potter, Rev. Michael, 203
Preston, Island, Coal Mines and Salt-pans, 317
Privy Council Registers, 53
Prosecutions for Contravention of Orders, 64, 65
Providence Road, 249, 460

REGALITY Court, 39, 40, 78
Register of Bands, 101
Representatives of Bo'ness, 202, 275, 351
Rennie, Rev. Robert, D.D., 205
—— describes houses and town in 1776, 253
Resurrectionists, 420
Riddell, Archibald (Covenanter), 142
Riddell, James, of Kinglassie, 67, 68
Ritchie, Captain John, 279
Ritchie, Declaratory action, 300
Roebuck, Dr. John, 152, 156, 235, 242, 405
Roman occupation, 2
Roman coffins, 8, 9
Roman Stations, 9, 10
Roman Tablet, 7

SALTMAKING, 22, 54, 55, 161
Secession Church, 210
Serf System, 308
Seton, House of, 11, 12
Seton, Sir Walter of Abercorn, North-bank and Carriden, 11, 12, 165
Shipbuilding (middle of 18th century), 258
Societies and Lodges, 335
  Sea Box of Borrowstounness, 335, 351, 425

Societies and Lodges—*continued.*
  Sea Box of Carriden, 349
  Trades Society, 354
  Beneficent Society, 355
  Freemasons, 358
  "Pythagoric," 359
Soap Work, 407
Spanish Invasion threatened, 62
Stewart, Archibald (Martyr), 132, 137
Stewart, Prof. Dugald, 377
St. John's Well, 257, 268
Stephens, James Brunton (poet of Australia), 392
Subsidences, 323
Surnames, examples, 108
Syver Well, 249

TAMBOURING and Silk Spinning, 402
Thomson, Rev. William, A.M., 203
Temple Pit Reservoir, 269
Thirlestane, 11, 164, 460
Tolbooth, Borrowstounness, 80, 115
Tolls and Toll Bars, 411

VOLUNTEER, Local Company, 424

WAGGON Road, Construction of, 247
Walton Farm, 9, 164, 165, 461
Water Supply, Early Difficulties, 254, 261, 266
Watt, James, 372
Waughe, Rev. John, A.M., 202
Whale Fishing, 239, 403
Wilson, Rev. Daniel, 224
Wishart, William (Prin. Edin. Univ., 1716-1729), 368
Wishart, Rev. Wm., Kinneil, 128
Witchcraft, 91, 111
—— Trials, 113